SELLING
the Profession
by David J. Lill

3rd Edition

Senior Project Manager: Martha Lill
Editor-in Chief: David J. Lill
Editorial Assistant: Gladys Hudson
Design Manager: Sally Longacre
Interior Design Assistance: Tracy Mitchell
Cover Design: Steve Longacre
Technical Consultants: Tony Marvelli, Adam Mason, Drew Sanford
Editorial Assistance: Valerie Scott, Mary F. Yost
Printer: Von Hoffman Graphics, Inc.

DM Bass Publications

6635 Broken Bow Drive
Antioch, TN 37013
(615) 941-2747
(615) 941-2458 (Fax)
lilld@mail.belmont.edu
or
dlill48@home.com

Address all correspondence and order information to the above address.
Please feel free to contact me if you want specific information on how to access
all aspects of the Web site I developed exclusively to assist you in the preparation
of lecture material, tests, case studies and other sales-related classroom
activities.

ISBN 0-9652201-9-2

Dedication:

Murphy, Jennifer and David, Jr.
The three loves of my life.

BRIEF CONTENTS

CONTENTS

PART III

Gaining Knowledge, Preparing, and Planning for the Presentation

6   PREPARATION FOR SUCCESS IN SELLING   129

7   BECOMING A MASTER PROSPECTOR   155

8 PREAPPROACH AND TELEPHONE TECHNIQUES   181

PART IV

The Face-to-Face Relationship Model of Selling

9 APPROACHING THE PROSPECT   209

10 IDENTIFYING NEEDS BY QUESTIONING AND LISTENING 233

11 MAKING THE PRESENTATION 257

12 NEGOTIATING SALES RESISTANCE 285

13 CLOSING THE SALE   313

PART V

Management Aspects: Personal and Organizational

14 CUSTOMER SERVICE AND FOLLOW-UP AFTER THE SALE   339

15 TIME, TERRITORY, AND PERSONAL MANAGEMENT   359

16 SALES FORCE MANAGEMENT   383

PREFACE

Approach and Purpose

I formed DM Bass Publications in 1995 for the specific purpose of self-publishing *Selling The Profession*. The 3rd edition is now complete and I am more excited than ever with the content of the book. As author, publisher and marketer of this professional selling textbook I have had the rare opportunity to interact with a significant number of college and university sales professors, as well as men and women employed fulltime in the field of professional selling. In addition, I am genuinely delighted with the relationship I have established with Surado Solutions, Inc. in Riverside, California. They have given me the authority to provide their contact management software to all professors who adopt and use my book. In addition, I now have a Web site devoted exclusively to assisting you in the preparation of lecture materials, tests and other sales-related classroom activities.

Updating and revising this professional selling book has been, and continues to be, an extremely satisfying experience. To write down all your thoughts and experiences in a way that makes sense and represents a legitimate contribution to the sales profession has been an enormous challenge. The years I have spent teaching sales courses to college students and conducting seminars for sales professionals, combined with almost 30 years of personal experience in various phases of the business of selling have helped to formulate the ideas, concepts, and style of this text.

There are a number of specific reasons why I decided to invest so much time and energy in the writing of this book. As a college professor, I personally wanted a textbook that concentrated on the relationship style of selling. It is this consultative or relationship-building style that spells success for a salesperson operating in a highly competitive business environment and dealing with today's sophisticated buyers who demand correct answers to complex problems. At the same time, I wanted a book whose style and organization made it fun to read, easy to comprehend, and very practical as a training tool for anyone really interested in developing their skills as a professional salesperson. My goal was to find a way to break the process into its most basic components, in an attempt to simplify the complex buyer-seller interaction that takes place in an actual selling situation. The result is an *eight-step sales cycle model* that is explored in depth in over one-half of the book.

In addition, because attitude is so important for achieving success in selling, I felt compelled to incorporate verbal and nonverbal communication and social style technology as the foundation stones in a relationship model of selling. A knowledge of these concepts allows you to appreciate more readily the complex, dynamic behavioral relationships that take place in selling. It also seemed essential to introduce the reader to the availability and usefulness of sales force automation and the numerous technology products available to the salesperson. Global competition has enlarged the playing field. As global competition brings new challenges, technology brings new tools that help sales professionals sell more effectively and efficiently.

Throughout the text, the reader is made aware of the "real world" of selling through review of the current sales literature, personal experience, and, most importantly, interviews with successful active sales professionals who put the theory contained in the book into everyday practice. As one top salesperson relayed to me, *"Practice without theory is blind and theory without practice is sterile."*

Finally, as a professor and as a person who dearly loves the sales environment and longs for improvement in the ethical business climate, I wanted a text that would: 1) show that selling can be an honest, respected profession; 2) convince the bright, creative students that selling is a profession they should consider—not just something you do until something better comes along; and 3) demonstrate that, if practiced as explained in this text, a sales career will be a source of financial, personal status, and self-esteem rewards.

ORGANIZATION/SPECIAL SECTIONS

The material in the text is organized into 16 chapters which are divided into five distinct parts:

PART I—Relationship Building and the Sales Cycle Framework

Part I discusses the consultative, problem-solving approach to professional selling. The various characteristics that successful salespeople possess are detailed. Relationship selling involves two-way communication, encourages prospect participation, employs empathy, is interactive and promotes a win-win environment. A principled style of selling has evolved that favors building close and trusting long-term relationships. Positioning your sales force as consultants or counselors creates a partnership with your customers. You are peers working to solve problems together. Establishing partnerships, not selling products, is the new function of sales.

A better understanding of the complete selling situation and the problems it generates may be gained by breaking the sale into its basic tasks. There are several steps to consummating a successful sale. An eight-step sales cycle is introduced in chapter two and explained in detail in chapters 7 to 14. It makes sense that if you understand what the steps are in the *Sales Cycle Framework for Relationship Selling,* and what is required to make each step a successful endeavor, then you will become a professional in selling much quicker than those who are simply stumbling through the process trying to figure it out. The chapters included in this section are:

1. A Career in Professional Selling
2. Consultative or Relationship Selling

PART II—Cultivating an Ethics Climate and Developing Communication Skills

Consultative, relationship selling is a challenging career field. Few professions, if any, give you more opportunities to be rejected on a daily basis than does the field of sales. You need strong ethical and moral character to sustain a sales career. Cheating, lying or short-changing the customer is a sure way to court failure for the future. Honest and caring service brings customers back and assures success for the salesperson.

Success in professional selling also depends upon your ability to have a productive exchange of information with prospects and customers. The more salespeople understand about prospects, the more readily they can discover what they need and want. An especially useful tool for gaining insight into the thinking of prospects is knowledge of the social styles model. A social style is the way a person sends and receives information. It is a method for finding the best way to approach a prospect and to set up a working relationship with that person. Part II has three chapters dealing with ethics and communication theory:

3. Ethical and Legal Issues in Selling
4. Consumer Behavior and the Communication Agenda
5. Finding Your Selling Style

PART III—Gaining Knowledge, Preparing, and Planning for the Presentation

The information in chapter 6 prepares the reader for success in a sales career by focusing on gaining product knowledge, developing a plan for self-motivation and goal setting strategies and introducing the use of sales force automation. The use of contact management programs is introduced in some detail in chapter 6. The electronic information age is here.

Chapters 7 and 8 discuss the procedures for locating and qualifying prospects and outline the information needed to prepare for an effective presentation. Chapter 7 is a very thorough look at the topic of prospecting. As the saying goes, "I'd rather be a master prospector than a wizard of speech and have no one to tell my story to." Chapter 8 discusses the process of gathering preapproach information and presents a six-step telephone track for making appointments for that all important personal interview. The three chapters in this section are:

6. Preparation For Success in Selling
7. Becoming a Master Prospector
8. Preapproach and Telephone Techniques

PART IV—The Face-to-Face Relationship Model of Selling

Chapters 9 to 13 are the very heart of professional, consultative selling. This is considered the "how to" portion of the book. I refer to this as the face-to-face cycle of the sale. You see, selling is a cyclical event. It is the valuable time spent in the actual sales interview; the time when a commitment is obtained and kept.

Chapter 9 focuses on the approach. What happens in the opening minutes is crucial to the overall success of the sales interview. Chapter 10 is devoted to the art of asking questions and listening effectively. A questioning sequence and listening guidelines are presented to carry through the entire sales interview. The **SPIN** Selling technique is explained and dramatized using a very practical example. Chapter 11 details the techniques to use in making the actual presentation. Units of conviction are the building blocks for creating and making a meaningful sales presentation. The five elements that comprise a complete unit of conviction are explained and illustrated. They are: features; transitional phrase; benefits; evidence; and the tie-down question.

The psychology behind overcoming resistance and closing the sale is presented in chapters 12 and 13. A plan to handle objections is introduced while a separate section in chapter 12 explains several ways of dealing with the difficult price objection. Chapter 13 stresses that closing the sale is the natural conclusion to a successful sales interview. A special section presents specific ways that help a salesperson deal with the rejection so common in selling. The chapters in Part IV include:

9. Approaching the Prospect
10. Identifying Needs by Questioning and Listening
11. Making the Presentation
12. Negotiating Sales Resistance
13. Closing the Sale

PART V—Management Aspects: Personal and Organizational

The service you give the customer after the sale has been completed can be as important, or even more important than the sale itself. Keeping current customers happy and regaining lost clients is the focus of chapter 14. Professional, consultative selling requires that you possess an ample amount of personal organization and self-management skills and habits.

Chapter 15 shows you how to get better control of your time and your activities. The chapter really is all about personal organization and self-management. You cannot manage time, but you can manage yourself and your personal activities. Administrative ability on the part of the salesperson is fundamental to success. Statistics indicate that only about 20 percent of a salesperson's time during a typical day is spent in face-to-face interviews with prospects. Finally, chapter 16 details the job responsibilities of the salesperson, and provides a useful introduction for more advanced sales management courses.

The chapters in this section are:

14. Customer Service and Follow-up After the Sale
15. Personal, Time and Territory Management
16. Sales Force Management

CHAPTER STRUCTURE

I have used a six-part structure as a guide for readers to follow as they study and learn the material in the various chapters.

1. *Learning Objectives.* These have been written to acquaint you with the important concepts to be gleaned from each chapter. They appear on the first page of the chapter and serve as guidelines to follow when searching for the most pertinent material.

2. *Profiles Of Successful Salespeople.* In nine of the chapters, a sales professional gives his or her thoughts and advice pertaining to specific concepts discussed in the chapter.

3. *Main Body Of Each Chapter.* They are organized in outline form to make it readily available for study and review. Each chapter is complemented by examples of actual "sales situations" that take the theory and put it into practice. The material in all 16 chapters is well documented with exhibits, tables, and figures, most taken from actual sales experience.

4. *Developing Partnerships Using Technology.* Technology boxes in chapters 6 to 15 illustrate how sales force automation tools will impact the "road warriors" of the twenty-first century. They will demonstrate how to increase sales efficiency in three functional areas: 1) Personal Productivity; 2) Improved Communications; and 3) Transactional Processing.

5. *A Summary Section.* This section ties together all the main points of the chapter to reinforce learning. Reading the various summaries gives the student a feel for the content of the chapter and provides a tremendous resource to use when attempting to pull together concepts from several chapters.

6. *Questions For Discussion/Exercises/Case Studies.* Each chapter ends with a series of questions to challenge the student's understanding of the material, along with practical exercises or activities designed to get them doing things outside the classroom. The case studies require the students to apply the critical skills discussed in the chapter and give them practice through simulation, role-playing, or experiential learning situations.

ABOUT THE AUTHOR

David J. Lill is a Professor of Marketing in the School of Business, Belmont University, Nashville, Tennessee. He earned his Ph.D. degree in Marketing from the University of Alabama. Dr. Lill is also an independent business consultant specializing in sales training, advertising strategy and communications skills development.

Dr. Lill is a dedicated teacher and has won awards for excellence in teaching. He currently spends some time outside the classroom conducting seminars and training courses on sales and advertising topics. His relationship selling model has been successfully used by companies in the insurance, telecommunications, publishing, banking, real estate, hospitality and automotive industries.

Dr. Lill has published over 85 articles on sales and marketing-related topics in various academic, trade and professional publications. Journals he has published in include: *Journal of Advertising, Journal of the Academy of Marketing Science, Journal of Pharmaceutical Marketing & Management, Sales & Marketing Management, Selling Power, Business Topics and The American Salesman.*

ACKNOWLEDGMENTS

Over the past twenty years I have been influenced by so many people that to mention each one individually is an impossible task. However, the following individuals and companies must be recognized for their help, encouragement and support.

Since one of my primary goals was to produce a text with "real world" concepts and applications, I could not have been successful without the assistance of all those in sales who took time to share their thoughts with me. The insightful comments made by the sales professionals highlighted throughout the book add an important dimension to student learning. The success they have achieved in all areas of their lives through hard work and dedication, while upholding high standards of business ethics, should serve as a model for our young, aspiring business people to emulate.

I want to especially recognize five individuals who have been a personal inspiration to me—Deryl Bass, Tanis Cornell, Tom Hoek, Robert Lambert and Emil Wanke—five consummate professionals, who each in their own way have had a profound effect on the way I think and the actions I take.

I want to thank Donald Silberstein, Director of Business Development for the Bureau of Business Practice, Inc., for his efforts in tracking down the 150 cases that he made available to me. Twenty-four are used as end-of-chapter cases in this book. Each case is based on an "actual" sales situation and provides the student with an excellent learning opportunity.

My personal thanks and appreciation to the following professors, business associates and colleagues. Their insightful suggestions, organizational ideas, and encouragement added significantly to the content of this textbook: Merlin Bauer, *MidState Tech College;* Tim Becker, *Point Loma Nazarene College;* Gary Benson, *Chadron State;* Dick Bickell, R.A. *Siegel Company;* L. Dean Bittick, *East Central College*; F. R. Bosch, *Snow College*; Steve Brown, *Southern Methodist University;* Frank Bingham, *Bryant College;* James Blair, *WRMX-FM Radio* (Nashville); Kenneth Blanchard, founder of *Blanchard Training & Development, Inc.;* Bob Bricker, *Pikes Peak Community College;* David Braun, *L.A. Pierce College;* Cindy Claycomb, *Wichita State University;* Dave Colby, *Mid-State Technical College*; Lester Conyers, *North Georgia College and State University*; Joe DePriest, *Three Rivers Community College*; Bruce Dickinson, *Southeast Technical Institute*; Claude Dotson, *Northwest College;* Donna Duffy, *Johnson County Community College;* Charles Edwards, *Mt. San Antonio College;* Don Ellers, founder of *SALESPRO International;* Timothy Elliott, *San Jacinto College* (Houston); Richard English, *San Diego State University;* Ken Erby, *Chesterfield-Marlboro Tech;* Sandra Fields, *University of Delaware;* Olene Fuller, *San Jacinto College* (Pasadena); Wil Goodheer, president of *International University* (Vienna, Austria); Sandy Haft, *Nassau Community College;* Debra Haley, *Fort Hays State University;* Tom Hoek, president of *Insurance Systems of Tennessee;* Norm Humble, *Kirkwood Community College;* George Johnson, *Marshalltown Community College*; Gary Karns, *Seattle Pacific University;* Gary Kritz, *Coastal Carolina University*; Desiree Cooper Larsen, *Weber State University*; Luis Martinez, *Manager Five Star Program, Chrysler Corporation;* Morris L. Mayer, *University of Alabama;* Cheryl McCarthy, Executive vice president, *Surado Solutions;* Barbara McDonald, *University of Illinois;* David Miller, *Panhandle State University*; Dan Moore, vice president of marketing, *The Southwestern Company;* Nancy Patterson, *Petit Jean Technical College;* Dr. Norman Vincent Peale, author of *The Power of Positive Thinking;* Phillip M. Pfeffer, former president of *Random House Inc.;* Robin Peterson, *New Mexico State University;* Lyn Richardson, *Ball State University;* John Robbins, *Winthrop University*; Andy Saucedo, *Dona Ana Community College of NMSU;* Allen Schemmel, *WSM-AM/FM Radio* (Nashville); Mary Lee Short, *Santa Fe Community College;* Kirk Smith, *Boise State University;* Sandra Taylor, *Athens Area Technical Institute;* Ray Thomas, *Edith Cowan University,* Perth, Australia; Ken Traynor, *Clarion University* and Walt Wyatt, *Cincinnati State University.*

One person warrants a special thank you: Gladys Hudson, former vice-president of *Success Motivation* in Waco, Texas. She was my original mentor, editor and creative inspiration for many ideas in this textbook.

To my wonderful wife, Martha, and my two fabulous children, Jennifer and David, Jr. There is absolutely no way this book could have been completed without their love, understanding and patience.

David J. Lill

PART I

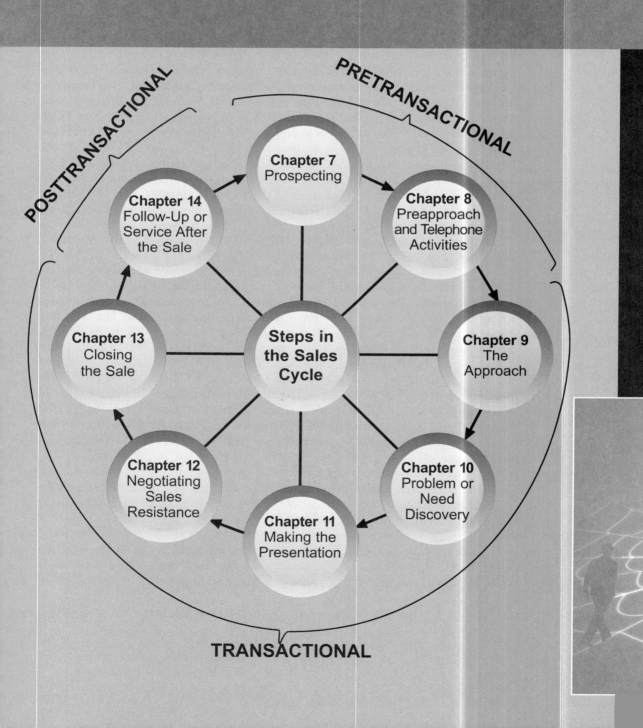

POSTTRANSACTIONAL

PRETRANSACTIONAL

Chapter 7
Prospecting

Chapter 8
Preapproach
and Telephone
Activities

Chapter 14
Follow-Up or
Service After
the Sale

**Steps in
the Sales
Cycle**

Chapter 9
The
Approach

Chapter 13
Closing
the Sale

Chapter 10
Problem or
Need
Discovery

Chapter 12
Negotiating
Sales
Resistance

Chapter 11
Making the
Presentation

TRANSACTIONAL

Relationship Building
and the Sales Cycle Framework

Part I discusses the consultative, problem-solving approach to professional selling. The various characteristics that successful salespeople possess are detailed. Relationship selling involves two-way communication, encourages prospect participation, employs empathy, is interactive and promotes a win-win environment. A principled style of selling has evolved that favors building close and trusting long-term relationships.

A better understanding of the complete selling situation and the problems it generates may be gained by breaking the sale into its basic tasks. It makes sense that if you understand what the steps are in the *Sales Cycle Framework for Relationship Selling,* and what is required to make each step a successful endeavor, then you will become a sales professional much quicker than those who are stumbling through the process trying to figure it out.

Qualities Of High Sales Performers

1. **Exchange information** rather than present products. They tend to ask a variety of questions that force the customer to analyze, evaluate, speculate, or express feelings.

2. **Know when to close.** They advocate their products only after they have identified or created an important need and involved the customer in developing the solution.

3. **Sell to people,** not organizations, and demonstrate a strong commitment to meeting customer needs.

4. Are perceived by prospects as **genuine advocates of prospects' needs,** even while actively promoting the company and its products or services.

5. **Provide value added** to the customer. They act as a resource able to directly provide expertise to the customer.

6. **Regularly establish trust within their own organizations** by sharing information, encouraging participation in decisions, and recognizing the contributions of the internal staff to their success.

7. **Engage in behavior** such as maintaining eye contact, showing enthusiasm, asking questions about customers' needs, restating accurately and being prepared with effective responses to buyers' objections.

C H A P T E R 1

Chapter 1

A Career in Professional Selling

LEARNING OBJECTIVES

- To gain an appreciation of the role of selling in our economy.

- To understand the purpose of personal selling.

- To learn about the different types of sales jobs and the requirements for success in each.

- To identify the personal characteristics that are needed for success in a selling career.

- To examine professional selling as a viable career opportunity.

THE SALES EDGE

Change is often desirable, frequently necessary and always inevitable.

Remember ... only you can give yourself permission to approve of you. Unlock your mind from negative thinking.

Envision yourself a success. What you think about, you become.

Attitude does determine your altitude. It's what's inside that makes you rise.

The right angle to solve a problem is the try-angle.

Eliminate failure as an option, and progress naturally emerges.

The best is yet to come. Yesterday's impossibilities are today's possibilities.

Have your dreams. They are the stuff great people are made of. Reach for the stars but keep your feet on the ground.

Extraordinary desire and persistence drives ordinary people to achieve great things. Achievers are not extraordinary people.

Seven days without laughter makes one weak.

A smile is the shortest distance between two people.

Listen twice as much as you talk. You were given two ears and one tongue.

Encouraging feedback is a process for learning about your impact on those around you.

Success is the progressive realization of worthwhile, predetermined, personal goals.

Excuses are for losers. Winners have ways. May we all find the way.

Determine never to give up. It's when things seem worse that you must not quit.

Goals are dreams with a due date.

Expect the best of yourself. Be SOMEBODY special. The best never consider success optional.

EVERYBODY SELLS

Many interactions between people involve selling. Of course, some are universally recognized as selling: Retail salespeople sell you clothes, furniture, or cameras; a salesperson sells you the car you drive; and your insurance agent sells you a policy. However, many other common transactions not usually recognized as selling involve the same skills, goals, and behavior patterns that professional salespeople use: Waiters attempt to sell you on trying a particular entrée, or adding a dessert to your order; students try to sell professors on agreeing to give them a makeup test; professors attempt to sell students on pursuing a particular major; politicians want to convince constituents to vote for them or convince other politicians to join them in promoting certain projects; trial lawyers sell themselves, their clients, and their interpretation of the law to judges and juries; diplomats work to sell other nations particular international policies; union leaders and management representatives sell one another their respective needs and desires; and family members influence decisions such as where to live, who can use the family car tonight, whether to borrow money for a vacation, and what to cook for dinner. In other words, you are already selling. You are selling yourself, your ideas, and your desire for cooperation and companionship to almost everyone you engage in anything more than the most casual conversation.

SELLING AND OUR ECONOMY

Understanding global strategies is essential in today's competitive marketplace.

Partnerships, customer relationship management, empowerment, team selling, strategic alliances and global strategies are more than mere words to a growing number of sales organizations today. They are the tools with which winning strategies are being fashioned. There is a growing competitiveness among the world's major corporations. Competing with yesterday's sales strategies is dangerous as global competitors battle each other. The latest and best marketing and sales practices are essential in gaining new markets and in defending those you currently serve. The sales profession must rise to the challenge because, as Will Rogers said, "Even if you're on the right track, you'll get run over if you just sit there."[1]

Product life cycles are shrinking and new products are obsolete almost before you can blink an eye. This is the century of "just in time selling," says Carl Everett, director of world wide sales at Intel Corporation.[2] Organizations must have flexible sales forces that can be quickly reconfigured and redeployed. You must take a proactive approach to corporate strategy and market changes.

Anyone considering sales should understand the business world today and what challenges customers face so you can really become a *solutions provider*. Sales professionals demonstrate their value to customers as a consistently productive information and solutions source.

Compensation

Because of their vital role in business, salespeople are among the best-paid employees of a company. More salespeople earn above $100,000 annually than people in any other profession.[3] Exhibit 1.1 is a composite summary of the findings from *Sales & Marketing Management*'s Sales Compensation Survey. In an *S&MM* exclusive survey of nearly 2,000 sales and marketing executives, they found out what people in sales are earning today. The respondents to the survey were asked to provide their own total compensation information (base salary plus commissions and bonuses) as well as that of the top performers of their sales forces, the mid-level performers, and the low-level performers. The top performers are walking away with the fattest wallets by far, averaging $125,844 in total compensation. They are even doing better than their bosses. These are just averages. Some salespeople make less, some make considerably more. Salespeople are catalysts of the economy. They are responsible for keeping goods, services, and ideas flowing.

EXHIBIT 1.1 - Salespeople's Compensation

Position	Total	Base Salary	Bonus & Commission
Sales Executive	$108,572	$71,693	$36,966
Top Performer	$125,844	$70,832	$56,687
Mid-Level	$88,734	$46,563	$42,515
Low-Level	$57,571	$36,906	$20,569
Average Rep	$84,004	$53,293	$31,441

"2001 Salary Survey," *Sales & Marketing Management*'s Sales Compensation Survey (May 2001). See pages 47 to 50 for more detailed information.

Importance of Sales Training

Comprehensive training programs are crucial in today's extremely competitive selling environment. Business is discovering the importance of investing time, money, and effort in training salespeople. All kinds of companies provide continuing sales training on a regular basis. Kodak spends over $20 million a year sending people through their courses at their Marketing Education Center.[4] Forty percent are Kodak's customers and dealers, while newly hired or veteran salespeople comprise the other 60 percent. They see sales training as the basis for winning all future competitive battles. For new reps, Kodak provides six months of formal training in sales skill development, understanding the marketing process, product knowledge, and on the philosophy and culture of the company. Kodak estimates up to $75,000 is spent on each new hire.

In a survey of 250 sales organizations conducted by the Krannert School of Management at Purdue University, the cost of replacing a single sales rep (including recruitment, training, and lost-opportunity costs) ranges from $50,000 to $75,000. A numbing report by Bill Ruch, president of Aptitude Testing for Industry, revealed that in a survey of 125 manufacturing firms every unsuccessful salesperson hired costs a company between $150,000 and $300,000.[5]

After spending $75,000 and devoting months to training, companies have made a significant investment in a salesperson. Productive salespeople are eager to receive this training because they know that learning never stops, and their companies are equally interested in their continued growth. Sales training should not be seen as an insult. Salespeople are most comfortable selling what they understand. By providing intensive hands-on training programs, companies build confidence in their sales force, enabling them to make superior product presentations. This ability also shows customers that they are dealing with a product expert.[6]

Web-Based Sales Training

Blended training involves both Internet and interpersonal sales training.

Gone are the days when the only method of sales force training was to either rotate people through a program or close down once a year for an annual sales seminar. Web-based technology makes training easy and affordable by maximizing flexibility and effectiveness for both the sales force and the sales managers. According to Dean Goettsch, sales training manager for Horizon Blue Cross & Blue Shield of New Jersey, one of the big issues here is the belief that selling time is a very valuable commodity. Any time spent out of the field is costly for your salespeople. The benefits of Web-based training are many, and include:

- 24-hour access – allows for fast and convenient training.
- Easier management of geographically dispersed teams.
- Instant new product information and current product updates – keeps sales force up to date on a daily or even hourly basis.
- Direct performance measurements – feedback can be immediate.
- Economical – reduces costs of airfare, hotel stays, and convention expenses.
- Sales reps can focus their attention on the specific training they need.[7]

One such Internet-based sales training system is *RedHotSalesTV*. It is an Internet training system that allows sales reps to watch streaming videos of Paul Goldner's Red Hot training seminars along with a synchronized PowerPoint presentation. There is also a workbook that can be downloaded by each participant.[8] E-learning is not where it needs to be when it comes to interpersonal sales training. Even the best Internet training cannot replace live sales training, role plays, and simulation exercises. The industry is really going toward *blended* training. You don't get rid of face-to-face training, and you don't get rid of *online* training. Together they form a mutually beneficial relationship.

Reliance on Salespeople

New and improved consumer and industrial products are never accepted automatically. Neither individual nor business consumers can keep up with all the product and service innovations that become available. Every year brings new models in automobiles, home appliances, and automation equipment for offices and manufacturing plants. Some, like DVDs, are designed for mass appeal; others appeal to a limited clientele (an example of the latter is presented in Exhibit 1.2). The service industry is just as busy developing innovations in communication services, new options for shipping methods, and faster methods for delivering mail and consumer goods. Banks and other financial institutions offer new services, consultants put together new service packages, and insurance companies offer new kinds of coverage for businesses and their employees.

How do businesses expect to keep up with pertinent developments just in their own fields? They rely on salespeople! Thomas Edison may have invented the light bulb and Alexander Graham Bell the telephone, but they are not responsible for the variety of electric lights and telephone systems in almost every home and business in the United States – a professional salesperson is responsible.[9] The job of salespeople is to identify customer needs, to determine ways those needs could be met by the products or services they have to offer, and then to provide that information to the customer. Salespeople also work in the other direction: They identify customer needs that cannot be satisfied by the company's present line and communicate those needs to the company for consideration in the development of new products.

EXHIBIT 1.2 - PowerTop SL™. A product designed for a specialized clientele.

At last you can raise and lower the convertible top on your Mercedes with the touch of a button. That's right, now you can avoid the strenuous and oftentimes socially awkward task of putting your top up and down manually.

AutoMagic, Ltd. has combined European design with American technology to develop a computer-controlled state-of-the-art hydraulic system to automate the SL top. PowerTop SL™ invisibly attaches to your existing top, a factory Mercedes switch is added to your console, and handles are permanently installed on the latches ... that's it! Then you

can enjoy the ease and convenience of having an automatic convertible top for your Mercedes.

In approximately thirty seconds the process is complete. No more trying to reach the lever behind the seat to release or lock the window or boot. Just remain safely in your car and push a button ... nothing else. The PowerTop SL™ unit tucks neatly into one corner of your trunk, leaving plenty of room for your golf clubs or luggage. The factory- looking cover conceals and protects the control unit.

THE POSITIVE NATURE OF PROFESSIONAL SELLING

The difficulty with recruiting talented new salespeople is made more challenging, particularly for those firms who seek college graduates, because many college students hold less than positive perceptions and attitudes toward selling as a career. Surveys taken over time indicate that a majority of college students see sales jobs as involving too much travel, interfering with one's home life and leisure time, a frustrating type of work, and requiring certain personality styles to be successful.

Why do these negative perceptions exist and persist? Most of us have had little opportunity to observe professional salespeople at work. Our only contact with salespeople has been with grocery store checkers, retail salespeople (many of whom have been put on the floor with too little sales training), and the telemarketing rep who calls you right in the middle of dinner. Unfortunately, most of us remember these models when we think about selling and tend to view sales as a job to accept if nothing better is available rather than as an exciting career option.

More accurate information and education today is helping to improve attitudes toward sales as a career. Table 1.1 indicates that attitudes toward the selling profession have become more favorable.[10] Students responding to recent surveys now support the view that selling is more challenging and prestigious, requires creativity, offers career opportunities, fosters increasing integrity, and provides better financial incentives than did students in earlier studies.

TABLE 1.1 - Attitudes and Perceptions Toward Selling		
	A 40-Year Comparison	
Perceptions and Attitudes	**1960s**	**2000s**
1. Just a job, not a career	Agree	Disagree
2. Must lie and pretend	Agree	Disagree
3. Little prestige/degrading	Agree	Disagree
4. No challenge/uninteresting	Agree	Disagree
5. No need for creativity	Agree	Disagree
6. Not much financial reward	Agree	Disagree
7. Arrogant/manipulate people	Agree	Neutral
8. Little job security	Agree	Neutral
9. Salespeople are money-hungry	Agree	Neutral
10. Frustrating at times	Agree	Agree
11. Too much travel	Agree	Agree
12. Personality is crucial	Agree	Agree
13. Interferes with home life	Agree	Agree
14. Little leisure time	Agree	Agree

An increasing number of sales managers who recruit at colleges and universities are quite pleased with the caliber of young men and women they are finding. Recruiting students from a college can uncover outstanding sales talent. "Get 'em while they're young." That's the advice of Jon Hawes, director of the Fisher Institute for Professional Selling at the University of Akron.[11] Students may not be as streetwise as someone with years of experience, but on the plus side, they tend to be a lot more technologically proficient. They also have an abundance of energy and enthusiasm, and can be hired before they develop bad habits. Chuck Harris, a vice president at Comdata Transportation Services in Brentwood, Tennessee, helped implement a program called Rapid Deployment that has provided his firm six top salespeople.[12] Comdata hires people right out of college and puts them into a three-month training program that grooms them for a field sales position.

An understanding of the personal attributes that a career in professional selling actually requires quickly dispels any outdated myths an individual may still possess. Four areas of your personality are involved.

Personal Integrity

Continued success in sales requires the highest possible ethical standards in dealings with prospects, established customers, and the salesperson's own company. A salesperson who lies or deceives customers in order to complete a sale is soon out of a job because customers do not place repeat orders and prospects soon get the word that this person is not to be trusted. An outstanding salesperson has high values and operates in the most ethical manner.

Personality Structure

Sales is a demanding career. The salesperson must have a strong internal personality structure, a positive self-image, and a sense of self-worth. A person who is unable to accept the reality that not every prospect becomes a client is devastated by the failure to make a sale with every presentation and feels an overwhelming sense of personal rejection. The persistent myth that salespeople are arrogant, overbearing, and excessively aggressive belies reality. Successful salespeople are instead highly empathetic, interested in other people and their needs, and eager to be of real service to customers and clients.

Personal Relationships

Successful salespeople are in an excellent position to attain status and recognition in the community. They are recognized as productive, capable professionals. Selling need never be personally degrading. Salespeople are not required to pretend, to abdicate their own personalities or needs, or to become doormats for customers. Success in professional selling does not call for assuming an inferior position socially, psychologically, or financially. The most successful salespeople find that their customers become friends with whom they form lasting social attachments. They derive great personal satisfaction from their ability to perform a needed service for their clients while earning a rewarding income for themselves.

Personal Abilities

Success in sales requires high levels of both intellect and developed skills. Salespeople must be able to understand—sometimes quickly and almost intuitively—a customer's business needs and problems. They must interpret those needs and suggest viable solutions even if customers themselves do not have a clear picture of their own needs or cannot verbalize those needs clearly. Salespeople need a broad knowledge of the field in which they operate, and they must understand people and how to relate to them positively. The development of these skills requires not only intelligence but also meticulous training.

DEFINITION OF PERSONAL SELLING

A comprehensive definition of personal selling which forms the basis around which this book has been developed follows:

Personal selling is the process of _seeking_ out people who have a particular need, _assisting_ them to recognize and define that need, _demonstrating_ to them how a particular service or product fills that need, and _persuading_ them to make a decision to use that service or product.

This definition is broad enough to include all types of selling in a number of different settings. It describes the commercial aspect of selling a product or service as well as the process used to solicit funds for charitable organizations or enlist leaders for youth organizations. It includes the activities of athletic coaches, political parties, clergy, and personnel officers in all kinds of organizations.

The fact that we begin learning and practicing basic sales skills almost from birth is a distinct advantage. The hungry baby who cries convinces an adult to provide attention. The child who suggests "Let's play hide-and-seek" is selling playmates on a particular solution to their need for a play activity. The teenager who wants to use the family car is often an exceptionally effective salesperson. Exhibit 1.3 is the story of one young lady who has become quite a sales and marketing professional at an incredibly young age.[13]

Selling is different for every salesperson because it involves the individual's values, personality, purpose, and current emotional and physical status. Selling is different in every situation because different prospects have varying needs, interests, ability to pay, and authority to make a decision. It also involves the prospect's past experience with a product or salesperson, as well as the prospect's values, emotional and physical status, and mental receptiveness.

Because every sales situation is unique, professional selling is an exciting and demanding career in which every day brings opportunities to develop new skills and sales strategies and polish existing ones. The potential for personal and professional growth never ends.

At the same time, personal selling requires a relatively short period of time to get started on the road to success. Other professions require long periods of study combined with various types of apprenticeship training. Physicians study at least eight years beyond high school, and attorneys spend

EXHIBIT 1.3 - The Whiz Kid

Mary Rodas is in her mid-twenties and already has 10 years experience as a vice-president of marketing for Catco Inc. Presently, Mary is president of Catalyst Toys. Mary says she's "the little girl with the toy company – or that's how everybody knows me, which is great. I'm always breaking new barriers, I guess half the time due to my age."

Don Specter, president of the parent company Catalyst Applied Technologies, says "Mary has a natural interest in her products that most people just don't have. She is a toy picker. She has great instincts."

Even at the age of four, she had an uncanny ability to identify and articulate problems. Making the rounds at a high-rise apartment with her father, an assistant superintendent, Mary noticed that a man was putting down tiles wrong and she told her father. As a nine-year-old, Rodas was already a paid toy consultant on weekends. At the age of fourteen, Mary Rodas became the youngest corporate vice-president in America. Her annual salary is over $200,000 along with a 5 percent ownership in the company.

It is the customer's opinion that is most important to Rodas. Her focus is so strong that she refers to Catalyst Toys' customers, not profit, as the bottom line. Mary is concerned with the customer because, as she puts it, "Without a customer there's no business."

In 1993, Mary helped create Balzac, a balloon protected by a stretchy cloth that came in vibrant colors. It was one of the hot Christmas products and turned Catco into a $70 million company. In each stage of development—from color selection, to packaging, to television commercials—she was instrumental. Mary's face has come to represent Balzac. In commercials, promotional materials, and personal appearances, her selling style is evident.

Mary Rodas understands the buying motives of kids. She is a diagnostician and a problem-solver. She says, "Kids like to play with things that look fun and are simple. They don't want to read directions. It's always the few simple, fun ones that remain outside the toy box."

from six to eight years in formal training. Cosmetologists, electricians, mechanics, and other skilled workers must serve a thousand or more hours of apprenticeship. Salespeople often just dive in and gain their expertise in the field.

Becoming a Master Salesperson

Too many people involved in selling have not attempted to learn the basic skills needed for success in the profession. They cop out by saying that they weren't born to be salespeople. They are called the 90-day wonders—because after ninety days they wonder why they ever got into the sales business. Professional salespeople read books, take courses, ask questions, study the techniques of successful salespeople, work for their customers, and continually strive to outperform themselves.

Selling requires a working knowledge of psychology, sociology, communication, and persuasion. It is not a natural process to "close" a deal. It is a skill set to be learned just like anything else. Most salespeople fail because they get to the point where they think they know it all. Success in selling is a constant learning process. You must be a student of your profession. Successful salespeople *are made, not born*, and they are made with concentrated attention, repeated practice, and goal-directed action.[14]

Exhibit 1.4 illustrates the ongoing debate "Can selling be taught?" We are all like computers in that we are only as good as we have programmed ourselves to be philosophically, emotionally, and intellectually. Becoming a real master salesperson takes a long time. Even the best salespeople are still learning and refining their professional skills throughout their entire careers.

EXHIBIT 1.4 - Can Selling Be Taught?

Get ready to retire! You're the father of a natural born salesperson.

Salespeople: Can selling be taught?

"Yes, absolutely," says Kevin Dunshee, an account executive with InterCall. Kevin's ultimate goal is to teach professional selling. He says, "I think there's a certain methodology that works during the selling process. Even if somebody is not a natural at selling, if they work this methodology, they can be successful." Karen Bowden, account manager with Rijnhaave Information Services, sees things a bit differently. "The skills and the techniques can be taught, but really great selling is a natural talent. You can teach a kid to play baseball, but not everybody is in the major leagues. Personally, I think you need both natural talent and discipline to be most successful."

REWARDS OF A SALES CAREER

Personal selling is a dynamic, challenging career for the right person, but it is not for everyone. In all professions, success comes to those who are willing to pay the price for the rewards offered. Consider the rewards offered by professional selling. If you decide those rewards are attractive enough to make you expend the effort necessary, success in personal selling can be yours.

The once popular "Wide World of Sports" television program promised the viewer "the thrill of victory—the agony of defeat." This thrill of victory makes sales an exciting and satisfying career, but the thrill is not just that of earning the monetary rewards or beating out the competition. That is actually a minor part of the satisfaction of successful selling. According to Nick DiBari, the actual monetary compensation earned by salespeople is often only a small part of the total picture of career satisfaction.[15]

The true victory a successful salesperson enjoys consists of moving up to satisfy higher personal needs.[16] Maslow's hierarchy of needs (see Figure 1.1) has special significance for professional salespeople. In the beginning, salespeople are concentrating on supplying their lower-order needs: earning a living, providing security for themselves and their families, and being accepted socially by their peers. As they satisfy these basic needs, salespeople can concentrate on the higher-level needs: self-acceptance (a positive self-image), making a contribution to life in general, and self-actualization (becoming all one can be; knowledge and achievement for its own sake).

FIGURE 1.1

Hierarchy of Personal Needs

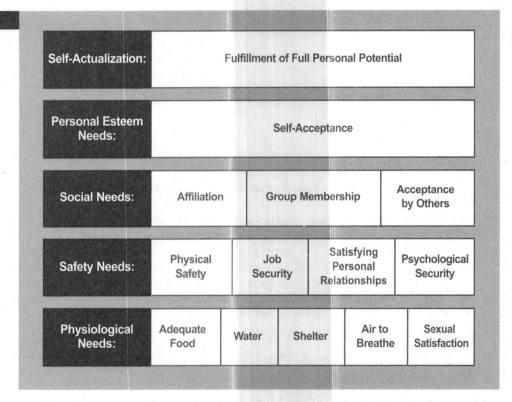

Self-Actualization:	Fulfillment of Full Personal Potential			
Personal Esteem Needs:	Self-Acceptance			
Social Needs:	Affiliation	Group Membership	Acceptance by Others	
Safety Needs:	Physical Safety	Job Security	Satisfying Personal Relationships	Psychological Security
Physiological Needs:	Adequate Food	Water / Shelter	Air to Breathe	Sexual Satisfaction

Variety and Independence

A sales career frees the individual from a locked-in daily routine. Salespeople are likely to work in a variety of places and deal with prospects who have widely different personalities. What works with one prospect may antagonize another. Consequently, salespeople must always be aware of every element of the environment and adjust quickly. Selling is never boring.

Salespeople can exercise a greater measure of control over their time and activities than many other professional people. Sales is not a nine-to-five job. The hours are usually flexible, long one day and short another. Because salespeople's jobs are not structured for them, they must be self-starters and exert tremendous self-discipline.

EXHIBIT 1.5 - A Potential Career Path for Professionals in Selling

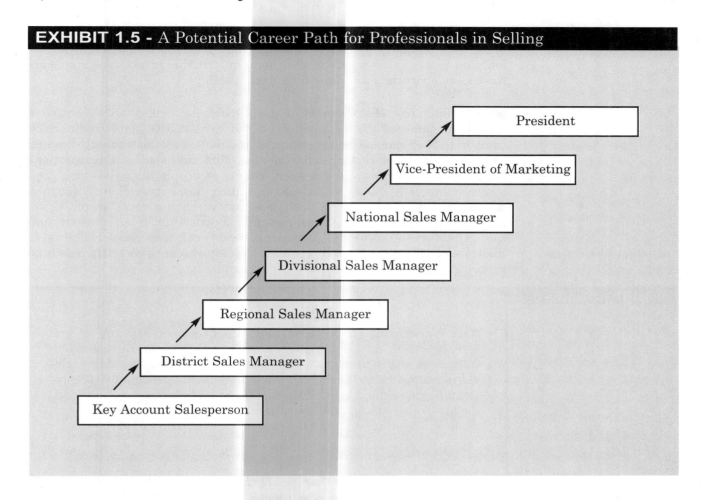

Opportunity for Advancement

Effective salespeople are not forced into any one career path. Almost any option for career advancement is open to them. Exhibit 1.5 illustrates a potential career path for a highly motivated salesperson. As you move up the corporate hierarchy, the various options require a different blending of personal skills and characteristics. As a result, there is simply no guarantee that a successful salesperson will also make a successful manager. Many talented salespeople refuse a promotion to higher managerial positions. They simply love what they do, and can often earn more money selling than they can moving into a middle-management position. Advancement comes by moving into a larger territory, moving to a different product in the same company, or moving to a new company that offers greater rewards.

Promotion to Sales Management. A sales manager may have either limited or extremely broad duties. The first step into sales management is often supervising two or three other salespeople—monitoring their activities, providing field training through joint sales calls, and/or recruiting additional sales representatives while continuing personal sales activities. More comprehensive sales management opportunities involve managing an entire local, regional, or nationwide sales division. Such a position might include budgeting, planning for sales training, sales promotion, and recruiting, in addition to executive status in the company. At this level, sales managers have less opportunity and time for personal selling.

Moving into Top Management. Sales experience makes an executive a valuable member of the management team. While CEOs have traditionally come from the financial and legal ranks, companies are increasingly tapping into the sales and marketing departments to find their leaders. Organizations are looking for CEOs who are good leaders of people and who have good strategic minds.[17] Many skills used in selling closely resemble those skills needed in top management. Both jobs involve having great people skills; maintaining control under stress; recognizing opportunities and threats; and the capability of locating, processing, and analyzing vast amounts of information. Figure 1.2 profiles two individuals who have certainly benefited from their backgrounds in sales.[18]

FIGURE 1.2	
Salespeople in the Executive Suite	**Mel Karmazin,** *CEO, CBS Corporation*, doesn't ask any of his salespeople to do anything he hasn't done. Karmazin attended college at night and sold advertising time during the day. He characterizes himself as a "relentless cold-caller," netting $70,000 in commissions in one year. Karmazin was admired as a salesperson for his preparedness and knowledge of his clients' business. These same skills earned him the top spot as CEO of *CBS* in 1999.
	Carleton (Carly) Fiorina, *CEO, Hewlett-Packard Co.*, has been described as a "selling powerhouse." This selling machine, who started as a sales rep for *AT&T*, has twice been named as *Fortune* magazine's most powerful woman in America. Her most impressive sale was selling herself to *Hewlett-Packard*. Fiorina had no computer industry experience and was in competition with other, more experienced candidates when she decided to turn her weakness into a strength. Fiorina knew her competition for the top position at *HP* had more computer expertise. This did not stop Fiorina. Instead of offering computer expertise, Fiorina convinced the *HP* board members they were missing strategic vision in their company. As a result of her persistence, Fiorina walked away with the job.

Entrepreneurship. Sales is an ideal introduction to the world of business for a young person interested in owning and running a business. No business can survive without a viable marketing organization, and an owner or chief executive who understands this part of the business is in an excellent position to launch and manage a new enterprise successfully. The entrepreneur can find people who understand manufacturing and finance, but the sales and marketing staff must share the founder's dream if the concept is to reach fruition.

Security

Every company will always need salespeople. In fact, the demand appears to be steadily increasing rather than decreasing. Good salespeople are eagerly sought, and most organizations provide excellent rewards and preferential treatment for their top sales performers. They know that good salespeople who become dissatisfied can easily go to work for a competitor and possibly take their established customers with them. Salespeople can directly affect their own income and security. Because they are usually paid according to their performance, they can directly determine their own income by deciding how much time and effort to invest in the job. Personal initiative is immediately and automatically rewarded. Unlike other employees of a company, salespeople are not forced to wait until someone notices their outstanding work, until annual performance evaluation time, or until the budget can stand raises to receive additional income. Their security comes from their own personal decisions about how hard and how efficiently they want to work. "Work, in many ways, is like money; if you are willing to expend enough of it, you can have almost anything you want."[19]

DISADVANTAGES OF A SALES CAREER

Like any other profession, selling has some drawbacks and reasons why it is not right for everybody. The same qualities of the profession that some see as advantages are distinct disadvantages to others. Some people view a fixed salary as more secure than an income dependent entirely upon their direct performance in a given time period. Others dislike the irregular hours or the traveling around to meet clients that salespeople see as the variety that gives spice to their lives.

Probably the greatest problem faced by every salesperson and everyone who considers sales as a profession is handling rejection. Not every sales presentation produces a sale. Not every prospect needs the service or product, and an ethical salesperson never presses for an order from a prospect whose needs will not be met by that product. No salesperson can ever be one hundred percent successful in closing sales, even when the prospect really needs the product or service. Successful salespeople learn quickly that rejection is not directed toward them personally. Prospects who do not buy are rejecting the *product or service—not the salesperson*. The decision seldom has anything to do with the salesperson's worth as a human being. Even the occasional prospect who reacts negatively to a salesperson does so as a result of the prospect's personal opinion—an opinion that may be colored by prejudice or completely unfounded. Rejection is not proof that the salesperson is in some way unworthy or inadequate. Salespeople who cannot separate their own personal worth from the product they sell may become too paralyzed by fear to approach another prospect because they face a renewal of rejection.

CLASSIFICATION OF SALES JOBS

Sales jobs are so diverse that they fit a wide variety of personal needs and interests. Variety exists from industry to industry. The responsibilities of a marketing representative who calls on large manufacturing companies to create awareness of computer systems for production-control are vastly different from those of the real estate salesperson who is selling homes to families. Sales careers vary within industries as well. In the computer industry, the work of the marketing representative just described bears little resemblance to that of the salesperson in a retail store who demonstrates and sells personal computers for home or small-office use. Similarly, the residential real estate salesperson is in a different world from that of the real estate developer who puts together multimillion-dollar projects for shopping centers, office complexes, and industrial parks.

As different as sales jobs may be, they all share some basic similarities:

- The need to understand the prospect's problem.

- The need for appropriate technical and/or product knowledge.

- The ability to translate product features into benefits that address the prospect's problem.

The type of people chosen by companies to fill sales positions varies according to the type of selling task as well as other factors such as pricing policies, the extent and complexity of the product line, types of distribution channels, and the type and amount of mass advertising employed.

Derek Newton developed a classification format for sales jobs that has become a standard model. Because it has been empirically researched, his format is presented here. Newton studied responses from over 1,000 sales executives from manufacturing, wholesaling, retail, and service firms. He identifies four types of selling found across this variety of industries.[20]

Trade Selling

The trade seller's primary responsibility is to increase business from present and potential customers through merchandising and promotional assistance. They usually deal with buyers who are resellers (wholesalers and retailers). Long-term relationships are important for success. In addition to delivering orders and replenishing inventory, this salesperson's tasks involve persuading the customer to provide additional shelf space, setting up product displays in the store, rotating stock as inventory is replenished, and perhaps conducting in-store demonstrations or distributing samples to customers. Companies usually do not encourage their trade sellers to conduct vigorous sales efforts. They are expected to generate increased sales, largely through assisting the customer move a larger volume of inventory.

Missionary Selling

The missionary salesperson's task is largely one of educating those who ultimately decide what product the consumer will use. The most familiar example of the missionary salesperson is the drug detail salesperson who calls on physicians to introduce and describe the pharmaceutical company's products and persuade them to prescribe their medications for patients who could benefit from them. In addition to pharmaceutical firms, food and beverage manufacturers, transportation firms, and public utility companies employ missionary salespeople.

Technical Selling

A fast-growing class of salespeople is the technical specialist group, the engineers, scientists, and others with the technical expertise to explain the advantages of the company's product. These salespeople sell directly to the firms that use their products. They are very important in such industries as chemicals and machinery. They act like management consultants in that they identify, analyze, and solve their customers' problems. In the past, technical specialists have been more concerned with explaining the product than with securing the order, but many decision-makers are now more knowledgeable about technology and more likely to respond favorably to the technical specialist. Consequently, many companies are teaching these salespeople basic selling skills to help them be persuasive in making presentations and closing sales.

New Business Selling

This type of salesperson *seeks out and persuades* new customers to buy for the very first time. They are extremely vital to firms putting their focus on sales growth. New business selling includes selling new products to existing customers or existing products to new customers. The characteristics discussed later in this chapter—perseverance, empathy, ability to ask questions, initiative, and resourcefulness—are vital to sales success for this category of salesperson.

Selling for a Manufacturer. Manufacturers' sales reps sell the products produced by the company that employs them. They might sell to other manufacturers, various marketing middlemen, or directly to consumers. Exhibit 1.6 lists five specific categories of salespeople and describes the content of their jobs.

EXHIBIT 1.6 - Categories of Salespeople

Five Types of Salespeople

Account Representative — A salesperson who calls on a large number of already established customers in, for example, the food, textiles, apparel, or wholesaling industries. Much of this selling is low key and there is minimal pressure to develop new business.

Detail Salesperson — A salesperson who, instead of directly soliciting an order, concentrates on performing promotional activities and introducing products. The medical detail salesperson, for example, seeks to persuade doctors, the indirect customers, to specify the pharmaceutical company's trade name product for prescriptions. The company's actual sales are ultimately made through a wholesaler or direct to pharmacists who fill prescriptions.

Sales Engineer — A salesperson who sells products for which technical know-how and the ability to discuss technical aspects of the product are extremely important. The salesperson's expertise in identifying, analyzing, and solving customer problems is another critical factor. This type of selling is common in the chemical, machinery, and heavy-equipment industries.

Industrial Products Salesperson, Non-technical — This salesperson sells a tangible product to industrial or commercial purchasers; no high degree of technical knowledge is required. Industries such as packaging materials or standard office equipment use this type.

Service Salesperson — A salesperson who sells intangibles, such as insurance and advertising. Unlike the four preceding types, those who sell services must be able to sell the benefits of intangibles.

Used with permission of *Sales & Marketing Management* magazine.

The Order Taker and the Order Getter. The order taker basically responds to requests and the order getter is a creative problem solver. The salesperson whose work is described as *order taking* responds or reacts to customers' expressed desires. Responsive selling jobs may be either inside or outside. Inside sales jobs include retail clerks in department stores, specialty shops, and other retail establishments. By being helpful and pleasant and by suggesting additional purchases, retail clerks may create a few sales, but they generally just assist customers in completing the purchase of goods they have already chosen. Outside order·takers are route salespeople who service retail clients to deliver orders or replenish inventory; the

"No nervous twitches, no history of anxiety, no high blood pressure, heart rate normal. How long did you say you've been in sales?"

main selling tasks are likely to be left to salespeople at higher levels in the organization.

The order taker may engage in *suggestive selling*—that is, ask you to purchase an additional item. The next time you stop at a McDonald's drive-thru and the person asks in a barely discernible voice, "Would you like an apple pie with your Big Mac and fries?" you are observing suggestive selling in action. And it works!

Order getting, or creative selling, requires ingenuity and the ability to generate demand for a product or service among potential buyers. The product may be tangible—such as automobiles, real estate, office equipment, water softeners, or swimming pools—or the product may be intangible—such as a complex telecommunications system, investment services, consulting services, educational or personal development programs, or advertising. Creative personal selling generally offers the greatest opportunity for high income because it demands the highest level of personal skill, dedication, and effort.

Creative salespeople are charged with developing new sales and maintaining relationships with previous customers by making additional sales to existing clients and supporting these clients in the use of the products and services they purchase.

Selling at Retail. The largest number of salespeople are employed in the various aspects of retail selling. A retail salesperson sells products or services to customers for their own personal use. They may be residential real estate brokers, retail store clerks, insurance agents, telephone salespeople, or direct-to-consumer salespeople who hold group meetings or sell door-to-door.

Several million direct-to-consumer salespeople represent firms such as Amway, Shaklee, Oxyfresh, Mannatech, and Mary Kay, to name just a few. There are literally hundreds of direct-selling companies employing millions of part-time and full-time sales reps.[21]

CHARACTERISTICS OF SUCCESSFUL SALESPEOPLE

No one list of traits exactly describes every successful salesperson. Salespeople are as diverse as members of any other profession. They include both extroverts and introverts—and all the degrees in between, shy and outspoken, talkative and quiet. However, certain core characteristics seem to be present to some degree in most successful salespeople, despite the numerous ways individuals express those characteristics and adapt them to their own styles. [22]

Enthusiasm

Ralph Waldo Emerson said, "Nothing great was ever achieved without enthusiasm."[23] In one survey, sales executives indicated that the most important characteristic in new salespeople is enthusiasm.[24] A distinction must be made between people who are enthusiastic about their product and those who are merely eager to take the prospect's money. Enthusiasm in salespeople is based on a genuine belief in the product and a conviction that it will serve the needs of the prospect. Such enthusiasm is communicated both verbally and nonverbally to the prospect in terms of the salesperson's own personality. Enthusiasm may be expressed as calm, quiet confidence or excited activity. However it is demonstrated, real enthusiasm is highly attractive and reassuring to prospects.

Empathy

"Nothing can stop the man with the right mental attitude from achieving his goal; nothing on earth can help the man with the wrong mental attitude."

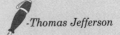

-Thomas Jefferson

Empathy, the ability to understand another person's concerns, opinions, and needs, whether sharing them or not, provides salespeople with the *sales edge* of being able to think and understand "with" the prospect during a sales call. Ken Germain, a successful stockbroker, says, "The key is truly to put aside your own needs and your ego and to listen to what the client is saying.... In the initial conversation, I will not, at any time, talk about a particular product.... I want to get a good handle on what problems or needs they may have, without discussing products."[25] By careful listening, effective salespeople absorb prospects' reactions, generate an upbeat environment, and sell themselves to prospects. The combination of sincerity and empathy enables them to tailor the presentation to mesh precisely with the prospect's stated problems.

Goal Direction

Stay focused on your goals and daily activities. A half-dozen things make 80 percent of the difference between success and failure. Ask yourself what things contribute the most to your success.[26] Goal-directed salespeople often respond positively to incentives such as money, prestige, recognition, and pride of accomplishment, which they see as tools they can use to reach their overall goals. When these incentives fit into their overall plan for achieving the goals that represent self-actualization for them, salespeople go all out to win them. Awards, plaques, prizes, and other sales recognition devices serve as a means of helping salespeople feel they have fulfilled their need for social and peer acceptance. They are then free to move up to satisfaction of higher needs—being of service to others and experiencing self-actualization—the levels at which they find it easier to exercise empathy and serve the needs of others, prime requirements for becoming master salespeople.

Ability to Ask Questions

Good salespeople ask questions; poor ones just keep talking. The salesperson needs to remain in control of the sales interview, and the person who is asking questions is the one in control. Salespeople who learn to ask the right kinds of questions get new prospects, discover qualifying information that points out the best prospects, uncover prospects' dominant buying motives, and prevent most objections and stalls. Asking questions is the salesperson's best tool for keeping the interview on track and moving toward a successful close, while also giving the prospect the feeling of remaining in control of the situation.

Resourcefulness

Top salespeople are resourceful. On the spur of the moment, they can think of new ways to make an old point, new applications and creative uses for products, and unique reasons for a particular prospect to make a buying decision. They can think on their feet under pressure. Resourcefulness operates like a reflex action, an automatic response. Resourcefulness comes from an agile and analytical mind and allows the salesperson to stay on the right side of *the fine line between being just right and very wrong*. In the sales situation, the right word or phrase clears away the fog and reveals the solutions. The wrong word or phrase is like putting a drop of ink into a glass of water; it obscures everything. Resourceful salespeople always seem to have at hand a barrelful of ideas and strategies. Their secret is that they work diligently at filling their barrels by keeping records of what has worked in the past, by studying product information and general industry needs, and by learning how to deal with people. Under pressure, their well-stocked barrels generally contain the right strategy.

Administrative Ability

Efficient self-management, especially the management of time, is essential to success in selling. Salespeople's most productive time is spent face-to-face with prospects. But they also are required to attend meetings, travel, wait, prepare for interviews, read, study, attend to paperwork, and conduct after-sale follow-up and service.

Salespeople must attend to a number of nonselling and administrative tasks. This means that only a small portion of their precious time can be spent in direct contact with prospects and clients. Efficient time management can make the difference between success and failure. Time and territory management is one of the most critical issues for salespeople today, A typical sales day, according to research done by the *Dartnell Institute of Business* in Chicago, is spent in the following way: 24 percent traveling, 21 percent waiting, 19 percent paperwork and administration, and 36 percent on sales-related activities.[27]

Initiative

All great salespeople have a powerful, unrelenting, internal drive to excel. This intrinsic motivation can be shaped and molded, but it cannot be taught.[28] Successful salespeople are self-motivated. They are self-starters who exercise initiative. They do not wait to be told to prospect, to be assigned calls to make, or to be urged to end the presentation with a close. They must see the work that needs to be done and take personal responsibility for doing it. Creative ideas that surface during a presentation must be implemented then and there— without time to ask the sales manager for advice. Salespeople who have self-confidence supported by adequate product knowledge and belief in their own ability to succeed feel free to exercise initiative. Initiative is supported by a high energy level, and a love of independence balanced with rigid self-discipline.

Perseverance

Setbacks often outnumber triumphs, and salespeople must have reserves of strength and resilience to fall back on when this happens. Depending upon the type of sales activity and the product or service being marketed, the number of sales closed compared to the number of presentations made usually ranges from 5 percent to 50 percent or more. Salespeople need perseverance in several areas:

- The ability to keep going to another prospect no matter how many have refused to buy.

- The ability to make repeated presentations to the same prospect over a period of time.

- The ability to continue asking for an appointment to make a presentation until one is finally granted.

Sales professionals have an abundance of persistence and respond competitively when challenged. Wall Street's *John Slade* is an inspiring example! In 1936 he came to New York after being booted off the Olympic German field hockey team for being Jewish. His job for the next few years, aside from running tickets on the exchange floor, was meeting immigrant boats at the docks and checking passenger names for those he recognized. Eventually, he had acquired 20 clients and a new position – foreign bond trader. Today Mr. Slade, who walks 23 blocks to work each day at the *tender age of 93,* continues to "work hard and remains loyal" to his brokerage firm Bear, Stearns and Company.[28]

**Pleasant
Personality**

The way to make a friend is to be one. The salesperson with a pleasant, outgoing disposition is remembered and favored. A key to forming a pleasant personality is to like people and genuinely enjoy knowing as many different kinds of people as possible. People respond to those who like them.

Department store entrepreneur J.C. Penney said, "All great business is built on friendship."[29]   How do you build friendships in today's tough competitive sales climate? Find out what the buyer needs, then make every effort to deliver it. Ask yourself: "What would I do if I really wanted to be friends with this person?" The answer will tell you how to build a long-term relationship.

SUMMARY

Selling is a basic component of all human interaction, although it is often given various other names. Because of the importance of selling in business, salespeople are among the highest-paid of all professionals and make the greatest impact on the profitability and success of the organization. Businesses are becoming more aware of the importance of selling, and more and more salespeople are coming to regard their work as a profession that offers many opportunities for advancement and career satisfaction.

Professional selling offers work that involves a number of different skill levels and a wide diversity of activities. People with all types of personalities can be successful in sales, but some special characteristics enhance the likelihood of success: Enthusiasm, sincerity, empathy, goal direction, administrative ability, resourcefulness, perseverance, a pleasant personality, and initiative make success in sales easier. Although professional selling is a demanding and challenging career, it offers outstanding opportunities for career satisfaction and for personal achievement and growth—advantages that far outweigh the hard work and dedication required for success.

QUESTIONS FOR THOUGHT AND DISCUSSION

1. In the sense that all persuasion is a form of "selling," name the types of situations in which you most frequently "sell." In which of these are you most often successful? If persuasion is an important part of selling, is selling also a form of leadership? Explain your answer.

2. What career limits are imposed on one who chooses sales? Illustrate.

3. Are salespeople born or made? Justify your answer.

4. Why is a feeling of rejection a problem for salespeople? Is this feeling an inevitable part of a sales career?

5. Describe the four broad classes of sales jobs and give examples of each.

6. For what does a company depend upon salespeople, in addition to securing orders for products?

7. What responsibilities belong to the salesperson after the order is signed? How does the discharge of these responsibilities affect the entire sales process?

8. Salespeople are interdependent with other members of the company. Why is this true in respect to the following factors: product changes, pricing, shipping and supply, and competition?

9. Name some qualities that seem to be shared by most successful salespeople. How do these qualities contribute to success? Can they be developed, or are they innate? Does this mean that a single type of personality is required for success in sales?

ACTIVITIES

1. Read the listings of sales job offerings in the Sunday classified section of your newspaper. What different types of selling jobs are available? What salaries and benefits are mentioned? What requirements in training, education, and experience are stated?

2. Interview a sales manager and ask what qualities that manager looks for when hiring salespeople. Also ask what personal qualities are evident in most of the top salespeople in that organization.

Case Study
CASE 1.1

Mary Landown will soon graduate from college with a degree in marketing. Mary entered college as a biology major but felt she might not be able to get a job in that field without going to graduate school. She has enjoyed her marketing classes, has been active in student government, and is eager to start earning some money, especially since she has been on a strict budget throughout college and has college loans to repay.

Concerned about what kind of job she should seek, Mary has recently taken a career interest survey that showed high scores in public speaking, sales, marketing, medical science and service, teaching, and writing; she made average scores in home management, agriculture, engineering, music, and drama; low scores were reported in nature, athletics, social science, mathematics, and clerical.

Mary has been offered the following three jobs:

1. SALES REPRESENTATIVE FOR A CABINETRY COMPANY

After a month's training at the home office, Mary would call on contractors, kitchen designers, and commercial interior designers. This offer includes a moderate salary plus commissions and an automobile allowance. Advancement to senior sales representative is possible after two years and to branch manager after six to eight years.

2. DETAIL SALESPERSON FOR PHARMACEUTICALS

Mary would, after three months' training, begin calling on doctors and pharmacists to explain the details and qualities of new drugs. She would also be expected to open new accounts. The job provides an automobile and travel allowance, and two or three nights per week of travel are standard. This company offers the highest total pay of any of the job possibilities, but the salary alone is relatively low if bonuses are not earned.

3. SALES REPRESENTATIVE FOR A MAJOR BUSINESS MACHINES COMPANY

Mary would start out selling memory typewriters to small businesses. If successful, she would move into selling small computer systems, primarily with financial applications. She would be on a straight base salary the first year and move to a base plus commissions thereafter.

1. Which job should Mary take? Why?

2. Which job would you take? Why?

C H A P T E R   2

Consultative or Relationship Selling

LEARNING OBJECTIVES

- To understand the role relationship selling plays in today's economy and how it differs from the past stereotype of selling.

- To learn the steps in consultative selling and the purpose of each step.

- To compare and contrast relationship selling and the traditional sales model.

- To introduce Customer Relationship Management (CRM) technology.

- To examine and understand gender issues in selling.

- To examine the usefulness of continuous quality improvement in a sales organization.

PROFESSIONAL SELLING IN A TECHNOLOGY WORLD

"Your professionalism is defined not by the business you are in, but by the way you are in business."

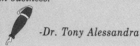

-Dr. Tony Alessandra

It is impossible to ignore the profound effects the Internet and technology are having on professional selling. Yet the e-commerce revolution may not be the most important change that's happening in sales. There is a second revolution occurring. This other revolution is in the consultative selling process where the buyer requires advice and expertise. It is here that face-to-face selling has been the most effective channel to the customer. Even Internet sales companies, such as Charles Schwab and Dell Computer, have created face-to-face sales forces to reach the segments of their markets requiring complex customized products and services. Their clicks-and-mortar strategies rely on sales professionals who can create significant customer value by helping clients define their problems and design unique solutions. This new selling is all about value creation: how the selling process itself can be used to create value for the customer. As Tom Dolan, president of Xerox North America, puts it, "Every call today must create such value that the customer would willingly pull out a checkbook to pay for it."[1]

Consultative selling—in which sales reps demonstrate not just a product's technical features, but how it can solve a business problem and save money—isn't a new idea. Yet experts estimate that only 20 percent of American companies have adopted the idea.[2] Positioning yourself as consultant and partner creates a more equal relationship with prospects and customers. The willingness and ability to meet each customer's needs is the cornerstone of building partnerships. Clients want business partners, not tennis partners.

When utilities giant ConEdision Solutions sells to clients, it doesn't just sell energy options; it sells cost-cutting solutions that offer ongoing savings. For instance, when the U.S. Postal Service needed to reduce its energy costs, ConEd sales reps explained that boilers, air conditioning units, and lighting systems within postal buildings could be preprogrammed to operate on alternating energy sources depending on the time of day. Doing so allowed 12 post offices in New York City to save $250,000 in one year. "You're always using the least expensive energy for that type of equipment for that time of day," says Steve Manning, ConEd Solutions vice-president of marketing and sales.[3] ConEd also gives its clients a follow-up mechanism to continually balance their energy usage at a level that's most efficient for them.

Build or Break a Relationship

Partnership is a positive word that makes customers feel that the sales rep is looking out for their best interests. The partnership formed between the buyer and seller is not a "legal" partnership. Rather it is a part of the continuous quality improvement process companies are implementing. To be successful, the salesperson takes time to get to know the customer's business situation, needs, cash flow problems, decision-making process, and the competitive environment. In sales, a partnership is a living demonstration of the attitudes sales reps have toward their customers.[4] Exhibit 2.1 illustrates the key elements that can build or break this trust-bond relationship between buyer and seller. Relationship selling allows you to grasp a company's needs by putting yourself on the customer's side of the desk. You are first a *diagnostician*.

EXHIBIT 2.1 - How to Build or Break a Relationship

Relationship Builders

1. Treat customers like lifelong partners.
2. Become a solutions provider.
3. Deliver more service than you promise.
4. Schedule regular service calls.
5. Develop open and honest communication.
6. Use the "we can" approach.
7. Take responsibility for mistakes made.
8. Be an ally for the customer's business.

Relationship Breakers

1. Focus only on making the sale.
2. Simply wait for a problem to develop.
3. Over-promise and under-deliver.
4. Wait for customers to call you.
5. Lie or make exaggerated claims.
6. Use the "us versus them" approach.
7. Blame somebody else. Knock a competitor
8. Focus on your own personal gain

Consultative salespeople create a relationship, an information transfer, a support for client goals and enthusiasm for their success. Mike Hill, business development director at PricewaterhouseCoopers based in Dallas, believes that we need to get away from a selling mentality and let the customer tell us their needs. His view is that they are building a relationship, based on trust in their expertise that can help clients solve problems. Hill says, "We talk about our approach to solving the client's problem and sometimes don't even need to ask for the business. The client often asks us."[5]

To be a consultant rather than just a salesperson you have to be resourceful, a value provider, and a friend to clients. If you're not, clients will shop for price, or these days, just go to the *Internet*. The consultative salesperson works hard helping others succeed – not just helping them purchase. Unless you are willing to commit to excellence, consultation will not occur. Lisa Ciampi, sales rep for Design Display Inc. in Birmingham, Alabama, feels consultative selling is all about being a marketing advisor and problem solver. She says, "Consultative selling is an attitude or mind-set toward the whole selling process. It's understanding the products you sell, your competition, and the market and making recommendations that are in the client's best interest, not necessarily in your own."[6] Here are some key characteristics of relationship or consultative selling:

"In professional selling, as in medicine, prescription before diagnosis is malpractice."

- Discover and understand the customers' problems and needs.

- Partner with the customers – become a valuable resource.

- Demonstrate to customers how they can achieve their goals with your product or service.

- Have a true conviction that your business, product, and/or services are the best.

- Believe in yourself. A positive attitude makes it all work.

RELATIONSHIP SELLING VERSUS TRADITIONAL SELLING

It just makes sense that if salespeople understand what the steps are in the *Relationship Model of Selling,* and what it takes to make each step a successful endeavor, then they will become professionals in selling much quicker than those individuals who are simply stumbling through the process hoping to figure it out. The *sales cycle model* in the actual face-to-face meeting between the salesperson and prospect includes these five steps:

1. The Approach
2. Identifying Needs
3. Making the Presentation
4. Overcoming Resistance (Handling Objections)
5. Gaining Commitment (Closing the Sale)

Figure 2.1 contrasts the amount of time the consultative salesperson and the traditional salesperson spend in each step. Sales trainer Brian Tracy indicates that "the old pyramid model of selling has been turned on its pointy head."[7] The 40 percent of the equation that used to be closing is now *building rapport and trust.* Meanwhile *reassuring and closing* has shrunk to just 10 percent of the model. The salesperson spends the vast majority of time in the first two steps, whereas the traditional salesperson exerts most of the effort and the majority of time on presenting features and trying to close.

Relationship selling involves not just thinking of your customers, *but thinking like them.* Visionary salespeople concentrate on understanding the unique concerns of prospects and clients. Relationship selling signifies a distinct method of selling. It combines understanding customer needs, alignment with customer vision, and creation of value through creative thinking. The goal for consultative sales professionals is to learn how to communicate with their

FIGURE 2.1				
Relationship Selling Versus Traditional Selling	**Phases**	**Relationship Model of Selling**	**Traditional Sales Model**	
			time spent in each phase	time spent in each phase
	Approach	Building Trust (Rapport)	40%	Telling 10%
	Identifying Needs	Probe, Ask Questions, and Listen	30%	Qualifying 20%
	Making the Presentation	Sell Benefits	20%	Presenting Features 30%
	Resistance and Gaining Commitment	Reassure and close	10%	Closing Long and Hard 40%

business partners and establish an alliance that is extensive in scope and relevant to the customer's own vision.[8] This viewpoint is not in accord with traditional sales thinking but is most compatible with the *relationship model of selling.*

Customers Buy Solutions

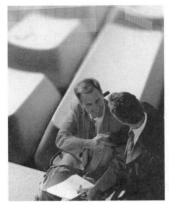

You are a solutions provider.

Technology has helped open new markets, speed communications between sellers and their prospects and customers, and frankly, created a whole new set of problems that salespeople can help clients solve. Customers can now conduct many of their transactions online and have little need for a salesperson that doesn't add value to the transaction. This requires a much more sophisticated and complex set of skills than those possessed by the traditional salesperson. Unless you can offer your clients expertise and guidance, you will be as dead as Willy Loman, the pitiable salesman in Arthur Miller's play *Death of a Salesman.*[9]

All advantage is temporary and the faster the clock ticks, the more temporary the advantage. FedEx was the first to-offer package-tracking information to customers. And it was the first to offer email service that allows the sender of a package to notify the recipient that a package has been sent. Then UPS went on the offensive by offering e-logistics that allows companies to increase the speed of business by sending their customers' orders directly to UPS. FedEx Vice President of Electronic Commerce Marketing David Roussain says, "Customers want to buy solutions and the key is to identify the business problems that your customers have so you can help them solve their problems.[10] Technology is a great enabler to help you, but you have to put together a solution that will actually save your customers time and money."

Low-end selling – essentially *transaction processing* and *order taking* – will continue to shift away from field sales forces into the more efficient, cost-effective, and faster venue provided by the Internet. But this doesn't mean that the Internet will replace the professional salesperson. Selling is simply becoming more strategic. It's moving up the food chain, and the need for relationship selling is increasing. Your company may sell accounting services, chicken wings, or do Web site design. However, that's really not what customers are buying. By demonstrating how you can help customers achieve the goals of their organization, you distinguish yourself from competitors. "Selling is still about relationships, and people buy from people they like," says sales force automation consultant David Hamacher.[11] Order-takers will vanish, but salespeople who know that selling is about building long-term partnerships will flourish.

In their book *MaxiMarketing,* Stan Rapp and Tom Collins stress that developing relationships with customers generates long-term repeat business. More importantly, building relationships is crucial to a company's survival in an increasingly competitive marketplace. They emphasize that relationship building is the new *vision* for sales and marketing professionals.

SALES CYCLE FRAMEWORK FOR CONSULTATIVE SELLING

A better understanding of the complete selling situation and the problems it generates may be gained by breaking the sale into its basic tasks. These steps are presented in a logical sequence, but they *are not necessarily chronological* and they do not always take place in any predetermined order. The ebb and flow of a sales interview defies attempts to package it into nice, neat compartments. Every selling situation has a beginning, an end, and a number of identifiable intermediate points. Regardless of account size or potential, certain predictable tasks must be performed by the salesperson. These tasks, such as identifying prospects and determining needs, may be called the *steps* in a sale or the *selling cycle.* When organized into a prescribed sequence they comprise an overall structure rather than a lock step approach to selling. The eight basics of successful selling described in Figure 2.2 are the focus of chapters 7 through 14. The eight steps are grouped into the categories of *pretransactional, transactional,* and *posttransactional* activities. These steps represent your guide to a successful sales career.

FIGURE 2.2

A Sales Cycle Framework for Consultative Selling

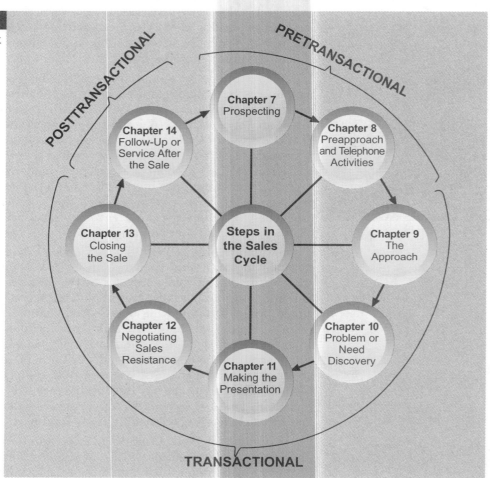

Pretransactional Activities

Identify Qualified Prospects. Prospecting is the process of searching for someone with a *need* for the product or service, the *ability* to pay for it, and the *authority* to make a buying decision. Review current accounts to see who needs service or who might want to increase the quantity purchased or buy new products for the first time. At the same time, survey the territory to identify new leads. Sales professionals study the people they want to sell. Product knowledge is only potential power. Preparation and planning are crucial.

Preapproach Activities. Allocate time for making an assessment of potential customer and current customer needs, determining who the decision-makers are, and establishing a definite purpose for each call. All of these activities

EXHIBIT 2.2 - The Web and CRM Technology Providing Preapproach Information

Until recently, Maidenform, the 77-year-old New Jersey-based company, was using an outdated ordering and tracking process with everything done via the fax and the telephone. So Maidenform aligned itself with *Fashionchain.com*, a provider of hosted services for the apparel industry. With *Fashionchain.com* the Maidenform sales force obtains real-time information on sales orders, including details such as quantity, size, color, and store location, all online. The sales reps are of greater service to their customers because they have better information. "They can see all sales and shipping information at any time from any place," says Mary Ann Lisclo, Maidenform's senior vice-president of operations. The sales reps are now more involved in closing sales and providing on-site assistance.

Customers can also enter their own orders over the Web through a wholesale Web order entry function. This is especially important since Maidenform has 900 mom-and-pop stores that order its products. Now, instead of being on the phone making orders during the day, the owners can spend their time with customers. And the telemarketing people at Maidenform can focus more on assisting their field sales reps in locating new leads.

equip the salesperson to interact with the customer. Then the salesperson can develop an action plan (call schedule) and set appointments. Exhibit 2.2 is one example of how a company is using the Web and Customer Relationship Management (CRM) technology to give its sales force timely preapproach information.[12]

Transactional Activities

Approaching the Prospect. Professional salespeople treat prospects as individuals and not as carbon copies of everyone else. What happens during the opening minutes of the face-to-face encounter affects the success of the whole presentation. Some people simply do not thaw out immediately, and as a salesperson you must find ice-breakers that help the prospect feel at ease with you. Spend time finding the prospect's comfort level. Most first-time meetings between salesperson and prospect produce an egocentric predicament arising from the salesperson's fear of being rejected and the prospect's fear of being sold something that is not really wanted or needed. By redesigning your approach to selling, you can calm the prospect's fear of buying and reduce your own fear of selling. This initial step in the sales process gives the salesperson an opportunity to find a peg upon which to hang the presentation. *In traditional selling*, this phase was extremely limited. It consisted of *telling* prospects what they needed and then moving quickly into the presentation to cover the salesperson's agenda. Sales can be made using this style, but it does not establish a sound, long-term basis for repeat business.

Discovering Needs. During this step of the sales encounter, the salesperson and the client discover whether the client needs or wants something that the salesperson can provide. Because the success of the whole process rests on this basic discovery, the consultative salesperson spends whatever time is needed to get to know the prospect's needs and problems. A basic goal for every sales situation should be to create an atmosphere within which an act of trust can occur—to make a friend rather than a sale, a customer who has confidence in the integrity and ability of the salesperson, and confidence in the company and its product or service.

Listen and takes notes to discover needs.

Active questioning (probing) and creative listening skills make this part of the sales interview productive. Helping the prospect define needs can be done only by asking a series of questions and listening carefully to the responses. Preapproach homework may give the salesperson some feel for the prospect's goals, but research is never a substitute for this step in the interview. *In the traditional model* the salesperson spends time thinking, "What am I going to tell this prospect about the product?" *In the relationship selling model,* the consultative salesperson determines what questions *to ask* the prospect.

Making the Presentation. Your evaluation of the prospect's situation should lead you naturally into the presentation of product benefits. Every product or service has both features and benefits. A *feature* is any fact about the product or service, tangible or intangible. It exists already and will continue to exist whether or not the product or service is ever purchased. For example, a feature of a particular automobile is front-wheel drive. However, prospects want to know about benefits rather than features. The front-wheel drive feature is meaningless unless it satisfies some need, solves some problem, or provides some benefit to the prospective customer. The benefits of front-wheel drive must be explained in terms of ease of handling, safety, or some other performance quality that promises to satisfy the prospect's need. The relationship salesperson presents and sells *benefits* rather than features.

Even better than showcasing the value of the product is to allow prospects to assess that value by discovering for themselves the benefits of owning it. The consultative salesperson is customer-oriented. A prospect does not buy without being convinced that what you are saying is true. People buy based on their expectations. *No one likes to be sold.* They like to see the value of what is being presented and then make their own buying decisions. Salespeople do not create sales; they set up levels of expectation to which prospects respond. Exhibit 2.3 illustrates how the power of expectation works. The salesperson who holds confident, positive expectations closes far more sales than the one who expects rejection.

EXHIBIT 2.3 - The Power of Expectation

Expectation is powerful. Three mess hall sergeants received large shipments of dried apricots. At first, they were all dismayed because they didn't see how they could ever use that many apricots. They each dealt with the problem differently. The first one "knew" no one in his outfit wanted apricots; so he cooked a large pot of stewed apricots, stuck a ladle in the pot, and set it at the end of the serving line. Sure enough, at the end of three days, his negative expectations were fulfilled; he still had most of the apricots. The second one adopted a more positive approach. He also cooked a large pot of stewed apricots; but he stood in the serving line with a big smile and a ladle in hand. "Let me serve you some apricots," he offered, as people came through the line. He disposed of more apricots than the first sergeant. The third sergeant decided to create a demand. He put up signs at the beginning and end of the serving line: "Coming Tuesday: Apricots just like YOUR Mother served. Your choice." On Tuesday at breakfast time, a big sign on the door announced: "It's Tuesday! Mother's apricots are here!" He had prepared stewed apricots and a mix of chopped dried apricots, raisins, and nuts to sprinkle on cereal. For lunch and dinner, he offered apricot fried pies, baked apricot pies, and apricot bread. His shipment of apricots disappeared quickly.

FIGURE 2.3

The Scale of Decision

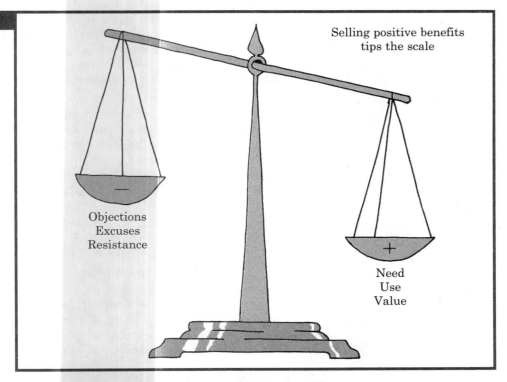

Selling positive benefits tips the scale

Objections
Excuses
Resistance

Need
Use
Value

Overcoming Resistance and Getting Commitment. Now is the time to verbally clarify and confirm what both you and the client will do to make the solution work. This part of the overall process helps to avoid misunderstandings by bringing any that exist out into the open so they can be handled. Each clarification and confirmation adds weight to the argument in favor of a positive decision. When the scale of decision tips far enough toward the positive side (Figure 2.3) the prospect can, and does, say yes. When that happens, everyone wins—the client, you, and your company. Consultative selling is a matter of presenting positive benefits that demonstrate need, use, and value. Selling in this manner reduces your need to deal with resistance, answer objections or excuses from the client, or haggle over price. All you do is add positive benefits, one after another, until the scales are tipped in favor of a buying decision. Since the client has been an active participant throughout, the commitment and close should be the natural conclusion to a successful sales interview.

Posttransactional Activities

Service After the Sale (Follow-Up). The final phase of consultative selling is service after the sale. Harvard Professor Theodore Leavitt said, "The purpose of a business is to create and keep a customer."[13] Service, service, and more service is what counts and gives you a competitive edge. Customer satisfaction is a moment in time. Plenty of satisfied customers do not come back unless the salesperson creates some kind of bond. Relationships will keep them coming back.

You should look at customer satisfaction as an economic asset just like any other asset of the company. Customer satisfaction is an income-producing endeavor. Too many salespeople perform service mechanically, without thinking of the impact their actions have on customers. Clients must sense that you truly care about them. Service after the sale is your way of expressing appreciation for their business. Service makes the difference and is as important as the quality of the product. Part of being a good sales consultant is revisiting clients to make sure your proposed solutions are occurring.

A successful sale does not end when the buyer says yes. The sale has actually just begun. Purchases that are expensive, require installation or instruction on maintenance and use, or involve a multiple buying decision should be followed up to make certain that the buyer receives maximum satisfaction from the purchase. The goal is to reduce post-purchase *dissonance* and pave the way for repeat business, a list of referrals, and a long, satisfying relationship. The professional salesperson sees to it that the order is completed and that all support arrangements, credit, delivery, installation, product design, and like matters are resolved. Exhibit 2.4 explains how the Eastman Chemical Company uses e-commerce to make customer interaction easy.[14]

How you relate to plant and office employees can make a difference in the way they treat your customers. It pays to be liked and appreciated by staff people, especially those in sales support, credit, billing, and shipping. Take a lesson from Mark Twain, who said,"I can live for two months on a good compliment." Take a moment from time to time to compliment and thank the support people in your company for the great job they are doing.

EXHIBIT 2.4 - Customer Interaction Made Easy With E-commerce

Eastman Chemical Company was the first chemical manufacturer to launch e-commerce capabilities. Eastman customers can log on to its Customer Center at *eastman.com* to place and track orders, reduce paperwork, obtain account information, and receive around-the-clock technical support. However, many of its customers had limited computer and Internet access. So Eastman established *partnerships* with Dell Computer and UUnet to help customers acquire updated computer hardware and Web access. They wanted to make the Web the preferred sales channel. Rexam Plastics, a North Carolina coating and laminates company, is an excellent example of what can happen. In an effort to reduce paperwork and to simplify procurement, Rexam turned to e-commerce. *Eastman.com* turned out to be a perfect fit. According to Bill Weinert, purchasing manager for Rexam, "We can check product availability, obtain price information, place orders, review company history, look at data sheets for a catalog item, all online." The Customer Center at Eastman Chemical has more than 500 users in North America and is expanding into Europe, Latin America, and Asia.

WOMEN IN SELLING

The rapid increase in the number of women employed in the sales profession over the past 30 years is having an important and dramatic impact. Although women experienced difficulty in the 1970s and 1980s in gaining entry into male-dominated sales organizations, saleswomen during the 1990s achieved success in a wide variety of sales industries.[15] They now account for an average of 26 percent across a sampling of industries, and they hold 10 percent of the sales management positions in those industries. Women have achieved greater acceptance in certain industries. For example, in the Amusement/Recreation Services, Communications, Business Services, Office Equipment, Apparel, and Printing/Publishing industries, women occupy 42 percent of the sales positions. However, in "traditional" male-dominated industries like Electronics, Machinery, and Chemicals, they make up just 4 percent.[16]

Emphasizing gender differences in management processes and interpersonal relationships can be a productive endeavor. However, there is no evidence to suggest differences in the productivity of men and women sales professionals. The attitude of sales managers and purchasing agents toward women in industrial sales is very positive. Exhibit 2.5 highlights the thoughts

EXHIBIT 2.5 - Tanis Cornell Talks About Success Characteristics for the Sales Professional

Is professional selling a viable career choice for an ambitious woman who wants to maximize her earning capacity, use all her skills and talents, and enjoy the satisfaction of knowing that she is personally productive? If you ask Tanis Cornell, her answer is a resounding yes.

Cornell, former vice-president of regional sales for WorldCom Group, is now a sales and business consultant. During her career in telecommunications, Tanis held several sales and operations management positions. Early in her career she was one of the few women. That has changed, however. Time has proven that sales is a level playing field and production and skills are what count.

"When I choose my people, I'm more concerned about attitude and skill set than gender. The new sales environment is result-oriented and based on the company's culture. So a woman can go far, particularly in a Web-based environment where decision-makers may be older and not as familiar with advanced systems and the Internet."

Sales has evolved from bartering to simple transactions to consulting to an exchange of information. So no matter whether you are a man or a woman, "you've got to know your product and inspire a deep sense of trust in the client."

In today's competitive market, many products, companies, and even salespeople start to look alike to the prospect. I look for men and women with the creativity to differentiate themselves from their competition. Much more emphasis is directed at keeping current customers happy and providing long-term solutions. Salespeople must not only excel at prospecting and finding that new customer but *excel at building long-term relationships* with existing customers.

Teamwork is especially important in today's sales environment. Many companies are taking a collaborative approach, cooperating with customers and suppliers to create an entire package. Females tend to be more comfortable with this team selling approach.

"In my years as a salesperson and as a manager, I noticed one very interesting thing. There are certain individuals, regardless of gender, that excel each and every year. You can change their compensation plan. You can move them to another job or another location. You can throw any number of challenges at them that would disturb the average salesperson. For top performers, it doesn't matter. If you have natural management skills, you will go up the ranks."

of Tanis Cornell, a highly successful sales manager and business consultant. Cornell says, "Good sales performance is not inherently or unalterably defined as male- or female-dependent." As Comer and Jolson point out, many aspects of gender-specific perceptions—such as closing skills, self-confidence, or questioning and listening skills—can be modified with the proper sales training and supervision.[17]

Gender Issues In Selling

As women enter the workplace, they bring with them different perspectives and experiences—and different ways of communicating. As females join both sides of the buyer-seller relationship, the managerial strategies for gender in the sales forces have changed.[18] Men and women may speak different languages, but they use the same words. Not only do they talk differently—they interpret language differently. Women use distinctly different styles and patterns of speech to deliver approximately the same message. There is an ongoing discussion about gender and language among communication specialists, psychologists, and business people. A number of books have been written on the subject. *You Just Don't Understand*; *In a Different Voice*; and *Men Are From Mars, Women Are From Venus* represent three of the books that discuss differences in men and women based on credible research.

It is ironic that early stereotyping itself may have fostered the development of communication styles that manifest themselves among men and women today. Research clearly shows that men tend to be more assertive while women tend to be more attentive listeners.

Boys learn the art of playing the game early. They learn about power and hierarchical order. When boys grow up, conversations for men become negotiations of power and achievement. Women have their own distinctive character and essence. By the time girls become women, they approach the world as a network of connections. Women weave webs of relationships; conversations are negotiations for closeness and intimacy.

Relating to the Opposite Sex. A research study by Russ & McNeilly concluded that managers who treat male and female sales reps the same will miss potential differences by gender.[19] A key question to ask is whether gender differences, in and of themselves, create different ways of thinking and behavioral relationships. If so, what are some things to be aware of when you're selling to someone of the opposite sex? When men and women find themselves sitting across from one another at the bargaining table, they must learn to adjust their styles. During the sales interview they should use the strengths unique to their gender. Women are often raised to be more accommodating and are therefore better at questioning and listening patiently. Research by Siguaw & Honeycutt found that women were engaged more frequently in customer-oriented selling than were their male counterparts.[20] Men are raised to compete and may be stronger closers but often lack people sensitivities. Women are more concerned with how a product or service will impact the company as a whole. Men are often more concerned with what the decision will specifically do for them. Women do not like to feel pressured or pushed, whereas men often respond better to a hard sell.

Use the strengths unique to your gender and social style.

Paula Zmudzinski, with Jon Goldman Associates in Orange, California, would agree that men and women are different, but believes it is far more important to take a *read* of the client, basing your sales approach on the client's style rather than the person's gender. Zmudzinski proposes that our society is changing, and one of the key ways she sees it changing, at least in the business world, is that men and women are becoming more alike. Just because something is written about the differences between men and women, it does not mean that it has value in every selling encounter between men and women. For example, when a woman nods her head, that doesn't necessarily mean she agrees with what a man is saying. When a woman crosses her arms, she is not automatically indicating she is closed to the idea being presented. She just may be tired or cold. Likewise, if a man doesn't look you in the eye when he is speaking, that does not necessarily mean he's hiding something—it may be his style. Acting on generalities, regardless of gender, can kill a sale more quickly than any thing else.[21]

Exhibit 2.6 provides some suggestions for dealing with gender differences. Salesmen must be prepared to work with men and women decision-makers. Similarly, saleswomen must communicate effectively with their sales managers and fellow sales reps, as well as the men and women decision-makers they call on. No one can make a sweeping statement about how all women or all men like to sell or be sold. In any selling situation it's vital to communicate in a way that substantiates what's meaningful to that individual, and gender may help determine what a client feels is important. Subtle, gender-based changes to your presentation may give you the edge you're looking for to boost sales.[22]

EXHIBIT 2.6 - How Can Men and Women Better Understand Each Other?

Salesmen:

Report talk vs. rapport talk. Male bonding through storytelling and anecdotes is fine; however, women are more interested in your product than your latest fishing trip.

Stop interrupting. Men interrupt women more often than other men. This is a good way to lose a sale. Learn to listen.

Feel the sale. There is more to selling than numbers. Women are interested in emotional satisfaction as well as the bottom line.

Control the language. Never again in a professional situation use the words "honey," "dear," or "sweetie." This is simply intolerable.

Saleswomen:

Speak confidently and clearly. It has been established that men will interrupt women, especially if they sound tentative or unsure.

Feed them data. Men love facts and the illusion of being cool and rational. Let them know you have also done your homework. Remain enthusiastic; just rein it in a bit.

Practice your humor. Women tend to use humor less than men. Being funny at the right moment is very important.

Watch your language. Avoid "girl talk" when presenting to men. Words like "lovely," "charming," or "adorable" should be excluded from your sales vocabulary.

CONTINUOUS QUALITY IMPROVEMENT

There has been so much written on the subject that Total Quality Management (TQM) has been dismissed by some as just another fancy theory. But to ignore the underlying principles of TQM is not wise. Many people do not ignore good nutrition and regular exercise despite the ceaseless promotion and discussion of the subjects.[23] These principles have practical implications for managing today's new breed of professional salespeople.

While there are variations in the language and scope of TQM programs, it is possible to discern five principles common to the practice of relationship selling:

1. Listen and learn from your customers and your employees.

2. Try to continuously improve the partnership.

3. Build teamwork by establishing trust and mutual respect.

4. Do it right the first time to ensure customer satisfaction.

5. Break down the walls in your own company. Everybody is involved in the relationship.

The Marketing Concept

The *marketing concept* emphasizes that the key task of a company is to determine the needs and wants of consumers, and adapt itself to meeting the desired satisfaction better than its competitors. Total Quality Management, like the marketing concept, also has a customer orientation. It is an *outside-in* approach to business. Continuous quality improvement is a philosophy, an overall style of management, that puts its focus on customer satisfaction. The center of all discussions is the customer; every one *inside* and *outside* the company is a customer. Federal Express Chief Executive Officer Fred Smith states, "Employee satisfaction is a prerequisite to customer satisfaction."[24]

Under the leadership of Smith, FedEx expanded into Asia and the Pacific. FedEx selected 25 of the region's best sales professionals to be field-based facilitators and recruiters, and brought them all to company headquarters in Memphis, Tennessee, for four months of training. Exhibit 2.7 illustrates FedEx's commitment to continuous quality improvement among its employees, but in this instance on a global basis.[25]

EXHIBIT 2.7 - Under the Leadership of Fred Smith, FedEx is Taking Aim at Asia

Fred Smith

Fred Smith, CEO of Federal Express, boasts that his company "connects more than 99 percent of the world's economy." Casey Zettler, vice-president of sales for FedEx, has no doubt about the company's future in Asia and the Pacific. FedEx believes that Hong Kong, with its spirit of entrepreneurship, will influence China far more than China will influence Hong Kong. The challenge, according to Zettler, is to get their salespeople in Asia to "manage locally, and think globally." The sales reps must also be trained on the features and benefits of the services we have to offer. And they must understand how our customers make money. Running FedEx's Asia operation requires hiring, training, and motivating a sales force of 250 men and women who speak different languages, represent different cultures, and serve different markets.

The key is a comprehensive approach to quality that cuts across functions and levels of an organization. Quality is an unyielding effort by everyone in an organization to understand, meet, and exceed the needs of its customers.[26] Key components include participative leadership, team-based management, flexibility in thinking, horizontal flow of communication and cooperation, and collaborative problem solving.

Service Quality

Continuous quality improvement means forgetting how work was done in the age of mass marketing and deciding how best it can be done now. Salespeople need to learn a different way of thinking about their work. They must think in terms of process rather than task. The necessary task improvements can be done using the process management *reengineering* techniques popularized by Michael Hammer and James Champy in their best seller *Reengineering the Corporation*. In actuality, the customer is a customer of the company, not just of the individual salesperson. Sales professionals know that their work is not simply calling on prospects. The goal is to make a sale, and that's a *process* in which the sales rep is only one player. The process includes production people, finance and marketing people, as well as customer service reps. So it's not left to the salespeople to solve a customer's problem; the whole organization gets behind the effort. Building customer relationships is everybody's responsibility.

TQM is established today thanks to the pioneering work of W. Edwards Deming. One of Deming's most important lessons for sales managers is his "85-15" rule.[27] When things go wrong in the field, there is an 85 percent chance the system is at fault. Only about 15 percent of the time can the individual salesperson be blamed. TQM means the organization's *culture* is defined by and supports the constant attainment of customer satisfaction, through an integrated system of tools, techniques, and training. Prospects and customers notice and think about everyone they come in contact with during the sales encounter. The relationship between perceived effort and customer service is a powerful one. When the salesperson and customer interact, the quality of the interaction itself is an important part of the relationship.[28] Figure 2.4 shows the dynamics of this interaction. Service quality has two dimensions: (1) *the process of delivering the service* and (2) *the actual outcome.*

FIGURE 2.4

The Service Quality Interaction

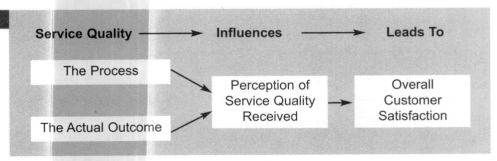

Most business success stories involve taking an old idea or product and doing a better job with it than the next company. Wal-Mart didn't invent discount selling; Sam Walton just did it better. And the executives who now run Wal-Mart are improving the way they buy and stock merchandise to drive their costs and prices even lower. Then there is Starbucks! Coffee shops have been around for a long time, but no one before Starbucks had figured out how to organize and run several thousand of them. The point is, you can get a lot out of a current product or service if you change the *processes* around it, or change the process by which it is *delivered*. The objective is to change those processes enough that you are delivering more value to your customers or, at the very least, hold on to those customers by offering a fair price.

The $332,000 Customer

Tom Peters, author of *A Passion for Excellence*, says, "A customer is not a transaction; a customer is a relationship."[29] The missing link in service often is intense awareness of the customer's point of view. The process of handling the problem is as important to customers as the solution of the problem itself. The logical inference is that every company better organize its service delivery system to answer every customer's implied question: "What are you going to do for me today?"

Peters uses the example of Dallas car dealer Carl Sewell, who has written a book called *The $332,000 Customer* because a loyal lifetime Cadillac customer buys that much from him. Peters goes on to suggest that happy lifetime customers generate four or five happy lifetime customers for you. So in fact, one Cadillac customer is roughly a $1,500,000 customer. Two investments Sewell has made illustrate his understanding of the value he places on customer satisfaction. Number one, he bought a street sweeper to keep the front of his dealership extra clean. First impressions count for everything, and people judge his dealership by the cleanliness of everything

Luis Martinez has a plan for implementing continuous quality improvement

Luis Martinez is manager of Daimler-Chrysler's Five Star Program. This multi-million-dollar program was developed to change the sales culture within Chrysler and among the carmaker's 4,500 dealerships. Martinez has the task of making everyone look at their jobs differently—That is, not to simply get people in the showroom door and sell them a car, but to do what is *best* for the customer no matter what.

Two things are taking place when a customer walks into a dealership: There is a *process and an outcome*. Even when the *outcome* meets 100 percent of the customer's expectations, it does not mean they will be satisfied with the *process*. Martinez explains, "The actual repair work done to a customer's car may have been terrific [outcome], but it took four full days and 15 phone calls to get it done [process]. The process was not user-friendly. We want to fix the buying and selling process.

These two worlds coexist in the dealership. Unfortunately, no one ever asked the customer, 'How do you want to do business with a dealership?' Long-term customer loyalty demands an answer to this question."

Martinez has a basic philosophy for success. He suggests that these five principles are essential for making the right presentation: (1) **Honesty and Respect**—Sell the customer what they need, not what you need to sell. Respect all people and never lie to them. (2) **Be Responsive**—Look for customer wants, always fulfill your promises, and be an active listener. (3) **Competence**—Know your product line and that of the competition. Customers will appreciate and remember you. (4) **Proactive**—Once you know the needs of your customers, don't put them through a canned presentation. Adapt your selling process to the buying process of the customer. (5) **Don't See Yourself as an Island**—Know all of the other support services available at the dealership. Someone will have the answer.

including the road in front of it. Number two, he convinced an upscale local restaurant to open a branch in his service bay. When it's a simple repair, a lot of his customers come in and enjoy a hot meal while the work is being done.

Figure 2.5 illustrates the kind of behavior wanted in a quality-driven sales organization and the kind that exists in the typical organization.[30] To move from left to right, use the 12 essential elements of TQM and your commitment to customer satisfaction to guide you. Some salespeople will read this and say, "This is nothing new; it is simply common sense." They are right, of course, but it has taken many years for men such as W. Edwards Deming, Philip Crosby, Joseph Juran, and Genichi Taguchi to refine and teach this philosophy. Generally speaking, salespeople understand the principles outlined here more easily than others in a company. Their livelihood has always depended on making the customer happy.

FIGURE 2.5

Culture Changes in a Sales Organization

Traditional Management Model	The TQM Model
Focus on product	→ Focus on service
Company knows best	→ Customer knows best
Transactions	→ Relationships
Individual performance	→ Team performance
Firefighting management	→ Continuous improvement
Blame/punishment	→ Support/reward
Short-term (year or less)	→ Long-term (years)
Intolerant of errors	→ Allows mistakes
Autocratic leadership	→ Participative leadership
Bureaucratic	→ Entrepreneurial
Top-down decisions	→ Consensus decisions
Inward-focused	→ Outward (customer)-focused

SUMMARY

The role of professional selling is evolving from the art of persuasion to the psychology of satisfying needs and solving problems. The consultative salesperson works by building relationships with clients instead of by pushing products. The basic process of selling begins with the approach to the prospect, during which the relationship is established; it then moves through the discovery of needs, the presentation of the product or service as the solution to those needs, overcoming resistance, and gaining commitment. Follow-up and service after the sale complete the cycle.

The purpose of the consultative approach to selling is to discover the needs or problems of the prospect that can be satisfied or solved by acquiring the salesperson's product or service. Selling, then, is customer-oriented and requires extensive knowledge about the prospect.

Women are entering the world of professional selling in record numbers. They bring different perspective and different ways of communicating. A key question to ask is whether gender differences create different ways of thinking and behavioral relationships. During the sales interview, use the strengths unique to your gender.

Business firms develop a philosophy that governs their operations. Total Quality Management, like the marketing concept, has a customer orientation. In its simplest form, TQM suggests that there should be a master plan for continuously improving quality in an organization. Such a concept helps salespeople orient their activities to the overall goals of the company.

QUESTIONS FOR THOUGHT AND DISCUSSION

1. Compare and contrast the stereotype of traditional selling and professional consultative selling.

2. What questions must a salesperson answer in the affirmative before it is possible to make a reasonable recommendation to buy?

3. What is the difference between the features of the product and its benefits? Which is most useful in the selling situation? Why? Should the other, then, be mentioned at all? How?

4. Name at least three reasons why a prospect may resist making a buying decision. For each reason, tell how the salesperson could have prevented this particular type of resistance.

5. If sales resistance is encountered, how can the salesperson close the sale in spite of the resistance? Is this always synonymous with what is regarded as "hard sell"?

6. What is the purpose of service after the sale? What does it include? Whose responsibility is such service?

7. Who needs to be conversant with the organization's basic philosophy of business? If that philosophy is not understood by all members of the organization, what types of problems might result? Why?

8. To what extent must a sales rep agree with the company's commitment to continuous quality improvement?

9. What are the key principles of the Total Quality Management philosophy?

ACTIVITIES

1. If you have had an experience with a traditional, "hard-sell" salesperson, share it with the class. Likewise, if you have had an experience with a consultative salesperson, share that with the class.

2. Go to a local car dealer and shop for a car of your choice. Take note of whether the salesperson tries to discover your needs. Did the salesperson use an approach and a needs-discovery phase, or move directly to a presentation of benefits? What was your reaction to the salesperson's total dealing with you?

3. Examine advertisements in magazines or newspapers or on television or radio. Choose three ads for which you believe there are follow-up salespeople and determine what features and benefits that salesperson would likely present.

Case Study

CASE 2.1

The Supreme Cookware Company has been in business for more than forty years. After a slow start, it became a leader in its field, but its record in recent years has been one of steady decline. The number of its accounts has been shrinking, and the sales volume of the average account has been declining as well.

An outside consulting firm was brought in to study the firm's situation and to determine, if possible, the reasons for its difficulties. After careful research, this firm reported that Supreme had fallen behind in styling. Consequently, dealers were reluctant to carry its line.

In implementing the suggestions of the consulting firm, Supreme made a careful market study to discover how best to correct its deficiencies. As a result, a completely new and modern line of cookware was developed. They also decided to begin a strong marketing campaign to introduce the new line and to reestablish the reputation of the company.

One executive was unhappy with the study. He raised the question of revitalizing the sales force and pointed out that most of the salespeople had been with the firm for two decades or more. Perhaps some or much of the firm's trouble stemmed from the fact that the sales staff had aged perceptibly and no longer had the energy or drive to go out and sell. He suggested that the firm release many of its older salespeople and bring in new blood.

This suggestion precipitated a near-violent argument, as the sales manager defended his staff. He emphasized that his salespeople had proved their ability in earlier years and that they would be successful with the new line if given a chance to show what they could do. How could they have been productive selling a line with admitted deficiencies?

The first executive argued that good salespeople should be able to sell anything. He said further that if the salespeople had really been communicating with their customers, they would have realized the problems the customers had with the cookware line and reported it to the company.

1. Do you think a good salesperson should be able to sell anything?

2. Do you think the sales manager was right in defending his staff so courageously?

3. What could the company do to aid salespeople in achieving success in selling the new cookware line?

PART II

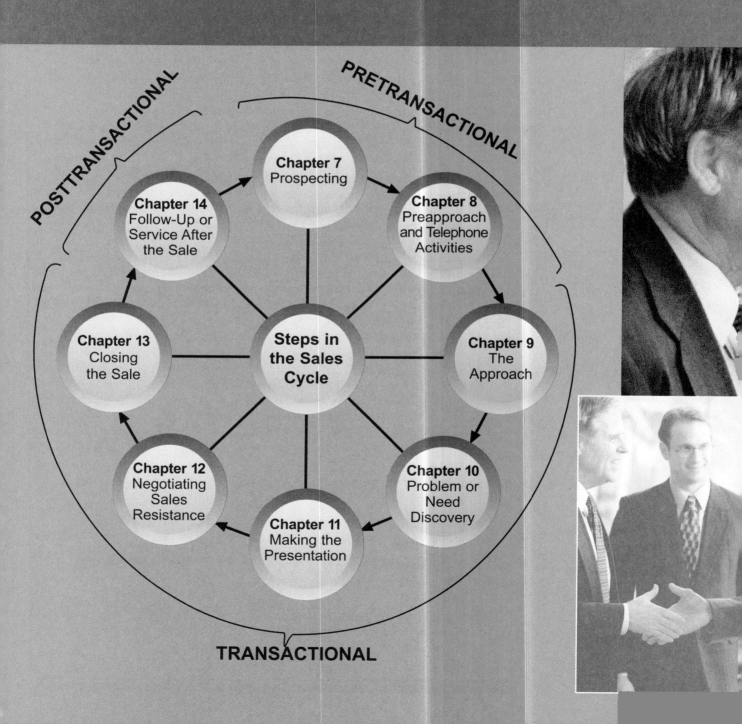

POSTTRANSACTIONAL

PRETRANSACTIONAL

Chapter 7
Prospecting

Chapter 8
Preapproach
and Telephone
Activities

Chapter 14
Follow-Up or
Service After
the Sale

**Steps in
the Sales
Cycle**

Chapter 9
The
Approach

Chapter 13
Closing
the Sale

Chapter 10
Problem or
Need
Discovery

Chapter 12
Negotiating
Sales
Resistance

Chapter 11
Making the
Presentation

TRANSACTIONAL

Cultivating an Ethics Climate and Developing Communication Skills

Professional selling is a challenging career field. Few professions, if any, give you more opportunities to be rejected on a daily basis than does the field of sales. You need strong ethical and moral character to sustain a sales career. Cheating, lying, or short-changing the customer is a sure way to court failure for the future. Honest and caring service brings customers back and ensures success for the salesperson.

Success in consultative selling also depends upon your ability to have a productive exchange of information with prospects and customers. The more salespeople understand about prospects, the more readily they can discover what they need and want. An especially useful tool for gaining insight into the thinking of prospects is knowledge of the social styles model. A social style is the way a person sends and receives information. It is a method for finding the best way to approach a prospect and to set up a working relationship with that person.

"It's OK, Kid, Everybody Does It"

by Jack Griffin

When Johnny was 6 years old, he was with his father when they were caught speeding. His father handed the officer a twenty-dollar bill with his driver's license. "It's OK, son," his father said as they drove off. "Everybody does it."

When he was 8, he was present at a family council presided over by Uncle George, on the surest means to shave points off the income tax return. "It's OK, kid," his uncle said. "Everybody does it."

When he was 9, his mother took him to his first theater production. The box office man couldn't find any seats until his mother discovered an extra $5 in her purse. "It's OK, son," she said. "Everybody does it."

When he was 12, he broke his glasses on the way to school. His Aunt Francine persuaded the insurance company that they had been stolen and they collected $75. "It's OK, son," she said. "Everybody does it."

When he was 15, he made right guard on the high school football team. His coach showed him how to block and at the same time grab the opposing end by the shirt so the official couldn't see it. "It's OK, son," the coach said. "Everybody does it."

When he was 16, he took his first summer job at the supermarket. His assignment was to put the overripe strawberries in the bottom of the boxes and the good ones on top where they would show. "It's OK, son," the manager said. "Everybody does it."

When he was 18, Johnny and a neighbor applied for a college scholarship. Johnny was a marginal student. His neighbor was in the top 3 percent of his class, but couldn't play right guard. Johnny got the scholarship. "It's OK, son," his parents said. "Everybody does it."

When he was 19, he was approached by an upperclassman who offered the test answers for $50. "It's OK, kid," he said. "Everybody does it."

Johnny was caught and sent home in disgrace. "How could you do this to your mother and me?" his father said. "You never learned anything like this at home." His aunt and uncle were also shocked.

If there's one thing the adult world can't stand, it's a kid who cheats.

> "It's OK, son," his father said as they drove off. "Everybody does it."

CHAPTER 3

Ethical and Legal Issues in Selling

- To become aware of the need for developing principles upon which to base ethical behavior.

- To recognize the various sources of influence on ethics and ethical behavior.

- To understand the salesperson's role in maintaining the ethical position of the organization and at the same time behaving in an acceptable ethical manner toward customers.

- To consider the question of what the salesperson's loyalty to the company requires in the event that it may be involved in questionable ethical behavior.

- To understand the implications of federal and local laws regarding ethical standards.

Ken Blanchard and Norman Vincent Peale

One of the significant books published in the field of business ethics is *The Power of Ethical Management*. This small book by Dr. Kenneth Blanchard and Dr. Norman Vincent Peale is especially significant for salespeople, who are on the firing line of relations between companies and their customers and clients.

Few individuals have had as great an impact on company management as has Kenneth Blanchard, co-author of *The One Minute Manager* and *The One Minute Manager Library*. Dr. Blanchard is the founder of a management consulting firm, Blanchard Training and Development Inc., in Escondido, California.

Dr. Norman Vincent Peale was the author of thirty-four books. *The Power of Positive Thinking* is one of the most widely circulated books ever published. It has been translated into forty languages and has enjoyed sales of over twenty million copies. He was also the founder of the monthly magazine *Guideposts,* which has a circulation of sixteen million.

The basic message of *The Power of Ethical Management* is simple: You don't have to cheat to win! Blanchard and Peale tell us that many people demand immediate tangible evidence that ethical conduct works, but such evidence is often not available. In fact, you may actually get farther in the short run by cheating. But in the long run, where it really counts, you never gain by unethical conduct. They remind us that "nice guys may appear to finish last, but usually they're running in a different race." Unethical behavior occurs in sales because people forget the real purpose of professional selling—to fill the needs of others.

Salespeople sometimes say near the end of the day, "I ought to make one more sales call before I go home. I wonder who I might be able to see this late?" Blanchard and Peale suggest that the better question might be, "I wonder if there is someone else I can help before I go home?" When salespeople focus on their purpose—solving the problems of clients and helping customers be more successful and more profitable—they understand the need for ethical behavior. Cheating, lying, and short-changing the customer on service may bring a satisfactory profit today, but is a sure way to court failure for the future.

THE ETHICAL DILEMMA

Betty Maloney feels as though she is being torn apart. The pharmaceutical company she works for is pressuring her to meet a sales quota twenty percent higher than last year's. She is a single parent with two children to support, and she sees an opportunity to meet her sales quota if she can beat out a competitor for a large order from a drugstore chain. She is tempted to plant some carefully worded negative comments about the competitor in the ear of the store chain's purchasing agent. What should she do? What would you do?

Betty Maloney is facing a situation that falls in the category of ethical considerations. Because salespeople are relatively free and independent operators, they may encounter more ethical dilemmas than many other business people. For this reason, those who choose a career in professional selling must think out their own positions on various ethical standards before getting caught up in something that gets beyond their control.

Today's renewed interest in ethics can be used by sales professionals to their advantage. Ethics is an old subject, but it is certainly not worn out. The Greek philosophers, for example, suggested that "a merchant does better to take a loss than to make a dishonest profit." A loss may be momentarily painful, but dishonesty does irreparable damage. America is reeling from the shocking, unethical, and immoral activities of a variety of business and government leaders and other public figures. It is not companies, institutions and political organizations, however,

Ethics in Selling, Honest!

Adapted from *Sales & Marketing Management*, Vol. 138, No. 7 (May 1987), p. 42

that are unethical; individual people are unethical. Ethics is a personal matter. The ethics of a business, government, or other organizations is merely a reflection of the combined value systems of its members.

Business ethics is an aspect of societal ethics. Traditional values seem to have given way to a widespread sense of "anything goes." Look at what we parade in front of people, implying approval, in the media and society: sexual allure, constant violence, conspicuous consumption, the soft life, "reach for all the gusto you can," and enjoy life now. As a result, many Americans want immediate personal gratification and will act in whatever manner seems to promise it.

Some say that business ethics is an *oxymoron,* a contradiction in terms. They suggest that business has no ethics or that ethics is something that people worry about on Sunday and not when they are out selling in the real world.[1] This thinking is ludicrous! The notion that honest salespeople finish last is poisonous; in addition, it is untrue. Unethical behavior is ultimately self-destructive; it generates more unethical conduct until a person hits rock bottom financially, spiritually, and/or morally.

The Origin of Ethics

A *legal* standard is enforced by statute, but an *ethical* standard is an outgrowth of the customs and attitudes of a society. Most of us have a shared idea of what we mean by ethics, but defining it in a way that everyone would accept is hard. Essentially, ethics is a systematic effort to judge human behavior as right or wrong in terms of two major criteria: truth and justice.

The root of the word *ethics* derives from the Greek word *ethos,* which means the character or sentiment of the community. A society cannot exist unless people agree fundamentally on what is right and wrong, just and unjust. Without shared norms of behavior, we would have anarchy in our political system and chaos in our daily lives. If we consider the United States to be our larger community, our ethical standards have been influenced philosophically by "Graeco-Roman thought, by the Judaic and Christian religions, by Enlightenment philosophy, and by the Scientific Revolution."[2] The three most important value-forming institutions in America are family, church, and school. Many people believe that the decreasing strength and changing roles of these three institutions have produced a society with lower ethical standards than those of its earlier history.

The Bases for Ethical Systems

Philosophers and ethicists point to two systems that have been named to describe ways of ethical thinking. The first of these is the *deontological* base, the use of specifically stated rules, for example, the Ten Commandments or the Golden Rule. Some believe these rules come from a higher power, some think the rules are intuitive, and still others hold that the rules are discovered by using reason.

The second system of describing ethical systems is the *teleological* approach. This system defines right and wrong in terms of end results. A study reported by Dr. Thomas Wotruba found that marketing executives' response to ethical problems is predominantly utilitarian.[3] The utilitarian model falls under this category and is illustrated by the idea proposed in the nineteenth century by Jeremy Benthem that society's goal is to produce "the greatest good for the greatest number." This approach says that in trying to determine a course of action in an ethical dilemma, the individual should assess what good or harm would come to the parties involved and follow the course of action that would have the most positive results for the most people.

With these two bases consciously or unconsciously affecting us, we can expect to experience ambivalent attitudes when faced with making ethical decisions. In the best seller *The Closing of the American Mind*, Allan Bloom theorizes that much of our moral and ethical ambivalence comes from family and educational system teachings in which almost everything is relative, in which there are no moral absolutes. He says that "the family's moral training comes down to inculcating the bare minimum of social behavior, not lying or stealing, and produces university students who can say nothing more about the ground of their moral actions than 'If I did that to him, he could do it to me,' an explanation that does not even satisfy those who utter it."[4]

Guidelines for Ethical Behavior

No matter which method of ethical decision making is followed, most Americans embrace three basic guidelines: universal nature, truth telling, and responsibility for one's actions. Without them, the free enterprise system itself would be threatened and any kind of business exchange would be difficult. Our society would disintegrate into a "dog-eat-dog" environment.

Universal Nature. The universal nature guideline is a derivation of the Golden Rule. We want others to play by the same basic rules by which we would play in a similar situation. This guideline sets up a basic level of trust between people and makes life predictable.

Truth Telling. A salesperson needs to believe that what others say is true. Most of us learned from teachers, religious leaders, or parents that lying is wrong. The idea of honesty may originate in a set of rules we have been taught, but truth telling makes sense on purely logical grounds as well. If lying were the general expectation, great amounts of time would be wasted in trying to determine the truth. Trust has been found to facilitate cooperation, buyer commitment to a salesperson, and the development and maintenance of long-term buyer-salesperson relationships.[5]

Responsibility for One's Actions. President Harry S. Truman kept a sign on his desk stating, "The buck stops here." He reminded himself that he had no one to blame when things went wrong. Individuals may choose to live by this attitude and accept personal responsibility for their actions, or they may attempt to follow the impulse of the moment and blame someone else for the consequences. Irresponsibility seems to be on the rise in our country. If we and our society demonstrated a higher level of trust and credibility based on universal willingness to accept responsibility for personal actions, our system would work more efficiently and in a less suspicious atmosphere.

INFLUENCES ON THE SALESPERSON'S ETHICS

Although individual salespeople each have a basic value system and may know what is right and wrong, they encounter many new influences and experience many new pressures on the first job. Nothing creates more consistency and direction for employee's decision-making, or a better suplement for judgement than ethical guidelines.[6] Knowing in advance what can be expected and having a feel for how to balance and integrate them into a personal code of ethics make handling ethical decisions easier.

Company Code of Ethics

Many companies have codes of ethics; some companies adhere strictly to the code as part of corporate culture and may have ethics training for new employees and an ethics committee to rule on ethical dilemmas. The growing concern about ethics is no longer restricted to business schools as demonstrated by Exhibit 3.1, which describes the General Dynamics ethics

EXHIBIT 3.1 - General Dynamics' Code of Ethics

General Dynamics' ethics program is considered the most comprehensive in the industry, and little wonder—it was put together as generals from the Pentagon looked on. The program was part of the amends the company had to make after being charged with deliberately overcharging the government on defense contracts.

Now General Dynamics boasts a committee of board members to review the company's ethics policies, a steering group to oversee policy execution, and a corporate ethics director. Hot lines let any of the company's employees get instant advice on ethical issues involving their jobs. Nearly all have attended workshops; those for salespeople include such things as expense accounts and supplier relations.

The company also has a 20-page code of ethics, which tells salespeople how to conduct themselves. For example:

- If it becomes clear that the company must engage in unethical or illegal activity to win a contract, that business will not be further pursued.

- All information provided relative to products or services should be clear and concise.

- Receiving or soliciting gifts, entertainment, or anything else of value is expressly prohibited.

- In countries where common practice might indicate acceptance of conduct lower than that to which General Dynamics aspires, salespeople will follow the company's standards.

- Under no circumstance may an employee offer or give anything to a customer or a customer's representative in an effort to influence him.

program. General Dynamics began a positive program to establish ethical standards and monitor its internal ethics problems after receiving bad publicity following an investigation that revealed the company, along with other government suppliers, had been grossly overcharging the government for small items like hand tools needed to perform maintenance on equipment supplied under contracts. These actions by some of the company's employees resulted in the publication of a clearly stated code of ethics for all employees whose compliance is monitored. Now the company has a 20-page Code of Ethics to tell salespeople how they must conduct themselves.

Federal sentencing guidelines have been established that reduce punitive damages based in part on what a company has done to prevent ethical problems.[7] Driven by these government actions and fear of retribution, companies are paying more attention than ever to the behavior of their employees. Ethics is a monetary issue as well! A survey conducted by the Center for Business Ethics at Bentley College reports that of 279 top U.S. companies responding to the questionnaire, 208 had written codes of conduct and 99 had formal training programs in ethics for their employees. Seventeen now have telephone "hot lines" to assist employees with ethical problems. Typical issues covered in these ethics programs for salespeople include:

1. The use of expense accounts.

2. The appropriateness of gift giving.

3. Dealing with a prospect's unethical demands.

4. Promises made to clients about product performance or delivery.

5. Loading the customer with unnecessary products. [8]

Some companies are as thorough as General Dynamics in implementing a code of ethics, but others keep their codes buried in filing cabinets; still others have no formal code of any kind. Implementing a code of conduct statement communicates to salespeople—and their customers—that companies have high moral standards. The findings of a recent survey by the Ethics Resource Center and the Society for Human Resources Management show widespread usage of ethics statements: 84 percent of surveyed companies have codes of conduct, and 45 percent have ethics offices. These guidelines can only be effective if sales managers are reinforcing them on a daily basis—traveling with reps, guiding them through the sales process, and engaging them in open, honest dialogue.[9] As a salesperson, you need to know where the company stands and whether its stand is consistent with your own. And the time to do this is before you're hired, not after.

Role Modeling by Executives

The likelihood that unacceptable selling practices will occur has more to do with how executives behave. If a sales manager gives the impression that you must do *anything* possible to make more sales, salespeople infer that dealing unethically is acceptable in order to succeed. More than anything an organization's culture influences sales reps behavior with clients. Dr. Eli Jones, co-director of the Program for Excellence in Selling at the University of Houston, says, "sales managers must emphasize ethical selling behavior in words and actions."[10] The company's top executives must keep in check the

"As a manager the important thing is not what happens when you are there, but what happens when you are not there."

-Dr. Kenneth Blanchard

pressure the managers put on their salespeople. If the CEO comes around once a year with a pep talk on moral behavior but proceeds the rest of the year to use underhanded methods of doing business, salespeople get a mixed message.

When confronting ethical dilemmas, individuals draw on various sources for guidance in making decisions. Salespeople's decisions are guided by organizational policies, codes, rules and norms, as well as interactions with other people in the organization. Ethical conflict may arise when salespeople's ethical values differ from those perceived to be held by their immediate supervisor or top management. Here are some ideas to consider that may foster ethical behavior within an organization:[11]

- Codes of ethics that are effectively communicated are likely to result in greater ethical behavior.

- The presence and enforcement of codes of ethics have been found to be associated with higher levels of ethical behavior.

- Corporate goals and stated policies strongly influence managers' decisions on whether to act ethically or unethically.

- When a climate is created where ethical values and behaviors are fostered, supported, and rewarded, more ethical behavior will exist.

Examples Set by Colleagues and Competitors

A salesperson sometimes discovers that colleagues and/or competitors are acting unethically. Imagine that you are riding in a cab one day, and a colleague asks the driver to provide a receipt for expense account purposes and to indicate a figure higher than the actual fare. As an observer, do you join in the activity, rebuke the colleague, report the colleague (commonly called *blowing the whistle*), or ignore it? A customer reports that a competitor has said you have an alcohol problem and are therefore undependable. Do you simply deny the charge, or do you retaliate by making detrimental remarks about your competitor?

The Bottom Line

One of the most powerful influences on salespeople is profits—their own and those of the company. Saul Gellerman, in explaining why good people can make poor ethical choices, says that "contrary to popular mythology, maximizing profits is a company's second priority—not its first. The first is ensuring its survival."[12] Its survival will surely be compromised if salespeople take casual views of the legal and ethical implications of their behavior. The company's short-term profits may be maximized by unethical behavior, but the company's very existence could be threatened if it were hit with huge fines or an unwanted exposure in the media. Although short-term profits are important for both the company and its salespeople, the long-term success and good name of the company must always be the first priority.

Groupthink and Gamesmanship

Groupthink refers to the pressure exerted on salespeople to be part of the group and not to buck the system—to be team players, no matter what. Being a team player is good if the team has ethical goals and plays by ethical rules, but if the group's thinking runs afoul of your own personal code of ethics, you must weigh your options carefully. Psychologist Irving L. Janis warns against "groupthink," which he suggests can cause flawed judgment.[13] Unfortunately there are examples of groupthink in every profession, and the pharmaceutical industry has not been spared its share of such activity. Two salespeople and three pharmacists pleaded guilty to their roles in a scheme involving the illegal sales of drug samples to pharmacies in New Jersey and New York. The operation generated more than a $1 million in illicit profits for **all** the parties involved. The salespeople, former Procter & Gamble reps, stole samples from doctors' offices and sold them to the pharmacists.[14] They also paid doctors and office personnel to obtain supplies. Here a number of people conspired to cheat others and somehow convinced themselves that what they were doing was all right. After all, if others in the industry were engaging in similar activity, making money at it, and not getting caught, then why shouldn't they? Groupthink is the same force that is called *peer pressure* when applied to teenagers.

Gamesmanship is becoming totally caught up in winning simply for the sheer joy of victory and a dislike of losing. Much of our culture nurtures this type of competitive spirit—from winning the high school football game to beating a friend at chess or golf. The typical gamesman in selling looks for shortcuts and is willing to use any technique to sell a product or service. To the gamesman, winning means doing whatever is necessary to make the sale. The dangers of gamesmanship are quite clear—the temptation to cross over the line into unethical or illegal behavior.

DEVELOPING A PERSONAL CODE OF ETHICS

Clearly many competing forces that influence a salesperson's decisions have an ethical dimension. Situations often arise in which a clear right or wrong is not easily apparent and discretion in behavior is up to the individual. Because the influences that come to bear upon a salesperson do not always agree and because conflicting demands are numerous, each salesperson must develop a personal code of ethics that supersedes all other claims.

Responsibility to Self

In the final analysis, the still, small voice of conscience is the arbiter of conflicting ethical claims. It provides the ability to say that you have made the best decision under the circumstances and take full responsibility for it. If you have personal integrity, then you cannot be dishonest with others—company, competitors, or customers.

Responsibility to the Company

Salespeople sometimes rationalize that cheating here or there in dealing with the company would not hurt. After all, the company makes lots of money and what you do would never be noticed. Several areas particularly lend themselves to temptations to be less than ethical.

Inaccuracy in Expense Accounts. Often padding expense accounts is relatively easy. A salesperson can add extra mileage, submit charges for a meal that was actually eaten at a friend's house, or take friends out to dinner and report the charge as entertaining customers. Tennessee Valley Authority officials discovered that about fifty TVA nuclear power employees conspired with hotel and motel representatives to bilk rate payers through travel expenses over the past few years to the tune of over $189,000.[15] Falsification of expense accounts is unethical and can lead to dismissal if detected. As a practical matter, it unnecessarily increases the costs of the company and may put it at a competitive disadvantage.

Honesty in Using Time and Resources. The temptation to do some shopping between sales calls, to linger over a third cup of coffee in a restaurant, and to sleep late in a hotel room are examples of ways a salesperson may misuse time. No time card is punched, and slipping in personal time may be relatively easy. This ultimately hurts both the salesperson and the company because fewer sales calls are made. Neil Snyder, a University of Virginia business professor, says losses of goods and cash to worker theft have reached an estimated $120 billion a year.[16] Misusing resources such as automobiles and selling samples for one's own profit hurt the company. These kinds of dishonest activities decrease the company's profits.

Accuracy in Filling Out Order Forms. Certain kinds of compensation plans, particularly contests, may tempt salespeople to withhold or delay orders or to oversell some items. This practice ultimately hurts the company because it results in unhappy customers. It also takes unfair advantage of co-workers who compete fairly to win contests.

Representing the Company. The salesperson is the spokesperson for the company and for that reason must accurately represent products and services and deliver the kind of follow-up service that the company promises. Exaggerating the capabilities of a product or failing to point out any problems that might be associated with its use is unethical and can be disastrous to a long-term relationship with a customer. In some instances, it is also illegal, with the potential for causing both the salesperson and the company serious legal consequences. In addition, a company that prides itself on service to customers will be sorely disappointed with a salesperson who makes a sale and neglects to check with the customer about any additional service needs.

Responsibility to Competitors

Being honest and refraining from taking unfair advantage are the basic guidelines when dealing with competitors. Making untrue, derogatory comments about competitors or their products is poor business. At the very least, the legal implications of this behavior simply make the risks too great. In the same sense, pumping a competitor's salesperson for information at a trade show in order to steal the competitor's customers is not ethical. Some salespeople go so far as to use sabotage, espionage, and dirty tricks to gain unfair advantage over a competitor. These tactics include hiding the competitor's products on a display shelf and planting "spies" in a business to hear a competitor's sales presentation. Persuading a customer to put out a fake request for bids to see what bids competitors would submit is another unfair tactic sometimes practiced. The basic theme in this area is to gain customers fairly and squarely by providing quality products and superior service.

Responsibility to Customers

Behaving honestly and providing quality information and services are the primary ingredients for establishing mutually satisfying relationships with customers. Fortunately, the stereotype of the silver-tongued, flattering, deceptive, door-to-door salesperson of the past is disappearing. Still, many opportunities for unethical tactics exist.

Overselling and Misrepresenting Products or Services. Some salespeople persuade customers to buy more than they need because the salesperson needs to meet a quota or wants to win a trip to the Caribbean. Overselling eventually catches up with the salesperson because customers realize that they have more than they need. In addition, repeat sales probably won't be possible for a very long time.

Lying about the capabilities of a product, the date the company can make delivery, or the nature of the warranty are all unethical ways to win a quick sale while running the risk of legal action or a permanent loss of the customer in the long run.

Keeping Confidences. Because of the relationship between the salesperson and the customer, the salesperson may be privy to valuable information about the customer. That information could be very useful to some other customer, and providing it might ingratiate the salesperson with the new customer. Failing to keep confidences is, of course, unethical, and eventually it results in a reputation for the salesperson as an untrustworthy gossip.

Gifts. Although giving a customer a token gift as a thank-you or as a reminder of the salesperson and the company is customary, the intent with which a gift is given usually reveals its ethical or unethical nature. If a gift is a way to get business or a bribe, then it is unethical and may well be illegal. The value of the gift in comparison to the sale is also something to consider. According to *Business & Incentives* magazine, approximately $3.5 billion is spent on business gifts yearly. Most companies usually spend around $25 on gifts, because it can be tax deductible as business expenses. Costs usually not included in this $25 limit are engraving, packaging, or mailing.[17]

Entertainment. Policies regarding entertainment are similar to those that cover gift giving. In some industries entertaining a client with a meal, an excursion, or tickets to the theater or a football game is customary. If the intent is as a means of saying thank-you to a customer or of developing a more personal relationship, entertainment may be acceptable and even expected. Finding out the rules of behavior in a particular industry and within an individual company is important. For instance, the United States government has a code of conduct letting executive-branch officials know precisely what is ethical regarding free lunches—corruption begins with the fifth lunch out. A bureaucrat can dine at the expense of a lobbyist or journalist provided the meal does not exceed $25. One official can only eat four times a year on any one organization's tab. The fifth one is unethical.[18]

Entertaining clients is a common sales practice

OPERATING IN A GLOBAL ENVIRONMENT

Salespeople today may operate not only in the United States but also in a foreign country where accepted norms of behavior may be different. Which morality should salespeople follow, their own or that of the country in which they find themselves? In the General Dynamics twenty-page code of ethics, the company instructs its sales force what to do in this event: "In countries where common practice might indicate acceptance of conduct lower than that to which we aspire, salespeople will follow the company's standards."[19] In some countries, "grease" or "speed" money makes the wheels of a government agency or a company move faster. In Japan, there is much gift giving in business relationships, and it is viewed as a time-honored tradition rather than a bribe. A company usually has guidelines for an employee to follow in a foreign country, but bribery is universally condemned and is in fact illegal whether it is practiced at home or abroad.

U.S. citizens selling overseas for American companies must abide by both United States law and the laws of the countries in which they sell. Patronage or payments to people in exchange for favors—actions that would be considered bribes here are the accepted way of doing business in many countries. Operating as a free and independent agent in a foreign country can be extremely difficult. To ease operations in countries with customs much different from ours, most companies align themselves with a local company or agent who can deal with ethical and cultural issues and cut a path through foreign laws and bureaucracy.

ETHICS AND JOB TENURE

When is it time to look for a new job? Of course, you want to be affiliated with a company of which you as a salesperson can be proud. Disagreements or issues of unethical behavior on the part of the company may, however, emerge during your employment. Deciding how to handle conflicts involving ethics can be stressful because your decision may mean either your termination or resignation. Weigh the options carefully and determine who is being helped and who is being hurt. Are there any alternative, creative options that minimize risk and allow career and conscience to be reconciled?

Whistle-Blowing

According to Nancy R. Hauserman, "In the pursuit of the goals of productivity and consumption, we have failed to preserve individual and community values. The individual has been reduced to a cog in the corporate wheel, a capital investment, a corporate property."[20] This attitude can make salespeople feel unimportant and fear that their ideas, suggestions, or revelations are not valid. This reaction is particularly true if they attempt to pass on valuable information to superiors and are rebuffed.

Consider the following scenario:

Six months ago Jim Hollis started a job with an industrial supplier selling valves for acid lines. A safety engineer at a chemical company has noticed that the secondary lining on the valve is not strong enough to keep acid from splattering in the event that the internal seal fails. Jim informed the appropriate people at his company that a major safety problem has been revealed to him, but they told him to keep selling the valves with no modifications.

What should someone like Jim Hollis do? A number of options could be considered:

- Negotiate and build consensus for a change in management's views.

- File away a memo that explains that he was outranked when he brought up the problem.

- Blow the whistle on the company.

- Ignore the whole situation and continue selling.

- Look for another job.

As careful as a salesperson may be when joining a company, an ethical dilemma such as this may arise eventually. In the best of all possible worlds, the violation should be exposed and those responsible punished, but what if pointing a finger at someone would cause the whistle-blower to be fired and put self and family in financial difficulties?

On the surface, the wiser course appears to be to keep quiet and let the problem resolve itself. Sometimes the best policy is to keep quiet until solid evidence can be accumulated or until the co-conspirators are identified, but silence as a long-term strategy is indefensible. The violation is likely to be exposed at some point, and being part of a cover-up is not a desirable position. Inaction can even be grounds for legal action. Harvey Pitt, an attorney who was a former Securities and Exchange Commission general counsel states, "If you're the head of the sales department and have some salespeople out there paying bribes and taking kickbacks but you decide not to do anything about it, you have a problem."[21] In such a situation, the head of a sales department certainly has an ethical problem but may also have a very real legal problem that is just as serious. Ethically, "the greatest good to the greatest number" is relevant. In the scenario involving the valve linings, the value of human safety must be given higher priority than saving the company and some of its sales in the short term.

The correct course of action may not be as black and white as the one described. In all but the most extreme cases, trying to negotiate a consensus probably makes good sense. If that is not an option, a wise move could be to go public. Recent rulings encourage whistle-blowers to follow their ethical urges. Settlements under the Federal False Claims Act are becoming larger. The act says a whistle-blower may receive 15 percent to 30 percent of any financial settlement won by the government. Chester Walsh, a former General Electric manager in Israel, received $13.4 million in a case involving a conspiracy between GE and an Israeli Air Force general who submitted bills for fictitious parts; the bills were accepted and paid by the Pentagon.[22] The newest way employees have of blowing the whistle is by e-mail. This type of computer correspondence is popular because employees feel secure in revealing improper company conduct.[23]

How the Company Treats the Salesperson

The company may treat its salespeople as partners joined with it in a common mission or simply regard them as cannon fodder out in the field. Salespeople are an extremely valuable resource to a company and deserve to be treated fairly, informed of decisions affecting them, and protected from situations in which they might be under pressure to make unethical decisions. Glenn Wilson discusses what companies can do to prevent unethical behavior among salespeople.[24]

- Avoid setting up management-incentive systems in a way that makes fudging the data tempting.

- Be accessible to salespeople in order to get early warnings on troublesome developments.

- Set up appropriate controls not only on financial accounts but also in customer complaints, salesperson dissatisfaction, and expense accounts.

- Set sales goals that are motivating but not impossible to achieve.

If salespeople know that their ideas are important and their judgment valued, they feel ownership in the organization and want to do a better job overall. Companies like Southwest Airlines and Levi Strauss have adapted to this new reality that workers need to feel valuable, so they are treating their employees not as forces to be controlled but as individuals to be empowered, in order to unshackle their skills, talents and potential. At Levi Strauss, for example, the predominant vision is that customer value comes from the values of its employees. That's why one-third of a manager's raise can depend on how well he or she lives up to the company's value-based philosophy.[25]

One of the most excruciating decisions salespeople face is that concerning territories. A salesperson may have spent years cultivating customers in a territory and then have it divided by management or even taken away. A key account that is the salesperson's bread and butter may be made a house account so that the salesperson no longer gets those commissions. One of the common e-commerce blunders is that companies do not consider the impact of their Web strategies on sales force compensation. The most important thing is to involve your sales reps in the decision and treat them in a straightforward manner. That's exactly what Tupperware Corporation did when it began selling its household products on its Web site. According to Christine Hanneman, "our salespeople are involved in all of our channels, including our Web site."[26] Customers who purchase the Tupperware products on the company's Web site are asked who referred them, and the referring salesperson gets the normal commission.

Other aspects of fair treatment are involved in firing, demotion, and payment. When salespeople must be fired or demoted, they should be told the real reason. Decisions concerning compensation for salespeople should be handled with kid gloves, especially if reductions are forthcoming. In addition, decreasing compensation calls for careful, ethical decision making; such action is, moreover, extremely demoralizing and may lead to losing salespeople who will cost the company money to replace and retrain.

SEXUAL HARASSMENT

A number of prominent sexual harassment cases have made the news in recent years. Perhaps the most famous was the case involving Anita Hill and current Supreme Court Justice Clarence Thomas. In today's legal environment, any institution's failure to recognize the consequences of workplace sexual harassment can be a capital blunder. For employees in organizations lacking sound policy practices, the negative impact from sexual harassment—including liability, embarrassment and lost productivity—can be extensive. Title VII of The Civil Rights Act of 1964 strictly prohibits sexual harassment.[27] The Equal Employment Opportunity Commission (EEOC) defines sexual harassment this way:

"Unwelcome sexual advances, requests for sexual favors, and other verbal or physical conduct of a sexual nature constitutes sexual harassment when submission to or rejection of the conduct explicitly or implicitly affects an individual's employment, unreasonably interferes with an individual's work performance or creates an intimidating, hostile or offensive work environment."

Sexual Harassment in Action

Read the following true-life situation (in disguised form) and imagine what you would do if you were in Sue's position.

"Yes sir, I'll schedule that with our driver for a Tuesday delivery," Sue said to the customer on the line, making a note of the request on her pad. "You're welcome," she responded to the customer's appreciative "Thank you."

But before she could put the phone down, another line began flashing. "Customer service, Sue speaking," her voice sang out into the receiver. "How can I help you?" While Sue was busy listening to the customer's request, Mike, her boss, came up behind her. He dropped a piece of paper on her desk and quickly left. He was bending over with laughter. Sue sensed Mike's presence and turned around to respond when the customer put her on hold. But Mike was already gone; however, the one page of paper lay on the top of her desk.

Sue recognized the paper as the company's standard performance appraisal. The scale ran from one to five, with one representing "unacceptable" and five saying "exceeds expectations." In the section where Mike was to fill in the key duties of her job and rank them, he had written the following:

1. Face = 3; 2. Breasts = 1; 3. Butt = 5; and Legs = 3

Sue's face turned red and her teeth clenched in anger as she tried to maintain her composure. When the customer came back on the line, she strained to keep a smile in her voice.

The situation just described is one of 36 authentic workplace incidents on sexual harassment documented by Dr. N. Elizabeth Fried in her book, *Sex, Laws and Stereotypes.* How would you handle such a situation if it were reported to you? What would you expect Sue to do? Would it make any difference if Sue had been a male receptionist and Mike harassed him in a similar way? Should the company itself be held liable for Mike's odious behavior (even though they had no prior knowledge of it)?

Sexual harassment charges filed with the EEOC have gone up 230 percent over the past decade. With the increasing incidents of sexual harassment in the workplace it is important for companies to institute effective policies in order to avoid liability. National surveys of more than 1,000 organizations found that sexual harassment had become one of the hottest topics in formal training programs.[28] In the past several years, sexual harassment consultant Maria Gottlieb says she has seen training requests on the issue rise by 75 percent, particularly in sales.[29] When considering employment with a particular company, make sure that there is a clearly defined sexual harassment policy firmly in place.

With a clear stand on sexual harassment a business can avoid liability and legal costs, perhaps keep talented people, and preserve the goodwill and trust of its customers. AT&T is an excellent example of a company whose sexual harassment policy has achieved these things. An AT&T employee sued the company for hostile-environment sexual harassment. When taken to court, AT&T was held not liable because they handled the situation promptly and took appropriate remedial action. In the future it will become increasingly important for businesses to develop and put into practice sound sexual harassment policies.[30]

ETHICS AS GOOD BUSINESS

Ethical behavior may sometimes appear to be an unattractive alternative. After all, for every inside trader, fraudulent salesperson, or immoral politician who gets caught, perhaps hundreds get away with unethical behaviors. However, the recent bumper crop of ethical scandals in corporate America has brought with it a renewed concern for ethics. Some of the newfound conscience in the corporations has filtered down to business people and individuals in every walk of life.

Gary Edwards of the nonprofit Ethics Resource Center in Washington, D.C., says that ethics is receiving more attention partially because of an awareness on the part of businesses of "the enormous costs of unethical activity—in fines and penalties, in increased government regulation, and in damage to their public image."[31] In short, companies are paying attention to ethics because it happens to be good business strategy.

Professional salespeople who are honest and aboveboard in relationships with employers, customers, and competitors alike become trusted and valued individuals. The key to making repeat sales is to build up these kinds of relationships and maintain them. A well-defined personal code of ethics as part of one's character and as a basis for behavior is an invaluable asset.

Checkpoints in Ethical Decision Making

When faced with an ethical conflict, a standard set of questions to ask yourself is helpful. Use the five questions suggested below to guide your thinking.

A Five-Question Ethics Checklist

1. IS IT LEGAL? LOOK AT THE LAW AND OTHER STANDARDS.

2. IS IT FAIR TO ALL CONCERNED?

3. WOULD I WANT SOMEONE ELSE TO ACT THIS WAY TOWARD ME?

4. HOW WOULD I EXPLAIN MY ACTIONS TO SOMEONE ELSE?

5. HOW WILL IT MAKE ME FEEL ABOUT MYSELF?

These questions first require careful evaluation regarding existing standards and personal liability. Next, the questions are designed to activate your sense of fairness and rationality. Last, realize that your personal feelings are important because negative feelings adversely affect positive performance. If your truthful answer to any one of these questions damages your self-image or causes you to be troubled by your conscience, then you should probably avoid the action in question. *There is no pillow as soft as a clear conscience.*[32]

LEGAL ISSUES FACING THE SALESPERSON

A serious problem faced by company sales forces today is a combination of antitrust law complexity and inadequate preventive legal guidance. Selling can sometimes be a mine field for salespeople who lack the legal expertise required to avoid violating various antitrust laws.[33] Often without realizing it, sales representatives violate legal regulations through various actions every day, and they can be held personally liable. Fines can be imposed up to $100,000 for individuals and $1 million for companies; criminal sanctions may also be imposed. Figure 3.1 illustrates some of the legal traps for unwary salespeople.[34]

Companies must properly train salespeople about required legal compliance to keep violations to a minimum. Actually, we would have practically no need for laws if all businesses played by the same ethical rules of the game. However, too many firms and individuals find the temptation to violate rules irresistible. Their violations, basically, fall into two broad categories:

FIGURE 3.1

Legal Traps for the
Unwary Salesperson

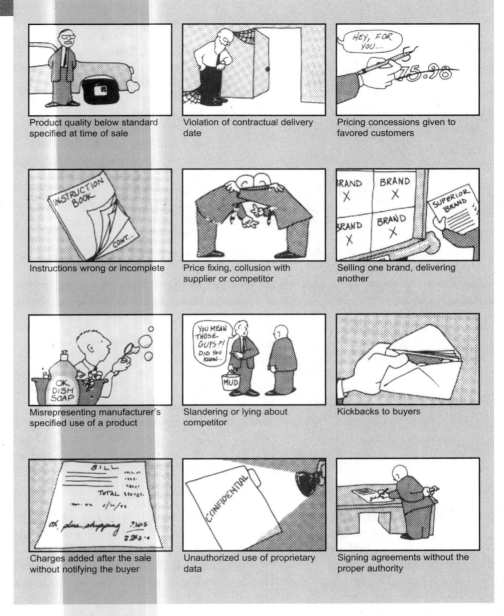

Product quality below standard specified at time of sale

Violation of contractual delivery date

Pricing concessions given to favored customers

Instructions wrong or incomplete

Price fixing, collusion with supplier or competitor

Selling one brand, delivering another

Misrepresenting manufacturer's specified use of a product

Slandering or lying about competitor

Kickbacks to buyers

Charges added after the sale without notifying the buyer

Unauthorized use of proprietary data

Signing agreements without the proper authority

1. Monopolistic actions, such as price-fixing or the acquisition of competitors.

2. Deceptive actions, such as false claims about products or services; disparaging remarks about or comparisons with competitors.

A number of laws have been passed to preserve fair competition. You might consider these government regulations to be your rules of the game. They serve to protect two groups: the consumer by preventing monopolies and eliminating practices that tend to be deceptive, and business competitors by establishing rules that prevent powerful rivals from depriving smaller firms free access to the market and by protecting competitors from those who would engage in deceptive practices.

Exhibit 3.2 outlines the antitrust legislation that most profoundly affect salespeople. Whenever you aggressively pursue an account, you can face temptations. In the heat of the battle, you may exaggerate or perhaps actually think you have said something clearly to the prospect. For example, the sales representative must completely, and in the clearest language possible, warn the prospect of any potential hazard connected with use of the product. Saying, "Use of this equipment at improper voltage levels will result in damage to the product and concomitant operator hazard" may not be good enough. A better statement would be: "It must be plugged into 115 volts only. If used at a higher voltage, it can fly apart and injure or kill you."[35] The courts may rule that the vague wording in the first statement is analogous to a sign in your yard that reads "Please keep off the grass," which is an insufficient warning if you know that the grass conceals rattlesnakes.

EXHIBIT 3.2 - Key Antitrust Legislation Affecting Salespeople

Sherman Antitrust Act (1890). Section 1 deals with competition. It prohibits contracts, combinations, or conspiracies in restraint of trade. Section 2 deals with market control. It prohibits monopolies or attempts to monopolize.

Federal Trade Commission Act (1914). Established the Federal Trade Commission, a five-member board of specialists with broad powers to investigate and to issue cease-and-desist orders. Section 5 of the act declares that "unfair methods of competition in commerce are unlawful" along with "unfair or deceptive acts or practices." (This latter phrase was added by the Wheeler-Lea Act of 1938, which amended the FTC Act.)

Clayton Act (1914). Supplements the vagueness of the Sherman Act of 1890 by prohibiting certain practices. For instance, Section 2 of the act deals with price discrimination; Section 3 deals with tying clauses and exclusive dealings; Section 7 with intercorporate stockholdings; and Section 8 with interlocking directorates. The key phrase stated in the law is, "where the effect may be to substantially lessen competition or tend to create a monopoly in any line of commerce." It provides that company personnel who violate the act can be held individually responsible.

Robinson-Patman Act (1936). Specifically amends Section 2 of the Clayton Act. It adds the phrase "to injure, destroy, or prevent competition." The law: (1) defines price discrimination as illegal (subject to certain defenses), (2) provides the Federal Trade Commission with the right to establish limits on quantity discounts, (3) prohibits promotional allowances except where made available to all "on proportionately equal terms," and (4) forbids brokerage allowances except to independent brokers.

The landmark lawsuit against the Microsoft Corporation is a compelling example of how the government wields the power of antitrust law to bring suit against a company they feel has become a monopoly that needs to be kept under control. Exhibit 3.3 highlights some of the key issues and provides plenty of food for thought.

EXHIBIT 3.3 - The Microsoft Corporation and Antitrust

The historic antitrust lawsuit against the Microsoft Corporation sought major changes in the design of the software that runs most computers. At the heart of the antitrust actions lies the issue of unbundling various Microsoft products, in particular its Internet Explorer browser, from the Windows operating system. The lawsuit against Microsoft represents one of the biggest antitrust battles since Standard Oil was forced to split in 1911.

Antitrust law was originally intended to protect consumers, not to help rivals. How interesting that in a country where freedom and innovation are applauded, our government wants to penalize a company that has worked hard and successfully to deliver what the consumer wants. In essence, the government wants to get involved in product development and design.

In June of 2001 the U.S. Circuit Court of Appeals reversed the finding that Microsoft's packaging of its Windows operating system with its Internet Explorer violated antitrust laws. In the next phase of the case the government will have to show that Microsoft unreasonably restrained competition with that action in order for it to seek a penalty. This decision is undoubtedly the most significant antitrust ruling since the court-ordered breakup of the AT&T telephone monopoly over twenty years ago.

This decision will likely face a Supreme Court challenge. In the meantime, the decision will vitalize and encourage Microsoft in several new initiatives it has under way to merge its popular software products. Government lawyers may see this new strategy, of extending the dominance of its Windows operating system to the Internet with new software that integrates with the core operating system, as leverage in the company's pursuit of monopoly power. On the other hand, Microsoft probably sees it as a result of their unquenchable passion for innovation.

The question for us to ponder: Is this an unavoidable consequence of advances in computer science, or just a clever monopolistic marketing strategy on the part of Microsoft?[36]

In view of all the laws affecting business, obviously sales representatives can say or do many things to get themselves, as well as their companies, into quite a bit of trouble. According to Robert Posch, the jail time for those who break antitrust laws has doubled, and they face much higher fines. He says, "In sum, crime simply does not pay; it's corporate suicide to commit antitrust crimes today."[37] Exhibit 3.4 points out six tactics for salespeople to consider following as protection for themselves and their companies when out in the field selling.[38]

EXHIBIT 3.4 - How Salespeople Can Protect Against Violating Antitrust Laws

1. Know the difference between "sales puffery" and specific statements of fact made during the sales presentation and avoid using unwarranted exaggeration to make your story sound good.

2. Thoroughly educate each customer on all aspects of the product before completing the sale.

3. Know the technical specifications, capabilities, design peculiarities, and special characteristics of the products you sell.

4. Read carefully any and all promotional literature published by your company on the products being sold. Challenge what you consider to be untrue or exaggerated claims.

5. Study the company's terms of sale policies. Overstating your authority to establish prices can legally bind the company.

6. Be up on all federal as well as state laws which affect warranties and guarantees.

THE UNIFORM COMMERCIAL CODE (UCC)

In addition to the federal antitrust laws, many other laws in all fifty states deal directly or indirectly with personal selling. Because of the diversity of these state laws, an attempt to cover them here is impractical. However, one set of regulations is consistent among the forty-nine states that have adopted it (Louisiana is the lone exception). The Uniform Commercial Code is a set of guidelines that spell out in some detail the conditions under which a sale may be consummated. The following aspects are governed by the UCC:

1. An offer to sell may be legally binding if it is made in writing or simply stated orally by the salesperson. A distinction is made between a legitimate offer to sell and an invitation to negotiate or deal.

2. The financing of the product or service must be explained clearly and completely. Salespeople must know the legal ramifications of any credit arrangements made with customers. Truth in lending also requires full disclosure of finance charges prior to closing the sale.

3. The salesperson must know the legal responsibilities if either party fails to live up to respective contractual obligations. For example, if the buyer is not able to pay the monthly finance charge, when can the seller take back the merchandise? If the goods are damaged or destroyed in transit, who is responsible for them?

4. Warranties and guarantees offered by the seller are basically the same and are governed by the UCC. The code defines both express warranties and implied warranties. *Express warranties* are statements and promises found in the advertising, sales literature, and labeling and in oral statements made by the salesperson. *Implied warranties* are a result of state law and the assumption that the product complies with those laws. Implied warranties are also in effect unless a disclaimer is made[39] To be on the safe side, the salesperson should state what is promised as well as what is not promised. In addition, the warranty statement should set time or use limits and clearly specify who is providing the warranty. For

example, if you are a distributor representing a manufacturer's product, make certain the customer knows that the manufacturer, not you, is providing the warranty.

COOLING-OFF LAW

In addition to the regulations provided by the UCC, nearly all states have additional laws regulating door-to-door selling. Much in-home selling has been characterized as high-pressure selling. The cooling-off rule gives buyers three days to think over their decision without a salesperson present. If buyers feel the decision is really not in their best interest, they may void the contract. This law applies to purchases for $25 or more. Firms selling door-to-door must typically provide potential buyers with information concerning these factors:

1. The number of days before the contract is binding.

2. How to cancel the agreement legally.

3. Any penalties involved in cancellation.

SUMMARY

In developing a personal code of ethics, a number of responsibilities should be considered. The ultimate responsibility is to oneself because it is that self to whom the salesperson always comes home. Without personal integrity, the salesperson cannot be responsible to other people or organizations. The salesperson must also ask what duties are owed to the company, to customers, and to competitors. If operating in a foreign country, additional conflicts may be present and must be dealt with directly.

Not only does the salesperson have ethical obligations, but companies have them as well. The salesperson should attempt to represent a company that has a reputation for honesty and fair dealing. Salespeople who find themselves in situations in which company violations are evident must make difficult choices about whether to blow the whistle on the company or settle on some other strategy that might well include finding another job.

A series of federal laws was passed beginning in 1890 with the Sherman Antitrust Act. It was followed by the Federal Trade Commission Act, the Clayton Act, and the Robinson-Patman Act. All these pieces of legislation make engaging in practices that inhibit fair competition or deceive the customer illegal.

In addition to the federal antitrust laws, forty-nine states have adopted the Uniform Commercial Code, which defines in some detail the conditions under which a sale may be consummated. It defines exactly what is meant by a sale, sets out required information for financing and truth in lending, and states a salesperson's legal responsibilities.

Because door-to-door selling has had the reputation of being high-pressure, special cooling-off laws have been passed in most states. These laws give the buyer a three-day period to break a sales agreement and specify what information the salesperson must give the buyer.

QUESTIONS FOR THOUGHT AND DISCUSSION

1. We have heard much about questionable corporate activities, insider trading scandals, defense contract fraud, health risk cover-ups, and so on. Does this mean that corporations are not interested in ethics—that the bottom line is that corporate greed takes precedence over moral responsibility?

2. What kinds of management tactics make salespeople more likely to exhibit unethical behavior?

3. Should there be any focus on morality in institutions? After all, you cannot have institutional integrity without first having individual integrity, and isn't that the domain of home, church, and school?

4. Does having a corporate code of ethics for salespeople really do any good? Out in the real world where salespeople compete for sales, is a code of ethics practical? Do salespeople need channels of communication and support structures along with an ethics code?

5. Ten years ago a Fordham University priest attended the Friday luncheon meeting of the Sales Executives Club of New York where he talked much about honesty in day-to-day business dealings. Asked why he did this, he replied, "What sales executives have to do puts them, among all business people, at the greatest risk of losing their souls." Do you agree with his statement?

6. Forty years ago the medical department at Johns Manville Corporation began to receive information implicating asbestos inhalation as a cause of asbestosis. Manville's managers suppressed the research and concealed the information from employees. The entire company was eventually brought to its knees by questions of corporate ethics. How can we explain this behavior? Were more than forty years' worth of Manville executives immoral?

7. Name the major pieces of legislation and their basic requirements that govern the ethical behavior of companies and salespeople.

8. Explain the operation of the cooling-off law.

9. When some specific safety precautions are needed in connection with using a product, what are the responsibilities of the salesperson in giving this information to the customer?

10. For your personal reflection: Do you believe you would ever be at risk of succumbing to groupthink or gamesmanship and participating in unethical or illegal activities? Have you ever been persuaded by peer pressure to do something for which you were later sorry? What can you do to lessen the possibility of compromising your own personal ethics?

ACTIVITIES

1. Interview a sales manager in a local company. Ask about the company's code of ethics: Does the company have a formal written code? Does it have an unwritten but specific set of ethical guidelines? How is the code communicated to salespeople? What penalties are exacted if a salesperson violates the code? Formulate your estimate of the sales manager's and the company's approach to the question of ethics. After your interview, would you feel comfortable and safe doing business with this company?

2. Interview a salesperson from another company. Ask about the company's code of ethics. Does the salesperson feel that the ethics policy of the company is strong enough? Too strong? How was the ethics policy of the company presented to the salesperson? Is the salesperson not sure what the company policy is in any area? Does the company actually enforce the policy?

Case Study

CASE 3.1

Dr. Donald Barnwell is a college professor teaching personal selling. One of his former students, Alicia Ramirez, called to ask his advice regarding what she considers to be an unethical situation. The company she works for gives each salesperson a $1,000 monthly expense allowance for entertainment of clients. After her first month on the job, she attempted to return the unused portion. The sales manager said, "Don't ever do that again. You must spend it all even it if means treating your friends, family, or former professors to free dinners. If top management discovers that we don't need that large an allowance, they will reduce it. We don't want that to happen, now, do we?"

Alicia felt confused. She asked Dr. Barnwell to go to dinner with her to discuss what she should do about this situation.

Questions:

1. Do you think he should go to dinner with her?

2. In attempting to understand the entire situation, what questions would you ask Alicia if you were in Dr. Barnwell's position?

CASE 3.2

Ray Morrison is a regional manager for a company that has just gone nationwide in the distribution of a non-contact system to detect the presence or absence of moving objects. Low-intensity gamma radiation is the detecting agent. This system is designed for applications where severe environmental conditions prevent the use of conventional devices such as infrared detectors, limit switches, and photoelectric and sonic sensors. Morrison has one major competitor in his region, a company that has had a virtual monopoly as a supplier of motion detection units in areas where severe environmental conditions existed. In addition, this company, Saferay Inc., was backed up by a complete service department that guaranteed that no system would ever be out of operation for more than six hours. When Saferay's competition established nationwide distribution, Morrison, who at the time was security chief for a large chemical company, was made a regional manager. Instead of being one of Saferay's best customers, he was now a competitor. The Saferay representative could not get used to the idea that a person he had considered to be a friend was selling in direct competition in the same territory.

One reaction of the Saferay salesman, Will Gager, has been to run down Morrison's products and services to every buyer he meets. Today's call at a new plant of a worldwide chemical company was no exception. Morrison was greeted by the chief of security with: "What do you think of the Saferay product?"

Morrison gave his standard answer to this often-asked question: "I think it's a fine system. And I know because I used it when I was a security chief myself."

"Well, they don't think much of yours," the prospect said.

"Oh, in what respect?" Morrison asked.

"Do you know Will Gager?"

"Sure, he's a good friend of mine. He used to call on me before I started selling," Morrison said.

"That's interesting. He tells me that the Security Council Lab almost refused to issue an approval label to your motion detectors because they just barely met minimum standards in a couple of environmental conditions," the security chief said.

Questions:

1. If you were Ray Morrison, what would you do?

2. What are the ethical issues involved?

Consumer Behavior and the Communication Agenda

CHAPTER 4

LEARNING OBJECTIVES

- To explore the differences between individual and organizational buyers.

- To understand the environmental influences on the purchase decision process.

- To understand the importance of communication.

- To learn what goes into the successful sending and receiving of a message.

- To develop knowledge of methods for overcoming communication barriers.

- To understand the importance of using the voice as a communication tool.

- To explore the effect of body language and proxemics in selling.

Lincoln's Gettysburg
Address

"Four score and seven years ago our fathers brought forth on this continent, a new nation, conceived in Liberty, and dedicated to the proposition that all men are created equal.

Now we are engaged in a great civil war, testing whether that nation or any nation so conceived and so dedicated, can long endure. We are met on a great battle field of that war. We have come to dedicate a portion of that field as a final resting place for those who here gave their lives that that nation might live. It is altogether fitting and proper that we should do this.

But, in a larger sense, we cannot dedicate—we cannot consecrate—we cannot hallow—this ground. The brave men, living and dead, who struggled here, have consecrated it, far above our power to add or detract. The world will little note, nor long remember what we say here, but it can never forget what they did here. It is for us the living, rather, to be dedicated here to the unfinished work which they who fought here have thus far so nobly advanced. It is rather for us to be here dedicated to the great task remaining before us—that from these honored dead we take increased devotion to that cause for which they gave the last full measure of devotion—that we here highly resolve that these dead shall not have died in vain— that this nation, under God, shall have a new birth of freedom and that government of the people, by the people, for the people, shall not perish from the earth."

The famous speech delivered by President Abraham Lincoln at the dedication of the Gettysburg National Cemetery on November 19, 1863

Figure 4.1 is the famous Gettysburg Address by President Abraham Lincoln. The entire speech lasted about two minutes. It has a total of 268 words—196 are one-syllable words; 52 two-syllable words; and just 20 words of more than two syllables. Today, the Gettysburg Address is recognized as a classical model of the noblest kind of oratory.

For centuries our finest writers, poets and orators have recognized the power of small words to make a straight line between two minds. Many of our proverbs employ terse monosyllables: "A bird in the hand is worth two in the bush," "A stitch in time saves nine," "If it is to be, it is up to me."

When asked to explain Britain's wartime policy to Parliament, Prime Minister Winston Churchill said: "It is to wage war, by sea, land and air, with all out might and with all the strength that God can give us." As Neil

Armstrong set his foot down on the moon he simply said, "That's one small step for man, one giant leap for mankind."

You don't have to be a great author or statesman to tap the energy and power of small words, so use them wherever you can. Small words are not only more understandable and exact than large words, they also add elegance to your speaking and writing. Salespeople realize and appreciate the persuasive power of a well written sales proposal. Just think how much more you could sell if you could talk and write equally well. If you must choose between a large word and a small word, select the small word everytime. Take a lesson from your local highway department. Place a sign at the boundaries of your speech that reads: *Caution—Small Words at Work.*

CONSUMER BEHAVIOR: WHY PEOPLE BUY

- A retail salesperson working at a Hickory Farms store in Denver convinces a young couple to purchase three pounds of Scandinavian butter cheese. They take it home and serve it to their guests at a reception honoring a group of foreign exchange students from Norway.

- An alumnus of a small private college in Prescott, Arizona, receives a personal call from the school's president, who tells him of a $20 million campaign drive now under way to underwrite expansion into the twenty-first century. The president convinces him to participate in the *Leadership Campaign* with a five-year pledge of $300 per year.

- The Mars Candy Company in McLean, Virginia, has decided to make and market a new candy bar with a peanut butter center coated in a creamy milk chocolate of a specific viscosity. Three competing salespeople offering a machine to make this product begin calling on Mars. This major capital investment requires consideration by top executives, tax specialists, production personnel, and marketing personnel. The three salespeople will have direct, frequent contact with all of these Mars personnel and will call in technical experts to assist. The purchase decision will take many months to complete.

Different consumers are influenced by a number of environmental factors.

These three situations involve consumer behavior and illustrate diverse aspects of the purchase decision process. *Consumer behavior* is the set of actions that make up an individual's consideration, purchase and use of products and services.[1] The term *consumer behavior* includes both the purchase and the consumption of products or services. The salesperson's role is vital in this process of matching the company's market offerings to the needs of the prospective buyer. However, this process does not end with the sale. The consultative salesperson is equally concerned with consumer satisfaction after the sale. This chapter introduces a model of the consumer's decision-making process, considers a number of environmental factors that influence this process, and then examines both the verbal and nonverbal elements of the communication process, with special emphasis on body language and *proxemics* (the use of space).

The Purchase Decision Process

The model of the purchase decision process presented in Figure 4.2 provides a useful tool for examining the buying process. It presents a view of the buyer as someone observed, not in a single act, but in a complex problem-solving process. Obviously, this model cannot provide all the answers for salespeople, but it does provide knowledge that can be used in individual sales situations as a guide for understanding what the prospect faces and deciding how to assist in the decision-making process.[2]

To understand why an individual makes a particular purchase decision, a salesperson has to look at events preceding and following the purchase act itself. A buyer generally passes through five stages: (1) problem recognition, (2) search for alternatives, (3) evaluation of alternatives, (4) the actual purchase decision, and (5) postpurchase evaluation.

FIGURE 4.2

Model of the Purchase
Decision Process

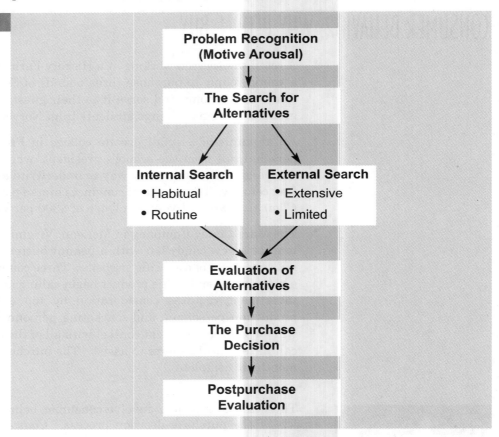

Problem Recognition. The purchasing process begins with mental recognition and acknowledgment that a problem or need exists and must be satisfied. A need is something regarded as necessary because it is essential to maintaining or improving a particular condition or circumstance. A need may also simply be something the buyer wants or desires and therefore perceives as a need. However defined, a need must first be aroused or stimulated before it can serve as a buying motive. No one takes action until motivated to do so, and motivation arises from awareness of needs. Therefore, the salesperson has to recognize needs that are already active or to find a way to arouse or stimulate a need of which the prospective buyer has not yet become aware.

All kinds of needs affect buying decisions. Some are quite *specific*: a senior graduating from college needs a business suit for job interviews. Some are *vague*: "I'd like to do something different today." Another need might be *physiological*: "A big pepperoni pizza would really taste good right now." Still another might be *security related*: "I need to buy some life insurance to protect my family if something happens to me." Abraham Maslow defined five levels of needs: *physiological, safety, social, esteem, and self-actualization*. Regardless of the kind of need, some buyers are not consciously aware of the nature of their needs until a salesperson brings them out into the open.

Search for Alternatives. After recognizing an unsatisfied need, the buyer begins to search for information concerning the available alternatives. The search may involve both internal and external sources. The internal search makes use of the buyer's previous experience, learning, attitudes, and occurs largely without conscious effort. For instance, if you run out of shampoo, your previous experience and attitudes take over and you are likely to purchase—from habit—the same brand you have always used. Even in the business-to-business markets, much purchasing is routine in nature. Pat Prewitt, a purchasing agent for Hooker Chemicals in New Orleans, says much of her purchasing is done through catalogs and list prices. A phone call to a regular supplier is all that is required.

The external search process involves added dynamics. It may require an extensive information search or a more limited search for alternatives. The extent of the search depends upon several factors: (1) the time commitment required, (2) cost of the product or service, (3) amount of past experience, (4) urgency of the need, (5) the perceived risk of making an incorrect decision, and (6) the value placed on the purchase.

Evaluation of Alternatives. The search process provides the buyer with knowledge of several alternative products. These products constitute an *evoked set* that probably contains only a few of the many possible choices. All individual consumers have specific criteria to use for making a decision—personal mental rules for matching alternatives with motives. These criteria are learned by actual experience with the product or derived from information obtained from commercial or social sources.

The implications for the consultative salesperson are important here. If salespeople can determine the buyer's *choice criteria*, they can tailor the presentation to focus on specific product or service benefits that differentiate their product from the competition. The buying process is actually a matching process, a harmonizing of the buyer's dominant buying motives with what the salesperson offers. Consumers' choice criteria involve both *salient attributes* (those used for evaluation purposes) and *determinant attributes* (the dominant buying motives used to finalize a decision). In buying a home entertainment system, for example, the salient attributes evaluated by a buyer might include freedom from audio and video distortion, strong signal capacity, remote control tuning, and channel capabilities. Once several models that satisfy these criteria have been identified, the determinant attributes come into play: price, reputation of the manufacturer, dealer's service capabilities, or cabinet design and finish. Identifying the dominant buying motives that determine a particular buyer's behavior in the actual decision-making process is vital to closing the sale.

Purchase Decision. After evaluating all the alternatives discovered in the search process, the buyer is ready to make the purchase decision—actually a whole set of decisions. These include style, brand, color, options, price, source, particular salesperson with whom to deal, and any number of other factors relevant to the product. Buyers want to minimize the risk and simplify the decision process as much as possible. The professional salesperson knows this and assists the buyer in making the decision. The salesperson finds out how the product or service fits into the buyer's entire consumption system by asking questions: Who else will use it? How is it to be used? Where? When? With what other products will it be used? The salesperson's role in assisting prospects to reach a satisfactory purchasing decision is what makes professional consultative selling so rewarding and fulfilling.

Postpurchase Evaluation. The purchase decision process continues after the product or service choice has been made. The buyer evaluates the purchase in terms of prepurchase expectations and decides whether it has been satisfactory. Sometimes the buyer experiences postpurchase anxiety—what psychologists call *cognitive dissonance*. The magnitude of the anxiety or tension depends upon the importance of the decision and the attractiveness of the rejected alternatives. To alleviate dissonance, buyers look for ways to reinforce their belief that they made a good choice.

BUSINESS-TO-BUSINESS BUYING

The five-stage purchase-decision process fits the ultimate consumer buyer adequately. Another category, the business-to-business buyer, follows a more complex purchase-decision process. Exhibit 4.1 illustrates this complexity. Understanding and profiling decision-makers within buyer groups, their areas of responsibility, and their buying process – whether formal or informal, centralized or decentralized – can be a critical business-to-business success factor.[3] The two processes are similar, but several fundamental differences in the behavior of this type of buyer should be noted.

1. *Decision maker.*

   The ultimate consumer is the decision maker in a purchase. In an organizational setting, decisions are often made by committees, commonly referred to as *a buying center*. The buying center is an ad hoc, cross-departmental, decision-making unit consisting of all individuals who play a role in formulating the purchasing recommendation.

2. *Buying criteria.*

   Ultimate consumers have a limited set of factors to weigh in making a buying decision, but organizational buyers may be bound by a highly complex set of decision-making criteria that must be considered.

3. *Buying motives.*

   Buying motives may be either rational or emotional. Ultimate consumers often buy based on emotion and later attempt to rationalize their decisions. Organizational buyers, however, must heed both rational or economic motives as well as emotional ones, but the rational motives are usually dominant.

EXHIBIT 4.1 - How Business-to-Business Buying Differs From Consumer Buying Behavior

1. Business-to-business buyers are far fewer in number, much larger in size and are concentrated geographically. This necessitates an emphasis on personal selling and specific trade publication advertising to reach these buyers.

2. Business markets often require products that are more complex, expensive and purchased in larger quantities. Because of this, buyers operate under purchasing constraints imposed by the company.

3. Derived demand influences business markets. That is, the demand for consumer products drives the purchasing decisions made by business organizations. There is no demand per se for organizational products.

4. There usually is a much longer period of negotiation. Before buying, firms may conduct a value and vendor analysis on the possible sources of supply. Their buying is subject to influence from multiple sources within the company (they are likely to form a buying committee to evaluate the purchase, especially for a new task buy).

5. They desire to stay with a supplier longer which results in the need for less frequent negotiation. This interdependence underlies the need to build a long-term relationship. As a result, many business buyers and sellers have formed what are referred to as strategic business alliances.

Classifying Business Customers

Business-to-business buyers include all organizations (profit and nonprofit) that buy products or services for their own use, or that resell to other organizations or sell to the ultimate consumer. They can be divided into four categories:

1. *Industrial producers* – Buy products or services to support their own manufacturing process or buy products that will be included in the products the company manufactures and sells. For example, U.S. Steel buys iron ore and converts it into steel and then attempts to sell the steel to DaimlerChrysler.

2. *Wholesale and retail firms* – Also known as resellers or marketing middlemen, buy products or services for the purpose of selling them to other businesses or directly to the ultimate consumer. To illustrate, Sears may buy their Kenmore washers and dryers from Whirlpool and then resell them to their retail consumer.

3. *The United States government* – Government buyers purchase products or services for use by the various local, state, and federal agencies they serve. The federal government accounts for more than one-half of these purchases, making it the largest customer in the world.

4. *Institutions (profit and nonprofit)* – This category includes churches, restaurants, universities and hospitals. Because of the complexity of selling to this disparate market, a packaged goods firm such as Del Monte will have one sales force calling on large supermarket chains like Kroger, and another sales force calling on large regional hospitals like the M.D. Anderson Cancer Center in Houston.[4]

Compared to ultimate consumers, organizational buyers are fewer in number, but the size or dollar volume of each purchase is usually larger. The United States has over 13 million industrial firms, about 475,000 wholesale organizations employing six million people, over two million retail firms employing 20 million people and 80,000 governmental units. The various federal, state, and local government organizations purchase more than $1.5 trillion in goods and services.[5] Success in selling to organizational buyers requires attention to their *purchase policies*, *multiple buying influence*, and *buying motives*.

Purchase Policies. Organizational buyers operate under the constraints of purchase policies established by the company or agency. Such policies range from strict specifications to general standards of performance. They may include guidelines for installation, warranty and repair service agreements, the availability and quality of technical assistance, and product performance standards. Product quality, delivery guarantees, and durability are additional policy items often considered. In addition, many companies require specific or customized products for their special needs.

Multiple Buying Influence. The responsibility for organizational buying decisions usually involves more than a single individual, especially when the organization is facing a new-task or modified rebuy situation. Many organizations set dollar limits beyond which purchase decisions must involve additional executives. Buying committees drawn from various departments become involved in decision making. The members of this committee, called a buying center, share common goals and knowledge relevant to the purchase decision. A major objective for a salesperson dealing with a *buying center* is to discover the key person or persons who actually make or strongly influence the final decision. Researchers have identified five specific roles played by the people who constitute a buying center:[6]

1. *Users.*

    Those who finally use the product or service purchased; for example, a telemarketing sales force who will be the primary users of a proposed new telephone system.

2. *Buyers.*

    Those who have formal authority to make the purchase, such as the purchasing agent.

3. *Influencers.*

    These are individuals who provide information directly or indirectly throughout the buying process to members of the buying center. For example, the supervisor for the telemarketing division may suggest certain features needed in a telephone system to make the calling process more efficient.

4. *Deciders.*

    Those who have the power and authority to choose from among the various suppliers. They make the final decision.

5. *Gatekeepers.*

    Those who control the flow of information into the buying center. Gatekeepers are invaluable to the group's decision making process. A purchasing agent, acting as a gatekeeper can decide which suppliers are notified and how much pertinent data these potential suppliers are given access to.

Buying Motives. Individual consumers or organizational buyers choose to buy a particular product or service as a result of *dominant buying motives* or reasons that are peculiarly their own. These dominant buying motives may be rational, emotional, or a combination of the two.

Every buying decision made—consumer or organizational—is based upon a dominant motive. Check the validity of this statement by examining what influenced your most recent purchase of clothes. Why did you buy a particular personal computer? What influenced you to buy the last compact disk you bought? Several motives may be involved, but one usually dominates. Table 4.1 lists the basic motives that lead to both consumer and organizational purchases.

TABLE 4.1 - Consumer and Organizational Buying Motives

Ultimate Consumer Buying Motives	Organizational Buying Motives
1. Increase wealth or income	1. Profit
2. Alleviate fear	2. Economy
3. Secure social approval	3. Flexibility
4. Satisfy bodily needs	4. Uniformity of output
5. Experience happiness or pleasure	5. Salability
6. Gain an advantage	6. Protection
7. Imitate	7. Utility
8. Dominate others	8. Guarantees
9. Recreation	9. Delivery
10. Improve health	10. Quality

ENVIRONMENTAL INFLUENCES ON THE PURCHASE DECISION PROCESS

Buying motives cannot be directly observed, but can be inferred from observing behavior. Many factors influence buying behavior. Figure 4.3 illustrates some of the psychological and sociocultural influences that affect a buyer's purchase decision process. Salespeople must understand the significance of the impact of these factors at the various stages of the decision-making process.

1. Behavioral concepts such as perception and the self-image impact *problem recognition*.

2. Sociocultural factors such as reference groups and social class influence the nature and scope of the *information search*.

3. Psychological factors like the mood of the moment, attitudes, and perception, as well as sociocultural factors including the physical environment and culture, influence *purchase decisions*.

FIGURE 4.3

Influences on the Buyer's Purchase Decision Process

Psychological Influences	Sociocultural Influences
• Perception	• Culture
• Mood of the moment	• Physical environment
• Attitudes	• Social class
• Self-image	• Reference groups

Buyer
(Psyche)

Salespeople can make positive use of these factors by becoming proficient in the art of communication—the sending and receiving of messages in a manner that results in understanding and agreement.

Psychological Influences

Several psychological factors affect a prospect's buying decision. The consultative salesperson must be cognizant of these factors and understand the role they play in the process.

Role of Perception.   Individual behavior is an organized, meaningful response to the world as that particular person sees it. Your perception of the universe constitutes reality for you and determines how you send and receive messages. It grows out of your past experiences, how you reacted to those experiences, and the resulting image you have formed of yourself.

We perceive situations according to our own personal needs, values, expectations, past experience, and training. Figure 4.4 illustrates the difference in individual perceptions. How many squares do you see? Check the answer given in the chapter endnotes.[7] If you didn't see that many, you may be exercising selective perception. Prospects often perceive not what the salesperson thinks is most important but what they select as important to themselves.

Mood of the Moment.   Perception is also influenced by an individual's psychological state or mood of the moment. On some days a minor mishap may be laughed off, but if nothing has gone right all day, the very same situation may be perceived in such a way that you become infuriated.

Attitudes.   Attitudes are merely habits of thought and habitual patterns of response to experiences. Because they have been used so often, they have become automatic and are used to save the time that would be required to think about a situation and make a decision. Salespeople often deal with prospects who have formed attitudes that affect the purchase decision process. For example, some prospects operate from an attitude that what has been done in the past is obviously the way to do things in the future. Their attitude is that change is bad. Some prospects adopt the attitude that anyone who tries to sell them anything is to be suspected of ulterior motives. Any attitude on the part of a prospect that makes the purchase decision more difficult can become a barrier that must be overcome before a sale can be made. Negative attitudes are a problem because they are often unconscious. Because they are habits of responding to experience, the individual involved no longer thinks about them and is unaware that they exist. In contrast, prospects who adopt attitudes of open-mindedness, enthusiasm, innovativeness and willingness to explore new ideas are a joy for the consultative salesperson to find.

An individual's self-image affects how he sees and reacts to circumstances.

The Self-Image. *Self-image* is an individual's unique and personal self-appraisal at a given moment in time. It affects what is perceived as reality and, as a result, how communication proceeds. People often see themselves in a particular role: a good teacher, an excellent student, a great joke teller, or a successful sales professional. Others, however, may see them as something entirely different. In choosing how to communicate, even more important than what is true is what the person *believes* is true. The salesperson who wishes to communicate effectively must learn to recognize these important dimensions of the prospect's self-image:

1. *Physical.*

   People picture themselves as tall or short, weak or strong, attractive or unattractive, lean or fat. They buy products that fit their self-image or that promise to change it to fit a desired goal.

2. *Social.*

   Individuals see themselves as liked or disliked, accepted or rejected, loved or unwanted, successful or failing.

3. *Moral.*

   Internalized values give people a picture of themselves as loyal or disloyal, honest or dishonest, straightforward or devious.

FIGURE 4.4

How many squares do you see in the figure? You may not see what others see.

Most psychologists suggest that by age seven or eight we have decided what kind of person we are, the kind of person we will become, how our world will respond or react to us, what kind of people we will deal with, and what our environment will be.[8]   The self-image includes dimensions that are not technically "self," but they are so closely identified with the self that in practicality they operate as though they are real. For example, people routinely talk about "my" company or "my" school, and some parents see their children as extensions of themselves. Every behavior can be explained if the self-image of the individual is understood. In one sense we are all self-centered, and we act in keeping with what we consider best for us at the moment.

Sociocultural Influences

In addition to psychological influences, sociocultural influences operate to determine how people think, feel, act, and communicate.

Culture. Culture is a way of looking at life that is handed down from one generation to another. It is completely learned. The effects of culture can be observed in what people do, see, and use and in how they reach judgments about people, events, and experiences. Individuals' values develop as a result of their reactions to the environment in which they live. The cultural environment exerts a powerful influence on how messages are both sent and received. For example, a large percentage of Americans attach a positive connotation to concepts such as success, competition, efficiency, freedom, and material wealth. The same positive reception to these words is not, however, universal. Even within the United States, subcultures of many kinds exist, each with its own set of values, priorities, and concepts.   Even more pronounced are cultural differences that affect communication among people from different parts of the world, a fact that has broad implications for sales and marketing people in today's global marketplace. Exhibit 4.2 illustrates that selling overseas (or to foreigners visiting the U.S.) demands cultural sensitivity. In Japan that means showing a business card the same respect you would show a person.[9]

EXHIBIT 4.2 - Treat a Business Card With Respect

Steve Waterhouse had the moment he had been waiting for. His firm had been courting a Tokyo meeting planning company for the past six months. At a National Speakers Association convention in San Antonio, Texas, Waterhouse had the good fortune (or so it seemed) to meet with the firm's representative to discuss services his company might buy. "He handed his business card to me in the traditional Japanese way," Waterhouse recalls – extending the card while holding onto both corners. "I took the card and scribbled a note on the back of it." Much to his dismay, Waterhouse looked up to find the man appalled at what he had just done. "I might as well have spit in his face," he says, "I quickly put it away and then apologized profusely, but the damage was already done." Steve Waterhouse lost a sale worth $100,000 to his company!

Cross-Culture Business Considerations a Global Perspective. Foreign cultures adhere to different business customs, protocol and body language for basic communication than we do in America. If you want to sell to international customers, whether here or overseas, you must establish rapport. Insensitivity to other people's customs and ways of communicating could derail your best selling efforts.

Some organizations operating domestically are encountering language problems once faced only by huge, global firms. Southern California Edison, for example, found five groups of customers deserving special attention: Cambodian, Chinese, Hispanic, Korean and Vietnamese. Their solution was to identify eleven bilingual employees to serve as company spokespersons and ambassadors. They then received special training in communication, public speaking and issues affecting the corporation.[10]

Those who sell to international customers may get by on a wink, a blink and a "see ya later" but only if they know how their language and gestures are going to be interpreted; *body talk* does not have a universal language. According to Diane Ackerman in her book *A Natural History of the Senses*, "Members of a tribe in New Guinea say good-bye by putting a hand in each other's armpit, withdrawing it, and stroking it over themselves, thus becoming coated with the friend's scent."[11] Thank goodness when we say good-bye to a client we can just shake hands, or can we?

In France the traditional American handshake is considered much too rough; a quick handshake with just slight pressure is preferred. Throughout Latin America, however, the greeting is often more exuberant. A hearty embrace is common among men and women. They often follow it with a slap on the back. But in Ecuador, to greet a person without shaking hands is a sign of special respect.[12] Throughout India it is quite rude to touch women, so never offer to shake their hands. Figure 4.5 illustrates several cross-cultural considerations when conducting business globally.[13]

Conducting business globally presents unique cultural challenges.

FIGURE 4.5 - Cultural Differences From a Global Perspective

1. Avoid slang or sports metaphors —"That proposal is way out in left field!" or "Are we in the ballpark on price?"—they may mean nothing to other cultures.

2. Always use your last name when answering the telephone in Germany such as, "Bond speaking." When you call a customer say your last name first: "This is Bond, James Bond."

3. Americans and Canadians will take a business card and pocket it without reviewing the information. In France, Italy, Switzerland, and Japan, the business card is an extension of the person who gives it so cards need to be treated with much respect.

4. After introductions, Americans and Canadians will tend to move quickly into business. However, in Latin America and China business can only proceed after a relationship has been built.

5. In Japan, you can never be too polite, too humble, or too apologetic. Make apologizing routine. This is one of the greatest areas of cultural difference between our two countries.

6. Always appear to be less informed and less skilled in the negotiation process than you really are. To the Japanese there is no such thing as a quick deal.

7. The British and Russians are masters at using the pressure of silence. Don't speak until your prospect has responded to your last comment.

Physical Environment. Americans usually keep their houses and offices at a cozy seventy-two to seventy-eight degrees, but the British prefer a cozy sixty to sixty-five degrees. Other elements such as sound level are also important in the environment. Most people of middle age and older like a quiet, restful environment; younger people tend to be stimulated by loud music and object less strenuously to machine noise. The perceptive salesperson won't attempt to make a presentation to a sixty-year-old prospect over dinner in a restaurant that features live rock music. The physical environment must be conducive to communication.

Social Class. A social class is a group of people who hold approximately equal social position in the eyes of others in the society. Almost every society has some class structure. In the United States, social structure is much less rigid than in some other nations in which it may be tied to religion, kinship, or inherited ownership of land. Americans often climb into new social classes by earning higher education and filling prestigious jobs. Social class groupings are based largely on source of wealth, occupation, education, type of house location. People tend to adopt buying behaviors, tastes, and characteristic ways of communicating that are in keeping with the social class of which they consider themselves members.

Reference Groups. The buying decision is also affected by the different reference groups by which individuals define themselves, including family, business or profession, religious, fraternal, civic, and political.

Any one of these groups can be important in the purchase-decision process. Prospects may buy a particular product because it is commonly approved by *members* of their cultural group or business. Some buy products that they hope will mark them as eligible for membership in some group to which they aspire to belong. A bigger house and a more luxurious automobile are common purchases of this type. Some prospects may even buy a product because it will prove that they do *not* belong to a certain group with which they *do not wish* to be identified. The alert salesperson identifies the relevant groups for each prospect and stresses the desirable traits of the people who buy the product to make the prospect feel comfortable with the idea of owning it.

THE COMMUNICATION AGENDA

Success in consultative selling depends upon accurate communication—the productive exchange of information between the salesperson and the prospect. Communication can be viewed as the verbal and nonverbal transmission of information between a sender and a receiver. However, for actual communication to take place the salesperson and prospect must share a common understanding of the symbols used to transmit that information. Each must understand the *intended* message. Thus, the goal of communication is a sharing of meaning.[14] Figure 4.6 shows the channel through which communication must flow in a selling situation. At each junction the potential exists for both problems and opportunities. Although the model considers communication from the salesperson's perspective, in any successful relationship both parties participate meaningfully in an active two-way process.[15]

FIGURE 4.6

The Communication
Model for Verbal and
Nonverbal Messages

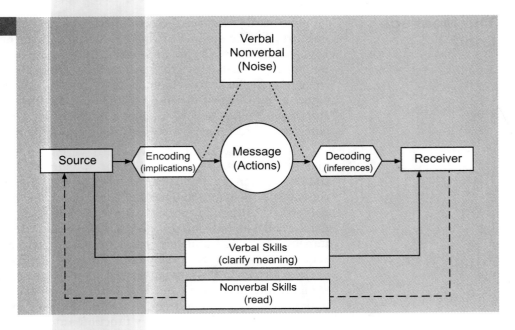

Encoding the Message

Encoding then is the process of putting meaning into symbols to be conveyed as messages in the communication process. In selling, this means converting an idea or concept by a salesperson into symbols the buyer can clearly understand.[16] The salesperson as *source* encodes the intended message, organizes it, and puts it into form for transmission to the prospect. Effective encoding of the message is based upon knowledge of the prospect's needs.

At this step in the process, either real communication or misunderstanding can occur. The message that exists in the speaker's mind must be transmitted by means of symbols—words, pictures, numbers, and the like—that merely represent the idea. Only implications can be sent. Prospects then make their own inferences. Communication is successful if the chosen symbols cause the listener to understand the speaker's original intent. The system breaks down if the salesperson makes any inaccurate assumption about the prospect's understanding or prior knowledge. On the other end of the communication channel, if the prospect makes erroneous assumptions about the salesperson or the message, the decoding process results in misunderstanding. The real challenge in communication is to transfer your thoughts, ideas, and intentions without distortion or omission.

Because communication is affected by the assumptions, the emotions, and the needs of both parties—as well as by outside factors such as time pressures, interruptions, and the environment—communication is often far from perfect.

In the process of encoding the message, the salesperson has at least three basic purposes:

1. To influence the attitudes and behavior of the prospect.

2. To move the buyer through a sequence of mind changes until a buying decision is made.

3. To obtain affirmative action upon five buying decisions: *need, product, source, price, and time.*

The Message Itself

The actual message is a combination of symbols that a salesperson uses to encourage a change in a prospect's attitude and/or behavior. Symbols merely represent objects or experiences. The most common symbols used in delivering a message are words, illustrations, numbers, sounds, physical touch, smell, body movement, and taste. To produce exact communication, symbols must have a common meaning for the speaker and the listener. *Automobile* is just a word and not a real vehicle. Unless both parties have the same understanding of the word, the meaning is unclear.

The message itself involves both verbal (words) and nonverbal (voice, visual) elements. In his book *Silent Messages*, Albert Mehrabian points out that *words* convey only seven percent of feelings and emotions, *tone of voice* conveys 38 percent, and *visual communication* conveys the remaining 55 percent.[17] Although not always consciously perceived by the prospect, nonverbal elements in the presentation make up the majority of the total impact. If verbal and nonverbal messages conflict, the listener invariably relies on the nonverbal message. Figure 4.7 illustrates the contribution of various factors to the messages we deliver to others and the amount of control we maintain over each one. The factors most easily controlled are those that make the least contribution, and those with maximum impact are the most difficult to control because they function automatically.

The process of delivering the message begins with visual impressions because they happen first. If a salesperson walks hesitantly into a prospect's office wearing a deadpan or worried expression, the prospect is immediately wary. The visual messages are unattractive. If the salesperson then extends a clammy palm with a "dead-fish" handshake, an unpleasant "touch" is added. If an unenthusiastic message is delivered in a monotone, the "sound" itself drowns out the words. The cluster of negative nonverbal cues completely masks the real message.

Research suggests that if the first thirty seconds of a communication result in a negative impression, the salesperson has to spend the next four minutes just to overcome that impression before any real communication can begin.[18] Unfortunately, the prospect may decide not to buy before the situation can be reversed.

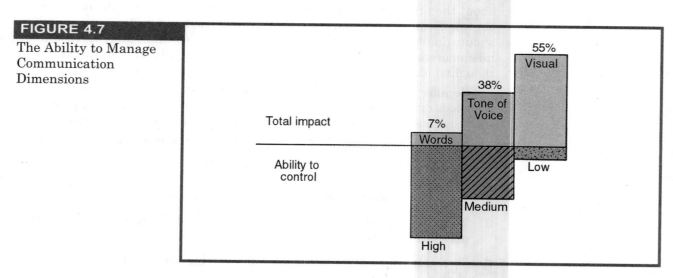

FIGURE 4.7

The Ability to Manage Communication Dimensions

Evaluating the Prospect's Decoding

Decoding is the mental process by which an individual interprets the meaning of the message. It is the process by which the receiver attempts to convert symbols conveyed by the sender into something meaningful. The symbols must be carefully chosen because the receiver will assign meaning to them in light of personal experience and knowledge. Successful communication depends upon the ability of the sender to evaluate the listener's decoding of the message. If the message was obviously both understood as it was intended and also accepted, there is no problem. If the prospect fails to understand the message or rejects part of it, the result is *noise*. A breakdown in communication has occurred. The prospect's reactions could include asking questions, expressing concerns, or simply refusing to consider any purchase.

Barriers to Effective Communication

Seldom does the buyer decode exactly the same meaning that the salesperson encoded. When the result of decoding is different from what was encoded, noise exists. Anything that interferes with or distorts understanding of the intended message is called *noise*. Noise can take many

forms and may affect any or all parts of the communication process. There are logical reasons why your sales message may not be understood or accepted. Some reasons for such miscommunication are:

Words. All language is a code. Even if you and your prospect use the same words, you are probably putting out different meanings.[19] Words only represent ideas. Noise is created when words are inappropriate: for example, the use of casual profanity that may offend the listener, language that seems to imply the listener is poorly informed, language that assumes too much knowledge on the listener's part, or language that obscures the real meaning.

Distractions. Any element that may focus the prospect's attention on something other than the message is a distraction. Some typical distractions are a salesperson's inappropriate dress, an uncomfortable temperature in the room, loud noise that makes concentration difficult, or a nagging personal or business problem occupying the prospect's mind.

Timing. If a prospect has some reason for not wanting to listen, no amount of communication skill on the part of the salesperson is enough. The prospect may be feeling under the weather, preoccupied with a family argument or an unpleasant disciplinary task, or facing a pressing deadline. Some prospects need time to *warm up* before getting down to business; others want to get right to your proposal and skip the small talk.

Interruptions. Phone calls, people walking in to ask questions, and emergencies represent the kinds of interruptions that cancel the impact of the message.

Technical Erudition. Information overload often obscures a message. The salesperson's unconscious desire to appear personally knowledgeable often results in talking too much, poor organization of features and benefits, or wrongly assuming that the prospect has adequate knowledge. As a result, the prospect fails to see a need for the product or service. Avoid the use of technical terms, jargon, or cliches without clarification. According to Gerard Nierenberg, "Jargon and cliches don't belong in the communication-negotiation process.... You'll just confuse or anger your customer."[20]

Interruptions cancel the impact of the message.

Poor Listening Habits. If the prospect is a poor listener, the salesperson is faced with a monumental challenge in designing a message and delivering it in an effective and successful manner. On the other hand, the salesperson who is a poor listener never picks up the prospect's cues that are keys to molding the message for quick acceptance.[21]

Making Use of Feedback

The buyer will draw inferences from the messages received and react accordingly. This *feedback* is crucial to a salesperson's success. During face-to-face communication, verbal and nonverbal feedback is immediate and quite revealing. Consultative salespeople are skilled in receiving feedback and can adapt their sales presentations to fit each individual buyer's requirements. They can use the circuits through which feedback passes from prospect to salesperson and back to bring the two sides closer to an exact understanding of what is being said by each. In this manner, the noise is filtered out so that the result is a clear communication.[22] Managing feedback by eliminating noise involves both verbal skills used to clarify the message for the prospect and nonverbal skills used to read feelings while listening to the prospect's verbal responses.

USING YOUR VOICE

Your voice is a major selling tool. The first impression you make is often based on your voice. When you call for an appointment, your voice is all you have for communicating. A voice that is pleasing and confident is a great asset. Your voice and how you use it play an important part in your success in selling. Several basic components of verbal communication deserve your attention.[23]

Clarity or Articulation. Do you recall the device Professor Higgins used in *My Fair Lady* to help Eliza Dolittle improve her speech? He had her talk with marbles in her mouth. To be understood at all, she was forced to form her words very carefully. As a result, her articulation improved. When you speak, do people hear separate words and syllables or *doyourwordsallruntogether*? If you have studied a foreign language, you may have listened to audio tapes in the language lab. At first, all the words seem to run together. Even though you have learned the assigned vocabulary, the normal speed of speech in the new language seems too fast and blurred. After a while, you become accustomed to hearing these new sounds, and you begin to understand. A salesperson with poor articulation leaves prospects as confused and bewildered as you felt at your first language lab session.

Volume. The normal volume of the speaking voice varies during conversation. The same is true of a sales presentation. Stressing a benefit may call for increased volume. Lowering your voice, sometimes almost to a whisper, may produce quite a dramatic effect; it causes the prospect to lean forward (a body position that signals agreement or approval) to avoid missing your words. Variation in volume should enhance the message; it must not be overdone to the point of melodramatic insincerity.

If the prospect changes voice volume, notice the direction of the change. Boredom and sadness, as well as indecision, cause a downward shift in volume, and increased volume suggests joy or enthusiasm. Of course, anger also shows up in increased volume. Be sensitive to changes—yours and the prospect's—and the accompanying verbal and nonverbal clues that can help you interpret changes correctly.

Silence. Silence is a powerful selling tool. Use it to give the prospect time to absorb the full impact of what you have said. Slight pauses between major points in the presentation suggest that you are thoughtful, intelligent, and analytical. Pauses also give the prospect an opportunity to comment, ask a question, or think about how the idea you have presented can be applied to an existing need or problem. Avoid becoming so enamored with the sound of your own voice that you must talk all the time.

Rhythm. The rhythmic pattern of your speech comes from your basic personality style and your emotions of the moment. Some voices seem to flow in long, continuous sentences, and others come in short, choppy chunks. Just as the rhythm in music changes to indicate that something new is happening, the same happens in speech patterns. Be alert to any changes in your own or the prospect's speech patterns. Changes are even more revealing than initial patterns. If the prospect suddenly shifts to a more drawn out rhythm, for example, the message may be "Let me think more about that" or "I don't believe what you are saying."

Rate of Speech. The tempo of your delivery should be comfortable for you as a speaker and for your listener. Speaking too rapidly may cause you to lose a prospect who customarily speaks more slowly and feels that your fast pace is pushing for a decision without allowing time for thought. Speaking too slowly may make the prospect want to push your fast-forward button. A moderate pace allows you to enunciate clearly, establish natural rhythmic patterns, or speed up or slow down for proper emphasis of some point.

SELLING WITHOUT WORDS (NONVERBAL COMMUNICATION)

Different people have different levels of competence in nonverbal communication skills, and some professions require more skill than others. The success of a professional gambler depends on the ability to exercise strict control of nonverbal messages to disguise a bluff. A mime depends exclusively on nonverbal skills to deliver a message. However, the consultative salesperson must possess skill in both verbal and nonverbal communication. Two particularly important components of nonverbal communication for salespeople to understand are body language and *proxemics* (use of space).

Body Language

Body language can be portrayed as messages sent without using words. The essential elements of body language include shifts in posture or stance (body angle), facial expressions, eye movements, and arm, hand, and leg movements. It includes every movement from the subtle raising of an eyebrow to the obvious leaning forward of an interested listener.

Through body language, prospects express their emotions, desires, and attitudes. As a result, body language is a valuable tool for the salesperson to use in discovering what the prospect is really saying. When body language and verbal behavior coincide, the verbal and nonverbal signals transmitted are said to be congruent and the climate is ideally suited for optimum communication. When you can *read* the prospect's body language and, in addition, control your own body signals to add impact to your words, you are likely to be understood.

Understanding the Language of Gestures. Important signals involve body angle, position of hands, arms, and legs, and the face—especially the eyes and lips.[24] All of these should be observed as a cluster of gestures that together state a message. A prospect sitting with arms crossed may be communicating doubt or rejection or may simply be sitting comfortably. In this case, you must also observe whether the legs are crossed, the body withdrawn, eyes glancing sideways, and an eyebrow raised. All these signs taken together surely suggest doubt or rejection, but one of them in isolation is inconclusive.

Body Signals. A hunched figure, rigid posture, restless stance, or nervous pacing may contradict what a person says verbally. Prospects allow you to sit closer if they feel comfortable and lean toward you if they like what you are saying and are intent on listening. John Molloy used videotape to study the behavior of successful and unsuccessful salespeople. One mannerism difference noted was the relative calmness of good salespeople in comparison to those who were less successful. Their body movements were smooth, unhurried, and without jerky motions, particularly when handing a contract or a pen across the table. Every movement was gradual. Less successful salespeople exhibited jumpy, nervous movements that were picked up— perhaps unconsciously—by prospects.

Look for the prospect's changes in body posture and gestures. For example, one who is ready to buy shows signs of relaxation—nodding in agreement, mirroring your movements, moving to the front of the chair, extending the palm of the hand outward toward you, and uncrossing legs or ankles. Your posture and gestures also communicate your feelings to the prospect. If you sit in an open, relaxed position, you are likely to be more persuasive and better liked than if you sit in a tight, closed posture.

Steepling of the hands indicates self-confidence.

Hand Movements. Rubbing the back of the neck may indicate frustration, but it can also indicate that the prospect has a sore or stiff neck from painting the bathroom ceiling over the weekend. Evaluate these hand gestures in the context of other nonverbal clues.

1. *Other gestures of hand and head.*

   Tugging at the ear suggests the desire to interrupt. Pinching the bridge of the nose and closing the eyes suggests that the matter is being given serious thought.

2. *Posture.*

   Leaning back in the chair with both hands behind the head communicates a sense of superiority.

3. *Involuntary gestures.*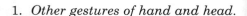

   Involuntary hand gestures that contradict a facial expression are likely to reveal true feelings. Tightly clasped hands or fists indicate tenseness.

4. *Steepling of the hands*

   Fingertips together forming what looks like a church steeple commonly indicates smugness, self-confidence, or perhaps superiority.

Facial Expressions. Eyebrows, eyelids, eyes, lips, jaw, mouth, and facial muscles all work together to communicate feelings and emotions. Research attributes as much as 70 percent of nonverbal message sending to the muscles of the face. Most people have developed some degree of skill in both message-sending and message-receiving by means of facial expressions. When you smile, frown, smirk, scowl, or even wink in reaction to what others say or do, you are involved in a most sophisticated element of nonverbal communication.[25]

The face is a highly reliable indicator of attitude. A person may avoid eye contact when trying to cover up true feelings. Increased eye contact signals honesty and interest. Be sure to maintain eye contact at critical moments of the presentation. For example, when describing technical characteristics of the product, direct the prospect's eyes to the product itself, the brochure, or the specification sheet, but when stressing the benefits of using the product, maintain eye contact. Lack of eye contact sends a negative message and neutralizes the impact of the intended benefit. Good eye contact makes a positive statement that words cannot.[26]

Suspicion and anger are shown by signs of tightness around the cheeks or along the jaw line. Muscle movement at the back of the jaw line just below the ears indicates an angry gritting of the teeth. A sudden flush of facial redness may warn that the situation has taken a bad turn; embarrassment or hostility may be radiating under an apparently calm exterior.

An isolated gesture or posture is seldom a reliable indicator of attitude or feelings. Obviously you have to take a look at the buyer in the context of the whole situation. The buyer may fold her arms just to be more comfortable. Generally, if there is an objection then the whole body will become more rigid. And you will see signals: skin texture will tighten up; voice tone will change. They may even have frustrated looks on their faces. When a cluster of gestures is consistent with verbal messages, accepting their validity is relatively safe. Exhibit 4.3 presents a number of ideas developed specifically for optometrists to keep their verbal and nonverbal communication skills in sync.[27]

EXHIBIT 4.3 - Doctor, Watch Your (Body) Language

When you communicate with your patients, you listen carefully and choose your words carefully. But your nonverbal language—gestures and expressions—is equally important. Here are some suggestions to keep both your verbal and nonverbal communication in sync:

1. Maintain eye contact when conversing with a patient. If you lean away or direct your gaze elsewhere, the patient will mistake your distraction for disinterest.

2. Keep your facial expressions pleasant, friendly, and encouraging. Listen with care and patience. Do not frown!

3. Speak with the patient at eye level. If you talk while standing to a seated patient, you may appear to be literally "talking down" to the patient.

4. Place your furniture so you can talk face-to-face or side-by-side with your patients. This encourages two-way conversation.

5. Keep your posture upright. Slumping or leaning back in your chair says, "I'm bored," or "I'm not really interested in you."

6. Check the messages your clothing relays. If your attire is stained or rumpled, you're sending a signal of unprofessionalism that tells the patient, "It's not important to me to look nice for you."

7. Evaluate your office. Good ventilation, proper temperature, cleanliness, order ... all go a long way to say, "I care about you and your comfort" to the patient.

Proxemics

Proxemics is the distance individuals prefer to maintain between themselves and others. Most people seem to consider observing desired distance a matter of courtesy. Violating distance comfort risks closing down the communication process. Highly successful salespeople tend to move closer to clients when closing a sale. Their skill in reading the individual prospect allows them to move as close as possible without causing discomfort for the prospect. The difference between how successful and unsuccessful salespeople use physical closeness can be observed in the prospect's reaction. Good salespeople do not move closer until they can do so without offense. The less effective salesperson moves in without considering the feelings or body signals of the prospect. Instead of positioning yourself where *you* feel immediately comfortable, attempt to estimate the needed distance from the prospect's perspective. Carefully test for the existence of comfort barriers; then place yourself just outside those barriers. Figure 4.8 shows the four basic zones or ranges that apply in the typical sales situation. Generally speaking, the intimate zone is about two feet (hence the expression, *to keep someone at arm's length*). Enter this range only if invited. To move inside the intimate zone, except for a handshake, is not a good idea. Beyond that, we all have a personal zone which is an envelope around us extending from two to four feet. Move into the buyer's personal zone only after invitation, which typically occurs only after a satisfying professional relationship has been established. The outer shell is the social zone, which extends up to 12 feet.[28]

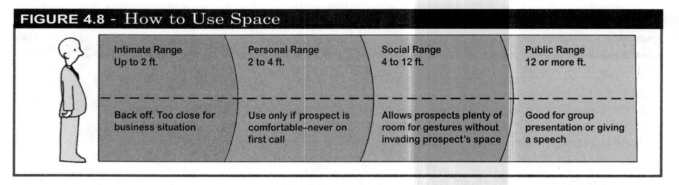

FIGURE 4.8 - How to Use Space

Intimate Range Up to 2 ft.	Personal Range 2 to 4 ft.	Social Range 4 to 12 ft.	Public Range 12 or more ft.
Back off. Too close for business situation	Use only if prospect is comfortable–never on first call	Allows prospects plenty of room for gestures without invading prospect's space	Good for group presentation or giving a speech

A number of factors enter into the amount of space various individuals need. Cultural differences, age, gender, and personality are important, as is the type of relationship that exists between salesperson and client. Peers tolerate a closer range of contact than people with a wide gap in age or status. Conversations between two women occur at closer range that those between two men or between a man and a woman. People with outgoing, open personalities are willing to be closer than those who are shy or withdrawn. Salespeople can move closer to long-term clients than to new prospects.

SUMMARY

The consumer's purchase decision process involves five stages: (1) problem recognition, (2) search for alternatives, (3) evaluation of alternatives, (4) the actual purchase decision, and (5) postpurchase evaluation. The salesperson is involved in each step: (1) arousing awareness of need and desire for satisfaction, (2) suggestion of alternatives, (3) presentation of the benefits of the suggested product or service, (4) reassurance and persuasion during the decision making stage, and (5) service after the sale to be sure that the customer remains satisfied.

Organizational buyers, while generally following the same process, are under additional constraints imposed by the organization and the need to satisfy a number of different people. They must fit into organizational buying policies, consider the ultimate user, consult with other executives, and meet budget restraints. Purchasing for organizations often involves a *buying center*.

Buying decisions are made on the basis of dominant buying motives or reasons that have particular meaning for the buyer. They may be rational, emotional, or a combination. Salespeople are successful in closing the sale when they are able to discover the dominant buying motives of the prospect and present benefits of the product that relate to those motives.

Both psychological and sociocultural influences are brought to bear on the purchase decision process. Psychological influences, including perception, attitudes, moods, and self-image, must be heeded by the salesperson in attempting to guide the prospect into a buying decision. Equally as important are the sociocultural influences that arise from the prospect's cultural background, physical environment, social class, and reference groups.

Communication—the exchange of information and ideas—is the vehicle for the salesperson's presentation of a buying proposal to any individual or organizational buyer. Because communication is a two-way process, the salesperson must be adept in understanding everything that affects it. Messages must be encoded—placed into symbols such as words and pictures—in a manner that the receiver can and will accept. At various points in the process, noise may block out the message. The salesperson needs skill in interpreting the prospect's understanding and acceptance of the message—the decoding.

Understanding body language and proxemics adds to the salesperson's ability to communicate with the prospect or customer. The majority of the message in communication is sent by nonverbal means—body position, facial expression, tone of voice, and gestures. When words and nonverbal cues are consistent, the salesperson readily knows how to proceed. When verbal and nonverbal messages are mixed, the salesperson has to locate the problem and resolve it before communication can continue.

QUESTIONS FOR THOUGHT AND DISCUSSION

1. Formulate a brief definition of consumer behavior.

2. Why must salespeople understand consumer behavior?

3. Name the six general classifications of dominant buying motives.

4. What are the five stages of the buying-decision process? What is a salesperson's function in each of these stages?

5. What is cognitive dissonance? How can a salesperson prevent it?

6. What differences exist between individual and organizational buyers?

7. What is a buying center?

8. What are the four purposes a salesperson may have in encoding a message to be presented to a prospect?

9. How can you be sure someone has received, understood, and accepted your message?

10. What is the role of perception in the buying-decision process?

11. What are some of the psychological influences on the purchase decision process?

12. What are some of the sociocultural influences on the purchase decision process?

ACTIVITIES

1. One student acts as a salesperson and another as a prospect. For two minutes, the salesperson chooses a product and describes the benefits of owning it. The prospect listens but says nothing. From watching the prospect's body language, the class determines whether the salesperson is likely to close the sale.

2. Does word choice affect understanding? What common saying has been reworded in each of the statements below?

   • A single in-and-out movement of a small cylindrical object with an oblong opening in one end through which an elongated fiber is passed produces the fortuitous circumstance of precluding the necessity of performing nine such procedures at some future date.

   • A wildly gyrating fragment of consolidated solid mineral matter is never encapsulated in a cutaneous layer of bryophytic living organisms that do not possess locomotive qualities in themselves.

   • You may succeed in conducting a large, solid hoofed herbivorous mammal of the family Equidae to the brink of a reservoir of liquid oxide of hydrogen, but there is no surety that you will succeed in coercing said mammal to imbibe a potation.

   • Members of the populace who sojourn in habitations of an amorphous inorganic transparent material made largely of silicates are well advised to eschew propelling concretions of earthy or mineral matter.

Case Study

CASE 4.1

Margie Barnes, sales representative for Easy-System Business Forms, has been assigned a sales territory that includes Kentucky, Tennessee, Alabama, and Georgia. Easy-System is a newcomer in the business forms field, and Barnes is its newest sales representative. Easy-System does little advertising and instead relies on its sales force to inform prospective customers about its products. The company as yet has no formal training program for sales personnel. It depends on the individual to be familiar with product features and company services.

Barnes's first selling effort was to a manufacturer of microchips. Future Chip is presently revamping its accounting and bookkeeping system; unfortunately, Barnes was unaware of this. In fact, she has taken very little time to acquaint herself with Future Chip's operations or with the microchip industry as a whole.

Barnes entered the office of Future Chip and asked to see the chief accountant. Although he usually saw salespeople by appointment only, Byron Glover consented to see her. They met briefly, and Glover called Ken Campbell, a systems analyst, and asked him to join them. Barnes emphasized the low price of the products, their convenient size, practicality, color coding to help the accountant, ease of ordering, prompt delivery, and easy credit terms. The meeting was interrupted by several telephone calls for Glover and Campbell and by a visitor looking for Campbell. Barnes tried to point out the merits of each form but failed to present them as an integrated system. Glover and Campbell asked several questions, but Barnes sensed that their interest was artificial. When she was ready to leave, she offered some sample forms that Glover and Campbell could examine and use. They declined the offer and told Barnes they would call her after they had better determined their needs.

1. Identify some of the barriers to effective communication in this case and suggest ways in which they might have been eliminated or reduced.

2. Did anything take place that should have given Barnes an idea that this prospective client was interested in a total system?

CASE 4.2

Bob Andrews was five minutes early for his 2:00 p.m. appointment with the purchasing agent for Belton County Consolidated School District. The purchasing agent, Dan Lane, arrived at the office at 2:30, nodded toward Andrews, and began discussing afternoon appointments and a golf game scheduled later that day with his receptionist.

At 2:45, the receptionist ushered Andrews into Lane's office. Lane said, "What's up?" and began sorting a stack of mail on the desk. Soon after Andrews started his presentation, Lane's golf partner called and chatted for ten minutes.

At that point, Lane instructed the receptionist to hold all calls and briefly turned his attention to Bob before he began to clip his fingernails. When the receptionist entered to remind Lane of an important meeting with the superintendent of schools, he apologized to Andrews for not having much time, rose, and thanked him for his call. Andrews quickly got up, said, "You're welcome," and stomped out.

1. What verbal and nonverbal communication cues were available for Andrews to evaluate when he called on Lane?

2. If you had been in Andrew's place, how would you have handled the situation?

Finding Your Selling Style

LEARNING OBJECTIVES

- To be able to recognize the various behavioral styles.

- To recognize your own favorite social style.

- To gain an understanding of how to deal with people who operate from each of the various styles.

- To understand the concept of versatility and how it affects your ability to relate to people of all social styles.

- To understand the basic concepts of neurolinguistic programming and how it can be helpful to salespeople.

Chapter 5

A DIFFERENCE IN SOCIAL STYLE

Six weeks into his job as a sales and marketing executive in a high-technology manufacturing company, Charlie Kromer realized that something was very wrong. Not the work itself—Kromer loved digging for the facts, arranging timetables, charting the development of new products. The job was fine. It was the boss he couldn't stand.

Recently Kromer had approached his boss with a new product development plan. Everything was detailed precisely: target dates, costs, sales approaches, presentation data, the works. Halfway through the presentation, the boss leaped to her feet and began tossing out ideas right and left. Some were impractical; all would throw the carefully thought-out plan completely out of whack. When Kromer pointed this out, his boss got miffed and charged out of the room, bellowing over her shoulder, "Now you've got the concept. Go to it."

"Go to what?" Kromer pondered. "All I've got to work with is a blast of hot air."

Some call such an incident a personality conflict. Others would say they are not on the same wavelength. They're not seeing eye to eye. Let's call it what it really is—*a difference in social style*. Conflict or miscommunication will exist not simply because of work pressures, but because of social style differences. Charlie, as you will learn when you study this chapter, has an *analytical* social style, while his boss has an *expressive* style. Unknowingly, they communicate disrespect to one another. This lack of understanding and knowledge concerning behavioral styles can cause lost sales, frustration, resentment, or resignation.

Charlie and his boss were like two ships that pass in the night with no communication. They were like the two old-timers who sat on the front porch in their rocking chairs reminiscing about days gone by. Both were so hard of hearing that neither ever knew for sure what the other was saying. They just took turns talking, each lost in his own memories, but content that there was someone nearby. For the salesperson who wants to succeed in a selling career, however, "being nearby" isn't enough.

Success and Behavioral Styles

Because of the importance of communication in the selling process, successful salespeople constantly search for new ways to make their communication more effective. They are eager to learn how they may better anticipate and avoid conflict situations. A selling transaction, whether it involves products, services, or ideas, is a communication exchange in which two individuals develop a mutually desirable solution to a problem about which both are concerned. The best sales relationships are long-term ones based on mutual trust and credibility. The pertinent question then becomes, "How can I sell so that I demonstrate respect for the customer, build credibility for myself and my product, and set up a win/win situation?"

Of tremendous importance for salespeople is the concept of behavioral styles, first developed by the Swiss psychologist Carl Jung.[1] Jung built upon and extended the knowledge of the adult ego state developed by Sigmund Freud. Jung's work on behavioral functions resulted in a theory of personality that included four functions: intuition, thinking, feeling, and sensing. Since his death in 1961, his work has become increasingly popular through the publication of his writings and the work of others in applying and interpreting his work. Several behavioral style models of special interest to salespeople have been developed and introduced by various authors. David Merrill and Roger Reid began the development of their Social Styles Model in the early 1960s. Dr. Paul Mok, working independently of Merrill and Reid, developed what he calls the Communicating Styles Technology Model. More recently the Wilson Learning Corporation and Dr. Tony Alessandra and Associates Inc. have expanded and added their own research to these original models. The material presented in this chapter has been gleaned from these four related approaches.[2]

THE BEHAVIORAL OR SOCIAL STYLES MODEL

Everyone learns as a child that family members and friends have different personalities. Perhaps you could always elicit sympathy from your mother but found that your father considered each situation and evaluated the circumstances prior to sympathizing or reprimanding you. You may have had a sibling who had a totally different personality from everyone else in the family. In your family, you had time to learn the ways you can best persuade or get along with various family members. In a business or social situation, you have less time to evaluate and adjust your persuasive prowess. The prospect's manner and social style are often deceptive and too many salespeople miss what is happening. The major mistake is not understanding how prospects think and make decisions.[3] Behavioral style models provide useful tools for making such an evaluation in the shortest possible time. The better you understand personality types, the more successful you will be in communicating with the people you meet.

Each person has a primary communicating style that is blended or fine-tuned by a secondary style. These primary and secondary styles shape others perceptions of you and filter your perceptions of other people. A second dimension to this model comes into play when you are under stress. At such times, you may shift to a different style of behavior. You may be aware of the shift yet feel unable to prevent it.

People use four basic styles to deal with the world. Each is based upon one of four basic functions of human personality.

1. The driver or *sensing* function of taking in here-and-now sensory information and reacting to it.

2. The expressive or *intuitive* function of imagination and abstract thought.

3. The amiable or *feeling* function of personal and emotional reactions to experience.

4. The analytical or *thinking* function of organizing and analyzing information in a logical fashion.

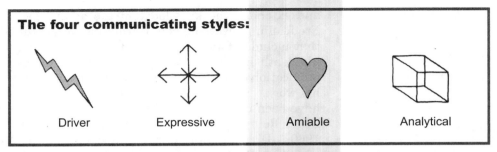

Everyone uses each of the four functions, but the frequency of use differs among individuals.[4] These styles can be observed even in young children. Behavior patterns, Jung claimed, are genetically determined and are seen in infants during their first days of life. Like adults, young children process experience according to their own individual styles.

Basic Concepts

Four basic concepts underlie the behavioral styles communication model presented in this chapter:

1. Everyone uses a *blend* of the driver, expressive, amiable, and analytical styles, although each person has a favorite style that is used more often than others. A *style* is an overall approach used to receive and send messages. It consists of verbal, nonverbal, and behavioral elements.

2. Every person operates the majority of the time from a favorite style. This is the *primary style*. Everyone also has a *secondary* or *backup* style that may replace or modify the primary style.

3. Because style is reflected in behavior, you can identify someone else's primary style by observing behavioral clues. These clues include use of time, manner of speech, typical reaction to other people, and approach to job performance.

4. People respond favorably to a style that is *similar* or *complementary* to their own primary and backup styles. When a salesperson's style is too different from that of the prospect, the resulting style conflict can be disastrous to the outcome of the transaction. *What* is said is often much less important than *how* it is said.[5]

Behavioral Styles in Selling

You tend to use one or two predominant styles as you sell. Your choice of style affects what you do and say. It also affects what prospects hear and believe during your presentation. Understanding the strengths and liabilities of your primary communicating style and learning to be *versatile* in your style can help you sell to more prospects more often.[6] The objective of this chapter then is to help you learn how to manage your daily interactions with customers and prospects more productively.

Figure 5.1 illustrates that your most damaging weaknesses (-) are merely exaggerations or over-extensions of your strengths (+). Your behavior responds to circumstances like the volume dial of a radio. When the volume is just right, the music is pleasing. Similarly, when a behavioral style is used in moderation it is seen as a strength; when overused (that is, when the volume is too high), it becomes a weakness and leads to ineffective communication. Professional selling is all about managing relationships. Remember that a customer is not a transaction, a customer is a relationship! Most people don't even think about working on relationships in their daily lives. On the other hand, consultative salespeople take time to think about and understand the people around them. The consultative selling approach will strengthen and enhance your selling style by turning you into a relationship-oriented helper. The consultative approach to selling is the 21st-century approach to helping clients and prospects buy.

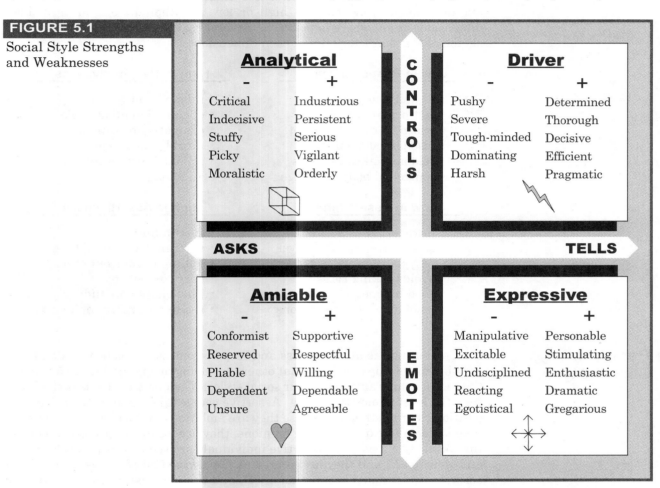

FIGURE 5.1

Social Style Strengths and Weaknesses

Remember that the emphasis in studying behavioral style characteristics is on *surface behavior*, not on in-depth personality analysis. Human behavior is predictable because ninety percent of our actions are controlled by habits and attitudes. The social styles model does not describe a person's complete personality because, according to Merrill and Reid, it omits reference to the individual's beliefs, ethics, abilities, and intelligence. What it does is describe three basic attributes or characteristics of behavior: *assertiveness, responsiveness,* and *versatility.*

Attributes of Behavior

When you meet someone for the first time, your mind subconsciously reacts to two main characteristics: assertiveness and responsiveness. *Assertiveness* represents the effort a person makes to influence or control the thoughts and actions of others. *Responsiveness* is the willingness with which a person outwardly shares feelings or emotions and develops relationships. *Versatility* is an individual's ability to adjust personal pace and priorities to facilitate interactions with a person of another style. Because people high or low in versatility can be found along all ranges of assertiveness and responsiveness this dimension is not used in forming the social styles profile.[7]

Assertiveness and responsiveness levels vary from one individual to another, and anyone may be high or low in either dimension or in both dimensions or anywhere in between. Several basic terms provide a thumbnail sketch of the characteristics of each dimension:

Low in Responsiveness	High in Responsiveness
• formal and proper • fact-oriented • guarded, cool, and aloof • disciplined about time • seldom makes gestures • controlled body language	• relaxed and warm • open and approachable • dramatic and animated • flexible about time • oriented toward relationships and feelings

Low in Assertiveness	High in Assertiveness
• introverted • supportive, a team player • easygoing • avoids taking risks • good listener • reserved in their opinions	• risk-taking • swift in decision-making • willing to confront others • very competitive • take-charge attitude • readily expresses opinions

Recognizing Social Styles

Combining the assertiveness and responsiveness characteristics makes it possible to develop a map of what others are doing or saying. Figure 5.2 shows the relationships among the four social styles. The horizontal axis is the range from the least to most assertive. Assertive people take a stand and make their position clear to others. Because they are ambitious, competitive, and quick to take action and express strong opinions, they are located on the *telling* end of the social style axis. Nonassertive individuals are seen as cooperative, silent, and slow to act, and they are located at the *asking* end of the axis. The least assertive individuals are in quartile D, and the most assertive in quartile A, with quartiles B and C representing intermediate levels of assertiveness.

The vertical axis indicates the range from least to most responsive. Nonresponsive individuals, those in quartile 1, are largely indifferent to the feelings of others, reserved, and no-nonsense in attitude. The responsive individuals found in quartile 4 are strongly people-oriented, concerned about relationships, and subjective. Those in quartiles 2 and 3 display intermediate levels of responsiveness.

Identifying the Four Behavioral Styles

Identifying the levels of assertiveness and responsiveness a person demonstrates is not a precise method of complete personality evaluation. With study and practice, however, Dr. Mok suggests that you can become seventy to eighty percent effective in using your observations to predict habitual behavioral patterns and be prepared to use your knowledge to improve the communication environment. Each possible combination of the two traits suggests one of the basic social styles. The four styles are linked to distinctive and unique habits of interactive behavior. The name given to each style reflects general characteristics rather than full, specific details. Keep in mind that no *one* style is preferred over another. Each has its own strengths and weaknesses, and successful people as well as failures are found in each style group, as are people of both sexes and all ethnic groups, ages, and other segments of the population.[8]

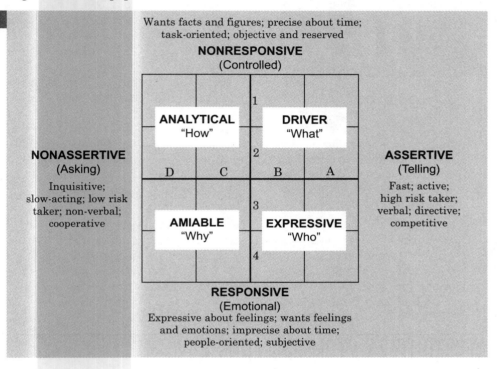

FIGURE 5.2

The Social Styles Profile

Drivers are tell/control people, high in assertiveness and low in responsiveness. They control others by telling them what to do and control themselves by remaining objective. They are task-oriented and combine personal power and emotional control in relationships with others. They are control specialists.

Expressives are tell/emote people. Like drivers, they are highly assertive, but they are also high in emotional responsiveness. They attempt to tell people what to do, but place more emphasis on their relationships with people than they do on the task itself. They are social specialists.

Amiables are ask/emote people, low in assertiveness and high in responsiveness. They rely on a personal feeling approach to get things done. They are support specialists, combining personal reserve and emotional expression.

Analyticals are ask/control people, low in both assertiveness and responsiveness. They are highly task-oriented but soften that style with low assertiveness. They ask rather than direct. They are technical specialists, combining personal reserve and emotional control.

Thomas V. Hoek understands social styles

Tom Hoek has earned what could be called a Ph.B. He is a Professor of Human Behavior. He says that we are all in the people business. As salespeople we observe and verify behavior and have a constant need to become expert at interpreting what we see. Tom is president of Insurance Systems of Tennessee, Inc., a training firm specializing in insurance and investment training courses. His firm has 19 instructors and five staff people with operations in Arkansas, Georgia, Kentucky, Missouri, and Tennessee.

In any personal relationship that you have, Tom suggests everybody has their own particular point of view. Ultimately, in every situation, the most persuasive person wins. When you understand Behavioral Styles Technology and what motivates each of the styles you can adapt your own style to meet the needs of others. Just exercise a bit of applied psychology. All of us have a way we like to be treated. Tom uses the phrase *Psychological Reciprocity* to describe what should happen in a sales situation. The salesperson makes the initial attempt to adapt or adjust to the prospect's social style. The prospect is then motivated to move toward him; to reciprocate. Real communication and understanding occur much quicker than if each person stays rooted in their own particular style.

Behavioral styles technology helps you present the right product in the right way. Tom suggests that styles are fixed early in life—it's what you do with your style (versatility) that makes a difference. Tom uses style flexing to *complement* the other person's style. He says this is truly win-win selling. Tom's motto is: "He who trims himself to suit everybody will soon whittle himself away."

VERSATILITY AS A COMMUNICATION TOOL

When people of different styles meet and behave strictly according to the characteristics of their own personal styles, conflict often results. A salesperson who is an amiable and a prospect who is a driver can quickly arrive at cross-purposes. A driver client wants to get facts and to accomplish the task at hand; the amiable salesperson wants to cultivate a personal relationship.

When such a situation occurs, the only way to avoid an escalation in miscommunication or a conflict is for one of the two people involved to engage in some style flexibility. In an ideal situation, both are willing to move part way, but the salesperson must be capable of making most or all of any necessary temporary adjustment. This willingness to try behaviors not necessarily characteristic of your style is called *behavioral flexibility or versatility*.

Versatility or behavioral flexibility is a person's willingness to control personal behavior patterns and adapt to other people as a means of reducing the possibility of ineffective communication. The salesperson's own personal style does not change, but rather techniques are applied that work in that particular situation.[9] For example, when meeting with an analytical, the expressive salesperson can incorporate versatility by talking less, listening more, and focusing on facts. Versatility should never be equated with either insincerity or mere imitation of the prospect's style. Versatile salespeople seek a reasonable compromise. They do not become so highly changeable that their pace and priority needs are constantly set aside for those of clients.

The prospect's preferences in pace and priorities must be recognized and given the importance that seems right to the prospect. Strive for *Psychological Reciprocity*. That is, as the salesperson, you make the initial attempt to get into the client's world. The person is then challenged to move toward you; to reciprocate. You connect! Rapport is established with the client much quicker than if each of you had stayed firmly entrenched in your own particular social style.[10]

The Interaction of Styles

The dimensions of assertiveness and responsiveness operate in people's pace and their priorities. *Pace* is the speed at which a person prefers to move. Those who are low in assertiveness (analyticals and amiables) prefer a slow pace; those high in assertiveness (drivers and expressives) prefer a fast pace in conversation, deliberation, and problem solving.[11]

Priorities concern what a person considers important and tend to be related to the dimension of responsiveness. Those who are low in responsiveness put tasks at the top of their priority list, and those who are high in responsiveness put relationships in first place. These conflicts may be summarized as follows:

Styles	Shared Dimension	Source of Conflict	Area of Agreement
Analytical/Amiable	Low assertiveness	Priorities	Pace
Driver/Expressive	High assertiveness	Priorities	Pace
Analytical/Driver	Low responsiveness	Pace	Priorities
Amiable/Expressive	High responsiveness	Pace	Priorities
Analytical/Expressive	None	Both	None
Amiable/Driver	None	Both	None

Conflicts that involve only priorities or only pace can be handled with relative ease; real trouble results when the styles of two people conflict in both pace and priorities.

Fortunately, few people are locked into a single style. Between the extremes of each dimension are many degrees of responsiveness and assertiveness. The descriptions of the four styles, then, do not represent absolutes. "If you deal with every customer in the same way, you will close a small percentage of all your contacts, because you will only close one personality style. But if you learn how to effectively work with all four personality styles, you can significantly increase your closing ratio."[12]

Salespeople who do not adjust their behavior to meet the style needs of clients face deteriorating situations. For example, an expressive salesperson's questions may be interpreted as a personal challenge or attack by an analytical prospect. If the analytical prospect responds to the questions merely to save face, the expressive salesperson then tends to talk more, move faster, and push the analytical into still greater conflict.

In any situation, conflict is finally relieved in a manner typical of the individual style. The expressive usually attacks verbally. The driver tends to become overbearing, pushy, and dictatorial. The amiable generally submits in order to avoid conflict at all costs but experiences resentment and distrust. The analytical withdraws—*flight* rather than *fight*. In a conflict situation, most people tend to move to the extreme dimensions of their favorite style.

To avoid distrust and ultimately a breakdown in communication, you must meet the needs of your prospects, especially their behavioral style needs. Treat them as *they* want to be treated, and move according to the pace and priority they desire.

Identifying Pace and Priority

How do you go about determining someone's pace and priorities? Ask yourself these three questions and observe the answers:

1. How fast does the person make decisions and get things done?
2. How *competitive* is the person? Not primarily in sports, but
   - Is the person competitive in a conversation?
   - Does the person fight for air time in a meeting?
3. How much *feeling* is displayed in a verbal and nonverbal communication?
   - How often does the person smile?
   - Do they gesture broadly?

Your goal is to identify pace and priorities accurately and respond in an appropriate manner. How can you find out your prospect's information preferences? Use one of these statements to assist you:[13]

1. *"Ordinarily I have an organized presentation and get right to it, but today maybe I should get to know you better. What would you like me to do?"*

2. *"I am prepared to get right into my presentation or if you prefer we can chat a bit so that I can learn about you and your organization. Which do you prefer?"*

3. *"There are a lot of ways I can start explaining exactly how this process would work based on the concerns you were kind enough to share with me at our meeting last week. Would you prefer I start with the end in mind and then work backwards, or would you like to hear the step-by-step details first?"*

The expressive and amiable styles would respond to these statements indicating a desire to chat and get to know one another. While the driver and analytical styles would want you to begin your presentation.

READING THE PROSPECT'S ENVIRONMENT

Important clues to a client's style appear in the environment as well as in verbal and nonverbal actions. Observe how the office is decorated and arranged, how objects are displayed, and what seating arrangements are available. Suppose that upon entering a prospect's office, you notice family pictures on the desk, nature posters, a round desk, and a separate seating area with four comfortable chairs. What would be your first impression of that client's behavioral style? Did you say amiable? If so, you are right. Next, you can confirm or adjust your initial impression by observing the prospect's actions and speech. If the prospect rises to greet you personally and sits in an easy chair your impression of amiable would tend to be confirmed.

Let's try another example. You enter the prospect's office and notice a diploma, an achievement plaque, and a poster on the wall that says "Why not?" The desk presents several jumbled stacks of paper and a generally chaotic appearance. Two overstuffed chairs by the open side of the desk provide seating. A bookcase with stacks of books and folders intermixed and a plant on the file cabinet complete the furnishings. The disorganization, the wall decorations emphasizing achievement, and the comfortable and accessible seating suggest that this office houses an expressive.

However, a word of caution is in order here. Roger Reid tells of a Texas company that mandated that all of its top executives display pictures of their families on top of their desks. He also notes that in some companies the top executives do not select or arrange anything in their offices. The pictures on the wall, chairs and desks, and office layout are selected and done for the executives by staff or consultants. Thus, you must confirm any initial environmental impression by noting the prospect's actions, tone of voice, speech patterns, and interpersonal behavior.[14]

Verbal, Nonverbal, and Behavioral Characteristics

As a salesperson, you can use knowledge of these styles to characterize the observable behavior of most prospects. Although we all possess traits from each of the styles, one style ordinarily dominates. Of course, identifying a social style does not provide a crystal ball that unerringly predicts a person's future actions and decisions, but it does provide a basis for forming reasonably accurate expectations about recurring behavior and for being prepared to respond appropriately. Both verbal and nonverbal clues are useful in identifying social style.

Examine the sales situation presented in Exhibit 5.1. See how accurately you can determine the social style of the prospect and determine how you would plan your own behavior to fit that of the prospect. Exhibit 5.2 summarizes the behavior typical of each of the four styles.[15] Study the exhibit and then apply the information to help evaluate the situation in Exhibit 5.1.

EXHIBIT 5.1 - Sales Situation

I arrived a few minutes early for my appointment and waited in the reception area. The client, meticulously dressed, came out of her office, acknowledged my presence with a smile, and gave some detailed instructions to the secretary. She invited me in, told me where to sit, looked at her watch, told her secretary to hold all calls, and said, "You have fifteen minutes. Go." During my presentation, she sat as a face on Mount Rushmore. But she asked for highly specific details and voluntarily extended the discussion. She asked specific questions about time, schedule, and cost, then closed the sale, and settled details herself.

Analysis—The clues indicate that her level of responsiveness is fairly low. She appears oriented to tasks, she is formal, and she hides her feelings. Her assertiveness level, however, is high. She set the schedule, directed the conversation, and confronted the issues. She is a _____.

EXHIBIT 5.2 - Typical Behavior Associated With Each of the Four Social Styles

ANALYTICAL

- Cautious in decisions and action
- Likes organization and structure
- Asks specific questions
- Prefers objective, task-oriented, intellectual work
- Wants to be right, so collects much data
- Works slowly, precisely, and alone
- Has good problem-solving skills

DRIVER

- Decisive in action and decision making
- Likes control; dislikes inaction
- Prefers maximum freedom to manage self and others
- Cool, independent, and competitive with others
- Low tolerance for feelings, attitudes, and advice of others
- Works quickly and impressively alone
- Has good administrative skills

AMIABLE

- Slow in making decisions or taking actions
- Likes close, personal relationships
- Dislikes interpersonal conflict
- Supports and actively listens to others
- Weak in goal setting and self-direction
- Seeks security and identification with a group
- Has good counseling and listening skills

EXPRESSIVE

- Spontaneous actions and decisions
- Exaggerates and generalizes
- Tends to dream and get others caught up in those dreams
- Jumps from one activity to another
- Works quickly and excitedly with others
- Seeks esteem and group identification
- Has good persuasive skills

Drivers

Drivers exhibit minimum concern for the feelings of others. A vice-president of marketing for a major theme park in Ohio was heard to say, "My secretary used to drive me to distraction. I'd ask her how her weekend went and she'd actually tell me. In detail! All I wanted to hear was fine or not so hot." Now those are the words of a true *driver*. If you say something harsh, they don't even seem to notice. They consider *yes-people* to be weak. Stand up to drivers. Sell to them by showing them what your product can do. Drivers' feelings are not easily hurt because they do not take things personally.

I am in control of the situation.

Drivers tend to be intense, competitive, fast-paced, and goal-oriented. They pride themselves on the ability to get things done. They like to *make things happen*. Convince them that your proposed action works and that it will provide all the benefits you promise. They are more impressed by what they see and hear than by what others say about you or your offering.

At their best, drivers are human dynamos. Resourceful, organized, and pragmatic, they impose high standards on themselves and others. As a result, they may be seen as impatient or tireless. They push to perfect their own skills but also invest time and effort in coaching other people in skill development. At their worst, they appear to give inadequate consideration to the long-range consequences of their actions. They draw criticism for seeking to impose on others their expectations for drive, speed and zeal. Under stress, drivers can seem anti-intellectual and may defensively overreact to any opinions differing from their own, especially to those that seem to resist action. Drivers are likely to feel that any failure is evidence that *others* were not loyal enough or willing to work hard enough to make the project a success.

When selling to drivers, be prepared and organized, fast paced and to the point. Remain professional and businesslike. Study their goals and propose solutions that are clearly related to those goals. Suggest several options and allow them to choose.

CUSTOMIZE YOUR SELLING STYLE TO HIT A HOLE IN ONE WITH THE DRIVER

Drivers do not care about developing a personal relationship with you. They are impatient and need to be in control. Therefore, spend little time attempting to relate to them on a personal level.

1. Move fast and isolate the most dollar-related product benefits that can be verified by producing concrete evidence.

2. Do not make a lengthy presentation citing all the benefits. Be brief and stress the bottom line.

3. The fewer visual aids you use, the better. Any visuals you choose to show must be absolutely relevant to the major points.

4. Ask questions to involve them, get them to talk, and allow them to lead. Depend on your choice of subject matter in asking questions to maintain control of the interview.

5. They will test you to see what you are made of; so be willing to joust with them. If you challenge them, challenge the concepts rather than the person.

6. Answer objections immediately, and never try to bluff.

7. Present several alternatives from which they may select their own solution. Avoid telling them what is best.

8. An action close stressing an immediate opportunity works well.

Expressives

I am sitting on top of the world.

Expressives temper assertiveness with concern for the feelings of others. You must compliment them. They desire success, but are recognition motivated. Show them how to win. Let them talk and they often sell themselves. Tell them who else uses your product. Testimonials from well-known people or people they respect are important.

Expressives pride themselves on originality, foresight, and the ability to see the big picture. Reinforce their self-image as visionaries and idea people, and they will be receptive to your ideas. At their best, expressives often see new possibilities and present fresh ideas and approaches to problems. At their worst, they seem to base decisions on opinions, hunches, or intuition rather than on facts. They want to delegate the details to someone who has time for it while they are free to dream. They may be impatient when others demand some documentation before accepting the vision or ideas they offer. Under stress, expressives run the risk of seeming detached. They appear indifferent to problems and seem to be living in an ivory tower. They may spend time defending their ideas instead of trying to make them work in practical manner.

The expressive's love of risk-taking makes it easier for them to take a chance on your product. Refer to the product as a "sure bet" or guarantee that you will "make this risk pay off big." Emphasize the importance of risk-taking to making progress and meeting goals, and show the expressive your product's payoff potential by sharing exactly what it can do and what that means to them. When you have a qualified expressive whose needs match your product's benefits, you should not have to do much persuading. Remember, expressives are intuition-driven.[16]

DEVELOPING A PRESENTATION STRATEGY FOR THE EXPRESSIVE

Expressives are visionaries and dreamers. Therefore,

1. Plan to show them how they can personally win and/or how their company can benefit.

2. Open with innovative ideas for them to grow and win with through your offering.

3. Ask open-end questions that allow them to talk at length about "their" plans for growth. Then relate your product's benefits to their plans.

4. Present proposals and seek feedback, using them as sounding boards. Convey respect for their intelligence, foresight, and prominence. Be careful, however, to avoid patronizing them.

5. Use some showmanship. They like to see the yellow binder, but are not necessarily interested in the details of what it contains.

6. Never argue or back them into a corner.

7. Ask if they want you to respond to their stated concerns. Often they respond, "No, I just wanted you to know how I am thinking."

8. Use testimonials, especially from well-known people because they identify with who else uses the product.

9. Allow them to carry out their own game plan, not yours.

Amiables

I am easy to get along with.

Amiables are submissive and willing to go along with the crowd. They need time to get to know you personally, so allow plenty of warmup time. They are undisciplined in the use of time. Agreeable in nature, they are also easily hurt. They want to be liked.

Amiables tend to be perceptive and observant individuals who are concerned with whether they like you, trust you, and can picture a positive long-term relationship with you. They are highly people-oriented in their management style and resent doing business with anyone who makes them uncomfortable or is unresponsive to their feelings. Their business decisions are markedly influenced by how their various options might impact the people in the organization. Before they accept your proposal or idea, they must be convinced that you personally believe in it. They must also know what risks are involved—especially risks to personal relationships.

Amiables at their best are truly perceptive and aware, skilled in communication, and empathetic listeners. Their insight enables them to assess organizational politics accurately. At their worst, they seem more concerned with the process of interaction than with the content of the matter at hand. They appear to be flying by the seat of their pants instead of relying in any measure on logic and thought. They seem to regard their own emotions as facts and act on the basis of their feelings. They may be criticized for being defensive, over-reactive, and too subjective.

To sell effectively to amiables, you have to show them you're a team player. Position yourself as their newest team member by first building rapport, then work side-by-side with them to accomplish the goals they've set. To minimize the amiable's insecurities, talk about the problems your product can solve and how solving them will help improve control and performance in the workplace, which will enhance management's image of them. It is the amiable's job to nurture the team, so don't forget to outline what your product will do for the people in the company.

A PRESENTATION STRATEGY FOR THE AMIABLE

Amiables must be convinced that you are authentic and have their best interests at heart. They have a difficult time saying yes. Therefore,

1. Plan to approach with as much personal information as possible.

2. Avoid a rigid or canned approach and presentation.

3. Make an informal presentation with visuals and testimonial information integrated.

4. Use empathy and show that you understand and accept their feelings.

5. Spend some time relating. Move to a first-name basis quickly.

6. Be open and candid. Develop a personal relationship with them.

7. Offer them money-back guarantees and personal assurances.

8. Avoid asking directly for their business. Instead, assume that they are favorably disposed to your proposition and suggest an easy next step.

9. Be prepared to use third-party references and case histories that link them to others.

Analyticals

I will have to think that over.

Analyticals need time to assimilate what they hear and see. They want to know just how things work and often say they want time to think things over. Product information is crucial. Know everything possible about your product, and don't expect to hear them say much.

Analyticals are highly logical, organized, and unsentimental. They tend to be fact-oriented. Their contribution to the management team is their ability to solve difficult problems and make sound, rational business decisions based on evidence and intelligent inferences rather than on imagination or gut feelings. They take a logical, ordered approach to responsibilities. The more supporting data you can provide for your ideas, the more likely you are to sell to them. They have little interest in your opinions and more in your ability to assemble and organize supportive data for use in weighing options and arriving at a systematic, well-thought-out solution to problems.

At their best, analyticals appear to be a consistent force for progress. They are top-flight planners and doers. They can cut through untested ideas and emotional fervor to find the core truth. They are effective organizers for research and planning. They are valuable in executing logical, painstaking, and profitable projects. At their worst, they are overly cautious and conservative. They emphasize deliberation over action. They may become so involved in evaluating all the various details of a situation that others may regard them as indecisive stumbling blocks to innovative action. Under stress, analyticals can become rigid and insecure. They may fear taking risks. They seem more concerned with being right than with seizing opportunities.

In sales interviews with analyticals, be well prepared and equipped to answer all questions. Be cordial, but move quickly to the task. Study their needs logically. Ask lots of questions that show a clear direction and pay close attention to their answers. Support your logical proposal with full documentation.

CUSTOMIZE YOUR SALES PRESENTATION FOR THE ANALYTICAL

Analyticals are data-oriented and slow to make decisions. They are naturally suspicious and extremely cautious. They read and study everything. Therefore,

1. Know their business thoroughly. Go in with facts and the evidence to back them up.

2. Use a logic-based, low-key style of relating.

3. Be sure prospects understand the structure of how you will present the information and solicit feedback.

4. Emphasize tested, proven, well-documented aspects of your product's benefits.

5. Make use of visual aids—charts, graphs, written "leave-behind" documents—in the presentation.

6. Present information in a controlled, professional, highly organized fashion.

7. Point out the pros and cons of your offering. They will be thinking about them.

8. Present a detailed summary of major points and use the summary as a close.

9. Avoid saying, "Well, in my opinion. . ." They don't care about your opinions, just facts that you can document.

THE EMERGENCE OF NEUROLINGUISTIC PROGRAMMING (NLP)

An entirely different approach to communicating effectively and understanding more about prospects is offered by neurolinguistic programming (NLP). When it first began to attract attention, many people considered NLP to be just another pop-psychology craze similar to the various communication approaches that have been offered as the ultimate answer for managers who wanted increased personal power and influence, for lawyers who wanted to sway judges and juries, and for salespeople who wanted to sell anything to anyone. Instead, however, NLP offers one more way to observe people and understand their needs. It is entirely different from the behavioral styles theory, but in no way contradicts it.

Neurolinguistic programming is the brainchild of linguist John Grinder and psychotherapist Richard Bandler. Both men insist that mastering the methods they teach for interpreting everyday language and nonverbal behavior enables you to discover how someone is thinking and influence how that person thinks and makes decisions—without calling attention to the process. NLP bears little resemblance to the numerous self-help theories that have attracted worldwide attention and earned millions for their inventors. NLP was originated by two people with impeccable academic backgrounds and a base of sound scholarship. Bandler is a successful Gestalt therapist with a master's degree in psychology, and Grinder is a recognized authority on linguistics. In the early seventies, they met at the University of California and together began the research that led to the development of NLP.[17]

Modes of Perception

NLP is based on recognizing and then appealing to the dominant modes of perception used by another person. We all use these modes to map reality and build a model of what the world is like that can guide us through our environment. NLP is the science of how the brain learns. All of us have a basic learning mode: visual, auditory or kinesthetic. Each is used in various situations, yet most of us will favor one mode.[18]

1. *Auditory.*

   Some people perceive the world largely by hearing. They learn more quickly by listening than by reading or seeing. Experiences presented through other senses are mentally translated into an auditory mode. These are the people who test ideas by how they *sound.* They often use responses like, "I hear what you're saying," "It sounds good to me," and "I'm hearing a lot of complaints about that situation."

2. *Visual.*

   Other people perceive the world largely through sight. They learn and form opinions from what they see. They are the ones who originated the saying, "Seeing is believing." They form mental pictures of their experiences as a means of interpretation. They frequently use sentences like, "I see what you mean," "I'm in a fog about the whole concept," and "Do you get the picture?"

3. *Kinesthetic.*

A smaller number of people perceive the world through the sense of touch. They feel life. Everything has a texture that either attracts or repels them. Subsets of the kinesthetic mode are the *gustatory* (taste) and the *olfactory* (smell) modes that sometimes come into play for kinesthetic people. Those operating in the kinesthetic mode say things like, "This deal just feels right (or wrong)," "That was a smooth presentation," "That transaction left a bad taste in my mouth," and "I smell something rotten about this deal."

Bandler and Grinder first used this information to teach therapists how to recognize these *representational* modes and use them to build rapport with the patient, to establish a climate of trust, and to improve communication. They soon realized that this powerful communication tool would work for people other than therapists. They began to train a number of people to teach these techniques. Reportedly, NLP has been used by people who have turned it into a powerful manipulative tool for their own benefit to the detriment of others. When used ethically, however, it is a helpful method for cutting down the time needed to build trust and rapport—a necessary process in consultative selling.[19] Its misuse does not discount its effectiveness; many kinds of knowledge can be twisted into tools for satisfying personal greed by those whose value systems allow such unethical action. If you look at NLP as an additional tool for interpreting the behavior, needs, and motivation of people, you can use it just as ethically and helpfully as you can use the information about behavioral styles and body language.

Tapping Into Prospect's Perception

Some salespeople seem to have a natural or intuitive ability to identify a prospect's behavior and personality traits and to adapt to them. They seem to possess an automatic radar system that instantly and unobtrusively sends out test signals, interprets the feedback, and then chooses the best tactics for establishing rapport. Developing such skills is one of the most difficult parts of sales training. NLP is one technique you can use to develop this ability.

Eye Cues

Our eyes are seldom still. The direction they move during a conversation reveals the system of perception that is active at the moment. Figure 5.3 illustrates the various eye cues that help to identify the operative system. Eye movements in most people are similar and can usually be expected to show these processes:[20]

FIGURE 5.3

Eye Cues Indicating Thought Processes

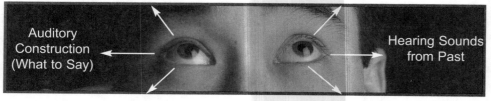

Construction (Imaging What It Would Look Like)

Visualizing Past Images

Auditory Construction (What to Say)

Hearing Sounds from Past

Feelings (Including Smell and Taste)

Talking with Self (Internal Dialogue)

Visual Perception

Looking up and left	Visualizing (remembering) from the past; picturing the past mentally
Looking up and right	Visually constructing an image to see what it would look like

Kinesthetic Perception

Looking down and right	Remembering past feelings

Auditory Perception

Looking sideways to left	Hearing sounds or voices from the past (remembering)
Looking sideways to right	Constructing a future conversation; thinking of the right words to use
Looking down to left	Holding an internal dialogue with oneself; how something sounds

Some left-handed people reverse the normal right and left eye cues; therefore, eye cues can be used only as clues to be confirmed by further observation.

Interpreting Predicate Words

Most people are fairly consistent in eye movements, body language, behavior style, and all the other ways anyone has devised to help salespeople tune in on their prospects. NLP teaches us to look at eye cues and test them against predicate words, that is, how people talk. Table 5.1 provides a list of *predicate words* that provide important information to confirm what is observed from eye cues. These words tell you how the other person is processing information. When these words match eye cues, you are on fairly safe ground in deciding which *mode of perception* is operating for the prospect at that moment.[21]

Salespeople who are good builders of rapport use a few initial questions to get the prospect to talk so they can discover which type of system is in use. Salespeople do not have to memorize a long list of specific questions to evoke the crucial responses needed to determine a prospect's system. The usual opening dialogue a salesperson uses to get acquainted and put the prospect at ease serves admirably. Compare these examples of the type of responses you might receive to such opening questions and determine which system the answer seems to indicate:

TABLE 5.1 - Predicate Words: A Guide to the Modes of Perception

Visual		Auditory		Kinesthetic	
analyze	look	announce	noise	active	intuition
angle	notice	articulate	proclaim	affected	lukewarm
appear	obscure	audible	pronounce	bearable	motion
cognizant	observe	discuss	remark	concrete	panicky
conspicuous	perception	dissonant	report	emotional	pressure
dream	perspective	divulge	roar	feel	sensitive
examine	picture	earshot	rumor	firm	shallow
focus	scene	enunciate	shrill	flow	softly
foresee	sight	gossip	silence	foundation	solid
glance	sketchy	hear	sound	grasp	structured
hindsight	survey	hush	squeal	grip	tension
horizon	vague	inquire	talk	hanging	tied
idea	view	interview	tell	hassle	touch

QUESTION: That's an impressive trophy. Do you play a lot of golf?

ANSWER A: I play in a club foursome almost every Saturday. I enjoy keeping active. It wards off some of the pressure. Sometimes when things get into an unbearable hassle, golf relieves some of the tension. Gripping the club, feeling the impact as I hit the ball, and getting into the swing of the physical motion seems to put me back on a concrete foundation and makes me ready to get back in touch with reality instead of lapsing into panicky emotions.

ANSWER B: I play on Wednesday afternoons and see it as an opportunity to get away from the work scene when the picture gets too crowded or blurred. On the golf course I have time to lose myself in a new perspective. I look down the fairway all the way to the horizon and dream of seeing my ball fly all the way to the hole in one shot. Of course, I've actually done that only once, but the dream lets me focus on what is most important, observe the obstacles, and picture a way to avoid them. Then when I get back to work, the whole view seems to have more clarity and the path around the obstacles becomes conspicuous where before it had been obscured because I was too close to the trees to see the forest.

How did you identify the systems used by these two different people? The first was *kinesthetic*. Did you note some of the key words?

active	feeling	panicky
pressure	motion	emotions
hassle	foundation	concrete
tension	touch	

The second answer was *visual*; note the key words:

see	look	picture
scene	horizon	view
picture	dream	clarity
blurred	focus	conspicuous

Be sure to take into account the eye cues, body language, and any other information you have about the prospect as you attempt to decide which system the prospect is using. Remember that we all use the different perceptual fields, often in quick succession, but most of us have one we use more often than the others. When eye cues fit the predicate words used, the salesperson has a fairly sound basis for deciding what is going on in the prospect's mind. Once you know the prospect's favorite system, you know how that person usually maps out the environment and plans a route to the solution of a problem or to the reaching of a goal. Then you can speak a language the auditory prospect can hear, draw a picture the visual prospect can see, or structure something concrete the kinesthetic prospect can grasp.

SUMMARY

The more salespeople understand about prospects, the more readily salespeople can discover what they need and want. Then a viable buying decision can be recommended and a sale closed. An especially useful tool for gaining quick insight into the thinking of prospects is a knowledge of behavioral styles. The social styles model, developed originally by Merrill and Reid, uses two dimensions of behavior to assess an individual's style: *assertiveness* and *responsiveness*. Recognizing typical behavioral cues related to these two personality dimensions makes it possible to classify people quickly as one of four basic personality types: driver, expressive, amiable, or analytical. A third dimension of behavior, *versatility*, is the individual's ability to adjust personal pace and priorities to facilitate interaction with a person of another style. Because the social styles model is, as are all attempts to classify people by behavioral cues, based on surface behavior, it is not a sure guide to character. It is only a quick method for finding the best way to approach a particular prospect and to set up a working relationship for communication.

A related tool for communication is neurolinguistic programming (NLP), developed by Bandler and Grinder. NLP uses observation of eye cues and typical predicate words to discover the particular perceptual field a person is using at a given time. All of us use different senses to perceive and interpret the world of experience. At any given point in time, we may use either the *visual*, the *auditory*, or the *kinesthetic* mode of perception, but most people have a favorite sensory path. By matching the prospect's perceptual field, the salesperson can communicate more directly. The prospect immediately receives and understands the message. If the salesperson persists in using a different perceptual field, the prospect must first translate the message into language that is meaningful before absorbing it.

The behavioral dimension of *versatility* and the NLP tactic of *matching perceptual fields* are both communication devices to help people meet on common ground so that communication is clear of barriers that produce misunderstanding or conflict. A salesperson should never attempt to adopt a style that is insincere pretense. Imitation of the prospect is a tactic that is usually seen as insulting. The salesperson, instead, takes the lead in finding common ground with the prospect.

QUESTIONS FOR THOUGHT AND DISCUSSION

1. What is meant by *assertiveness* and *responsiveness* as dimensions of behavioral style?

2. Which style is characterized by each of these pairs of dimensions?

    Low assertiveness and high responsiveness

    Low assertiveness and low responsiveness

    High assertiveness and high responsiveness

    High assertiveness and low responsiveness

3. What is a backup style and what is its importance to the salesperson?

4. Explain this statement: The strengths of a particular behavioral style are the source of that style's typical weaknesses.

5. Point out some strengths of each of the four behavioral styles and show how they can be used as assets in selling. Identify some of the weaknesses of each and tell how they can damage sales effectiveness.

6. What is a perceptual field? How is it observed in a person's behavior?

7. Read the statements below and determine what perceptual field the speaker is probably using:

    a.   There is so much noise in here, I can't hear myself think.

    b.   The atmosphere was heavy and damp; there was an oppressive stillness, thick with apprehension.

    c.   I am watching developments in that particular stock; before I buy, I want to see the progress it makes this quarter and get a picture of what to expect in the future.

    d.   The rookie quarterback was calling the first play of his career. He repeated the coach's instructions in his head, and the murmur of the crowd filled his ears. He could hear his heart pounding with excitement.

    e.   The rookie quarterback was calling the first play of his career. He could still see the coach's face in his mind, imposed on the vision of the great sea of faces in the stands, with all eyes focused on him—a tiny speck on the playing field.

8. What kind of sales aids would you use in making a presentation to a person with a *visual* perceptual field? What changes would you make when talking to a prospect with an *auditory* field? How would you deal with a prospect with a *kinesthetic* field?

9. Is it ethical for a salesperson, by employing behavioral flexibility or versatility, to alter personal behavioral style or to match perceptual fields with a prospect? Are there limits to which such adaptation should adhere? Explain.

ACTIVITIES

1. What social style do you see in the individuals below? Consider assertiveness and responsiveness dimensions and the behavioral characteristics of each style to determine your answer.

   Jay Leno, star of the "Tonight Show"
   Dan Rather, anchorman for CBS News
   Charles Bronson, movie star
   Ronald Reagan, former president of the United States

2. In this chapter, two examples were given of prospects' answers to the question, "That's an impressive trophy; do you play a lot of golf?" One answer revealed a kinesthetic perceptual field at work, and the other a visual perceptual field. Construct a similar answer that might be made by a prospect using an auditory field. Review Table 5.1 for the appropriate types of predicate words that you might use.

Case Study

CASE 5.1

Karen Bradfield, a financial planner, is calling on Sue Johnson, self-made president of an employment agency. As Bradfield enters Johnson's office, she notices good-quality furnishings, a large backlog of work on Johnson's desk, and stacks of files on the credenza. Johnson is dressed casually in a skirt and sweater. The conversation begins like this:

BRADFIELD: Good morning, Ms. Johnson. I am Karen Bradfield, and as I told you on the phone, I have my own financial planning firm.

JOHNSON: Sit down, Karen. I've been making more money lately and want to do something with it besides investing in CDs. I'd like to see what kind of plan you could suggest for me.

BRADFIELD: Yes, I will. I couldn't help noticing that you've acquired more office space. This company has really been growing, hasn't it?

JOHNSON: Yes. Now I have fifty thousand to invest, and I was thinking about some municipal bonds or some mutual funds.

BRADFIELD: Oh, there are many to choose from, and I'm sure we will find something suitable. Oh, I see from your diploma on the wall that you went to my alma mater. When did you graduate?

1. What two communication styles are operating here?

2. Do you think Bradfield will make the sale if she continues as she is now?

3. What change, if any, does Bradfield need to make in her procedure to be successful in selling to Johnson?

CASE 5.2

John Long is a sales representative for a commercial office furniture supplier. He has already called once on Larry Lavine, president of Evergreen Savings and Loan Association. At that first meeting, Lavine appeared to be running behind schedule. He had multiple projects going on simultaneously and had taken phone calls while telling Long to continue with his presentation. During the middle of the interview, he seemed to become more relaxed when Long asked him about his golf game and his fly fishing. At the time, Lavine offered to play golf with Long but said he would beat him and take all of his money.

Lavine's office was full of his ego—pictures of himself shaking hands with the mayor, receiving awards, fly fishing, and playing golf. During that first interview, he regales Long with stories about his community involvement and the positive changes he had masterminded at Evergreen. Long had found it difficult to get a word in.

1. Long is now preparing to call on Lavine a second time. What is Lavine's social style?

2. What kinds of strategies should Long employ in this second interview?

THE SALES EDGE

The following chart summarizes some of the key features of the four social styles. Salespeople are only as good as their reflex actions allow them to be. We are in the people business. In selling, we observe and verify behavior styles every day. We need to be experts in understanding people. Rather than a Ph.D., perhaps a salesperson should have a Ph.B.–Professor of Human Behavior. Study the chart below; learn how to read behavioral styles. There's an old saying–if you want to get better at something, learn more about it.

SOCIAL STYLE SUMMARY

	Driver	Expressive	Amiable	Analytical
Backup style	Autocratic	Attacker	Acquiescer	Avoider
Measures personal value by	Results	Applause or approval	Security	Accuracy, "being right"
For growth, needs to	Listen	Check	Initiate	Decide
Needs climate that	Allows to build own structure	Inspires to reach goals	Suggests	Provides details
Takes time to be	Efficient	Stimulating	Agreeable	Accurate
Support their	Conclusions and actions	Dreams and intuitions	Relationships and feelings	Principles and thinking
Present benefits that tell	What	Who	Why	How
For decisions, give them	Options and probabilities	Testimonials and incentives	Guarantees and assurances	Evidence and service
Their specialty is	Controlling	Socializing	Supporting	Technical

PART III

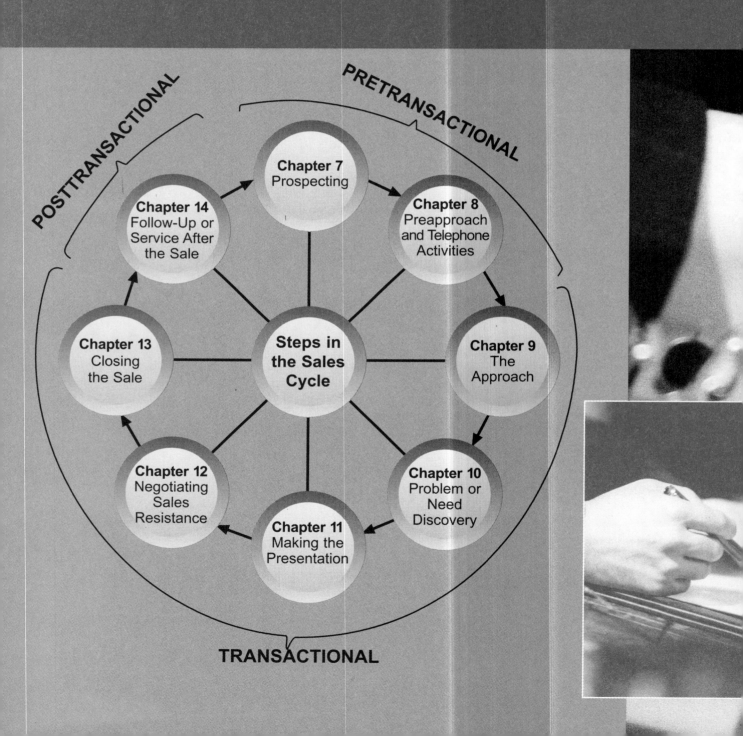

POSTTRANSACTIONAL

PRETRANSACTIONAL

Chapter 7
Prospecting

Chapter 14
Follow-Up or
Service After
the Sale

Chapter 8
Preapproach
and Telephone
Activities

Chapter 13
Closing
the Sale

**Steps in
the Sales
Cycle**

Chapter 9
The
Approach

Chapter 12
Negotiating
Sales
Resistance

Chapter 10
Problem or
Need
Discovery

Chapter 11
Making the
Presentation

TRANSACTIONAL

Gaining Knowledge, Preparing, and Planning for the Presentation

The sections in Chapter six prepare the reader for success in a sales career by focusing on gaining product knowledge, developing self-motivation and goal-setting strategies, and introducing the use of sales force automation. The electronic information age is here. The use of contact management software programs is introduced in this section.

Chapter 7 is a very thorough look at the topic of prospecting. As the saying goes, "I'd rather be a master prospector than a wizard of speech and have no one to tell my story to." Chapter 8 discusses the process of gathering preapproach information and presents a six-step telephone track for making appointments for that all-important personal interview.

Goal setting is the strongest human force for self-motivation

CHAPTER 6

Preparation for Success in Selling

PREPARING TO SELL

Once you have chosen to pursue a career in sales and have been hired as a salesperson, how do you begin? Will one or two sales courses in business school give you all the preparation you need? Who has the responsibility to prepare you for success in this particular job?

Of course, any background, training, or education is helpful, but academic training is not enough. Adequate preparation for success in sales involves a combination of the information and training provided by the company and your own active preparation in learning and personal commitment. The more help the company gives, the easier your job is. Because the company's success depends upon your success, your preparation is a major mutual concern. Adequate preparation for success in selling involves at least three areas that are considered in this chapter.

1. Product knowledge
2. Sales force automation
3. Motivation and goal setting

Some elements in each of these three areas are the primary responsibility of the company; some are primarily your responsibility. No matter who bears the primary responsibility, both salesperson and company are active participants; neither can be passive because too much is at stake.

PRODUCT KNOWLEDGE

Newly hired salespeople may have some general knowledge of the company's field or industry and may even have some knowledge of the specific product they will be marketing. However, salespeople are often hired with little or no knowledge of the company and its products or even of the industry. Obtaining product knowledge is one of the first prerequisites of success. "One of the most important things you can do for a new salesperson is give them enough product knowledge to make them feel comfortable on their sales calls," says Mike Killen, executive director of sales for Carrington Laboratories Inc., a research and development biopharmaceutical company.[1]

What do you need to know about the product? One answer to that question is *everything!* Nevertheless, you cannot delay beginning sales activity until you have had time to learn everything, and you cannot cease to learn about the product or service once you begin to sell. Gaining product knowledge is an ongoing process.

The Product Itself

Product knowledge begins with the product itself: what it does, its size, color, how it is operated or used, its specific features and benefits, and its acceptance in the marketplace. Product knowledge includes knowing all available options—how it can be adapted to the particular customer's needs, and how it performs under varying conditions. Detailed product knowledge prepares you to answer any question a customer might have and to offer whatever reassurance is necessary in the process of helping the customer reach a decision. When you know the product backward and forward, you can answer detailed, technical questions from expert buyers or explain in simple terms to one who is considering a first purchase of a product of this kind. You seldom tell anyone all the information you have, but having all the information gives you a whole library from which you can choose the best items for the current situation. Exhibit 6.1 shows how two salespeople used specific product knowledge with varying results.

EXHIBIT 6.1 - Use of Product Knowledge to Close the Sale

A computer salesman called on the owner of a small business who was looking for a solution to the mountain of paperwork that was burying his accounting department in red tape and slowing up shipping of orders. The salesman had been well trained in product knowledge and was eager to demonstrate his expertise. He overwhelmed the prospect with computer jargon—bits and bytes and megabytes, CPUs and I/O devices—and he peppered his sales talk with terms like EDI and GPS. He left without an order.

Later, another salesperson called. She told the prospect how quickly the equipment she proposed would process orders so they could be shipped, and how time and paper handling could be cut in preparing and mailing invoices. Then she explained that daily reports could be produced to summarize orders received and shipped, cash received, and other transactions that would provide solid information upon which good business decisions could be made in a timely manner. She got the order!

Performance

Performance information about the product is another vital area of product knowledge. How long will it last? What kind of wear and stress does it tolerate? How fast does it run? What is its output? How much training is necessary for an employee to operate or use it? How much fuel or power is needed to run it? Can it be repaired? How much maintenance is required? Who can perform needed maintenance? Are spare parts readily available? In the more technical industries, salespeople have access to company engineers and technical advisors who furnish engineering and technical information when it is required; sales knowledge in this case means knowing who to call on and when to ask for backup.

Manufacturing

Product knowledge includes thorough knowledge of the manufacturing process and methods that affect the quality, performance, or durability of the product. These vital ingredients of quality affect buying decisions. Knowledge of the manufacturing process also enables the salesperson to explain why the price that seems high to the prospect is actually reasonable or why delivery takes longer than the buyer had expected.

Distribution Channels

The company's distribution methods are an important area of product knowledge. What channels are used? Why? Are exclusive dealerships granted in certain areas? Is distribution selective? Do discount houses and chains sell the product in competition with other types of retail dealers? How do these channels affect any particular dealer's success with sales of the product?

Another important element of distribution concerns pricing policies. How much the dealer pays, availability of quantity discounts, applicable credit terms, and whether the company will consider negotiating special deals are all elements of distribution about which customers are concerned.[2] The company's advertising policy is also important: how much, what methods, its general thrust, and how it affects consumer demand, as well as what advertising allowances and promotional assistance are offered by the company.

You must be aware of the needs of the market in your assigned territory. Are marketing efforts directed toward industrial buyers, wholesalers, retailers, or direct to the consumer? How does the buyer actually use the product? Salespeople who are marketing security systems, for example, need to know what security their typical customers need before they can propose a workable system. Do they need primarily burglar alarms to protect the premises when no one is working? Do they need devices to prevent shoplifting from a retail location? Do they need sprinklers to protect against fire? Many large companies assign sales territories on the basis of types of customers in an area rather than purely upon the basis of geographical division. This gives salespeople the opportunity to become real experts in one class of products; identifying and helping to solve the customer's problems is then easier.

Service Available   Once a product is sold, your responsibility has just begun. Service after the sale cements the client-salesperson relationship and ensures repeat orders. You must know the company's service policy: What repairs, replacements, or adaptations are considered the responsibility of the company? What charges are made for service? Who performs the service? Where? On what kind of time schedule? What kind of consulting service is available to adapt or adjust the product to the customer's needs?

APPLICATION OF PRODUCT KNOWLEDGE

Product knowledge is sterile and unproductive unless you can use it and apply it to the problems or needs of a particular client. Knowing the materials and specifications used in manufacturing enables you to advise a prospect to order your product and expect it to perform as desired. This knowledge also helps you suggest what custom changes might be made in the product to fit a particular need of the client.

Product knowledge can be either a help or a hindrance, depending on how it is used. Exhibit 6.2 illustrates how salespeople can use their special knowledge to close—or to lose—a sale.

EXHIBIT 6.2 - Using Product Knowledge to Fit the Need

An automobile salesman was showing a new car to a husband and wife. They told him that the wife would be driving the car primarily for neighborhood errands. The salesman spent a lot of time explaining that the car had front-wheel drive and that the motor was mounted at a ninety-degree angle to the traditional position. He loaded his sales talk with terms like engine ratios, rpm's, and torque, and bragged about the car's ability to accelerate from zero to sixty faster than any of the competition. The woman's questions about what that meant for her needs produced even more complicated explanations that did not interest her or her husband. The couple bought a car demonstrated by the salesman from another dealer. He stressed styling, real leather upholstery, the comfort of adjustable seats, and the added visibility provided by the rear-window defroster, and then invited the wife to test-drive the car.

Knowledge of the Competition

Knowledge of the competition is often overlooked as an element of product knowledge. Today customers have easy access to product information; they can quickly find application data, and competitive comparisons on product performance by searching the Internet. The product-focused salesperson of the past can no longer compete successfully. In the 21st century, professional salespeople know how to leverage information technology and assume the role of trusted advisor to the client's business. Learn about the products of your major competitors; know their credit terms, their prices, their delivery schedules, and their reputation for service. Most buyers—either personal consumers or company purchasing agents—are not weighing the advantages of buying against those of not buying; they are trying to decide *which* product to buy. Your product is one of the possibilities; the others are your competitors. If you know that your competitor's price is a little lower than yours, you can make a special effort to show the advantages of your prompt delivery, your company's excellent customer service department, or generous credit terms. One of the advantages of studying your competition is that you see afresh the good points of your own product or company. Your commitment to and belief in the product is enhanced, and your enthusiasm for it increases. Knowledge of the competition allows you to highlight your product's advantages with confidence that you are right. Exhibit 6.3 provides an overview of the four possible areas of competitive advantage.

Information About the Company

Product knowledge also involves gaining as much information as possible about the company you represent. You need to know something about the history of the company: who founded it and when, how the present product line evolved, the company's position in the marketplace, its past and present performance and growth, its principal customers or clients, and any other information that may be of interest to prospects.[3] Knowledge of the company also includes tactics and strategies that affect the customer—service, delivery options, and company policies.

EXHIBIT 6.3 - Differential Competitive Advantage

Product Superiority		Service Superiority	
Versatility	Design	Delivery	Installation
Efficiency	Mobility	Inventory	Maintenance
Storage	Packaging	Credit	
Handling time	Life expectancy	Training	
Safety	Adaptability	Merchandising	
Appearance			

Source Superiority	People Superiority
Time established	Personal knowledge and skill
Competitive standing	Knowledge and skill of support personnel
Community image	Integrity and character
Location	Standing in community
Size	Flexibility of call schedule
Financial soundness	Interpersonal skills
Policies and practices	Mutual friends
	Cooperation

SALES FORCE AUTOMATION

Crumple up your paper calendar, burn your Post-it notes, and put your Rolodex in the closet. The electronic information age is here! A generation of salespeople is emerging who are not only computer-literate, but who also are being taught about the information superhighway, e-mail, Internet, integrated marketing, and database marketing. For them, the computer is being used as a tool to foster and build relationships with customers, and to manage information and key accounts with greater efficiency.

Sales automation has created the opportunity to integrate sales and marketing efforts, making the entire company stronger as well. The practical implications for the future are clear. Companies will need a highly trained sales force to keep abreast of the technological advances. Salespeople must adapt or fall by the wayside. Fax machines have cut the length of time needed for proposals, routine orders, and correspondence. Laptop computers outperform even the most sophisticated equipment of the last decade. Desktop publishing has completely changed the way visual aids, sales proposals, and group presentations are developed.

Computers in Selling and Sales Training

Sales was one of the last professions to accept personal computers (PCs) as an important tool. But today the sales industry is experiencing an explosive trend toward automation.[4] Salespeople can have a clear direction and the right incentive, but if they don't have the right tools, sales will suffer despite their best intentions. For example, Jim Hill, former director of sales for Sun Microsystem's Asia Pacific region, said, "I sent five managers into the field to talk to reps, and they all said the same thing. These guys were burning a lot of time sitting in front of their workstations trying to figure out all the administrative stuff." The sales reps just needed some tools that would help them reduce their administrative time so they could spend more time selling.

So Hill and his managers created the *One More Deal* program, which gave each of the 500 direct sales reps Web-based tools, such as standard proposal templates and better customer data so that they didn't have to "reinvent the wheel" every time they worked on a proposal for a prospect. As a result, the reps cut their administrative paperwork by over 50 percent, and sales in the region went up 45 percent.[5]

To keep up with the increasing demands of the continually changing, competitive marketplace, salespeople are being asked to become more productive at everything they do. They have to talk to more people, provide more value, and do a better job with each customer they call on. Computers relieve salespeople of many administrative duties, and allow them more time for planning and selling. The salesperson is able to analyze the information collected and thus gain a better understanding of the company and the product. Exhibit 6.4 illustrates the impact technology is also having on the product and selling skills training received by a sales force.[6]

EXHIBIT 6.4 - Interactive Sales Training at the Prudential

Interactive learning has revolutionized the way Prudential trains its sales representatives. The company has implemented the Prudential Learning System (PLS), a PC-based training program, that will enable Prudential's representatives to take 75 percent of their in-house training courses on their PCs or on special learning terminals. When the company was planning its reorganization, they asked, "What can we do from the standpoint of education and development to help our field representatives become more effective?" Craig Miller, director of field education and development, says, "PLS was created to focus on an individual's training needs, which results in better customer service and an increase in both representative and client retention."

PLS has 60 courses available on topics such as Prudential's products, core selling skills, quality service, and prospect management.

PLS's core curriculum has a preliminary sequence of 25-30 courses. Local managers, however, can adjust that sequence to meet the specific needs of an individual rep. New reps are expected to complete the core curriculum within the first 30 months of their employment with Prudential.

To access PLS, Prudential's 16,000 reps use their PCs or special learning terminals to connect—via an 800 number, a modem, and Prudential's proprietary software—to a central computer. Reps can also use their PCs to study anytime, anywhere.

Online Sales Training

For most sales organizations the ideal solution will involve a combination of Web and face-to-face training. The sales training market is ideal for an Internet-based approach. Product knowledge, specific selling skills, and knowledge of the competition are accessible through the Internet. With audio and video streaming becoming popular, interactive training programs hold real promise. Web-based training can range from simple text-based product information to intricate simulations that mirror a real-life sales interview.[7] There has been a definite movement to online education. The two examples that follow illustrate what is happening in the world of online sales training.

In The Know How Zone. Alan Hupp, CEO of *KnowHow*, has created a series of online sales training courses using concise, practical modules designed to challenge and test sales reps at all levels. The Web site *(www.knowhowzone.com)* is an Internet source for a library full of fast-track training courses featuring some of the most respected names in sales training. For example, your sales team can learn to qualify from Tom Hopkins, handle price objections from Brian Tracy, and improve interpersonal skills from Tony Alessandra.

Each of the modules covers a specific sales skill—pre-call qualification, relationship selling, prospecting, qualifying, and handling customer objections. *KnowHow* uses multimedia techniques—pictures, text, and sound—to reinforce learning. It is an affordable alternative to bringing sales training experts and salespeople to a central location. *KnowHow* delivers anytime, anywhere as long as the rep has a personal computer, a modem, and a browser. Hupp says that a one-hour module can cover about the same material as a three-hour live seminar. The modules first quiz students on their existing skills, thus allowing experienced reps to skip what they already know.   The lessons have been developed as cases or sales problems. The system also scores and stores the reps' responses, enabling managers to track the progress of their salespeople. Hewlett-Packard used the system to train distribution staff, who received a reward of $200 for completing the course successfully.[8]

Red Hot Sales Seminars Online. In a similar venture, Paul Goldner, head of the Sales & Performance Group in Katonah, New York, has tapped into Internet-based sales training. Goldner originally built his business by talking to people face-to-face during his Red Hot Sales Seminars. However, to keep up with the needs of many sales organizations, Goldner switched tactics and joined the Internet revolution. He admits that Internet-based education isn't necessarily "better than a classroom, but it's the next best thing to being there."

RedHotSalesTV is an Internet-based training system that lets sales trainees or experienced sales veterans watch streaming videos of his Red Hot training seminars along with a synchronized PowerPoint presentation.

The advantage of *RedHotSalesTV* is similar to the advantage offered by all online education, including *KnowHow*: It saves time and a considerable amount of money. Jack Gordon, a Minneapolis-based training expert, believes "the biggest cost advantage of computer-based training is that you don't have to bring people together...the farther you have to bring people, the greater the economies of the situation." Essentially, selling time is a precious commodity and online training enables the salesperson to download or go online when it is convenient for them – at the airport, in a hotel room, or at home – without losing any selling time.

However, even the best e-training should not, and cannot, replace live sales training. Paul Goldner believes "where the industry is really going is toward blended training" or a mix of online and face-to-face training.[9]

THE IMPACT OF SALES TECHNOLOGY TOOLS

The companies that find ways of responding quickly to customer needs and making information easily available to their business partners will have a competitive edge. The implementation of an effective sales force automation program provides numerous company benefits which correlate directly to improving the bottom-line profit picture.[10] Sales force automation can help increase sales efficiency in three functional areas:

Personal Productivity

a. *Laptop Computers* – provide the sales force with desktop power wherever they go. Palm Held Computers–salespeople now have important contact information, sales scripts, and documents in their pockets. Palm Handheld computers come with such built-in core applications as a calendar, contact book, memo pad, calculator, and expense report program. To find hundreds of applications that can be downloaded to the Palm, try *www.Palmgear.com*.

b. *Contact Management Software* – no more paper mess and scribbled notes.[11] In addition to providing the functionality of an electronic Rolodex listing all your customer contacts, these products offer sales reps powerful tools for tracking detailed customer information; scheduling appointments, activities, and to-dos; and integrating a number of Web resources into a single sales force automation solution.[12] Some of the better-known software programs are Surado Solutions' *SmartContactManager*, Interact Commerce Corporation's *ACT!,* and FrontRange's *Goldmine*.

c. *Mapping Programs and GPS technology*—the road warrior will never be lost or late to an appointment with these new field guides and real-time location finders. With the information plotted on a map, the administration of territories becomes immeasurably more accurate.

Improved Communications

a. *Internet and Videoconferencing*—face-to-face interaction with clients globally without the travel costs. Also great for proposals and presentations. The personal selling medium of the future.

b. *Telecommuting* (Virtual Private Networking)—no more fighting rush-hour traffic! Not only can salespeople check e-mail, but they can update databases, product information, and appointments from the comfort of their homes and hotel rooms.

Transactional Processing

a. *Electronic Data Interchange (EDI) Technologies*—the entire company has up-to-date order, processing, and fulfillment information. Ordering customers can have instant access to product information, just like e-mail. Automate the selling chain to include customers, distributors, and suppliers.

b. *Corporate Contact Management and Custom Reporting Programs*— shared contact information that is modified and updated by everyone in the sales office. Salespeople can customize reports to their specific needs for each of their individual customers and prospects.

c. *Internet Database Development Technologies*—providing online order and product information and order entry for salespeople or their customers. Utilizing Internet Web sites is an effective method of advancing information between a company, its sales channel members, and its customers.

Individual applications of these technologies will be discussed in the technology boxes highlighted in chapters 6 to 15. The illustrations will provide the reader with a detailed look at how sales forces are using these productivity, communication, and transaction-processing tools to improve relationships with customers and prospects.

Developing Partnerships Using Technology describes how a salesperson's time management skills are enhanced because of the various contact manager systems available to the *Road Warrior*. An entire sales plan for the day can be scheduled, worked on, and prioritized while you are having your morning coffee. Because of advances in hand-held computers, all of this information can be taken along and updated on the road. Time has now become an ally of the salesperson rather than an adversary.

Developing Partnerships Using Technology
Manage your time with ruthless efficiency using your contact manager.

Here is what the traveling salesperson's typical scheduling program might include:

Customizable Calendar. A calendar program gives you a range of dates by day, week, or month. They can be further broken down by hour or appointment. It enables the salesperson to look ahead and modify or change appointments according to circumstances.

Appointment Reminders. These clever programs remind you of appointments with sounds or messages. The reminders can come days, hours, or minutes before the meeting is actually scheduled.

Task Lists. Instead of losing track of what activities need to be accomplished, you can make "to do" lists on the computer. Now your daily and weekly goals are always available to examine or update whenever necessary.

Smart Card Reader. Transfer business card information directly into a database with the Smart Business Card Reader. Users can search for contacts based on these notes. For example, contact information can be transferred into Surado Solutions' *SmartContactManager*.

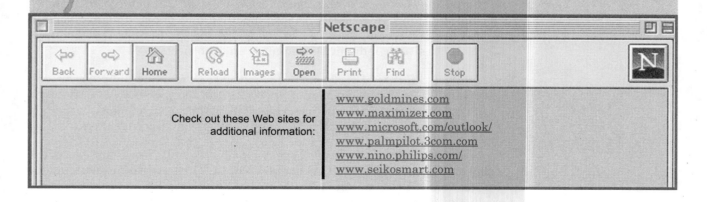

Netscape

Back | Forward | Home | Reload | Images | Open | Print | Find | Stop

Check out these Web sites for additional information:

www.goldmines.com
www.maximizer.com
www.microsoft.com/outlook/
www.palmpilot.3com.com
www.nino.philips.com/
www.seikosmart.com

PRODUCT POSITIONING

The level of competition today is just amazing. There are so many brands, and so many salespeople trying to get everybody else's business, and they're coming at you from all over the world. Just in the past 30 years, the number of new automobile models increased from 140 to 260 and the number of over-the-counter pain relievers went from 17 to 41. That makes **positioning** – the marketing strategy of differentiating a product or company in the mind of a prospect – more important than ever. Once a business identifies what makes it *unique* in the *eyes of the consumer*, that idea should be the focus of its entire marketing and sales strategy. You must give your salespeople that differentiating idea. Exhibit 6.5 gives sales professionals five points to consider that will enable them to go into an organization and say–*"Allow me to explain to you how and why my company and its products are different."*

EXHIBIT 6.5 - Key Points for Developing a Powerful Market Position

FIND OUT what qualities of your products and services are most important to your customers. Then use the information to create a unique niche for yourself.

PUT TOGETHER a marketing strategy built around several features that are important to your customers and that will set you apart from the competition. And then develop an integrated marketing communication message that reinforces those attributes in the customer's mind.

REMEMBER the way you service your customers or sell to them can be a powerful difference. For example, if you are in an industry where the prevailing culture stresses face-to-face selling, the ability to buy directly online can be very attractive.

RECOGNIZE that focusing on the few attributes that really set you apart means you can't be all things to all people. When you shout, *"Hey, everybody,"* you end up satisfying nobody. Zero in on those customers that are a part of your specific target market.

KEEP an eye on how your competitors are positioning themselves. Be ready to respond to their claims and make sure you maintain a differential competitive advantage.

Positioning was popularized by Jack Trout and Al Ries in their book *Positioning: The Battle for Your Mind.* The term "positioning" refers to developing a specific marketing mix to influence potential customers' overall perception of a brand, product line, or organization. **Positioning** is the place a product occupies in potential customers' minds relative to competing offerings. Once a position is selected, product, price, place, and promotion strategies and tactics are designed to promote and reinforce the sought-after position. These marketing-mix components represent a bundle of individual dimensions that are designed to work together to create a differential competitive advantage.

To illustrate this, the Otis Elevator Company has positioned itself as an innovator that offers tangible benefits for its customer base. For instance, their Remote Elevator Monitoring system (REM) allows Otis to monitor the performance of its elevators in their clients' buildings, so mechanics can fix minor problems before they cause a major shutdown. Otis has created an e-commerce plan that gives prospects and customers the opportunity to research and buy its elevators on the Web, and moves the REM system online, enabling existing customers to monitor the service of their elevators on the Web as well. Another competitive advantage is a display panel inside new elevators showing information from the Internet. These innovations have helped Otis expand its relationships with customers. Mark Granato, Otis' vice-president of communications, says, "In a competitive industry that is exceedingly price-conscious, having the reputation of a leader is increasingly important—and takes constant planning. You get a head start on them—that's the key."[13]

Integrated Marketing Communication

Setting in motion all the pieces in a sales and marketing program takes coordination. *Integrated Marketing Communication* uses computerized databases to orchestrate the conception, timing, and execution of all the marketing elements. Each of the seven modules shown in Figure 6.1 has a specific function, and they should be designed to work together as a company-wide, interactive, closed-loop communication system. *Integrated Marketing* should provide management the ability to measure quantitatively the impact on sales and/or customer perceptions a specific action has and determine the optimal level of sales stimuli—such as price, advertising, sales promotion, direct mail, and personal selling—needed to bring a specific reaction in the market. The logical solution is to create a marketing database accessible to all parties. The people who go through the process will know more about their prospect and customers than anyone else in the company.

FIGURE 6.1

A Closed-Loop, Integrated Marketing Communication System

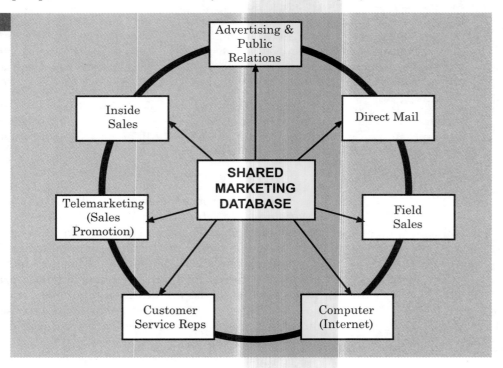

The goal is to deliver marketing communications tailored to the unique needs of a target audience. In the consumer goods field, for example, Avon delivers a series of coordinated messages by using a combination of communication vehicles: sales promotion, telemarketing, mass media advertising, cable TV, and response-specific direct mail. As a total package, these marketing tools allow Avon to communicate directly with the millions of people in its database.[14] This is a truly integrated approach to sales and marketing.

Integrated marketing is a communication campaign in which all the elements come together to form one comprehensive and consistent **positioning** strategy. Depending on the situation, an organization selects what kinds of communication should be used and when. This may include direct mail, telephone selling, customer service, public relations, trade shows, or face-to-face selling. Schuster Electronics—a regional distributor of amplifiers, relays, and similar gear in Cincinnati, Ohio—designed an Integrated Marketing Communication system to keep up with and service the 6,000 customers in its database, with both in-house telemarketers and field salespeople working off the same database.

Schuster is able to target not just a company, but individuals who may have radically different responsibilities within that company. When a field salesperson pays a personal visit, he doesn't try to see everyone but comes away with names of influencers in, say, production, quality control, or engineering. These names go into a database for follow-up by mail or by telephone. Integrated marketing enables Schuster to view the actual sales call as just one among many marketing tools at their disposal. Similarly, in its business-to-business markets, Kodak **positions** itself by using a blend of marketing, trade shows and exhibitions, displays, and personal selling to reach prospects for its copiers and desktop publishing business.[15]

MOTIVATION AND GOAL SETTING

Textbooks, journals, and periodicals of all kinds dealing with business—especially the areas of sales, marketing, and management—discuss motivation. Salespeople often find that they have the needed product knowledge and sales and computer skills but have trouble getting around to using them, or else they work hard and long but find that what they accomplish fails to bring them lasting satisfaction. The missing ingredient is motivation.

Numerous definitions have been given for motivation. Perhaps the simplest is that motivation is the reason for taking action. This definition can be expanded slightly to say that motivation is the *impetus* to begin a task, the *incentive* to expend an amount of effort in accomplishing the task, and the *willingness* to sustain the effort until the task is completed.

The question most asked of business consultants is, "How can we motivate our employees?" The answer most given by consultants is, "You can't." The reason for this answer is that the question typically implies that somewhere there are strategies, techniques, or gimmicks that, once discovered and implemented, will double or triple employee motivation and productivity. Consultants realize that genuine and lasting employee motivation is not something management does, but rather a process that management fosters and allows to happen.[16]

The primary responsibility for developing and sustaining motivation rests with the individual salesperson; the company's role is to provide a supportive climate in which the development and sustaining of motivation is encouraged. Bob Nelson, author of *1001 Ways to Reward Employees*, says, "What motivates people the most takes just a little time and thoughtfulness." Recognize them as individuals and you're giving them what they most crave. What follows is a concrete example to spark your creativity in providing a rewards program that will support and energize your salespeople. Read the insert below for an inspirational idea that cost just a few dollars but paid enormous dividends.[17]

The Lighthouse Story

Jonathan Berger, director of strategic accounts for Square D/Schneider Electric, had a salesperson on his team close a very important account that put a fairly large bonus in the sales rep's pocket. So Berger decided to take the extra step that made this sale a truly memorable triumph. He knew the sales rep's wife had a passion for photographing lighthouses, so he sent her a small crystal lighthouse with a note that recognized her husband's achievements and thanked her for her support and the time she had invested. The wife wrote Berger back and said, "Never has anyone in any company ever acknowledged my existence or the contribution I make to my husband's career." This story is good enough to pass on. So relate the story to a sales manager friend of yours!

Practical Motivation for Salespeople

Because all motivation theories agree that motivation arises as a response to either an external or internal stimulus, recognizing those stimuli that operate in your own experience can help you discover ways to control either the stimuli or your responses to them in a way that produces a positive, sustained motivational power and the success you desire. Motivation may arise in fear—the fear of punishment or withholding of acceptance if behavior does not conform to expectations. It may come from incentive—the promise of reward for desired behavior. But the most effective type of motivation is that arising in attitude—behavior chosen because it fits the values and standards chosen by the individual as guiding principles for living and performing.[18]

Fear Motivation. Fear as a motivating force has some value. Fear is a natural emotion designed as protection from danger. The parent's warnings against playing in the street or touching something hot are examples. Negative warnings are often reinforced with threat of punishment. Fear motivation has some advantages.

1. It protects the individual from self-destruction or harm.
2. It protects society from undesirable behavior.
3. It is sometimes the quickest way to accomplish a desired reaction.

In spite of these advantages, fear motivation has serious disadvantages that more than offset its benefits.

1. *Fear is external.* It is effective only as long as the enforcing power is stable. When the parent, teacher, or sales manager is out of sight, fear motivation is materially weakened. A natural desire to "get away with something" may assert itself and produce behavior opposite to that desired.

2. *Fear is temporary.* Threats or punishment may control behavior for a time, but people tune out warnings if they discover that threats are not always fulfilled. Even if the threatened punishment is assessed, they learn they can live with it and do as they please. For example, a salesperson who learns that the penalty for failure to complete required paperwork on time is only a "chewing out" by the sales manager may go on neglecting paperwork. The reprimand is only momentarily unpleasant and never seems to lead to anything more serious.

3. *Fear is negative.* It is directed largely toward not doing something or toward doing something unpleasant merely because it is an imposed duty rather than a chosen activity. A warning not to do something creates a void that may be filled by another equally undesirable behavior. A duty or activity performed under the motivation of fear may be satisfactorily completed, but there is no desire for special effort or creative thinking that goes beyond the actual requirement. As a result, the individual's potential is overlooked or unused.

Incentive Motivation. The use of incentives for motivation is generally considered more enlightened than the use of fear. An *incentive* is the promise of a benefit or reward to be earned in return for certain behaviors. Parents and teachers often see incentives as learning aids. The attempt to produce motivated activity through offering incentives is also common in sales organizations. Some common incentives used by sales managers include the appeal to work harder to earn increased commissions; contests, certificates, and plaques for quotas reached; bonuses; the promise of an enlarged or better sales territory; and perks such as a reserved parking place, a private office, a personal secretary, or a company car. Greg Christensen, Branch Manager for Oracle Corporation's department of defense, says, "You have to understand what motivates each individual on your team and use that information."[19] Like fear motivation, incentive motivation has advantages.

1. Incentive motivation calls for extra effort. When a promised reward is highly desirable, salespeople put forth almost superhuman effort to win it.

2. Incentive motivation is positive and promises something desirable. Salespeople are not frozen into inaction by fear of being punished or deprived.

Like fear motivation, however, incentive motivation carries built-in disadvantages.

1. *Incentive motivation is external.* Behavior depends upon the initiative of the person who offers the reward rather than upon the salesperson who will earn it.

2. *Incentive motivation is temporary.* A salesperson may put forth a great deal of effort to win a sales contest or to earn some desired reward but not continue that level of activity or effort once the contest is over. When the expected reward level returns to normal, so does behavior.

3. A promised reward that is *not perceived as desirable* provides no motivation for action. A multinational company with sales representatives in many parts of the world conducted a big sales contest. A number of awards for productivity were given at intermediate points in the contest, but the grand prize for the top salesperson over the whole contest period was kept a secret. Finally, the contest was over. The sales manager called the winner with the good news. "You won the top prize! You and your wife will be guests of the company president at the Super Bowl." There was dead silence. Finally the winner asked, "What's the Super Bowl?" No one had anticipated that the winner might be uninterested in sports. The next time a contest was announced, that salesperson wanted to know what the top prize would be before he decided to enter the contest.

4. Incentives once earned often come to be regarded as *rights* instead of a special privilege for outstanding performance. For example, salespeople who qualify for a company car by high productivity and enjoy this reward for several years feel incensed if the requirements for having a company car are raised and they fail to meet the new quota, even though they improve their sales for the year.

Producing a particular behavior in others through offering incentives and threatening punishment depends upon constantly increasing the

value and attractiveness of the incentive to compensate for previously satisfied needs or upon constantly increasing the severity of the threatened punishment to overcome the growing ability to endure hardship. The *chief problem* with both fear and incentive motivation is that the individual whose behavior is the focus of the motivation effort is not in control. This means that someone else must give constant attention to keep the person moving. For sales managers, the prospect of providing all the motivation for all the salespeople in the organization is depressing. How can sales managers know what will motivate so many different people? How can they find out what specific rewards will appeal to them, or what punishment they will fear enough to produce the desired behavior? Fortunately, there is an answer.

Attitude Motivation. Attitude motivation operates on the concept that the only lasting and uniformly effective motivation is the personal motivation that emanates from the internal structure of the individual. It is based on a strong self-image and a belief in the possibility of success. Attitude motivation is self-motivation. It is also referred to as intrinsic motivation. All great salespeople inherently possess this powerful, internal drive. Self-motivation can be shaped and molded, but it cannot be taught.[20]

Self-motivation is the result of the choices made by individuals in response to conditioning influences. Fear and self-doubt are the habitual attitudes of some people, but others choose, instead, to respond to life positively. For example, some salespeople who are told they're too inexperienced decide that they are and always will be. Then they wait for someone to tell them what to do. They are motivated to act only when someone else provides an external stimulus. Others choose to remain "too inexperienced" and use this excuse to manipulate others to help them or do things for them. However, others respond to the statement by choosing to believe that their condition is temporary. They strive to grow and prove their worth. As a result, they are willing and eager to try new activities, stretch their imaginations, and attempt new goals. They do not wait for someone else to motivate them; they are always reaching out for new experiences. These salespeople are self-motivated. What you are, then, is not entirely a result of what happens to you. *What you are is a result of how you react to what happens to you, and your reactions are a matter of choice.*

It's All a Matter of Perspective

Two salesmen fell on hard times and ended up broke in a small town in Montana. They needed money to move on and learned that the town paid $20 each for wolf pelts. They sensed the opportunity. That night they set out with a couple of clubs and some borrowed supplies and made camp in the distant hills. They were no sooner asleep than one was startled by an eerie howl. He crawled outside the tent to find himself surrounded by hundreds of snarling wolves. Back into the tent he crawled and shook his buddy. "Wake up!" he cried. "Wake up! We're rich!"– It's all a matter of perspective![21]

The advantages of attitude motivation are the opposites of the disadvantages of fear and incentive motivation:

1. Attitude motivation is *internal*. Because attitudes come from within, the salesperson does not need to wait for an outside stimulus to make appropriate choices and take action. Lack of outside stimulus is a problem only for those who want someone else to take responsibility for their behavior.

2. Attitude motivation is *permanent*. An attitude, once thoroughly established, continues to operate on an automatic basis until you do something to alter it. Self-motivation is the only kind of motivation that can be sustained over a long period of time despite setbacks, uncontrollable environmental problems, and other people's actions. It cannot be developed overnight, but it cannot be destroyed by isolated obstacles.

Attitude Motivation Through Goal Setting

The single most important tool for developing self-motivation is a program of personal goals. A personal goals program creates desire—one of the most powerful emotions operating in human experience. Desire cannot always be explained or defended to the satisfaction of others, but people who possess desire sometimes produce amazing feats of achievement. If you want to be able to choose where you will go with your sales effort, and how you will get there, you need clear goals and strategies. Only then will you have the power to direct your efforts.[22]

Figure 6.2 is the Million Dollar Personal Success Plan that Paul J. Meyer, founder and chairman of the board of SMI International, developed for his own use at the age of nineteen. It provides a workable plan for achieving success in selling.

Crystallized Thinking. You must know what you want to achieve. If your goals are hazy and poorly defined, you cannot plan concrete action steps for their achievement. You must write down and date your goals. Gary Bachelor, a national sales trainer and consultant, says it is absolutely necessary to write down your goals. Monitoring your status keeps you focused.[23] Without specific action plans, much of your time and effort is wasted.

The Million Dollar
Personal Success Plan

THE MILLION DOLLAR PERSONAL SUCCESS PLAN

by *Paul J. Meyer*

FOUNDER & CHAIRMAN OF THE BOARD
SMI INTERNATIONAL, INC.
WACO, TEXAS

I - Crystallize Your Thinking

Determine what specific goal you want to achieve. Then dedicate yourself to its attainment with unswerving singleness of purpose, the trenchant zeal of a crusader.

II - Develop a Plan for Achieving Your Goal, and a Deadline for Its Attainment

Plan your progress carefully: hour-by-hour, day-by-day, month-by-month. Organized activity and maintained enthusiasm are the well-springs of your power.

III - Develop a Sincere Desire for the Things You Want in Life

A burning desire is the greatest motivator of every human action. The desire for success implants "success consciousness" which; in turn, creates a vigorous and ever-increasing "habit of success."

IV - Develop Supreme Confidence in Yourself and Your Own Abilities

Enter every activity without giving mental recognition to the possibility of defeat. Concentrate on your strengths, instead of your weaknesses ... on your powers, instead of your problems.

V - Develop a Dogged Determination to Follow Through on Your Plan, Regardless of Obstacles, Criticism or Circumstances or What Other People Say, Think or Do

Construct your Determination with Sustained Effort, Controlled Attention, and Concentrated Energy.
OPPORTUNITIES never come to those who wait ... they are captured by those who dare to ATTACK.

A Plan of Action with Deadlines. A written plan of action keeps you on track and headed toward the achievement of your goals. You know exactly what to do next. A written plan also reveals conflicts between various goals so that you can plan ahead and make a reasonable schedule for the time and resources needed to reach all your goals. Deadlines provide you with the needed time frame for achieving your goals. They give you something to aim for.[24] Because most of us now use such a small percentage of our real potential, target dates serve the purpose of drawing out more potential and using it to bring desired goals into being. Deadlines help you maintain a positive attitude of expectancy toward goals achievement. They eliminate distractions and help you to think creatively.

Sincere Desire. A burning desire to achieve the goals you want often makes the difference between a *wish* and a *goal*. A *wish* is something you would like to have but are not willing to invest enough time or effort in to achieve; a *goal* is something you want so intensely that you will exert whatever effort is needed to reach it. The more goals you achieve, the more desire you develop. The greater your desire, the more you can achieve. Desire is an ascending spiral of success.

Supreme Confidence. Success demands supreme confidence in yourself and your ability. Self-confidence enables you to undertake challenging goals and believe you can succeed. Self-confidence lets you see problems as opportunities and obstacles as stepping-stones to success. Self-confidence builds credibility for the salesperson so that the buyer is open to considering the solutions suggested. Self-confidence makes it easy to ask for the order—not once, but again and again until the sale is closed successfully. The secret to developing this kind of confidence is a growing list of goals accomplished. Each time you succeed in reaching a goal you have set and worked toward, you gain added belief in your own capability to achieve. Confidence in your own personal ability is the greatest source of security you can possess.

Dogged Determination. Determination to stick to your plan of action until your goal is achieved is an outgrowth of desire and confidence. When you have a burning desire to achieve your goals, you are not easily swayed by others' thoughtless comments, by the disapproval of someone who does not understand your goals, or the active opposition of those who fear to be compared with you in either effort or results. Determination is the quality that enables you to continue calling on a difficult prospect until you close the sale. Determination gives you the creative freedom to discover new tactics for achieving your goal when your first effort fails and to think up more ideas until you discover a way that works.

All of these success essentials are interdependent. Use of each increases your power to use the others. Success in any one intensifies your belief in the others. Self-motivation is the only real and lasting motivation. Its development is your responsibility. The company and the sales manager can provide a climate in which self-motivation is easier to develop and operate, *but even the most negative climate cannot demotivate you without your permission.*

SUCCESS AND THE TOTAL PERSON

Organizations emphasize that their employees are essential to corporate success. They especially stress salespeople's contributions to organizational success because of the direct relationship between the daily results salespeople produce and the income that is a prime factor in the achievement of many organizational goals. However, organizations seldom pay much attention to what constitutes success for an individual. Too often success for salespeople is measured only in terms of the amount of sales generated; furthermore, the same criterion seems to be applied as a measure of the worth of the people themselves. This narrow view of success has been responsible for destroying the self-confidence of untold numbers of people. An understanding of what really constitutes success frees individuals to become all that their potential allows.

One of the most comprehensive definitions of success is this: "*Success is the progressive realization of worthwhile, predetermined, personal goals.*"[25] This definition is especially applicable to salespeople, who can begin their careers with relatively little training compared to that required of other professionals. Because success is *progressive*, a beginning salesperson can be successful immediately just by choosing to pursue goals that are personally fulfilling and then beginning to work toward them. Obviously, such a beginning is not made at the level expected of a master salesperson with long experience but at a level consistent with present reality. When salespeople learn this truth, they have the patience to study, learn the art of selling, and practice their skills.

Too many people fall into the same erroneous thinking that organizations often follow in measuring success. Those "worthwhile, predetermined goals" must involve more than money and position or the success that is achieved is likely to be hollow. Student athletes, excited by the acclaim of peers, alumni, and press, must often be reminded of this truth. Mike Singletary, former all-pro middle linebacker for the Chicago Bears, is a much sought after speaker by Christian youth groups all over the country. In his motivational and inspirational talks, Singletary encourages his young audiences to develop their potential in all areas of life, not just their athletic skills. Likewise, salespeople who concentrate only on career success and neglect other areas of life find their lives less than happy. Money and position are fairly low on the hierarchy of needs that all people experience. For this reason, *goals must be set in every area of life:* physical and health, mental and educational, family and home, spiritual and ethical, social and cultural, financial and career. Total personal growth in these areas is effectively pictured in Exhibit 6.6 as spokes on a wheel. If some spokes are uneven, the wheel that represents total life achievement is not round. The ride is bumpy, and the passenger feels dissatisfaction and a vague sense of uneasiness or unhappiness. Unmet needs prevent the enjoyment of achievements in other areas. Monetary success means little to the salesperson whose family life is shattered, health ruined, or the respect of friends lost. All areas of life must be included in a plan for becoming a "total person."

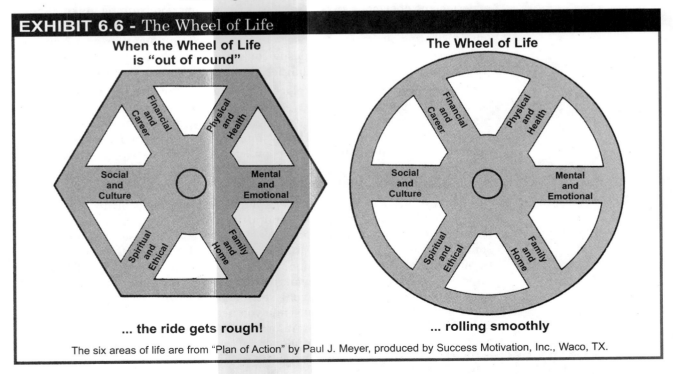

EXHIBIT 6.6 - The Wheel of Life

When the Wheel of Life is "out of round"

Financial and Career · Physical and Health · Social and Culture · Mental and Emotional · Spiritual and Ethical · Family and Home

... the ride gets rough!

The Wheel of Life

Financial and Career · Physical and Health · Social and Culture · Mental and Emotional · Spiritual and Ethical · Family and Home

... rolling smoothly

The six areas of life are from "Plan of Action" by Paul J. Meyer, produced by Success Motivation, Inc., Waco, TX.

This definition of success also implies that success has different meanings for different people and that not every salesperson belongs in a particular organization selling a specific product or service. To succeed, salespeople must market a product or service in which they *personally believe*. Selling a product that seems worthless or even damaging to the prospect prevents the salesperson from sincerely offering to help prospects solve their problems or fulfill their needs.

Once salespeople know what they want from a selling career and dedicate themselves to achieving those goals, the responsibility for reaching success is largely in their own hands. Too many people confuse *action with progress and effort with results*. Trying hard does not guarantee success. Success comes as a result of determining the desired goals, finding out what activity is required to reach those goals, and then completing those actions based on a personal commitment to oneself. *Real success never comes by accident.*

SUMMARY

Preparing for success in a sales career includes three areas of special importance: product knowledge, sales force automation, and motivation and goal setting. Although your company assists in each of these areas, the primary responsibility rests with you, the salesperson.

Product knowledge includes knowledge of the entire industry or field as well as specific knowledge about your product or service. It should include information about the performance of the product, how it is manufactured, the company's distribution system, service offered in support, the competition, and the company that makes or markets the product.

A generation of salespeople has arrived with computer skills that were unknown to most of the sales world just a decade ago. The sales industry is now experiencing enormous growth in sales force automation training. As companies downsize and trim staff people, sales forces are being forced to do more administrative activities themselves. Sales force automation and computer technology help increase a salesperson's personal productivity, internal and external communications capabilities, and transaction-processing efficiency.

Positioning refers to the place a product occupies in customers' minds relative to competing offerings. Once a position is selected, product, price, place, and promotion strategies are designed to reinforce the desired position. Develop a marketing-mix strategy built around several features that are known to be important to your prospects. And then put together an Integrated Marketing Communication strategy that reinforces those attributes in the customer's mind.

Motivation—the force that keeps you in action—comes primarily from one of three sources: fear, incentive, and attitude. Both fear and incentives used as motivating forces are limited in effectiveness because they depend on someone else as a source. Attitudes as a basis for self-motivation provide a permanent source of inspiration, intention, and initiative. One of the most important support systems available for self-motivation is setting goals for personal success. Successful goal setting begins with crystallized thinking about what is important to you. Then you need to develop a plan of action with deadlines for achievement. Reinforce your plan of action with desire for achievement and supreme confidence in your ability to succeed. Continue to act with determination, and success is within your reach.

QUESTIONS FOR THOUGHT AND DISCUSSION

1. What contribution can business school courses make to success in selling? How much academic work in sales or marketing is necessary to guarantee success in professional selling?

2. Does the company that hires you have any responsibility for preparing you for sales success? If so, what specific types of knowledge, information, or other input is the company's responsibility?

3. Name at least four areas of product knowledge that are important for salespeople.

4. What advantage does knowledge of the competition's offerings provide for the salesperson?

5. What would you do about product knowledge if you were hired to sell a highly technical product for which you have little background or understanding?

6. Sales force automation can help increase a salesperson's effectiveness in at least three distinct ways. Discuss each one and give an example to illustrate.

7. Explain how fear and incentives are used as sources of motivation. Can you give an example from your own experience of how both of these were used by someone else in an attempt to motivate you?

8. What limits the effectiveness of fear and incentives as motivating forces?

9. What are the advantages of attitudes as a basis of motivation?

10. Explain how goal setting affects self-motivation.

11. How does a personal goals program produce self-confidence? What is the value of self-confidence to salespeople?

ACTIVITIES

1. There are now a number of sites that offer online Customer Relationship Management (CRM) functions. You can literally have CRM access from almost anywhere. These sites virtually eliminate the need for software. These services also offer the ability to access your data from a Palm Pilot or with Microsoft Outlook. Check out any one of these four Web sites and report back to your instructor the types of information available. This would make a great term paper topic as well.

   www.sales.com
   www.upshot.com
   www.salesforce.com
   www.salesnet.com

2. Interview a successful salesperson about the importance of product knowledge. Ask how that person acquired product knowledge initially, how much help the company gave, and how much time was required to become familiar enough with the product to feel fully prepared to answer prospects' questions. Inquire also about how that salesperson keeps product knowledge current. Write a brief report of your interview.

Case Study
CASE 6.1

Ted Ransom has been one of the top salespeople for the industrial division of Islander Paint and Varnish Companies for the past ten years. His territory covers the New England industrial area. He is respected by his clients as an authority on finishes of all kinds. He likes prospecting and making cold calls, and his obvious product knowledge pays handsome dividends in the form of a growing customer list.

When he read in the financial section of the newspaper about the opening of a new firm, ElecMotor, in the Boston area, Ted was right on the job with a call on the company. When he told the purchasing agent that he sold industrial paints, he had a pleasant surprise. "Talk about good timing," the purchasing agent said. "I was talking to our production manager about a line of mini-motors that is going into production in a few weeks, and he said we needed to talk to some paint salespeople pretty soon. Let me see if he is available."

When Ted met the production manager, Dan Miller, he was glad to learn that they wanted a soft green paint for the motor housing, a color that would complement the company trademark. Ted's all-purpose paint came in the exact shade they desired, and his knowledgeable presentation brought him a nice order. The order went through promptly and delivery was made in five days. Ted planned to follow up with Dan the next time he was in Boston, but Dan called in less than two weeks with a disturbing report. They had applied the paint, but during testing, Dan reported, as soon as the motors began to heat up, the paint peeled off every one.

"Every one?" Ted asked incredulously.

"Yes, every one." Then Dan added, "I guess my decision to buy was too quick. I'd better talk to some other paint companies. And I'm returning the full shipment to you for a refund."

1. Is there a possibility that Ted's product knowledge is less complete than it should be? Remember his good reputation in this area.

2. Is it possible that a prompt follow-up service call could have saved the account? How?

3. The production manager has declared his intention to return the paint for a refund. What should Ted do at this point?

CASE 6.2

Debbie Adamek had just taken a job as a manufacturer's representative for a new line of cosmetics being introduced by Grayson's Laboratories. The new line, called Capture, was designed to appeal especially to teenagers. Debbie's job was to call on wholesale distributors and chains to obtain orders for distribution to their retail outlets. Grayson's had conducted an extensive media advertising campaign and anticipated considerable demand for the new products.

Debbie, along with other salespeople who were to introduce the new line, was given a week's intensive training on the new products. Frankly, Debbie was bored. She had taken this job because she wanted to get away from the classroom scene, the load of reading she had hated in college, and people telling her what to do. She thought selling cosmetics would be easy because she considered herself an expert makeup artist; she knew exactly how to use every kind of aid imaginable to take advantage of her best points. Customers should know just by looking at her that any cosmetics she had to offer would obviously be the top of the line.

Before she made her first sales call, Debbie experimented with every item in the new line. She became familiar with the color-matching scheme and learned the best way to apply each item. Imagine her shock when her first prospect began asking questions: Is it necessary to observe any precautions about temperature where the products are stored? What percentage of customers are likely to experience adverse skin reactions to the products? What kind of customer response was received when the products were field-tested? Will users experience any special difficulties in extreme hot weather or extreme cold weather? What cooperative advertising plan is available? How much advertising is planned for this state, in what media, and when?

It took only two or three days for Debbie to come to the sobering realization that she didn't know enough about her product to sell it to wholesalers.

1.   What are Debbie Adamek's options at this point?

2.   Would Debbie's type of product knowledge be adequate for another selling situation?

3.   Can someone who begins a sales career on such a naive basis achieve success? What would success require?

What Causes Low Sales

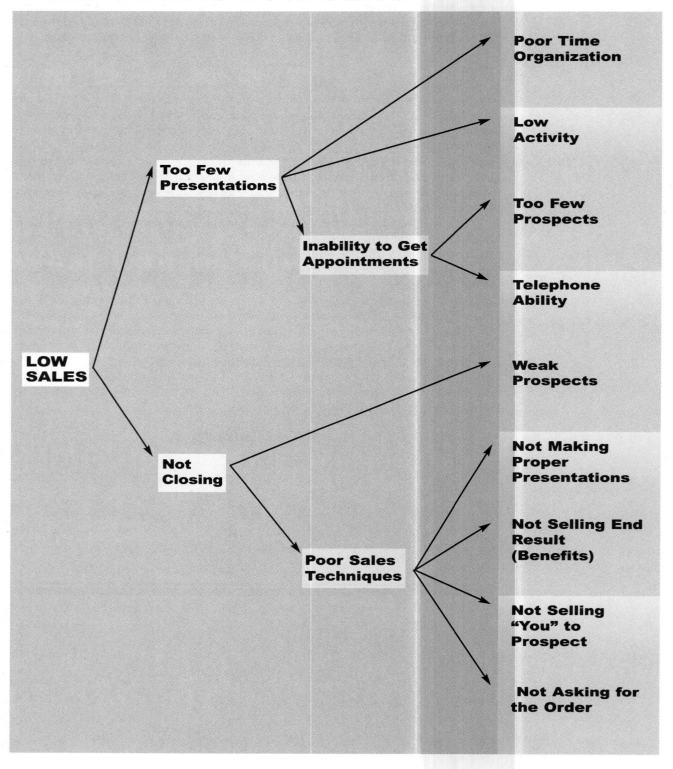

LOW SALES

Too Few Presentations

Not Closing

Inability to Get Appointments

Poor Sales Techniques

Poor Time Organization

Low Activity

Too Few Prospects

Telephone Ability

Weak Prospects

Not Making Proper Presentations

Not Selling End Result (Benefits)

Not Selling "You" to Prospect

Not Asking for the Order

CHAPTER 7

Becoming a Master Prospector

LEARNING OBJECTIVES

* To understand the nature and importance of prospecting.

* To develop an awareness of who is a prospect.

* To learn how to qualify prospects.

* To become familiar with different prospecting methods.

* To see the importance of managing prospect information accurately and consistently.

* To see the value of computer technology in the management of prospect information.

THE CONCEPT OF PROSPECTING

Becoming a master salesperson begins with becoming a master prospector. A salesperson without prospects is as out of business as a surgeon without patients. Great salespeople ask smart questions, know how to close a deal, and have excellent follow-through. But the one trait they demonstrate more consistently than any other is constant prospecting enhanced by creative approaches that build value and relationships. They see opportunities everywhere and they know it's not just the numbers – but the numbers are what count.[1] Mastering the basics of prospecting puts you at the top. Competent prospecting saves time, and time is money.

"I'd rather be a master prospector than be a wizard of speech and have no one to tell my story to."

-Paul J. Meyer

If your closing ratio is lower than you like, your major problem may be that you don't have enough good prospects and not that you are a poor closer. If you see enough people, sooner or later you sell to someone, but selling to one of three is better than selling to only one of twenty. Confucius taught, "Dig the well before you thirst." To succeed in professional selling, locate qualified prospects in advance—before you need them. Develop multiple sources from which names of prospects flow constantly. A fertile river valley quickly becomes a desert when the river dries up.

Prospects are everywhere. The key to successful prospecting is learning where the best prospects are and how to reach them. Some prospects are merely leads. You do not know enough about them to make a presentation that appeals to their real needs or even to determine whether they need your product or service. Other prospects are obviously custom-made for what you offer. They could benefit from your product or service, they have the money to buy it, and they possess the authority to make a buying decision. When you have such a prospect, successful selling is both possible and enjoyable.

Generating leads is akin to building the Alaskan pipeline. So how do you build the pipeline and get that oil flowing? Exhibit 7.1 highlights six specific ways that work for Janelle Patterson, Honeywell service account specialist.[2]

EXHIBIT 7.1 - How One Salesperson Keeps Her Pipeline Flowing With Prospects

Janelle Patterson

1. Spent days digging through the archives of everyone who had ever purchased Honeywell's products or services out of their Washington, D.C., location in the previous 15 years.

2. Targets companies via the Internet. Janelle looks at what markets Honeywell has been successful in and then researches those types of companies and learns from their Web sites. The Internet allows her to do her homework before she calls.

3. Acquires a lot of leads from Honeywell's field technicians. They find out first hand if a customer has a service contract. If not, it's a lead for her.

4. Practices competitive sightings – If Janelle sees a competitor's van at a building, she knows that prospect uses Honeywell's type of services. She then calls and asks if she can send them her business card in case they decide to switch vendors.

5. Gets involved in her community – She may teach a course, coach a team, sponsor a charitable event or join a civic, nonprofit or networking group. The possibilities are endless.

6. Uses current customers – She says her existing client base offers the strongest opportunities to help generate new leads. Janelle keeps an open line of communication by giving regular and newsworthy feedback that serves to further endear her to clients.

QUALIFYING THE PROSPECT

Cultivate prospects who
pass the *MADDEN* test:

M—oney

A—pproachable

D—esire

D—ecision-maker

E—ligible

N—eed

Establish a pattern for prospecting. You can waste a monumental amount of time calling on leads who are not prospects for your product or service. When all you have is a name and address, you have only a possibility of developing a prospect. Figure 7.1 illustrates the process of moving a name from the status of lead to that of qualified prospect. Truly qualified prospects are those who are exactly right for you because they possess the necessary characteristics that make them logical buyers for your product or service. Applying a detailed screening process to each lead greatly increases your chances of successfully completing a sale.[3] One good definition of the best prospect is this:

A *Class 'A' qualified prospect* is one to whom you have been referred by a person the prospect respects, one who has the ability to make a buying decision and to pay for the product or service, and one about whom you have all the personal information you need to make a good presentation.[4]

FIGURE 7.1

Action of the Salesperson
in Developing Leads into
Qualified Prospects

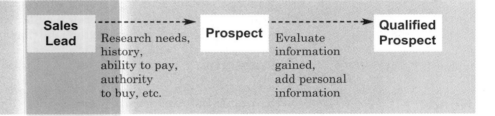

Money

Separate the talkers from those who actually have the money to buy. Does the individual prospect have enough money to pay for your product or service? Is a corporate prospect solvent enough to pay its bills? If your company subscribes to a credit-rating service such as Dun & Bradstreet, you may wish to check the prospect's standing. You will save yourself and your company many headaches by determining a prospect's ability to pay before spending your time and energy gaining a client who may quickly become more of a liability than an asset.

Approachable

Can you get an appointment? The president or chairperson of the board of a large company may grant an initial interview only to a senior level executive in your company. Do not hesitate to ask for such help when there is real possibility of gaining an important client. Individual prospects are often approachable only if you are willing to fit your time schedule into the unique time needs of their business or profession. Be flexible. Your chances of success increase if you and the prospect meet at a time that is mutually convenient and comfortable.

Desire

The prospect may be quite satisfied with a present supplier and have no desire to change. You can sell such a prospect only if you *create or discover a desire* that will motivate the prospect to move from the present supplier to you. The prospect may desire to save money, to enjoy a wider variety of services, to receive more dependable service or quicker deliveries—all of which may have been the basis for selecting the present supplier in the first place. A desire to own the product or use the service is also important. A person without such desire is not a prospect.

Decision Maker   Be sure the person you visit is the decision maker. No matter what enthusiasm for your product or service you are able to create in one manager, if that manager does not have the authority to sign the order, you will be forced to repeat the entire sales process with another person. If you are not sure who makes the decisions in a particular company, start the sales process with the head of the company. If you do reach the CEO or COO conducting business may be easier than you think. They earned the top spot by making tough calls and can appreciate the tough call you've just made. Let that executive tell you who to see. A survey made by McGraw-Hill's Laboratory of Advertising Performance discovered that over 90 percent of purchase *decision-makers* interviewed had not been called on by a salesperson within the previous two months.[5] Obviously, salespeople spend a great deal of time talking to people who are not in a position to make a buying decision. When you first contact a prospect, ask who else will be involved in making the decision and set up an appointment with all individuals at one time.

Eligible   Determine whether the prospect is eligible to buy from you. Some prospects are already committed to a competitor and cannot buy from you. Others need a product with greater or smaller capacity than you can offer or a service that is more or less extensive than yours. Some prospects for insurance obviously cannot pass the necessary physical exam or are beyond the set age limit.

Need   Determine the need level for your product or service. To accomplish this you must ask questions and listen carefully to determine what the prospects buying motives are in order to uncover their specific needs, and then decide if your company has the products that can effectively satisfy those needs. Ask yourself – will the business your company gains be worth the amount of time you must invest to get it?

METHODS OF PROSPECTING

Does the mere idea of prospecting for new customers sound difficult, time-consuming, or boring to you? It doesn't have to be any of those if you use your head instead of your feet. Always keep in mind that you need customers to replace those lost through attrition factors, including:

Develop a prospecting consciousness—a prospecting awareness; it is the key to your success in professional selling. Prospecting is to successful selling what breathing is to living. There are prospects by the millions if you open your eyes and see them.

1. Customer's company goes out of business.
2. Competitor takes client from you.
3. Customer moves or dies.
4. Merger with another company causes a change of suppliers.
5. Customer-salesperson relationship deteriorates.

In addition, you need new customers for new products as well as new users for existing products.

Practice in prospecting invariably develops skill, provided the methods of practice are correct. Incorrect practice on a musical instrument produces only a greater ability to make errors. So it is with prospecting; aimless, hit-or-miss prospecting, no matter how much of it is done, generally leads only to failure. To streamline the job of prospecting and produce better results, master a number of different methods and use the ones that work best for your particular situation. Exhibit 7.2 summarizes eleven prospecting techniques that are discussed in this chapter.

Referrals

The use of referrals is one of the most powerful prospecting techniques. WorldCom, a major telecommunications company, suggests that as much as fifty percent of its sales comes from referrals. A *referral* is a name given to you as a lead by a customer, a friend, or even a prospect who did not buy but felt good about you and your product. The factor that makes this prospecting method so valuable is its *leverage*. Until the proper time to use that leverage arrives, a referral is just a lead like any other.

When you have qualified a referred lead by securing all the information needed to show that this person fits the pattern of prospects you call upon, you are then ready to use the valuable leverage that is yours by reason of the referral. The people who provide referrals should be willing either to make an initial contact for you or to allow you to use their names. Referrals work because people are naturally fearful or skeptical of strangers, especially those who try to persuade them to make some kind of decision. People accept you and your product more readily if someone they know and respect has sent you to see them.

EXHIBIT 7.2 - Eleven Useful Prospecting Techniques

1. *Referrals*—Names given to you by a customer, friend, or someone else who feels good about you and your product.

2. *Center of Influence*—A person who believes in what you are selling, influences others, and is willing to give you names and help to qualify them.

3. *Group Prospecting*—Bringing a number of people together at the same time and place and capturing their names and other information about them. Some examples are trade shows, speaking engagements, and meetings.

4. *Planned Cold Calling*—Calling on a lead without first making an appointment and knowing very little or perhaps nothing about the person.

5. *Direct Mail*—Choosing a mailing list of individuals, businesses, or professional people who appear to be at least partially qualified and sending them a communication that requests a reply.

6. *Observation*—Prospects are everywhere, so keep your eyes and ears open. Scan local newspapers, trade publications, and the financial pages of major news magazines and papers.

7. *Civic Groups*—Membership in various civic groups gives the salesperson opportunities to meet people who can become prospects for a product or service.

8. *Networking*—Salespeople from different businesses share information about the sales climate and exchange prospect information.

9. *Directories*—Directories help identify possible prospects and provide information to determine whether they actually have the potential to become customers.

10. *Company-initiated Prospecting*—A company may provide initial prospecting for salespeople. This frees them to have more face-to-face interviews with qualified prospects.

11. *Web Sites*—A company can market its products and find customers utilizing the power of the Internet.

Salespeople do not have more referrals because they don't ask or because they don't know how to ask. The fear of rejection is probably the reason many salespeople avoid asking for referrals. One way to overcome the fear of rejection is to make asking for referrals an automatic, habitual part of every sales presentation. When you believe in the product or service you sell, you should feel that you have done your customers a favor by introducing them to it. Offer your customers the opportunity to do their associates the favor of introducing them to your product or service.

Gaining More Referred Leads. If you don't know how to ask for referrals take the time and make the effort to develop this important skill. There are two reasons why people do not immediately give you referrals. The first is that they find it difficult to think of names to give you. Basically, they just do not want to exert the mental effort to decide who might be interested. The second reason is they consider themselves to be "conscientious objectors" – they say they just do not give referrals. Sales professionals estimate that 20 percent of clients *won't give* referrals no matter what you do. Another 20 percent of clients *will give* referrals no matter you do. It's the other 60 percent where a plan of action is essential.[6]

A small percentage of salespeople are loved by their customers. Why do these few enjoy the admiration and trust of their clients? These sales reps come across as helpers and as both problem finders and solution providers. They are welcomed because of the reputation that preceded them and because of the obvious spirit of caring these salespeople show from the first moment of contact.[7] Exhibit 7.3 illustrates a step-by-step approach to use when asking for referrals. Practice and rehearse it with clients who think your great or have given you referrals in the past. Customers think of themselves as professionals and they like to buy from professionals.

EXHIBIT 7.3 - A Seven-Step Approach for Gaining More Referred Leads

1. Ask for referrals with respect. Open the dialogue something like this, "I have an important question I want to ask you." It will capture your client's attention and indicate to them just how significant this is to you.

2. Ask for their help. Soften them up by saying, "I'm trying to build my business and I would value and appreciate your help."

3. Explain the course of action you are proposing in detail. Tell them what will happen if they give you a referral, and let them know that you will remain professional and report back to them.

4. Gain their permission to explore. You might give them another softening statement: "I can understand how you feel." Then go on to say, "I was wondering if we could agree on who you know who might also benefit from the types of products I have to offer. Are you comfortable with that?"

5. Narrow their focus by describing the prospect profile you are looking for. Once you have been given names, make a first step toward qualifying them. Ask your client, "if you were in my place, who would you see first?" Ask why. Then find out which one to contact next.

6. Report back to them. Whenever you receive referrals, be sure to report back to them on the result of your interviews with these prospects.

7. Be sure to thank the clients for giving you referrals regardless of whether they did or did not buy from you.

The Million-Dollar Referral

Michael Twining, sales rep for a large distributor of agricultural products, has a very clever way to secure more referrals. Whenever he gets a referral by an existing customer he quickly mails a handwritten thank-you note and includes a lottery ticket with the message – Thanks a million for the referral. I hope you win a million! It costs very little and always creates a lot of good will and laughs on his next visit with that customer. Michael says and, "it almost always gets me one more referral."[8]

A Referral Call to Take Action. The referral call to action gives your clients clear-cut steps to take to help you make contact with a person they are recommending.[9] A referral call to action includes:

- The kind of prospects you are looking for. This serves as a way for your clients to think of specific people.
- What are you prepared to do and why it is beneficial for both your clients and the referred leads they give you?
- How you would like to get in touch with those leads.

There is one guiding principle in asking for a referral: Place the focus on your client and the lead, not on you. Be sure to express your appreciation for the client's continuing relationship with your company. If the client knows of others who might benefit from your assistance, say you would be pleased to help those individuals meet their needs. Real caring is an attitude that is conveyed to customers. You can't fake it, at least not for long. People buy from people they like and trust and, in turn, provide referred leads because you have earned their trust. Here is one specific statement that can be used to make the client feel comfortable about giving you names:

- *"I'm not asking you to recommend me or my product. I am merely asking you to give me an introduction to some people you know. I will talk to them, as I have with you, in a professional manner and give them an opportunity to learn about me and my company."*

What to Ask For: The Issue of Control. The principal thing you are asking for in a referral is for your client to make it easy for you to contact the prospect. The big variable is how this contact should be made. What to ask for depends upon your client's need for control of the situation:

- Some customers want to handle the communication themselves. This is great because they are making the contact for you and will tell you what to expect.
- Others want minimal involvement. They prefer that you initiate the contact.
- Still others may have very specific instructions on what they want you to do or say with their referrals.

The best way to find out how much control your client wishes to have is to simply ask, using an *alternate of choice* type question: "Would you prefer that I call Mr. Singletary, or would you want to personally call and talk to him on my behalf?"

When to Ask for a Referral. Make asking for referrals a part of the selling cycle. A logical time to ask for referrals is right after the close. A customer who buys is sold on you and likely to feel good about giving you names. Sometimes, however, a customer wants to use the product or service before giving any referrals. Salespeople are taught to go after referrals at the wrong time. They start asking for referrals before the ink on the contract is even dry. Marty Levenson has developed what he calls *The Referral Principle*.[10] You can't ask for referrals; you must earn them. The best referrals come from satisfaction, not a signature on a contract. Good referrals come about at those "moments" when the customer is particularly pleased with either your service or the performance of your product. It's at these moments that they are ready to tell the world about you and your company. This is the time to ask for referrals because the customer is motivated to go to work for you. A referral climate has been created!

Centers of Influence

The best sales tool you can have is a person who believes in what you are selling, is influential with a number of people who are potential customers for you, and is willing to give you the names of these people and help you qualify them. Such a person is called a *center of influence*. When you have several centers of influence, you always have plenty of prospects. Centers of influence are especially valuable because the names they give you are at least partially qualified prospects and more than mere leads.

This method of prospecting is a specific application of the referral method. In both methods, you begin with a satisfied customer or with a person whose interest in you and your product has developed to the point of desiring to help you make additional sales. The important distinction between the two is that the center of influence can give you many more prospects and is both willing and able to provide new names on a continuing basis; in addition, people respect the center of influence to the extent that an introduction from this source virtually assures you of a sympathetic hearing.

Every community has people whose popularity, charisma, character, and leadership make them influential. Regardless of their personal financial position, they have earned the respect of many other people. As a result, their introductions carry a great deal of influence. Prospects are interested, or at least attentive, out of respect for the person who sent you. A center of influence may come from any one of a number of areas of life. You can find them among community leaders—social, political, business, cultural, or religious leaders. Cultivate their friendship, sell yourself to them, and ask them to help you. Centers of influence *may or may not* be actual customers of yours, but they must be sold on you and the value of the product or service you represent.

Consider a prominent individual active in the community where you sell. Getting that person on your team can open many doors that otherwise would remain closed to you. If an influential person is willing to write a letter, make a few phone calls, or give you a personal introduction, you are likely to find qualified and interested prospects. Think how you would react if such a person called you and said:

I had lunch this past week with Dennis Gentry, a business associate of mine. I think he is a person you would like to meet, and I told him about you. He will be calling you this week; I hope you will meet with him.

Centers of influence are one of the most valuable assets you can have as a salesperson. Follow up every lead they provide; then report your results to them and thank them for their help. Find a way you can show your gratitude by being of service to your centers of influence. A two-way relationship is rewarding to both parties.

Group Prospecting

Some companies use group prospecting with great success. The idea is to bring together a number of people, from eight to twenty or even more. The group may meet in a home, a conference room in a hotel, or in an office. The purpose is to inform prospects about the product or service. Network 2000, based in Kansas City and representing US Sprint nationwide, is one company that uses this technique successfully. They describe their service to a group and ask those who would be interested in exploring the value of the service to their own needs to sign a card asking a representative to call. Some prospects, however, sign up on the spot. A number of direct sales companies use this method for finding prospective

Yvette Kuester recruits and manages students who sell door-to-door

Yvette Kuester is a young professional. She has been a field sales manager for the Southwestern Company since graduation from college. Yvette has now been employed by Southwestern for the past three years and is responsible for recruiting, organizing and leading a sales organization of nearly $1 million in retail business during the summer months.

Yvette is from Creston, Nebraska, and is a graduate of the University of Nebraska. Her college major was advertising and public relations. During her freshman year of college, Yvette was looking for a summer opportunity that would challenge and reward her based on her own performance. A fellow student told her about the opportunity with the Southwestern Company.

The Southwestern Company is a Nashville-based marketer of books and software aimed at families through a unique sales program. All sales are made during the summer months by teams of college students who are recruited and trained during the school year. The students from a single college generally stay together and work as a team in one area. The typical student makes fifty or more cold calls a day.

Yvette was immediately successful. Her enthusiasm, work effort and persistence paid off her first summer with a personal profit of over $8,000 which is well above the company average of $5,600. She has increased her profits incrementally each summer throughout her college years. The summer after her senior year, "her money summer," she was one of the top five students out of over 3,000 student dealers with a personal profit of over $45,000.

The Southwestern Company recruits at 500 campuses throughout the United States, Canada, the United Kingdom, Ireland and France. Yvette continues to build her direct-selling organization as a field sales manager. Her organizational name is "F.O.R.C.E.," which is an acronym for "For Opportunity Rarely Comes Easy."

Yvette says, "In college Southwestern was like having my own mini-career. It was a blend of academics during the school year and real-world skills about business and management throughout the summer. I have been fortunate to have an opportunity to be exposed to many successful habits, attitudes and philosophies early in my career. Not many people have an opportunity of this kind until well into their adult life. The experience in recruiting, training and motivating sales people has given me valuable skills at a young age."

distributors or salespeople. Among the well-known organizations that use this approach are Tupperware, Amway, Shaklee, and PartyLite Inc. Companies that use party-plan selling not only expect to make sales at the parties but also hope to find prospects who will agree to host parties at which additional new prospective customers and party holders are likely to be present. The dynamics involved in this technique are powerful. As one person either expresses interest or agrees to buy, others jump on the bandwagon and take similar action.

A variation of this method is to look for groups of potential prospects and offer to be a *guest speaker*. Members of civic clubs like the Toastmasters, Kiwanis, Lions, and Optimists may be ideal prospects for you, and they are always looking for speakers who have information that would make them more productive or successful. If you establish your credibility and sincerity, you may be able to close your speech with a brief presentation of your product or service. If this is inappropriate, you will at least be given an introduction that tells what your business is. Be sure to meet as many members of the audience as possible before and after the meeting, ask for their business card, and give them yours. You may also be able to provide cards for those interested in learning about your product or service to sign to indicate that they want you to call. Because these people have heard you speak, they already feel they know you. If they were impressed enough to want you to call, you know you have a qualified prospect.

Planned Cold Calling

One prospecting method that is available to any salesperson is cold calling.[11] *Cold calling* is the procedure of approaching a business, office complex, or someone's home without an appointment and introducing yourself to whoever will talk to you. Cold calling can become an enjoyable part of your day if you accept

Golden Opportunities

Most salespeople would agree that cold calling is the toughest part of selling. But, at the same time, the rewards can be great. "When I started making cold calls I decided to call them warm calls because most prospects want to be treated with friendliness and in a positive manner," says Irby Stewart with Positive Communications in Thunder Bay, Ontario. Because he took this positive approach, Irby became the top salesperson across Canada selling Brian Tracy's two-day video seminars.

Recently he developed another point of view toward cold calls. It struck him that he should be calling them opportunity calls. That's what they really are. Viewing cold calls as golden opportunities gives him even greater incentive for selling to clients and prospects. Now go out and create some golden opportunities for yourself![12]

the reality of the situation. Each year 15 percent of all firms become dissatisfied with a supplier and want to change. This means that one of every seven cold calls you make a prospect is probably receptive to what you have to say.[13] Cold calling serves as an excellent supplement to other prospecting efforts if it is carefully planned for maximum effectiveness, and some firms, such as *The Southwestern Company, use it exclusively.* Here are some guidelines for cold calling:

Supplement Your Prospect List. Because cold calling is designed to augment your current prospect list, be careful that cold calls never take so much of your time that you neglect calling on qualified prospects and existing clients. Set aside a specific amount of time each week for cold calling but never at the expense of more profitable sales activity.

Preplan Cold Calls. Develop several effective door openers and experiment until you find which ones work best for you. Give the prospect something related to your product or service, such as a circular, newsletter, brochure, or calendar, or share an idea that can save the prospect time or money. Your door opener should be something that causes the prospect to remember you when you later call for an appointment to make a formal sales presentation.

Remain Enthusiastic. Set a goal to turn every cold call into a *warm call.* When you make cold calls, the person you should see is almost certainly not in or too busy to receive you. If you remain enthusiastic in spite of such responses, you make a positive impression on the receptionist or secretary. You may actually get enough information to qualify prospects without meeting them. When you call again in person or by telephone, you will be remembered, and receptionists and secretaries exert a great deal of influence on who gets to see the boss. Impress them with your professionalism and you will find those inner doors to the buyers open more easily. Keep rejections in their proper perspective, and you will eventually benefit from cold call prospecting.

Direct Mail

Surveys show that consumers tend to favorably respond to direct mail, with eighty percent saying they sift through mail received and read what is of interest. Also, forty percent said they sometimes like reading direct mail if it proves to be useful in obtaining product information.[14]

The success of direct-mail prospecting depends upon the management of mailing lists. Some lists are better than others, and the best investment of your time and budget demands careful planning and analysis. The product or service you sell has a great deal to do with what kind of list you use. The goal is a list of people or businesses that are already at least partially qualified as prospects. If you are selling heavy industrial machinery, using the residential telephone directory doesn't make much sense; using the membership list from a trade association whose members use the kind of machinery you sell would be much more profitable. If you are selling a product that appeals largely to home owners, the city directory might be a good starting place, but be sure to identify specific segments of the city so that you eliminate apartment complexes and neighborhoods that are largely rental property or for some other reason are unlikely to provide good leads. Exhibit 7.4 has some suggestions for sources of direct-mail lists.

EXHIBIT 7.4 - Suggested Sources for Building Direct-Mail Lists

– **Membership rosters:**
- Professional societies and trade associations (for example, medical, accountancy, manufacturers, air conditioning, electricians)
- Country clubs
- Civic clubs (for example, Kiwanis, Lions, Civitan, Optimist)
- Fraternal organizations
- Women's organizations (for example, Altrusa, AAUW, Junior League)
- Special-interest groups (for example, Audubon Society, garden clubs, environmental protection groups)

- Community business groups (for example, Chamber of Commerce, Jaycees, Business and Professional Women)

–**City directories**

–**Telephone books**
- (white or yellow pages, depending upon need)

–**Religious groups**

–**People you have done business with in the past**
- (for example, home repair or building, banking, auto service and repair)

Manage your database of direct-mail lists wisely. If you are using a computer to store lists, develop a coding system to show which types of lists produce the highest percentage of responses. Code the names of people who actually respond. Even if you do not sell to them immediately, they have some interest in your product or service and might become active prospects at some later date.[15]

One advantage of using direct mail for prospecting is that it opens new segments of the market to you. The U.S. Army developed a system of ZIP code analysis that pinpoints the demographics of young male Americans. Their database also includes every high school in the nation and indicates those from which a relatively high percentage of top high school graduates consider military service over college.[16] ZIP code direct-mail prospecting is also used by political organizations. *USA Today* reported that people in the New York City ZIP code 10021 gave nearly $1 million in political contributions within one year—more than 32 states combined.[17]   Although referrals produce a high percentage of appointments, they are likely to produce clients of the same income bracket or job type as the people who provided them. If you want prospects in a higher income bracket, direct mail may produce the first leads you need; referrals from customers developed from these leads can establish you into the new market segment.   Ron Knox, a 25-year veteran with Northwestern Mutual Life Insurance Company, wanted a systematic way of contacting existing clients and prospects on a regular basis. Ron sends out a cover letter attached to a newsletter to 400 clients and 100 prospects, four times a year. He has never received less than two *reply cards* back and often gets eight or more. Ron knows: (1) this database marketing tool provides useful information, a value-added benefit to his clients and prospects; (2) it keeps his name in front of them; and (3) it gives people the opportunity to say they have had a change in their situation and want to review their insurance needs.

Observation

No matter what other methods of prospecting you elect to use, your own keen powers of observation provide many of your best prospects. Keep your eyes and ears open because prospects are everywhere. The daily newspaper, for example, is an excellent source of prospects.   Exhibit 7.5 tells of one salesperson's success in using the newspaper for additional prospects and sales. Whether you sell paper clips, stone crushers, or fiber optic systems, scan the paper for pleasant personal items about people or businesses in your community. Wedding announcements, business promotions, reports of civic activities, winners of contests, lists of graduates, notices of new business openings, new partnerships or planned mergers—all these and many others focus your attention on people who may be prospects. Clip an item, attach a personal note of congratulation, and mail them to the person or company featured. These news items provide such good leads for certain purposes that even a newspaper's circulation department may use them for prospecting. The *Milwaukee Journal*, with a very high subscription rate for Metro Milwaukee households, assigns a sales representative in the circulation department to call all couples whose names appear in the wedding or engagement section of the paper to solicit their subscription to the *Journal*. Prospects are everywhere you look.

EXHIBIT 7.5 - Creative Observation in Prospecting

Marilyn Hooks, a telecommunications salesperson living in Euclid, Ohio, read about Gary Granger, president of a local company, whose recent successes had been outstanding. A story in the Cleveland Plain Dealer mentioned that Gary was a 1980 graduate of Case Western Reserve University. This gave Marilyn an idea! She obtained a copy of the 1980 yearbook of that University and cross-checked with the local telephone directory to see which of the graduates still lived in the Cleveland area.

Marilyn was successful in selling Gary a telephone communication system that would save his company $3,000 a month. As usual, she asked for referrals. But her keen observation and the initiative to make creative use of random information paid off in the personalized manner of her request. She asked Gary, "By the way, do you happen to know Bob Tight and Shirley Meggitt who were in your class at Western Reserve?" Gary did, and helped her arrange interviews with them. Marilyn sold both of them her service and eventually made sales to eight of the fourteen names she had found in the yearbook. A little extra effort and creativity paid rich dividends.

Read local newspapers and the trade magazines of the professions or industries in your target market. News of mergers, acquisitions, and expansions give you valuable ideas for developing new business. A company's decision to expand plant capacity or to diversify by seeking international markets might open the doors to you and your company. Richard Pluntron, manager of a Seattle commercial real estate firm, says he spends time each day online looking for business news or anything that will help his salespeople. Here are two sites Pluntron visits regularly:[18]

1. www.commercialsource.com - This is the official site of the National Association of Realtors. This gives us news and industry updates on the things we need to know.

2. www.seattletimes.com – The paper has an excellent local business section that we can gather solid business leads from. If any new building is being built, we need to know about it, and this is a good place to find out.

Joining Civic Groups

Membership in civic groups and other organizations can give you opportunities to meet people who are prospects for your product or service. Their meetings provide you with regular times to meet more people and to build relationships. Exhibit 7.6 lists some tips for using membership in civic clubs as prospecting opportunities.

In selecting groups to join, consider the kinds of prospects you need to meet. Then evaluate various groups to find which ones have members of the type you should meet. Choose organizations to which decision makers belong. Join a group whose purposes you can wholeheartedly support and one that will stimulate your own thinking and creativity. Look for ways you can assume a place of leadership in the organization, preferably in a position with high visibility so that you become known to most of the members as soon as possible. Perform your leadership role competently so that your name is automatically associated with excellence in the minds of all the members, and give unselfishly of yourself to the group. If you are interested only in what you can get from the group (prospects), other members will soon see through your facade of insincerity.

Set goals to meet a certain number of new people at each meeting and to *remeet*—or establish stronger relationships—with a certain number of others.

EXHIBIT 7.6 - Tips for Using Membership in Civic Clubs for Prospecting

1. Carefully select the groups you join.
2. Assume leadership responsibilities.
3. Work for positive visibility.
4. Set contact goals for each organization meeting.
5. Follow up with contacts.
6. Maintain an information file on the contacts made in each organization.
7. Use "remeet" goals to help you develop closer relationships with people.
8. Reach out to new members.
9. Use active listening to learn more about the financial goals and needs of others.
10. Look for appropriate opportunities for further business-oriented discussions.

Be especially attentive to newcomers; help them get acquainted. This gives you an opportunity both to meet new members and to strengthen your relationships with others. Keep an active file of the organization's members as you meet them and learn about them. You should *avoid active selling* at the meetings, but you may ask someone to tell you the best time to call to set up an appointment. Building relationships through these contacts lays the groundwork for active selling in the future. Listening to others at meetings pays much bigger dividends than advertising yourself or your company. Listening tells you what you need to know to turn contacts into real prospects.

Networking

Networking is the active cooperation between people in businesses to share information about the business climate, specific happenings in the business community, and prospects.[19] Networking incorporates the three C's—connecting, communicating, and cooperating. In a sample of 1,500 job hunters, statistics indicated that 61 percent of these individuals found employment through networks.[20]

In many cities, formal networking groups are organized specifically for the purpose of sharing business information. Alina Novak, founder of New York City's Networks Unlimited, calls such networking the planned acquisition of contacts for mutual support, the exchange of information,

Networking around the world

and the transaction of business. Members meet weekly and bring their business cards and sales brochures. Its 250 members, who are 95 percent women, are learning to use influence and power to accomplish their career goals. Such formal networking groups appeal to the increasing numbers of women who have been entering the selling profession because they often discover that they are excluded from the informal *good old boys' network* that their male counterparts have long operated and taken for granted. They had not necessarily been excluded because of any overt discrimination; the networking activity so often occurred in situations when women were not present. Now the value of the organizations has become obvious to both men and women, and many of the groups contain both men and women from the business world who find value in sharing information and ideas.[21]

Networks may be as large as the New York group or as small as a group organized by Peg Stanfield in San Francisco. The group she formed serves a small, specialized group of saleswomen, all of whom offer office products or services, including commercial office design and furnishings, phone systems, copiers, and moving services. Each member brings the names of three customers to meetings and passes them out to the group. Every two weeks, each member of the group receives thirty new leads.

One innovative way to gain information is an organization entitled LeTip International, which has over 400 chapters across the U.S. and Canada. Most of the members are salespeople who exchange tips and leads. Each chapter meets precisely for 75 minutes once a week between 7:16 and 8:31 a.m. You must attend 90 percent of the meetings and pass on at least two qualified leads a month—or else be terminated from the club. One particular member made six sales which he credits to receiving information directly from his chapter of LeTip.[22]

Sharing information and names of prospects makes good sense. For instance, if you are a realtor involved in a pending real estate development, it could be to your own advantage to alert a banker acquaintance who may prove helpful to your client in arranging financing. You benefit, your client benefits, and the banker has new business. When you regularly serve customers or clients with your product or service, you have opportunities to learn about additional needs that you cannot fill. If you are the CPA firm for a small manufacturing company, you may learn that your client needs to replace some old air-conditioning equipment. A friend who sells such equipment would appreciate your referral. Sharing your customers' names and information about them with other salespeople who can help is a tangible service to your customers.

Using Directories

Many salespeople overlook directories as a source of prospects. The most accessible directory is the *Yellow Pages*. We are accustomed to looking there when we want to buy something, but telephone books also tell you where to look when you want to sell.

Directories are gold mines of information if they are used correctly. They cannot replace other means of prospecting, but they are excellent supplements. Some directories are useful in identifying possible prospects; others are helpful in learning more about prospects to determine whether they have the potential to become customers. Many companies have copies of the directories that supply information directly related to their businesses. Other directories are available at public and university libraries. In this age of information technology, many directories are now available on computer disks and CD-ROMS. Become familiar with these directories:

1. *Moody's Industrial Directory* is an annual publication with a wide range of statistical information about particular firms that might be prospects for your product or service. Names of executives, description of a company's business, and a brief financial statement for over 10,000 publicly held firms.

2. *Standard & Poor's Register of Corporations, Directors and Executives* is an excellent source of personal information about individuals in companies. You can use such information for qualifying prospects and for learning enough

about them to plan an effective approach and presentation. This annual publication lists names, titles and addresses for 50,000 firms.

3. *Thomas Register of American Manufacturers*, published annually, provides information about who makes what, and where almost anything may be purchased. Information is also provided about the corporate structure of the manufacturer and about its executives.

4. *Polk City Directory* supplies detailed information on individuals living in specific communities. Polk publishes over 1,100 directories covering 6,500 communities throughout the United States and Canada. Your local chamber of commerce should have access to this directory.

5. *Trade Shows & Professional Exhibits*. Lists over 3,500 trade shows, including their location, when they are held, and attendance expected.

6. *Business List (infoUSA)* has 12 million businesses and 120 million households in their databases. They provide Prospect Lists (perfect for sales lead generation and telemarketing). Visit Web site: *www.directoriesUSA.com*

Specific industrial groups publish directories, too. Use them to locate architects, contractors, air conditioning manufacturers, computer software companies, and many others. If the library does not have a directory that fits your needs, ask one of your customers what directory would help you find other customers in that same field.

Company-Initiated Prospecting

The purpose of company-initiated prospecting is to free up time for salespeople to concentrate on the top priority of all sales activity—face-to-face interviews with fully qualified prospects. This is where results are generated. Everything else is merely preparation for the true sales arena.

Telemarketing. Telemarketing is an industry that is experiencing incredible growth, selling over $300 billion in products and services yearly.[23] Some firms rely almost completely on a particular chosen form of telemarketing for gaining leads; others use it as a supplement to other prospecting methods. Those at the Houston Chronicle credit telemarketing (phone sales) with providing 40 percent of ad revenue.[24] Other companies train their telemarketing specialists to ask additional questions and attempt to set up an appointment for the sales representative. If an appointment is made, the salesperson is almost sure to make a presentation. The closing average can be improved, however, if the salesperson uses some ingenuity to discover additional information about the prospect before the presentation.

Empire Associates established a center to manage direct mail, tele-marketing, and advertising for its member agencies. They took over the entire responsibility of prospecting and allowed the salespeople to concentrate all their time on face-to-face contacts with qualified prospects. They developed a profile of the desired prospect for each agency they serve and then designed mailings and advertising campaigns targeted to produce the leads needed. After their telemarketing staff qualifies the leads, agents receive detailed information that enables them to begin their sales activity at the point of calling for an appointment with the prospect.[25]

Personalization With Web Marketing and Advertising. Reebok International makes its customers feel like they are the center of the universe. They do it through personalization – the latest trend in Web marketing. Reebok turned to Internet designer Mindseye Technology Inc. to design a Web site that creates an interactive dialogue between them and their customers. Mindseye created a membership application that features personalized content and encourages return visits. Members can register their location, favorite sport and such demographic data as age group and gender. Reebok then runs specialized promotions, sending personalized emails to targeted groups, for example, all female runners in the Northeast.[26]

Because retail stores are Reebok's primary sales channel they also created a product catalog of all Reebok shoes. The catalog functions as an information tool to educate customers about different types of running shoes, and provides pictures, specifications, and prices. The Web site can determine the customers' location and sends them to the nearest Reebok retailer.

Computer technology is making advertising a more effective prospecting tool. The lists used for mailings can be coded to indicate past responses as well as characteristics that make each prospect a possible target for a particular mail piece. The computer can also be used to manage the information gained by responses to advertising in newspapers, magazines, or trade journals. The value of computer technology in managing lists depends upon the care with which the lists are compiled so that the salesperson who receives the leads has the best possible information. The more the salesperson knows about the prospect, the more efficient the process becomes in producing sales.

Make Use of Current and Past Customers. In a cross-sectional survey of 183 company executives conducted by the Patrick Marketing Group (PMG) of Calabasas, California, they found that 70 percent said expanding relationships with existing customers is the biggest factor challenging the success of their sales forces. These numbers suggest the importance of existing customers as sources of new revenue, says Craig Shields, senior marketing consultant at PMG. Firms realize that it is easier and less expensive to penetrate existing accounts and fully flesh out their potential than to prospect for new clients. It is estimated that it costs 5 to 10 times more to go out and get a new customer than to keep the customer base you currently have.[27]

Some companies take the initiative in furnishing salespeople with the names of past customers who, for one reason or another, are no longer active. If they do not, the salesperson can certainly ask for this information. If the business was lost because of some communication or service problem, the account often can be reestablished by a sensitive salesperson who is willing to work with the customer. If conditions changed so that the customer no longer needed the product or service, conditions may have changed again, and the customer may now need the same product or some new product you can offer.

Trade Shows. Trade shows in the United States attract over 100 million visitors each year. And, globally, trade shows are a more significant part of the marketing process than in the United States. Companies use trade shows to demonstrate new and exiting products, enhance their corporate image, provide information to those who visit the booth, and also use the opportunity to examine competing products.[28] The decision to exhibit at a trade show is a complex one that must be based on consideration of a number of variables:

1. Which trade shows will produce the largest number of prospects and the best-qualified prospects?
2. Is the goal on-the-spot sales or discovery of leads for future sales?
3. What kind of display should be planned?
4. How many salespeople will be needed to staff the booth, and which ones are the best choice for this activity?
5. How can we ensure high visibility for our exhibit and our name?
6. How will we preserve the information gathered?

According to Philip Gelman, a company has just 20 seconds to send out a powerful message to get people to visit their booth. For example, to generate traffic for its booth, PepsiCo company created a memorable exhibit developed around the theme "Liter of the Pack." PepsiCo hoped it would be a traffic generator for Kentucky Fried Chicken franchisees, a group they were particularly anxious to have as customers. Built around a nostalgic motorcycle theme, the franchisees had the opportunity to win a brand new Harley-Davidson motorcycle if they entered a drawing at the booth. PepsiCo was very successful signing up 40 percent more than the goal they had set for the event.[29]

Trade show attendance is off in some industries. However, some organizers and exhibitors say that in hard times, trade shows are the best way to spend marketing dollars. Trade shows are a relatively low-cost setting for marketing and making sales. You can purchase a booth and arrange for travel and people to work the booth, for less than ten thousand dollars. The booth can lead to literally thousands of face-to-face interactions with highly targeted individuals. A report from the Center for Exhibition Research says it costs 56 percent less to close a lead generated at an exhibition than a lead generated in the field — $625.00 versus $1,117.00.[30]

Nearly one-half of trade show visitors are using the Internet to plan their attendance. Time constraints have created a new breed of attendees who use the Net to plan their time at exhibitions. Response rates to well-designed Web sites are high. *Investors Business Daily* estimates that Internet promotions get five times the response of direct mail. It's quite possible that one sale will often pay for the cost of the virtual exhibit and the Web site. Companies are capitalizing on this by making a "virtual exhibit" part of their pre-show preparation.[31] A Web version of your show booth can acquire leads from people who use the Internet yet cannot attend the show, and, at the same time, can drive qualified buyers to your booth at the show. These "Web shoppers" want to know the following types of information: 1. What products will you display at your booth? 2. Will the CEO of your company be there? If not, what "experts" will be there? 3. What new applications will you have available? 4. Will there be any special offers or incentives for us to visit your show booth?

Using Web Sites

A Web site is a collection of information, text, pictures, sound, video and other communication media stored and posted on the Internet for public use and viewing. Salespeople and small companies can set up a home page with a nominal initial expense and use their home pages to advertise their services, offer special deals, tap into lucrative foreign markets or add sales reps halfway around the world. People can market their businesses very inexpensively because of the power of the Internet and as a result of the online relationships they form.

Streamline the Sales Process. Suppose you need distributors to sell your product in Spain and Italy. Just five years ago you would have had to contact reps who sell there, find a list of reputable firms and secure one or more to sell for you. The process would take months. Now you get on a search engine (Yahoo, Lycos, Infoseek, HotBot, etc.) type in photography, bronze sculptures or whatever the product is you sell, probe the entire world and in a few hours have a number of solid leads who you then e-mail. Not only have you located and identified your prospects, you have also contacted them. Contracts can be e-mailed to the ones you select, and they can make modifications, and fax it back. The Internet connection and e-mail are basically free and you've spend a few days rather than a few months putting the deal together. Those individuals in sales and marketing who recognize the power of this opportunity are destined for big-time success.

Affiliate Program Marketing. The Internet is also a great prospecting tool, especially as a way to partner with others. Are there Web sites that sell to the same types of customers that also buy what you sell? If so, your products might complement what they're doing in a way that would allow for an affiliate-type of arrangement. An innovative e-marketing tactic to drive traffic to your Web site is to target your marketing at specific groups of prospects that are likely to have an interest in your product. This is done by compensating the referring site for any sales that are made to customers that link from its site to yours. Unlike banner advertising, where you are ostensibly paying for impressions, this approach allows you to only pay for results.

Amazon.com's affiliate program is a prime example of a marketing initiative that operates through thousands of independent Web sites.[32] Here's how it works – Web site operators offer books for sale on their sites. The orders are placed and fulfilled through Amazon, which compensates the site operators with a percentage of each sale. It is a win-win situation for everyone. The site operator is able to offer books that are of value to their customer without having to invest in inventory or worry about the operational hassles of fulfillment. Amazon, meanwhile, extends its reach into the marketplace and only has to pay when an actual sale is made.

Turning Web Leads Into Online Sales. Toshiba America Business Solutions Inc. is obtaining more than 80 percent of its sales revenues from the Net. Their business-to-business site is getting about 15,000 hits per month.[33] The highlight of the Web site (www.copier.toshiba.com) is the Dealer Lead Referral System that allows customers to locate the Toshiba dealer closest to them. "It's a persuasive selling tool, and it lets our dealers go out and follow leads," says Anthony Codianni, director of marketing communications.

Customers can't proceed until they say how they ended up on the site. The customers must then enter their contact information and the model numbers they're interested in purchasing. The information is then forwarded to a local dealer. A checks-and-balances system is in place as well – the dealer is given two hours to respond to the request or one of the sales managers will take action for him.

MANAGING PROSPECT INFORMATION

All your good work in prospecting goes down the drain if you do not have a system for managing and using the information you find about prospects. The type of system you use is not the primary consideration; what is important is accuracy, completeness, and ease of use. You can use a file box and individual cards. However, if you use a computer, you can easily achieve the same results with the added advantages of handy printouts and provisions for additional listings of names by any category you desire that can be added to your coding system. Whether you use manual or computer records, the purpose and result are the same.

Initial Recording of Leads

The initial information you need about prospects depends a great deal upon the product or service you sell, but it will, in all likelihood, include these items:

1. Prospect's full name, address, and telephone number (both business and home)

2. Name of company, address, and telephone number; type of business

3. Position in company

4. Family: spouse, names and ages of children

5. Personal information: hobbies, clubs and associations, civic leadership

6. Approximate income (if your product or service is to be sold to the individual rather than to the company)

Classification of Prospects

When you first find the name of an individual or company prospect, assign a classification indicator to the name. One handy classification system uses the letters A, B, and C. *Class A* prospects are those about whom you have adequate information to make a good presentation. You know they have the money to buy and the authority to make a decision. Ideally, you also have a referral from someone they respect. *Class B* prospects are those about whom you have inadequate information to make the best possible presentation. You may not know enough to be sure they need your product or service. You may not know whether they have the authority to make a decision or whether they can afford to buy. You may not have a referral to help open the door. When one or more of these items is missing, your proper action is research rather than approach. *Class C* prospects are people whose names you have found in some way, but about whom you have little or no information other than a name. They are leads, not prospects. Prospecting activity involves not only finding new leads but also qualifying existing leads by adding information that allows you to move them up to *Class A* status.

Scheduling Contacts

When you have classified a prospect as *Class A,* determine when you will initiate contact, either by telephone, personal visit, or direct mail, according to the method of approach you choose. The various methods of preapproach and approach are discussed fully in chapters 8 and 9. Use a *tickler* file arrangement of your prospect cards or computer records to see that you take the proper action on the date assigned. The same tickler file will help you schedule later contacts if your first attempt to schedule an interview is not successful for some reason. Once a prospect's name enters your file, it stays there permanently until you close a sale or determine that the person is a prospect for any product or service of your company. If you make a presentation and do not close, choose a time for a new attempt and schedule an appropriate time for contacting the prospect again. When you discover that a person is not a viable prospect for you and will probably not become one in the foreseeable future, that person can still be an important contact. The impression you have given of your company by your professionalism may cause that person to recommend you to someone who will prove to be an excellent prospect. Someone who is not a prospect for you may be an excellent prospect for another salesperson. Passing on the information you have is the basis of networking among salespeople.

USING TECHNOLOGY TO AUTOMATE PROSPECT INFORMATION

Sales professionals no longer have time to organize prospect information on 3 x 5 blank file cards or in loose-leaf binders. It would be very difficult to go through handwritten or typed notes every time you're on the phone or in a client's office. However, as your client base grows the need to interact with them, and other individuals from the various departments within your own company requires the use of computer technology. This is why the most widely used software programs in selling, outside of word processing, are contact management programs. These powerful programs were developed to help the salesperson collect, organize, classify and keep track of prospect information. It's like having a super *Rolodex* for your desktop or laptop computer. Most sales contact management software automatically includes features such as appointment tracking, call reminders, software generated telephone dialing, import/export features, order entry and tracking, address label creation, extensive sales management reports and links to accounting software invoicing programs.

Developing Partnerships Using Technology describes some of the common features found in contact management programs.

Developing Partnerships Using Technology
Contact Management Programs Track a Variety of Prospect Information

Pre-defined Fields. These are used for general entry information when building the database (name, company, phone, fax, e-mail...etc.). Some of the programs have fields for specialty items such as birthdays and other special occasions. Advanced users can generate their own personal fields for all their contacts.

Keyword Searches and Queries. The salesperson can take the entire database and ask the contact management program to find specific words, phrases, notes, names or any information from the other fields. Information on any *one* of a countless number of prospects can be sifted through and found in a matter of seconds.

Synchronization With Laptops and Palmtops. In true *road warrior* style, salespeople literally have prospects in the palm of their hands. They can transfer contact information to a palmtop or take the whole database with them on a laptop. Information obtained in the field can be transferred back just as easily to an existing database or the office network server.

Journals and Histories. A salesperson can locate every instance where a contact has been updated, reclassified or added to the database. The program can also track what documents, e-mail, and phone conversations a salesperson has had with each client. A running tally of time you spend with a prospect or client is only a few mouse clicks away.

E-Mail and Internet Integration. This is one of the newest additions to contact management software. Now contacts can be generated directly from e-mail or from special Internet submission forms online. Literally thousands of new pre-qualified prospects can be added every day with these new sources.

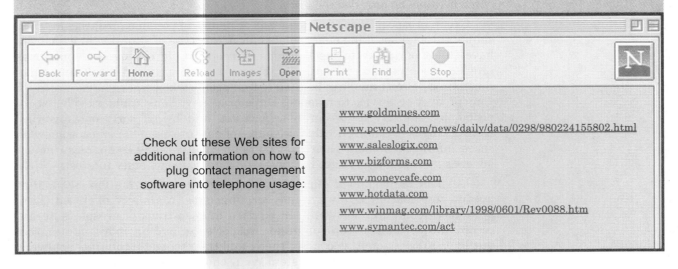

Netscape

Back | Forward | Home | Reload | Images | Open | Print | Find | Stop

Check out these Web sites for additional information on how to plug contact management software into telephone usage:

www.goldmines.com
www.pcworld.com/news/daily/data/0298/980224155802.html
www.saleslogix.com
www.bizforms.com
www.moneycafe.com
www.hotdata.com
www.winmag.com/library/1998/0601/Rev0088.htm
www.symantec.com/act

Data mining — computers hunting through stacks of records in search of useful information — has been a reality for over a decade. There is simply no excuse for making a cold call anymore. In today's world you can go into a call knowing about the prospect. Technology has created the solution. Hotdata, recently acquired by Group 1 Software, is one example. Just type a company name into HotData, an intelligence-gathering tool that integrates or plugs into such leading contact managers as Act!, Goldmine, Pivotal and Siebel.

Applications for database technology are limited only by the creativity of the salesperson. For example, salespeople with Sovran Leasing Corporation begin their day by calling up a list of follow-ups from the corporate database. They check the best way to organize the day based on where they'll be, and what prospects or customers are in that area. Then they order form letters to go out to all the customers and prospects they visited the day before and print them on their own letterhead. In addition, they can generate call schedules and short-range forecasts, provide scheduled contact lists in chronological order and account summaries, expedite long-range forecasting and sorting by a variety of criteria (zip code, alphabet, amount of last sale), and prepare graphs showing likely trends in sales for current customers.[34]

SUMMARY

Prospecting is the skill that keeps salespeople in business. Without prospects, you cannot sell. Once you have the names of people you might see, you have to qualify them to determine whether they are true prospects who have a need for your product and are in a position to make a buying decision. Develop a profile of the type of person who constitutes a *Class A* prospect for your product or service. Match the information you gain about leads to this profile to determine which ones are most likely to become your clients.

Eleven methods of prospecting are presented in the chapter. Two of the most effective methods are referrals and centers of influence. When you are introduced to people by someone they respect, you have a built-in sales assistant—the influence of the person who provided the lead.

Group prospecting is securing leads or names of possible prospects at trade shows, through speaking engagements, or in any type of situation in which you have the opportunity to meet groups of people. Cold calling can sometimes provide a source of new prospects, but is psychologically difficult and time-consuming. Direct mail can be used to find people who have enough interest in your product or service to respond. Directories of various kinds provide lists of people by industry, by geographic location, and by all sorts of categories. Networking is becoming a valuable source of new prospects for salespeople who share information about their customers or clients. Many companies conduct advertising campaigns to get responses that indicate customer interest.

Efficient management of prospecting records and information means that needed information is always at your fingertips. Manually operated filing systems or computer software can be used to keep track of prospects as you record initial information, upgrade prospects by adding more information until you know enough to contact them, and then schedule the time you want to contact each one. The system you choose should also provide for transferring prospect files to customer files when a sale is closed.

QUESTIONS FOR THOUGHT AND DISCUSSION

1. How does your skill in prospecting exert a direct effect on your ability to close a sale?

2. What characteristics make a qualified prospect?

3. What is a referral? How do you get referrals?

4. What is the advantage of having referrals from your clients?

5. What is a center of influence?

6. Name several directories that might be helpful sources of prospects. Where would you look for these directories?

7. What is observation prospecting? Name several places a salesperson might find prospects through observation.

8. How does networking work for salespeople? Why were women active in organizing formal networking groups in the 1970s? Is this an important activity for men as well as women?

9. What methods do companies use to provide leads for salespeople? Why would the company be interested in providing leads instead of having individual salespeople do all the prospecting?

10. What kind of records are needed for keeping track of prospects?

11. How long should a prospect's name remain in your prospecting system?

ACTIVITIES

1. Go to a computer store and review the software available for salespeople to manage prospecting records. If possible, see a demonstration of a program in operation or get a brochure describing its features. Write a brief description of what it does and give your opinion of its effectiveness. If your school has a computer lab with sample software, ask if they have a prospecting program or some type of filing program that could be used for that purpose by salespeople.

2. Choose an organization that you might consider establishing on your campus. Define its purpose and then write a profile of the type of people who would make good members for it. For a week, prospect for the organization. Consider using at least three methods. For example, you might ask a professor (a center of influence) to suggest students who fit the profile. You might find information in the student directory or other lists of people that would suggest prospects. Use your imagination, your powers of observation, and your creativity, and see how many prospects you can find in a week. Classify them as Class A, B, or C. Write a brief report on your experiences. Which method worked best for you?

Case Study

CASE 7.1

Gil Robinson studied the monthly report of his sales that had just come in from the home office. He knew things had been slow lately, but he had no idea that things had reached quite the low that the report revealed. The figures were in front of him in black and white. "Should be red and white except for the fact that black suggests mourning," Gil thought to himself. He decided going around feeling sorry for himself wouldn't do any good. What he needed was a big push to get back in the win column.

Just then the phone rang. His sales manager, Dick Porter, was calling. "Did you get your monthly report?" he asked.

"Yes, I did. Pretty sad, isn't it?" Gil said.

"It's kind of strange, too. The thing I don't understand is that the rest of the sales force is going great guns. What's causing your slump?" Dick wanted to know.

"Well, for one thing, I've lost a few customers. Plants are closing or moving out of my territory. None of my real big buyers, so I think things will start picking up pretty soon," Gil predicted.

"How are you doing with your steady customers?"

"Fine, no problems there," Gil answered.

"You know, we've set a pretty stiff quota for your territory," Dick said. "The way it looks, you're going to have to go some to meet it. Do you have any ideas about how to do it?"

"I've got a few ideas. I think things will get better soon."

"Okay, Gil," Dick said. "We're expecting a lot from your territory. Don't let us down."

After hanging up the phone, Gil turned to another item that had come in the mail. It was a listing of selected sales from all over the country. The home office had developed it to give salespeople an indication of what types of companies are buying which products. Gil glanced at it. "There's never anything in this to help me. Maybe I'll look it over later. Right now, I've got to get on the ball and find some customers to replace those I've lost."

1. What do you think is Gil's major problem?

2. What do you think about the conversation between Gil and his sales manager? Did they identify the problem? Did they find a solution for it?

3. How is Gil's problem related to prospecting?

CHAPTER 8

Preapproach and Telephone Techniques

LEARNING OBJECTIVES

- To recognize the importance of the preapproach in the overall sales cycle.

- To know the objectives of the preapproach and the planning needed to make it effective.

- To learn how to prepare for an effective preapproach.

- To understand how the preapproach fits into the sales cycle as an extension of prospecting.

- To learn effective methods for making telephone calls that are successful in leading to sales interviews.

- To understand the six-step telephone track and how to make it work.

THE IMPORTANCE OF PREAPPROACH PLANNING

The path to success in selling is often described by this formula: seeing enough of the right people at the right time. That sounds logical enough! The most exacting part of the formula however, is the "right people." How can you be sure that you are investing your time in calling on qualified prospects? The answer lies in your diligence in collecting information about the leads you record in your prospecting system. When someone gives you a referral, ask questions to learn what you need to know about that prospect. Do some research about the prospect's business or industry and about the company itself. Discover some personal information that will help you know what kind of personality to expect. The various activities that provide this necessary personal and business information are called *presale planning* or the *preapproach*. The *preapproach* is the planning and preparation done prior to actual contact with the prospect.

Read the Don Ellers success story below. His contact management software program gives salespeople an integrated system for organizing prospect and client information. In gathering such information, you are learning *who* to call on, *why, when, and where*. What seems to be insignificant might be the key to the exact approach that spells the difference between success and failure. Leave nothing to chance. For example, details such as

Don Ellers developed his own software program to manage information

Don Ellers lives in Atlanta, Georgia. His love of selling and interest in being personally productive led him to the development of a product that is designed to make salespeople more productive.

Early in 1983, he joined a dealer who was the only computer retailer in a three-state area marketing the "new" Apple Lisa computer. As outside sales manager for the Lisa line, Don participated in a seminar his company conducted for people interested in computers. Six hundred people attended the seminar, and Don found himself buried under a shower of 3 x 5 cards as he tried to manage the prospecting records and follow up all these leads. To help with the job, he decided to use a simple *tickler file software program* on his desk top computer. Immediately, his sales went through the roof. At that time, he knew he had the germ of an idea that would revolutionize selling.

In 1985, Don started SALESPRO International, and began development of computer software for salespeople. His company introduced *Sales Producer*, a comprehensive software program for management of sales information. The program gives salespeople an integrated system for organizing prospecting information, keeping track of contacts with prospects and clients, generating sales letters and mailings, and tracking sales results. The company's clients range from large companies who provide the software for their salespeople to individuals who purchase it on their own because they want to be more productive. "I like to know," says Don, "that I can go out to lunch and when I come back to the office, *Sales Producer* will have a hundred sales letters written and ready for me to mail. I also feel good about going to work in the morning knowing that I can punch two or three keys and display a list of people I need to call, and have all the information about those people right in front of me. For new prospects, I have everything I have learned about them and where I got the names. For clients and people I have contacted before, I have a complete file including the size and date of their previous purchases, when I contacted them last, and what happened in that interview—and even have the computer dial the phone for me."

"What makes this business exciting," he says, "is hearing from clients that they have increased their sales by 50 percent or more from using our product. What could be more satisfying for any salesperson than to help another salesperson in that way?"

the correct pronunciation of the prospect's name can be secured in advance. Roger Capps, an industrial salesperson, thought he was well prepared to call on an important new prospect, only to find himself sent on his way after less than a minute. The prospect, Mr. Hajovsky, had no time for Capps, who made the fatal error of mispronouncing Hajovsky's name. Capps could have avoided the lost sales opportunity by taking a few seconds to ask the receptionist for the correct pronunciation.

EXTENT OF THE PREAPPROACH

The sales cycle is a continuous process with no clear break between one phase and the next. Chapter 7 dealt with prospecting, this chapter and the next treat the preapproach and the approach, and Chapter 10 discusses asking questions as a means of need discovery. All these parts of the sales cycle are concerned with gathering information about the prospect. In practice, you cannot separate these elements into different segments. They seem to blend together and become one. They are discussed separately for convenience, but the exact point where one phase ends and the next begins is never clear. Figure 8.1 illustrates the absence of clear dividing lines between these steps in the consultative selling process.

FIGURE 8.1

Four Phases of the Sales Process Work Together Turning a Lead into a Qualified Prospect

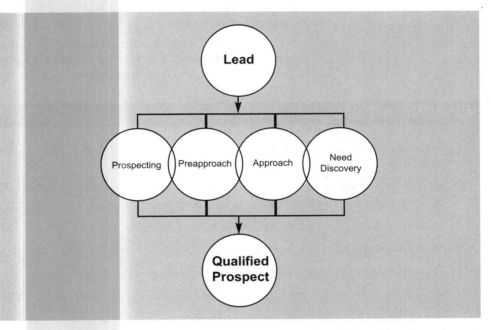

The numerous types of selling vary so widely that few broad generalizations can be made about the amount of preapproach information that should be gathered. Some salespeople handle only one account; others call on hundreds of accounts. Some handle the sale from start to finish; others operate as part of a team. Some locate and open new accounts; others handle only established accounts. Some have little contact with customers except across a counter; others have close, continuous contact. Depending on the type of selling job to be done and the product or services being sold, the preapproach differs considerably. The retail salesperson, for example, typically has little opportunity either for prospecting or for preapproach activities until the customer appears in the store. Qualifying prospects must therefore be accomplished during the approach and need discovery process by asking questions and through observing, listening, and interpreting verbal and nonverbal signals. By contrast, a salesperson selling investment and estate planning services is required to gather a great deal of information about prospective customers. Sometimes months are spent in gathering preapproach information, and several more months in face-to-face meetings with the prospect before the salesperson is ready to make a buying recommendation.

PREPARATION AND PREAPPROACH

The type and quality of information uncovered during the preapproach is vital. Just as students dislike doing homework after school, many adults have a similar aversion to the preliminaries to the "real work" they prefer to do. However, this step is a must. Successful sales professionals rarely make even a *cold* call without some sort of preparation.[1] When they are ready for a formal sales call, professional salespeople have studied and analyzed the prospect's personality, company, operations, needs, and financial position before ever entering the office. One of the most thorough ways to prepare is to develop a checklist of questions to answer before you make the sales call. Exhibit 8.1 presents a checklist designed to help gather the essential sales information you need.

For Dean Cormier, sales manager for Catapult Systems, thoroughness is what it is all about. Before giving a sales presentation, Cormier gathers information about the company, researches the industry, interviews potential

EXHIBIT 8.1 - Checklist of Sales Essentials for Collecting Preapproach Information

1. What business is the company in? What are its products and markets? Who are its primary customers?

2. How big is the company? Where does it rank within the industry? Can this company give us enough business to make this call worthwhile?

3. Who is the actual decision maker in buying the product or service I sell?

4. Who else influences the buying decision?

5. How often does this company buy my type of product or service?

6. Who is the company's competition? Does my company do business with that competitor?

7. What plans does the company have that could affect its future need for my product?

8. How well is the company satisfied with its present supplier?

9. What are the background and personal interests of each person concerned in the buying decision?

10. Is the company's staff technically well informed? Can we help them develop greater expertise?

11. Do we (or can we) use their products or services in our company?

12. Do any of our top executives know any of their executives personally?

"So You Want to Be a Salesperson," Burnett Temporary Personnel, Houston, TX. Compliments of Rick Burnett.

clients, and finds out exactly how his product can benefit a specific company. Cormier says, "when I give a presentation to a dot-com company, I know exactly how a dot-com company works; when I give a presentation to an oil company, I know exactly how an oil company works."[2] Maren Rupel, a human resources executive at Chevron, cited Cormier's in-depth knowledge and confidence in his product and its capabilities for their business needs as the key in her company's decision to buy from Catapult Systems.

Predict Likely Objections

Rarely does a sales interview proceed without some objection or question. Your past experience tells you what objections are raised most often. The preapproach information you have gathered tells you what objections or questions a particular prospect may have. A prospect who is concerned about costs will probably have price-related objections. A prospect who is an efficiency expert will be concerned about the effect your product or service will have on overall productivity.[3] The more you know about the prospect, the easier it will be for you to predict the questions and objections that will arise, and develop good answers in advance.

Prepare for the Presentation

Plan specifically for each sales call. Do your research to find out about the prospect and develop a purpose for the call, linked to a potential client benefit.[4] Set a goal for each contact with a prospect, know what you want to accomplish, and how you plan to do it. There is much more to preparation than simply gathering and reviewing information. *Rehearsal* eliminates the stammering, nervous speech habits, and repetition that sometimes result from lack of preparation. Allow time in your daily schedule to prepare the sales approach and presentation you will use in each call. Decide how you can make the best possible use of sales literature and other tools provided by your company in this specific call. Plan how to incorporate visual aids into your approach and presentation for maximum effectiveness.

Videotaping their presentations allows salespeople to see how they really look. "That's the best way to coach people," says Ken Taylor president of Decker Communication Inc. Videotaping also allows presenters to hear their use of what Taylor calls non-words — fillers like "um," "ah," and "you know." He suggests the following rehearsal tips:[5]

- Reps should practice presentations with specific customers in mind.
- Videotape presentations to show reps their strengths and weaknesses.
- Encourage salespeople to make large, exaggerated motions until they feel comfortable making more natural-looking gestures.

Visualize Successful Selling

Salespeople can learn a great deal from the training habits of world-class athletes. Many track stars use visualization techniques to help them focus on a specific event. An integral part of their training consists of what is called "mental toughening sessions." They run the race over and over in their minds. Edwin Moses, over a 10-year period, won 122 consecutive races in the 400-meter hurdles. His power of visualization became so acute that when he mentally visualized hitting a hurdle, he actually felt the pain in his leg. To further illustrate just how powerful visualization can be, consider this amazing example:

After the Vietnam War, an Air Force captain who had been a prisoner of war for over seven years was interviewed by a reporter. The former POW had just played a superb game in a golf tournament. When the reporter mentioned his surprise at the captain's skill after so long an absence, the captain said, "I've played this course perfectly for the last seven years." The reporter replied, "I thought you hadn't played golf in the last eight years." The captain said, "Well, actually I haven't physically played the game in the last eight years. However, for the last seven years in my cell as a POW I have been playing this course mentally."[6]

As a salesperson, you can practice this same type of mental exercise. You can positively affirm the feeling you want to create and visualize the outcomes you want to obtain. Think about what you will say and anticipate the prospect's responses. Create a mental hologram and live it over and over in your mind. Practice out loud; your mind believes the sound of your own voice. *Remember that your mind cannot separate a real experience from an imagined one.*

Used with Permission of United Feature Syndicate, Inc.

SOURCES OF PREAPPROACH INFORMATION

When you know what information you need, you can identify a number of valuable sources for obtaining it. The information you gather will help you get in to make a presentation as well as guide you in preparing a strategy for the interview itself. For example, you can ask colleagues on your company's sales team for information they have on particular prospects. Current customers are also excellent sources of information, and they may be happy to share what they know with you. There is nothing wrong with calling

---

IMITATION IS THE SINCEREST FORM OF FLATTERY

Kelly Immoor, national sales manager for Bedford Communications Inc. in New York, says, "If you want to stand out, then blend in." Before sending anything to potential clients she researches their product lines, Web sites and media advertising. Companies place "about us" links on their products and Web sites for a reason. With this unlimited company information available she puts together communication pieces that match the particular style of the company being targeted. She finds their slogan, the motto the company lives by, and uses the phrase as a headline in the proposal. Immoor further tailors her proposals by including such subtle features as the prospects' colors and images. Based on the company's mission statement and goals, she specifies how her product will help them reach their objectives.[7]

personally on prospects without an appointment. At the very least, this *cold call* gives you the opportunity to observe their facilities and you learn something that validates them as, at least, partially "qualified" prospects. You simply cannot predict the most beneficial sources of information. Keep your eyes and ears open![8]

Do some reading. The business pages of the local newspaper, trade magazines, company newsletters, government reports, and the business section of Sunday papers. Here's a useful tip—read magazines and newsletters that are related to your customer's industry. You read publications that are pertinent in your field, so obviously your clients also read publications relevant to their fields. This is a great way to uncover ideas to serve their needs better. Janelle Patterson targets companies via the Internet. As an account services specialist with Honeywell, she looks at what markets Honeywell has been successful in and then researches those types of companies and gathers preapproach information from their Web sites.[9] The Internet allows her to do her homework before she calls. Not only is she gathering valuable preapproach information, but also building a way to make more sales. However, just researching and reading are not enough. You must know what to look for.

1. *Mergers.* Will new alliances give you better opportunities to see companies that have denied you access in the past?

2. *Personnel Changes.* Watch for new appointments by your customers, prospects, and competitors.

3. *Changing Product Lines.* Firms that drop or add products may be suggesting a new emphasis that gives you a reason to call.

4. *Advertising Plans.* Have your competitors or customers changed advertising agencies? Are they creating a new approach or pushing certain products?

5. *TV and Magazine Ads.* Television commercials and print ads are a source of invaluable clues for a salesperson. Look at the features being stressed and the image being portrayed.

6. *Sales Training.* The news media highlight new sales training endeavors. Is your customer or prospect developing a sales training program you can somehow make use of?

On a much more personal level, there are numerous online sites that may make pounding the pavement a thing of the past.[10] Even your fingers don't have to do much walking. Just a few mouse clicks and you can literally find thousands of employment opportunities on the Internet. If you are seeking employment in sales, or in any other career for that matter, Exhibit 8. 2 lists six online sources to assist you in gathering a significant amount of preapproach information:

EXHIBIT 8.2 - Researching and Finding a Career Position for Yourself

Career Magazine (www.careermag.com) – The Web site has job listings, a recruiter directory, listings of job fairs, relocation services and career links.

Careermosaic (www.careermosaic.com) – Access is free to this Web site for job seekers. You can search opportunities by zip code anywhere in the United States. The site has the capability of notifying you via email of new listings that match your criteria.

Hotjobs (www.hotjobs.com) – You can narrow your search by keyword, region or by type of job. In sales, for example, options include client services, inside or outside sales, sales rep, sales engineer, and telemarketing.

Monster.com (www.monster.com) – Job seekers have access to interactive, personalized tools such as My Monster and Resume Builder. You can see real-time job postings and complete company profiles to guide you in your search for the "job."

Workseek.com (www.workseek.com) – The Web site includes a network of vertical sites targeted to specific careers, industries and demographics: SalesSeek, RetailSeek, GradSeek, FinanceSeek, WorkSeek, and yes, GeekSeek.

Yahoo! Careers (www.careers.yahoo.com) – This site lists hundreds of thousands of jobs nationwide. You can post your resume, research companies and get advice on preparing resumes, interviewing techniques and legal tips.

Excellence in selling requires an awareness that the hardest work takes place during the preapproach, but all that hard work adds up to a closed sale.[11] You must be prepared to answer the questions that are in the minds of prospects when you first contact them. Exhibit 8.3 lists ten questions that buyers have, although they don't often volunteer to ask you these questions.

Building Your Self-Confidence

One of the key benefits of preapproach planning is to build personal self-confidence. Knowing that you are prepared gives you an added measure of self-confidence that is transmitted to the prospect. The opposite of self-confidence is fear, and fear comes primarily from the unknown. Children who are afraid to enter a dark room lose their fear like magic the minute the light is turned on because the light reveals the unknown. The light of preparation reveals the unknown about every prospect: needs, buying motives, credit rating, ability to buy, authority to make a decision, unique personality style, and anything else you can use to design an effective presentation.

A definite plan for each prospect means you are more likely to be accepted. A purchasing agent for a big food processing plant who sees many salespeople described his reactions like this:

I turn away salesman after salesman because they come in like lost sheep. . . . They hope that somehow they'll stumble into an order. I get the impression that they figure I'll do the selling for them. I haven't got time for people like that.[12]

Particularly in business-to-business selling, salespeople call on professional buyers whose job is to make sound purchasing decisions for their companies. These professionals expect to interact with another professional, not an unprepared amateur. If you walk confidently into the buyer's office and get down to business immediately without wasting the prospect's time with unnecessary questions, you increase the likelihood of a successful close. By emitting an air of self-confidence, you add to your perceived value.[13]

SETTING UP THE SALES INTERVIEW

Timing

With a little research, you can determine the best time to call a prospect you have not previously met. For example, Powell Kenney, vice-president of Clampitt Paper Company in Fort Worth, sees salespeople only between 5:30 and 8:30 a.m. each weekday morning. He does not want his regular work routine *disrupted* by listening to sales presentations.

Ordinarily, sales calls can be scheduled for almost any time during the business day. Like Mr. Kenney, however, most prospects have a time when they are more receptive to your presentation. Some like to see salespeople the first thing in the morning. Others prefer to handle routine matters first. Fortunately, people have different preferences to the extent that salespeople can fill the workday with appointments. If every buyer insisted on appointments before 8:30 a.m., salespeople would be in serious trouble. If a particular prospect does not seem to have a preference for a time of day to see salespeople, try to discover when most salespeople call on this prospect. If most call in the morning, schedule your call for late in the afternoon. Many executives work past 5:00 p.m. and will see you. In fact, they may well appreciate your work ethic.

EXHIBIT 8.3 - Ten Buyer Questions

1. What are you selling?

2. Why do I need it?

3. Who is your company?

4. How much will it cost?

5. Who else is using it and are they satisfied?

6. What kind of a person are you?

7. Is your price truly competitive?

8. How does your solution compare to other alternatives?

9. Why do I need it now?

10. What is your record for support and service?

Gaining Entry

Before an actual face-to-face meeting can be arranged, you must choose a way to contact the prospect and set up the interview. Appointments can be set up in three basic ways, and each way has a number of variations. You may send a *letter* requesting an appointment, make a *cold call* or *telephone* the prospect and schedule a specific time and date for the interview. Writing a letter for an appointment may produce no answer or may require several contacts to set a mutually convenient time. Cold calls have a low probability of finding the prospect available for an interview. Today, more and more business is being conducted by telephone. Just a few minutes are required to make an appointment. Good telephone techniques and habits are important to anyone in professional selling. The number of companies using the telephone for selling purposes has grown dramatically. In a recent survey, it was emphasized that the telephone is an essential tool for sales reps in all types of industries.[14] The results of the poll indicate the top six ways sales reps make use of the phone.

Customer Service	89.6%
Follow-up	83.6%
Prospecting	83.6%
Scheduling	76.1%
Qualifying	74.6%
Cold calling	71.6%

Using the telephone successfully requires the same basic selling skills as a face-to-face call, plus some additional skills to meet the special challenges of telephone use. Finding a prospect in a bad mood or under a time constraint, the surprise element of a call, and the lack of visual contact are some of the elements that prevent salespeople from feeling as comfortable with the telephone as they do in a personal contact.

Of the three basic methods for gaining entry to a prospect, a letter requesting an appointment is the *weakest*. A letter is too easy to discard. Often the person to whom the letter is addressed never sees it. Busy executives have receptionists or assistants who screen incoming mail and quickly discard anything that threatens to consume time. These so-called *gatekeepers* also do an excellent job of protecting and conserving the time of their superiors by determining who gets in and when. Gatekeepers have many names, and they can range from receptionists, secretaries, and even managers. It is important to build a relationship with these gatekeepers, because statistics show that approximately 60 to 80 percent of them have "significant influence" over the purchase of certain products and services. It is a mistake to view them as barriers to overcome, and the best way to get to the main buyer is to sell yourself at the door. Exhibit 8.4 outlines eight ways to build rapport with gatekeepers.[15]

EXHIBIT 8.4 - Building Rapport With Gatekeepers

1. *Adjust Your Attitude*—be friendly, but not fake. Gatekeepers appreciate respect, and they can recognize insincerity.

2. *Honesty Is the Best Policy*—don't lie just to increase your chances of seeing the purchaser. Gatekeepers will discover your fib, and once this happens the possible sale has ended before it has begun.

3. *Get Personal Information*—find out the names of gatekeepers, their interests and family names without being too nosy. They appreciate being remembered by name.

4. *Sell to the Gatekeeper*—gatekeepers have influence over buying decisions. So if you show them how their company can benefit by using your product or service, the chances of you making the final sale increase.

5. *Question Gatekeepers*—ask them what the needs and goals of their company are, and they just might be willing to tell you.

6. *Be Thoughtful*—remember to thank gatekeepers for their help, but also remember special occasions such as birthdays and holidays. Don't go overboard, and don't use these gifts as payoffs, gatekeepers are intelligent and know what's going on.

7. *Keep a Sense of Humor*—this keeps things light, and maybe this will encourage the gatekeeper to accept you in a favorable way.

8. *Be Patient*—it may take longer than you expect to get through the door, but if you keep your patience and persistence, a positive outcome is the result.

TELEPHONE TECHNIQUES

Because of the ever-increasing cost of a sales visit to a prospect, the telephone call for many companies is replacing the unsolicited or cold call approach in making the initial contact with a prospect. *The average cost of a personal sales call* – factoring in compensation, benefits, travel and entertainment costs – is $169.64. However, for companies using a value-added sales approach that stresses consultative selling over price the average cost of a sales call is $211.56. Figure 8.2 shows the average cost of a sales interview using four distinct presentation styles or approaches to selling.[16] The proper use of the telephone helps you qualify prospects, budget time, and save money. In addition, good telephone technique enhances your image and preconditions the prospect to receive you favorably. Phoning for an appointment implies that you are courteous and considerate of the prospect's time. The phone call helps to create a selling situation because, just by agreeing to see you, the prospect tacitly indicates interest in your product or service.

FIGURE 8.2

Cost of a Sales Visit by Sales Approach or Method

Presentation Style Matters	Average Cost of a Personal Sales Interview
TRANSACTIONAL (sell on price; product is a commodity)	$56.52
FEATURE/BENEFIT (prices and features equally important)	$142.63
SOLUTION (tailor product to clients' needs; price is secondary)	$164.97
VALUE-ADDED (use team-sell approach; solution more important than price)	$211.56

Appointment as a Mini Sale

You must regard the use of the telephone to set up appointments as a true sales activity and not just a necessary evil. You must also remember what you are selling. The _mini sale_ is selling the prospect on the idea of giving you an appointment; your purpose is not to sell your product or service on the telephone.

Using the telephone to set up appointments is a great time-saver. A North Carolina furniture-manufacturing company conducted extensive advertising of a new line of grandfather clocks to boutiques, craft stores, and furniture and department stores. It received a large number of inquiries, but sales representatives could not make enough personal calls to cover them. In addition, only one in twenty of their calls produced an order. After three months, the company considered dropping the line. Instead, they trained sales reps to follow up inquiries by telephone and to make appointments with the prospects. One day a week was used for this purpose, and the other four for keeping the appointments. They found that calls made with an appointment not only reduced waiting time, but prospects were more receptive because those who were not really interested did not schedule appointments. The closing ratio increased from one order in twenty to one in three.[17]

First Impressions

Do you come across as being sincere, honest, confident, strong, knowledgeable and likable? The quality of your voice, the hesitation in your voice, the volume, the strength of your speaking style all convey an image to another person. If you sound weak and tentative or use words like _well, sort-of, kind-of, maybe, perhaps,_ that says to the prospect, "Gee I'm not one bit sure that this is going to a good investment of time for you." Lots of people also include phrases like, "_Well, to be honest with you,_" which says to the prospect that you aren't always honest.[18] Consider how you would react to this type of telephone call:

Hello, Michael—uh, my name is—uh Karl Malone—uh I'm with the Utah Jazz and—uh we've developed an—uh idea I—uh think you might find—uh interesting and—uh valuable. Uh—Michael, are morning or—uh afternoon appointments more convenient for you?

A salesperson with this type of delivery does not make a professional impression. Verbal hesitancy seems to signal a weak, unsure personality.[19] An essential element in telemarketing that helps overcome this is a script, whether it is general or written out word-for-word. Scripts are helpful in guiding the salespeople by capturing the prospect's attention. The first ten to thirty seconds of a telephone sales call are crucial; they go far toward determining whether your request for an appointment will be successful.

People buy from the people they like. Remember your projecting your personality over the phone.[20] How you say something can be as important as what you say.   Try to put a smile in your voice. The most successful salespeople project positive voice qualities such as sincerity, courtesy, and confidence. A survey conducted for Jacobi Voice Development revealed the type of voice characteristics prospects are most annoyed by. Table 8.1 illustrates the most negative or annoying qualities.[21]

TABLE 8.1 - Most Annoying Voice Characteristics	
1. Whining and complaining	44.0%
2. High-pitched or loud tone	28.0%
3. Mumblers	11.1%
4. Too fast or too weak	8.5%
5. Monotone voice	3.5%
6. Strong accent	2.4%

Organizing the Call

Inadequate preparation reduces the effectiveness of your delivery. Using a last-minute mental checklist helps you stay on track.[22]

1. *Why am I calling?* Do you want to make an appointment, check on customer's need to reorder, or follow up an inquiry?

2. *What is my proposal?* Your plan should have two parts: (1) what do you want from the person you call, and (2) what commitment you will make. Jot down some notes. Be specific!

3. *What would make this person want to grant my request?* Before calling, determine why the person you are calling will do what you request— grant the appointment, place the order, or provide the information you want. Recognize the customer's reason for acting rather than yours.

4. *Finally, review your telephone script.* Identify those key words or phrases in your telephone sales call that you can emphasize to make your message more convincing.[23]

Before you ever pick up the telephone, go through a mental checklist to ensure that you are fully prepared. Exhibit 8.5 presents ten strategic checkpoints to consider when you are preparing to use the telephone to set up appointments. An organized, professional salesperson knows what to say in advance of placing a call.

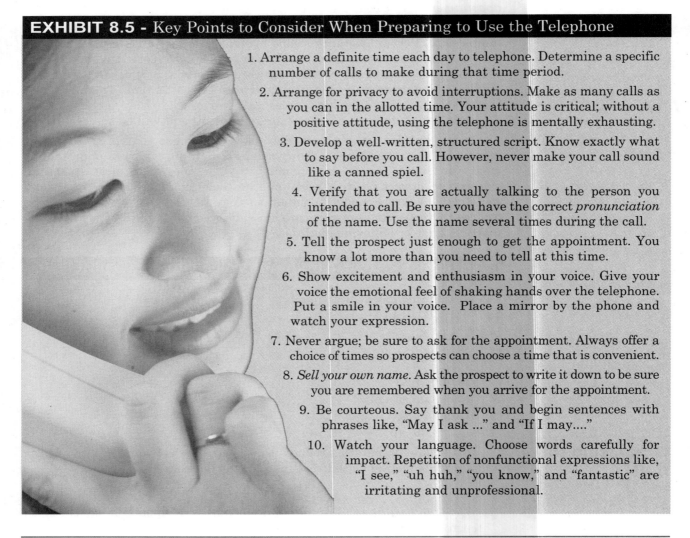

EXHIBIT 8.5 - Key Points to Consider When Preparing to Use the Telephone

1. Arrange a definite time each day to telephone. Determine a specific number of calls to make during that time period.

2. Arrange for privacy to avoid interruptions. Make as many calls as you can in the allotted time. Your attitude is critical; without a positive attitude, using the telephone is mentally exhausting.

3. Develop a well-written, structured script. Know exactly what to say before you call. However, never make your call sound like a canned spiel.

4. Verify that you are actually talking to the person you intended to call. Be sure you have the correct *pronunciation* of the name. Use the name several times during the call.

5. Tell the prospect just enough to get the appointment. You know a lot more than you need to tell at this time.

6. Show excitement and enthusiasm in your voice. Give your voice the emotional feel of shaking hands over the telephone. Put a smile in your voice. Place a mirror by the phone and watch your expression.

7. Never argue; be sure to ask for the appointment. Always offer a choice of times so prospects can choose a time that is convenient.

8. *Sell your own name.* Ask the prospect to write it down to be sure you are remembered when you arrive for the appointment.

9. Be courteous. Say thank you and begin sentences with phrases like, "May I ask ..." and "If I may...."

10. Watch your language. Choose words carefully for impact. Repetition of nonfunctional expressions like, "I see," "uh huh," "you know," and "fantastic" are irritating and unprofessional.

PLUGGING CONTACT MANAGEMENT INTO THE TELEPHONE

Of all the daily administrative tasks performed by a salesperson, using the telephone to set appointments is certainly one of the most critical. With sales force automation, telephone time becomes much more efficient and productive. All of the leading contact management programs have some integration with the telephone. This powerful tool can help you maximize the use of your precious phone time. A salesperson can review preapproach information gathered or any past conversations with the prospect or client.

Developing Partnerships Using Technology accentuates how contact management programs assist the salesperson in setting up appointments for a personal visit with a prospect or client. These programs give salespeople an integrated system for organizing prospecting information. The information might include the size and date of the previous purchases, when you contacted them last, and what happened in that interview—and even have the computer dial the phone for you.

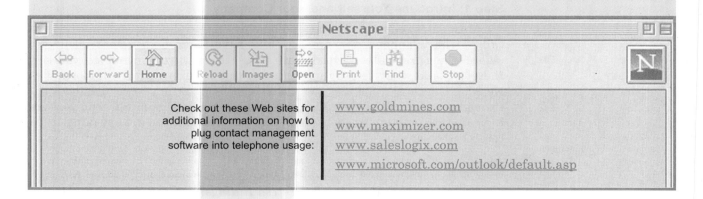

Developing Partnerships Using Technology

Plugging Your Contact Management Program into the Telephone

Full Information. A salesperson can review preapproach information gathered or any past conversations with the prospect or client. If a particular document or previous correspondence with an individual is needed, the salesperson can easily open the file (i.e., to review a price quote, check inventory, content of the last e-mail or memo sent, etc.). After the phone conversation, the prospect's file can be instantly updated with the new information.

Auto Dialing. Most programs are equipped with automatic dialing features. This requires a connection to the office phone system or modem. Instead of pounding away at the keypad, the salesperson can have the program dial the number. Calling is faster and more accurate, especially for international contacts with complex dialing codes.

Caller ID. Advances in telecommunications technology are making sales calls more effective. Caller ID can recognize incoming calls. This allows for screening calls without needing an administrative assistant. Contact management programs have these same advantages. The programs are able to pull up a contact's file whenever they call so it is right on the screen when the salesperson answers the phone.

Road Warrior Sidekick. Road warriors working out of their virtual office (their cars) now have the *virtual assistant* traveling with them. Contact management software dials, answers, screens calls, and finds files in the blink of an eye. Maybe one day soon, they will also make your morning coffee!

Netscape

Back Forward Home   Reload Images Open   Print Find   Stop

Check out these Web sites for additional information on how to plug contact management software into telephone usage:

www.goldmines.com
www.maximizer.com
www.saleslogix.com
www.microsoft.com/outlook/default.asp

THE SIX-STEP TELEPHONE TRACK

The key to using the telephone effectively is to engineer conversations that sound like talk. They have to be two-sided, but cleverly get people to sell themselves on seeing you. When you try to set an appointment by phone, you don't have the advantage of being able to show your prospect what a great product you offer. Instead, you need a careful strategy that allows the prospect to take an interest in what you're saying and agree to meet with you face-to-face. Use the six-step outline in Figure 8.3 to plan your appointment-setting calls so that the next time you talk to prospects, you're sitting in front of them.[24]

FIGURE 8.3

The Six-Step Telephone Track

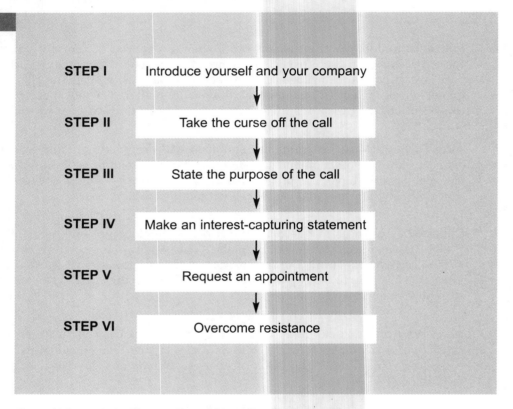

STEP I   Introduce yourself and your company

STEP II   Take the curse off the call

STEP III   State the purpose of the call

STEP IV   Make an interest-capturing statement

STEP V   Request an appointment

STEP VI   Overcome resistance

Step 1: Introduce Yourself and Your Company

Most sales relationships depend heavily on initial impressions. When you call on the telephone, the prospect will have made a judgment about you before your first fifteen words are said.[25] How you introduce yourself, therefore, and what you say immediately thereafter are vitally important. A weak or tentative opening puts a salesperson at a severe disadvantage throughout the rest of the call. Your opening words should tell who you are, indicate the company you represent, and confirm that you are speaking to the correct person:

Good morning ... I am Larry Henley, sales representative for Investors Daily. Am I speaking to Mrs. Teresa Ridings? ... Good. Mrs. Ridings, ...

Be sure the person you reach on the phone is someone who can make or influence a buying decision. Smile as you speak so that you transmit the impression of a warm, friendly personality. Watch the rate at which you speak. Prospects instinctively pay more attention to someone who speaks at a moderate rate. A too rapid rate of speech seems nervous or sounds as though you are reading a canned pitch. If you are too slow, you come across as lazy or unconcerned, or the prospect feels that talking to you will be a long, time-consuming process.

Step II: Take the Curse Off the Call

The telephone call is an *interruption* of your prospect's work. To sell people on the idea of granting you an appointment, you must detach their attention from what they were doing or thinking when the phone rang and attract it to what you propose. It helps if you think and talk about your call as a service you are offering rather than as an interruption for which you must apologize.

Put yourself in the prospect's position. People generally have a negative attitude about the telephone. Mention telephone selling, and they immediately think about photography, aluminum siding, or credit card salespeople. People particularly dislike robot-like voices reading canned scripts. You can take the curse off the call with a statement and a question to soften the impact of the interruption. For example,

1. *It will take just about a minute to explain why I'm calling. Is it convenient for you to talk now?*

2. *Mrs. Ridings, do you have a minute to speak with me now, or did I catch you at a bad time? ... (If the prospect indicates the time is inconvenient ...) ... When would be a better time?*

A prospect who is totally preoccupied with other matters may refuse to speak with you. In this case, calling back at a time the prospect suggests is better. When you do call back at the suggested time, the odds will be greatly improved that your message will receive a favorable hearing.

Step III: State the Purpose of the Call

Follow Step II (assuming the prospect does have time to speak) with a brief, hard-hitting, lead-in statement about why you are calling—just enough to capture the prospect's attention but short of describing the benefit(s) you will present in Step IV. Use these ideas to spark your creative thinking about possible lead-in statements you can use:

* Refer to a direct-mail piece you have already sent to the prospect.

* Mention the person who referred you to this prospect.

* Say that your company has designed a program or service to benefit clients like the prospect.

* Point out that your company's Web site is getting 15,000 hits each month. Ask if they have seen your latest product models and specifications.

A letter, product literature, a newsletter, or any other direct mail piece sent to a select sampling of prospects gives you the opportunity to call and inquire if they received it. This tactic gives you a purpose for calling and provides an acceptable type of lead-in statement. Here is a sample:

> *Mrs. Ridings, thank you for taking a minute of your valuable time to speak with me. My purpose in calling is to find out if you received the newsletter I sent you last week describing a specialized investment service that my company has recently developed for professionals like you.*

Whatever the answer, you can use this beginning to move on to the next step.

Perhaps the best reason you can give for calling is that you have been referred by a third party the prospect respects. The value of using a third party as an introduction is the immediate endorsement it provides. The prospect automatically assumes that you are reputable and reliable and that you deserve a hearing. In the majority of instances, a referral alone is enough to get the prospect to hear you out during this first telephone call. Then you must generate enough interest to motivate the prospect to agree to give you an appointment.[26]   Here is an example of how to use a referral as a purpose for calling:

> *Mrs. Ridings, I recently performed a service for the DM Bass Company that was extremely well received by their employees. Martha Bass was so pleased with the service and the results that she asked me to get in touch with you and see whether it might also be helpful to you.*

After you have established a legitimate purpose for the call, you are ready to move to the next step.

Step IV: Make an Interest-Capturing Statement

Once you have the prospect's attention, your task is to convert attention into interest so that you can expect a favorable hearing. Interest is established primarily by promising a benefit or offering a service. Use product benefits, company services, or financial rewards to answer the prospect's unspoken question: "What's in it for me?"[27] Offer the prospect a benefit from listening to you, offer a service, or offer to do something *for*—not *to*—the prospect. Be sure to say how long the actual personal visit will take, and assure the prospect that everything you have to say can be covered in that length of time unless the prospect wants to explore certain areas in greater detail. Here are two examples:

1. *Mrs. Ridings, we have designed a service for companies similar to yours that could increase the effectiveness of your business from 10 to 25 percent with a decrease in the cost of operation. It will take about 20 minutes for me to show you how.*

2.   *The benchmarking results from our design department show that many managers have been pleased with the quality and reliability of our new design simulator. Our clients report saving tens of thousands of dollars. In fact one client, Shelby Engineering, saved more than $50,000.*

Rather than making a statement, you may ask a question to capture the prospect's interest:

My company has an idea that could give complete protection to your entire plant and decrease your present costs. You are interested in cutting costs, aren't you?

Most business people want to see their operations run more efficiently and would answer this question in the affirmative. You could then suggest that you have a specific plan and request a personal visit to discuss it with the prospect.

Sales representatives of Transworld Systems Inc. (TSI) must give presentations in person because they use visual aids and review a prospect's receivables aging report, but they use the telephone to set appointments. TSI's corporate offices are located in Rohnert, CA. Paula Wilson, district manager for TSI, emphasizes the importance of creating interest in the first phone call. Prospects have to be given a valid reason to be interested in doing business with TSI. Our clients want to know—*what's in it for me?* The basic approach is to find out if the prospect is using a percentage agency or not using an agency at all (collecting internally). The prime objective for the TSI sales rep, according to Wilson, "is to set an appointment with the prospect." This is achieved by sharing information about the prospect's industry and causing them to wonder what their competitors know that they don't know. It is important that the sales rep control the flow of the telephone conversation. You don't want the prospect to make a rash decision regarding the service before a presentation is even made. Ms. Wilson recommends that sales reps use this language, "Transworld Systems works with over 40,000 clients nationwide including over (give number specific to the industry, i.e., 10,000 medical practices, over 500 heating and air conditioning contractors, over 800 CPA's, etc.) helping them to recover their slow paying and delinquent accounts without paying up to 50 percent of the collection as charged by a conventional agency. I would like to meet with you to let you see some results from other (physicians, contractors, accounts, etc.) who are using our service. Would Tuesday or, perhaps, Thursday of this week be better for you?"[28]

Step V: Request an Appointment

Remember that your goal at this point is to secure an appointment with the prospect so that you can make a complete presentation. Avoid giving interview information over the phone. The prospect can easily say, "I'm not interested" into a telephone. Then you have nowhere to go. The end of the story could be much different when you give an excellent presentation in person. In his book *Reach Out and Sell Someone*, Gary Goodman says that salespeople provide prospects with too much information over the phone; the more information you give, the more problems the prospect may see. He recommends the KISS approach to selling the appointment: *Keep It Simple, Salesperson!* The telephone itself encourages brevity. Ask for the appointment confidently and directly.

1. *I'm sure you agree that we should get together to discuss how we can accomplish this for you. Would this Thursday at nine be good for you? . . . or perhaps Friday morning would be better?*

2. *The best time for me would be tomorrow afternoon at 2:00 or Thursday morning at 11:00. Which would be more convenient for you, Mrs. Ridings?*

Notice that in each example the prospect was given a choice of times rather than asked, "When would it be convenient to see you?" which makes saying no too easy. You simply want to create enough initial interest to set up an appointment. Resist every temptation to get into specifics on the telephone. You are *selling an appointment*, not the product or service. After you have set up the appointment, be sure to say "thank you" and then allow the prospect to end the call. It is important for the salesperson to *hang up* last, because the prospect may think of something at the end and should hear your voice instead of a click.[29]

Step VI: Overcome Resistance

Using the telephone to set up appointments gives rise to two types of objections: an objection to receiving a telephone call and an objection to granting an interview. A prospect who was engaged in an activity of interest or importance may feel irritated by an interruption and prefer to resume that activity. This prospect's goal is to get you off the phone by refusing to become interested in what you have to say.

Prospects who do not want to grant an interview often fear that they cannot successfully defend their own ideas or decisions when faced by an experienced salesperson. They are afraid that they will buy. This type of objection can be overcome in three steps:

1. Agree sympathetically with the objection. This builds the prospect's ego.

2. Switch from the prospect's objection to your idea or purpose for the interview.

3. Ask for the appointment.

Here are two typical objections or types of resistance you are likely to encounter and possible ways to overcome them:

Prospect:

Salesperson: *I can certainly appreciate how busy you must be. That's why I phoned. Significant dollar savings, Mr. Ridings, could make this a priority for you. I am sensitive to people's schedules, and for that reason I use a planning calendar; I've got mine open as we speak. Would next Tuesday morning at 7:30 be good for you, or would 10:30 be even more convenient?*

Prospect: *Give me additional information while we are still on the phone.*

Salesperson: *Mr. Ridings, a phone conversation would not serve you very well. Using a series of charts and graphs in a personal meeting with you will take about 20 minutes and will help give you a precise picture of our approach. Would this afternoon at 3:00 be acceptable or would 4:30 tomorrow be better?*

Design the telephone approach in the six-step format presented above and then practice it until it feels comfortable and natural. *Internalize it rather than just memorize it.* Exhibit 8.6 is an example of an actual telephone script written by Ben Phillips an agent with Northwestern Mutual Life Insurance Company. Ben's example is a referred-lead telephone script. This is just one of five scripts he has developed depending upon the type of prospect he is calling. You can see how closely Ben follows the six-step telephone track.

EXHIBIT 8.6 - Referred-Lead Telephone Script

STEP 1: INTRODUCE YOURSELF

Good morning, I am Ben Phillips with Northwestern Mutual Life Insurance. Am I speaking with Mr. Jones? Good!

STEP 2: GET APPROVAL TO CONTINUE

Mr. Jones, it will only take a minute to explain to you why I am calling you today. Is it convenient for you to talk now? Thank You!

STEP 3: STATE YOUR PURPOSE FOR CALLING

Mr. Jones, as I mentioned I am with Northwestern Mutual Life. Our mutual friend Mrs. Smith is a customer of mine, and she felt that some of the ideas that I shared with her might also be of interest to you. Mrs. Smith has been pleased with the service that I provide and thought that it might be good to check with you to see if you too might benefit from my services.

STEP 4: CAPTURE INTEREST

Mr. Jones, I would like the opportunity to share with you how Northwestern Mutual is helping people just like you explore their family's financial security. It will take me about twenty minutes to show you the kind of work I do, and if you feel like some of the ideas I share with you would improve your situation I would consider it a privilege to help you in that way.

STEP 5: REQUEST APPOINTMENT

Mr. Jones, I am sure that you are interested in providing financial security for you and your family aren't you? Then I think we should get together for a few minutes and explore how our services may help you accomplish that.

STEP 6: OVERCOME RESISTANCE

Prospect: I already have insurance!

AGENT: *GREAT! BECAUSE OUR SYSTEM TAKES INTO ACCOUNT YOUR EXISTING INSURANCE. SO WE CAN TAKE A LOOK AT YOUR ENTIRE SITUATION.*

Prospect: I have enough insurance!

AGENT: *I AM GLAD YOU MENTIONED THAT. MANY PEOPLE FEEL THE SAME WAY, BUT A CURRENT REVIEW IS NEARLY ALWAYS BENEFICIAL. THAT WAY YOU WILL KNOW THAT YOUR PROGRAM IS STAYING CURRENT.*

Courtesy of Mr. Ben Phillips of Murfreesboro, TN.

SUMMARY

Planning and preparation are the keys to a successful preapproach and therefore to securing an appointment for a sales interview. The planning and preparation needed here are an extension of the prospecting activities through which you obtained the prospect's name. Now you are continuing to learn about the prospect and how you can best make an approach that will result in scheduling a sales interview that will eventually produce a sale.

Preapproach may be by personal call to meet the prospect briefly and request a later appointment, by letter to introduce yourself and your company to be followed by a personal call or telephone call to request an appointment, or by telephone. Each of these three types of preapproach may be used effectively under the appropriate conditions. The telephone is probably the most frequently used because of its cost effectiveness.

The attempt to set up a sales interview may be regarded as a mini sale in which the product is a sales interview and the purpose of the call is to sell the prospect on the idea of granting the interview. You have to keep the discussion focused on that purpose and that purpose only. Save the description of the product or service and its features and benefits for the interview.

The ideal telephone preapproach call proceeds through six steps:

Step I: Introduce yourself and your company
Step II: Take the curse off the call
Step III: State the purpose of the call
Step IV: Make an interest-capturing statement
Step V: Request an appointment
Step VI: Overcome resistance

QUESTIONS FOR THOUGHT AND DISCUSSION

1. What are the steps to follow in preapproach planning?

2. What information do you need about a prospect before you call to request an appointment for a sales interview?

3. What are the important sources for obtaining information about a prospect?

4. In what way may a telephone call to request an appointment serve to qualify the prospect?

5. What can you do to make sure your timing is appropriate for making a telephone call to a particular prospect as well as for the time you suggest for the appointment?

6. What advantages and disadvantages does calling for an appointment present in regard to the first impression you make on the prospect?

7. What is the six-step framework for making a telephone presentation?

8. How should a salesperson deal with prospects who say they are too busy for a sales interview?

9. If the prospect asks you to describe your proposition over the telephone, how would you handle the situation?

10. Who should be in control of the flow of the preapproach telephone call? How do you make sure control is in the proper hands?

11. Suppose that you telephone to make an appointment with a prospect. When the secretary answers, you say, "Mr. Steele, please, Joan Gray calling." If the secretary responds, "May I ask the nature of your call?" What answer would you give? If you give your answer and are then told that Mr. Steele is too busy to see you, what do you say then?

ACTIVITIES

1. Suppose you are a financial planner and learn from a friend that Joe Green has just received a promotion and a raise. These two items alone give you enough information to put Joe in your prospect file. What kinds of additional information would you attempt to get about Joe before meeting with him? Write a sample telephone script for obtaining an appointment with Joe. Then visualize and write a scenario for your first meeting with him.

2. Assume you are a salesperson for USX Corp. and call on industrial customers. Assume, also, that you work in a specific city for which you have access to newspapers, magazines, and other public information. During a one-week period, review these materials and any other available information and write a report in which you judge the quality of this information as a basis for assessing prospects.

3. An office supply salesperson uses the following telephone approach when in doubt about a prospect's authority to buy: "Mr. Crew, my presentation will take approximately fifteen minutes. I realize your time is precious and I want to be certain that you are the person with whom I should be talking. Are you the one I should see about purchasing office supplies, or does someone else have that responsibility?" What is your reaction to this approach? Why?

Case Study

CASE 8.1

As Kevin Warren drove to his next scheduled stop at Baker Products, he thought to himself, "I wonder if that call was worth the time it took. I did get an order for some bubble pack, but sitting 25 minutes in the waiting room didn't add much to my commission. Oh, well, some days it goes like that." Kevin's company produces a complete line of packaging materials used by a wide range of manufacturers and wholesalers, so most firms that ship products are potential customers. Kevin was making a living but wasn't setting the world on fire. Just last week, his sales manager mentioned that he should be making more calls per week. "You know the old saying, the more people you see, the more sales you make. Maybe your territory is poorly organized. Why don't you take a look?"

Kevin did take a look — and found nothing to criticize. He had divided the territory into segments to eliminate backtracking. Although he had not been able to do away with every lengthy drive, they were at a bare minimum.

Parking in the visitor's lot at Baker Products, he took a few minutes to review his file to refresh his memory about their past purchases and his contact person there. Then he went into the office and asked for Mr. Lewis. The receptionist said, "I'm sorry, but Mr. Lewis is visiting our other plants and won't be back for three weeks. I'll let you see his assistant, Miss Alexander." Kevin greeted her, "Miss Alexander, it's nice to meet you. I'm Kevin Warren; I've been supplying your company with packaging materials for a couple of years. According to my records, this is the month you usually order. Did Mr. Lewis mention it before he left?

"No, he didn't—at least not to me. I'm afraid I can't help you. Mr. Lewis will be back on the 17th. I know he'll be swamped for a few days. Can you come back after the 20th? Mr. Lewis should be able to see you then." Kevin was committed for that time to another part of his territory, and he was almost sure he wouldn't be able to get back before his next regularly scheduled time in this part of his territory. Walking to his car, Kevin thought, "A thirty-mile drive out here and nothing to show for it. Now it's thirty miles back to the city, and it'll be too late for another call. I guess the boss is right; I need to make more calls. But even more than that, I need to make each call more productive, too. The boss suggested calling ahead for appointments, but I'm not very good at that. I've got to do something, though."

1. Are telephone calls to set up appointments the answer to Kevin Warren's problem? As he has not been successful with this technique previously, how can he make it work for him?

2. What else could Kevin do when a prospect is not available other than just come back later?

3. What other sources for ideas would you suggest for Kevin?

CASE 8.2

Barry West hung up the phone and slumped in his chair. "It happened again. I get more stalls than an old battery!" Barry couldn't understand why it happened so often. His line of business products, particularly the ultramodern microfilm system for indexing and filing documents, should have been of prime interest to the Merchant's National Bank trust officer to whom he had just talked. Before he had managed to tell Mrs. Blevins about more than one or two of the system's unique features, however, she cut him off, saying she couldn't consider anything of that sort until after the bank's planned remodeling project was complete and she knew just what space would be available. The next call was no better. Davis Brothers Department Store should certainly have been interested in something in his line, but when he asked for an appointment he heard the same old story. When Ms. Kingsley, the office manager, asked the purpose of the appointment, Barry told her he wanted to show her all the various products he had to offer so she could see what she needed that he could supply. Ms. Kingsley replied that she really didn't know of a thing she needed at this time, that she was in the midst of an especially busy season, and that Barry should call at some later time if he had anything specific to show her.

"Maybe it would be better if I just dropped in to see prospects without any warning. Maybe they couldn't think of so many stalls that way," Barry mused.

1.   Can you account for Barry's problem with stalls? What two principles of telephone use did he violate in these two calls?

2.   Is he right in thinking he would do better by calling on prospects without an appointment? Is he likely to find that they would not offer stalls if he called in person?

3.   Write out a plan of action for Barry to follow that could improve his results in gaining appointments by telephone.

PART IV

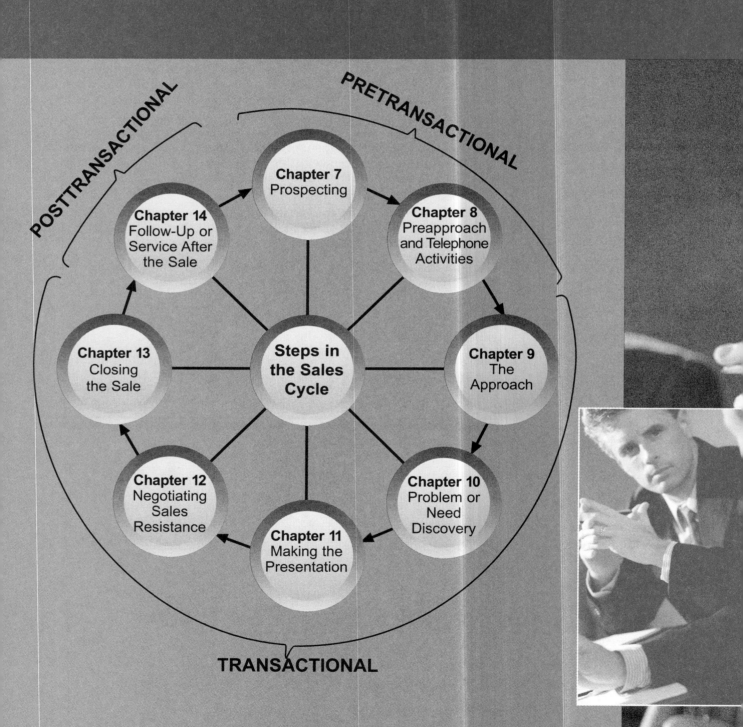

POSTTRANSACTIONAL

PRETRANSACTIONAL

Chapter 7
Prospecting

Chapter 8
Preapproach
and Telephone
Activities

Chapter 14
Follow-Up or
Service After
the Sale

**Steps in
the Sales
Cycle**

Chapter 9
The
Approach

Chapter 13
Closing
the Sale

Chapter 10
Problem or
Need
Discovery

Chapter 12
Negotiating
Sales
Resistance

Chapter 11
Making the
Presentation

TRANSACTIONAL

Chapters 9 to 13 get at the heart of professional, consultative selling. This can be considered the "how to" portion of the book. It is the valuable time spent in the actual live sales interview. The time when a commitment is gotten and kept.

Chapter 9 focuses on the approach. What happens in the opening minutes is crucial to the overall success of the sales interview. Chapter 10 is devoted to the art of asking questions and to listening effectively. A questioning sequence and listening guidelines are presented to carry through the entire sales interview. Chapter 11 details the techniques to use in making the actual presentation of features and benefits.

The psychology behind handling objections and closing the sale is presented in chapters 12 and 13. A plan to handle sales resistance is introduced while a separate section in chapter 12 explains several ways of dealing with the difficult price objection. Chapter 13 stresses that closing the sale is the natural conclusion to a successful sales interview. A special section presents specific ways that help a salesperson deal with the rejection so common in selling.

excellence

Excellence is never an accident. It is achieved in an organization only as a result of an unrelenting and vigorous insistence on the highest standards of performance. It requires an unswerving dedication to continuous quality improvement.

Excellence is contagious. It infects and affects everyone in an organization. It charts the direction of programs. It establishes the criteria for planning. It provides zest and vitality to the organization. Once achieved, excellence has a way of penetrating every phase of the life of an organization.

Excellence demands commitment and a tenacious dedication from the leadership of the organization. Once it is accepted and expected, it must be nourished and continually reviewed and renewed. It is a never-ending process of learning and growing. It requires a spirit of motivation and boundless energy.

Excellence inspires; it electrifies. It potentializes every phase of the organization's life. It unleashes an impact which influences every program, every activity, every committee, every individual. To instill it in an organization is difficult; to sustain it, even more so. It demands adaptability, imagination and vigor. But, most of all, it requires from the leadership a constant state of self-discovery and discipline.

Excellence is an organization's life-line. It is the most compelling answer to apathy and inertia. It energizes a stimulating and pulsating force. Once it becomes the expected standard of performance, it develops a fiercely driving and motivating philosophy of operation.

Excellence is a state of mind put into action. It is a road-map to success. Success is getting what you want. Happiness is liking what you get. Successful people form the habit of doing what unsuccessful people don't like to do.

Excellence in life is important...because it is everything. The quality of a person's life is in direct proportion to their commitment to excellence regardless of their chosen field of endeavor.

Approaching the Prospect

LEARNING OBJECTIVES

- To discover the purpose of the approach in a sales situation.

- To explore the importance of first impressions and ways to control them as a means of improving sales performance.

- To understand how surface language affects the ability to establish rapport with a prospect.

- To examine the elements of the greeting in a sales situation and how to choose and control them.

- To discover ways to get the attention and capture the interest of the prospect.

- To explore different types of approaches and understand the best circumstances in which to use each one.

Chapter

YOU NEVER GET A SECOND CHANCE TO MAKE A GOOD...

Follow the river and you will find the sea. Determination is the key.

Individuals cannot consistently perform in a manner which is inconsistent with the way they see themselves.

Remember...If you fail to plan, you plan to fail.

Some people dream of worthy accomplishments, while others stay awake and do them.

The single most important ingredient in the formula for success is knowing how to deal with people.

If you don't take care of the customer...somebody else will.

Manage your time and your choices—and you'll manage your life.

Prepare yourself for leadership. Be a living example of the excellence you expect from others.

Running a business is no trouble at all as long as it's not yours.

Everything you say and do is a reflection of the inner you.

Singin' in the rain of life is better than letting it dampen your spirits.

Self-esteem, commitment and action determine your outcome.

If we could kick the person responsible for most of our problems, we wouldn't be able to sit for a week.

One way to avoid criticism is to do nothing and be a nobody. The world will then not bother you.

No one is useless in this world who lightens the burden of another.

*Choose a job you love
and you will never have to work a day in your life.*

PURPOSE OF THE APPROACH

The *Road Warrior* in full battle gear!

Your prospecting and preapproach efforts have uncovered potential clients, and you have successfully arranged a personal meeting with a prospect. What happens during the opening of the face-to-face encounter profoundly affects the success of the whole presentation and your ability to close the sale. The approach is important because it determines the character of your future relationship with a prospect, including how receptive the prospect will be to your presentation and whether the close will be difficult or easy. Although the overall success of the interview depends on more than the approach, an effective approach creates a favorable buyer-seller environment. The approach is often overlooked or taken for granted. Although the approach is usually considered in the context of the first call on a prospect, every meeting with a client—new or long-established—begins with an approach.

Salespeople tend to use the same approach over and over, but prospects and situations are not the same; instead, salespeople ought to make a practice of using various types of approaches that fit the needs of a specific situation, whether calling on new prospects or on old customers. An effective approach achieves four key objectives:

1. To make a favorable or *positive impression* on the prospect
2. To gain the prospect's *undivided attention*
3. To develop *positive interest* in your proposition
4. To lead *smoothly* into the fact-finding or need-discovery phase of the interview

FIRST IMPRESSIONS

In his book *Contact: The First Four Minutes*, Leonard Zunin says that the first four minutes of initial contact with a prospect are crucial. He suggests that four minutes is the average time the prospect takes to decide whether to buy from you. Impress the prospect with a show of good manners, clear enunciation, good grooming, and appropriate dress; when you look and act like a professional, the prospect, consciously or subconsciously, begins to trust you. People make quick decisions based on feelings, emotions, or hunches. The more positive their feelings, the more they hear and accept what you say. The opening moments of the approach must be designed to create an atmosphere of trust. The first twelve words you speak tell volumes about you.[1] Every personal characteristic is watched and evaluated; your approach must be impeccable. Exhibit 9.1 presents some guidelines for making the first impression favorable. *After all, you never get a second chance to make a good first impression.*

Although some buyers base purchasing decisions on first impressions, others do not. Doug Bartulis, a sales representative with Applied Data Systems Inc., based in New Haven, Connecticut, has several clients who admit that they did not like him at first. Remember, too, that you are not forced to like all prospects personally; you can sell to them in spite of a lack of personal attraction. A consultative salesperson must be able to work effectively with a prospect even in the presence of a personality clash. Look further than your first impression of a prospect before making an unalterable judgment.

EXHIBIT 9.1 - There's No Second Chance to Make a Good First Impression

When meeting a prospect for the first time, pay attention to:

Visual factors
- Correct any detail that could become a visible distraction: a tattered briefcase, a messy car, or inappropriate grooming.
- Nonverbal communication is powerful. Pay attention to what the prospect sees in your body language as well as in what you wear.
- Don't wear jewelry such as lapel pins, tie pins, or rings that advertise your membership in a specific organization that may not be recognized or admired by some people.

Organization, professional habits
- Be prompt, even early. Set your watch five minutes ahead if necessary.
- Present a clear agenda. State the purpose of your call right away. Make it clear that you are not there to waste the prospect's time.
- Be prepared with as much information as possible about the prospect (individual and/or company).

Building rapport
- Be sure to pronounce the prospect's name correctly. A person's name is a personal identifier; mispronouncing it takes away some of the owner's status.
- If you pay the prospect a compliment, make it specific and of personal interest.
- Recall the importance of proxemics. Respect the prospect's personal space.
- Look for common ground like mutual friends, membership in the same religious or civic group, or similar hobbies.

Actions
- Shake hands, maintain eye contact, and greet the prospect warmly, but never say, "How are you?"
- Refrain from personal habits like smoking or chewing gum or careless language that might be offensive to some people.

Attitude
- Be enthusiastic. Enthusiasm is infectious if it is sincere.

Although first impressions may be dependable signposts, first impressions do have some weaknesses:

- They are likely to be based on feelings and emotions.

- All behavior traits do not show up simultaneously, and an initial short interview may not provide enough time for all traits (either favorable or unfavorable) to surface.

- The prospect may deliberately control behavior and allow you to see only certain chosen personality traits.

- Some event immediately preceding the interview may strongly influence the prospect's current behavior.

Be willing to wait before you conclude that you and a prospect have a personality conflict that cannot be overcome. At the same time, remember that the prospect may not be aware that such a suspension of judgment is needed and may judge you on the first impression you present. As a professional salesperson, your job is to establish rapport, build confidence, and make the prospect feel comfortable. Do everything in your power to satisfy the needs of your prospects, and refuse to allow first impressions to prevent a mutually beneficial sales experience.

SURFACE LANGUAGE (APPEARANCE, ACCESSORIES, CLOTHES)

Surface language—including grooming, clothing, accessories, posture, and all other aspects of appearance—vitally affects first impressions, even though surface language factors actually provide limited or shallow insight into the true person. Salespeople must be sure the statements they make with their surface language are favorable because the impressions formed during the first few minutes of an initial encounter between two people could be lasting. Successful salespeople increase the odds in their favor by taking advantage of the power of first impressions. Visual impressions almost always come first. Fortunately, you can do a lot to shape the visual impact you make when a prospect first sees you.

Projecting an Image

"As an effective salesperson you want your clothes to command respect, inspire credibility and create trust – you must come across as the authority on the product that is offered," points out Sherry Maysonave, head of Empowerment Enterprises in Austin, Texas.[2] Your clothes speak volumes about you, your company, your work, and how you relate to customers. Clothes, grooming, and accessories work together to make a statement that can either make or break you in sales. You can kill a sale by being too casual or by overdressing. When you know that you are dressed appropriately, you feel good about yourself. When you are confident and at ease, you emanate an air of competence that the prospect unconsciously accepts and interprets as credibility.[3] Total appearance is important because the prospect's initial attention is focused on you and not on your proposition. If you want to be successful, you must look successful. A salesperson who wears an obviously cheap suit, for example, creates a negative impression and sets up this line of thinking in the mind of the prospect:

1. This salesperson is dressed cheaply. He must not be making much money.
2. Because he's not making much money, he must be having difficulty selling his product.
3. If the product is not selling, something must be wrong with it.
4. I don't want an inferior product.

Joe Girard, who according to the *Guinness Book of World Records* is the world's greatest salesman, says, "I believe a salesman should look as much as possible like the people to whom he sells.... I never wear clothes that will antagonize my customers and make them feel uneasy."[4]

Dress Conservatively. Your objective as a salesperson is to focus the prospect's attention on the benefits of buying your product or service. Anything that detracts from that focus works against you. Conservative dress gives the prospect the impression that talking with you is safe and that you are familiar and dependable. Excessive flamboyance in dress or lack of attention to generally accepted norms raises a red flag and warns the prospect of undefined danger. Although "conservative" varies from one region to another and from one industry to another, that variation is not extremely wide. The color and pattern of clothes should be conservative. Dressing conservatively suggests stability and dependability; following extreme fads of color, cut, and pattern may suggest just the opposite. Casual corporate dressing has become a trend, and it appears to be a growing one. Exhibit 9.2 discusses how a conservative approach to this trend must be taken to achieve a professional, yet laid-back, style.[5]

Choose Accessories Carefully. Accessories are intended to enhance your appearance. Make sure they do not call attention to themselves. Jewelry should be simple. One good piece is more impressive than three or four cheap pieces.

Jewelry that announces your association with some organization or belief—unless shared by the prospect—may call attention to itself and away from the purpose of your call.

Accessories should be of good quality. High-quality pen and pencil sets and top-quality leather attaché cases make a quiet statement of your personal pride in your profession and mark you as successful.

Avoid sunglasses or lenses that noticeably change color with shifts in light. People may not believe what you are saying if they cannot see your eyes. Hiding your eyes seems to say you are hiding something else as well.

Dress Appropriately. You should plan to dress as well as your prospect. People feel comfortable dealing with those who seem to fit into their own lifestyle. Jean Louis Decaix is the number one salesperson for his firm in

EXHIBIT 9.2 - What Is Corporate Casual?

Salespeople today are suffering from what might be called the "casual confusion syndrome." Just what is business casual? Some sales reps think business casual means a two-day beard and faded jeans! Salespeople today have to be a lot like Superman. Bob Kiel, a consultant in Silicon Valley, has changed clothes four times in one day for various appointments. The casual look is not easy to achieve. "There has been an uproar about corporate casual," says Marc Streisand, founder of Inside-Out, a New York-based image consulting company. "People still don't know how to do it. It's not weekend casual." The problem lies in that being told what *not* to wear doesn't help people know what *to* wear. This new trend is not intended to convey a lack of professionalism, just a more comfortable, perhaps less boring way of projecting one's best.

Streisand says that "professional" is the key word to remember. If you are still left wondering what to wear on casual day, he offers this advice: "It's like going on a blind date," he says. "You want to look good, but not overdone. You want to be able to go to a good restaurant and not be embarrassed."

Perhaps the biggest mistake made is dressing too casual. Your clothes should reflect your position.

For Men – A suit is still quite appropriate, but for those more casual customer visits, try wool pants or quality cotton slacks worn with one of the following: a blazer, tie, and dress shirt; a cotton, silk, or merino wool sweater; a rayon, silk, or cotton shirt.

For Women – One staple should be a sheath or shift dress that can be worn alone or with a matching jacket; sweater sets and tailored pants are also adaptable to business casual. You may want to keep handy (i.e., under your desk) spare flats to dress down an outfit or heels to dress it up.

Paris, France, in medical diagnostic equipment sales. He says, "I refuse to wear jewelry. I don't wear loud ties and prefer a quiet, elegant appearance that is more in line with the tastes of my clients. Customers buy the salesperson long before they buy the product."[6] If your clothes are too formal or carry too much of an aura of power, you cause the prospect to feel overpowered; the result may be rebellion against what is perceived as your snobbish attitude. If you dress too casually or carelessly, prospects may unconsciously feel that you do not consider them or their business important.

Geography plays a part in your choice of clothes. When selling in international markets, it is vital to know what is appropriate attire. For example, when in Rome, dress sharp! Italy is famous for being the birthplace of all things bella. Understandably, fashion plays a role in business negotiations, where looking good is seen as a reflection of success.[7] On the other hand, large cities in the United States call for more formality in dress than do smaller towns and cities. The high-pressure climate in large cities also calls for a stronger authority statement in clothing. Smaller cities and suburban areas may accept Ivy League styles and other more casual styles. Sun Belt cities and towns accept lighter colors and more casual styles than would be acceptable in the Northeast. People perceive what you wear as your statement of who you are and what you do. Exhibit 9.3 indicates what the clothes you wear say about your image.[8]

EXHIBIT 9.3 - Dressed to Sell

What do your clothes say about you? That you're sophisticated? Disorganized? Powerful? Your professional image should work for you, not against you. How you look goes a long way toward establishing your identity. Your clothes say much about your character and credibility.

Consider these nine style tips:

1. Clothes should be professional and understated. Flashy clothes detract from your image and take attention away from the work at hand.

2. Absolutely nothing you wear should be wrinkled, frayed or sloppy.

3. Always wear suits to meetings; jackets give the appearance of authority.

4. The most powerful color is blue. This is why police uniforms are blue.

5. Keep your shoes shined (men often judge others by the condition of their shoes).

6. Make sure your socks match your suit and shoes.

7. Keep accessories simple: ties, watches, jewelry. Clients should be looking at you, not your accessories.

8. Dress in line with your superiors, but never more casually than subordinates.

9. Dress appropriately for your business. Bankers always look like bankers.

10. Be prepared for unexpected meetings. Have a spare sports jacket/blazer cleaned, pressed, and ready in your office.

Give Attention to Grooming. Grooming, like dress style, should be conservative. Men's hair should look neat and recently trimmed. Women's hair is usually best between collar and shoulder length. The style should be simple and easy to manage. Extreme hairstyles for women are sometimes perceived by prospects as a subtle sexual statement, regardless of the saleswoman's intention. Women's makeup should be used in moderation so that it enhances the general appearance without calling attention to itself. For both men and women, neatness and cleanliness are obviously necessary. Avoid hair preparations that leave a greasy, shiny look; keep perfumes and other scents light and unobtrusive. Obsessiveness about neatness is not desirable, but reasonable attention to appearance is good common sense.

THE PROPER GREETING

Choice of Greeting

In order to increase the odds of making a good impression, use the business etiquette *Rule of Twelve*. The first twelve words you speak should include a form of thanks: "Good morning, Mrs. Eubank. Thank you for agreeing to see me," or "Good afternoon, Brian. It's a pleasure to meet you." Casual questions like "How are you?" or "How ya' doing?" have lost all semblance of meaning. How does the prospect respond? "Great" or "Just fine, thank you," but what if the prospect is not feeling great and what if business is not going great? If a prospect covers up real feelings with a conventional answer, a vague feeling of uneasiness results from the untruth. If the prospect responds to your question with a long list of ills or problems, no response you make can turn attention naturally toward your sales presentation. How might you answer the simple question "How are you?" You may want to try the response used by Pat Shemek. When prospects or clients ask Shemek "How are you doing," his response has become a real attention getter. Pat replies, "Super duper"—an answer certainly different from the typical response, but it seems to give him an edge over competitive salespeople. The clients have come to expect this response. They look forward to it. Shemek's attitude seems to be—fake it until you make it! If this sounds too impracticable for your style, come up with your own unique response delivered with a smile on your face and enthusiasm in your voice. Your customers will appreciate your positive attitude.[9]

GEEK BOY SERVICES

Remember the movie *The Revenge of the Nerds*? Well, now there is a company serving their needs. For about $1,000, Geek Boy Services, a Silicon Valley consulting service, provides image makeovers to admitted computer geeks who want to spice up their T-shirt-and-khakis wardrobe. The consulting service also advises their clients on nightclubs where they can go to try out their new looks and test their dating skills.[10]

The Handshake

Your voice inflection and how you shake hands are as important as what you say. These three elements of the greeting taken together tell a prospect your mood. The handshake, particularly, is a revealing form of nonverbal communication. Exhibit 9.4 presents helpful guidelines for an effective handshake.

The prospect's handshake can provide useful information for your presentation. People with a dominant, assertive behavioral style (a classic *driver*) have a very strong handshake and may even indicate a desire to dominate by turning their wrist to position the hand over yours. This type of

---

EXHIBIT 9.4 - Guidelines for an Effective Handshake

1. Maintain eye contact for the duration of the handshake.

2. You may wait for the prospect to initiate the handshake (to avoid offending those people who "do not like to be touched").

3. Apply firm, consistent pressure on the hand. Avoid the limp-wristed, wet-fish or bone-crusher handshakes.

4. If your palm tends to be moist from nervousness, carry a special handkerchief with powder and pat your hand several times just before entering the prospect's office. Be careful not to leave a residue of powder on your hand that might be transferred to the prospect's hand or to your clothes.

5. The hands should meet equidistant between the prospect and the salesperson in a vertical position. If you turn your wrist so your hand is over the prospect's, this nonverbal gesture implies the intention to be dominant. If you turn your wrist so that your hand is on the bottom, you are signaling a submissive nature.

person wants to win at everything. People with less assertive personalities (*amiables*, for example) tend to shake hands with little eye contact and with less aggression.

The handshake is also an indispensable tool to consider when selling to customers around the globe. Several tips for *international* handshaking are presented in Table 9.1.[11] The customs and mannerisms of our overseas partners are equally

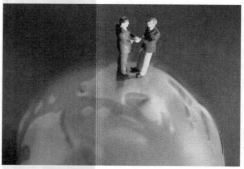

International handshake

essential to understand and accommodate. Be sure to make use of this information as one aspect of surface language to assist you in establishing rapport with people, regardless of nationality or personality style.

Small Talk or Get Down to Business

In the initial face-to-face meeting, both parties may experience what might be called *relationship tension*. Prospects fear being sold something they do not want, and salespeople face the fear of being rejected. The opening few minutes of conversation are designed to find a comfort level for both parties so that rapport can be established. The purpose of small talk at the opening of the interview is to gain an advantageous, positive beginning that breaks the ice and eases the tension. Small talk may be a discussion of topics entirely

TABLE 9.1 - Shaking Hands Around the World

Four noteworthy tips when greeting international prospects and customers:

1. **Shake hands with everyone.** International etiquette demands that the salesperson shake hands with everyone in the room. Not shaking hands with someone is noticed, and considered a personal rejection.

2. **Initiate the handshake.** An American saleswoman should extend her hand to a European male. Not doing so causes her to lose credibility. Women should initiate handshakes, and shake hands with other women and men.

3. **Culture-to-culture differences.** Latin Americans tend to use a lighter, lingering handshake. In Arab countries, handshakes are limp and last longer than the average American handshake. Japanese salespeople shake hands with one firm gesture. The handshake is often combined with a slight bow.

4. **Shake hands a lot.** Western and Eastern Europeans reshake hands whenever they have been apart, even if just for a very short period of time.

unrelated to what you are selling. Topics like mutual friends, similar interests in civic organizations, hobbies, and family life are frequently used. Al Angell, a very successful sales professional in Dallas, says this warm-up period usually takes him five minutes or more. Al calls this time "chit-chat with a purpose." He asks four basic questions that he feels are nonthreatening, easy to answer, and objective:

1. Are you a native of this area?
2. Were you educated there? (Based on answer to Question 1)
3. Are you a family person?
4. How did you happen to get into this business?

This type of socializing at the beginning of the interview eases tension and may give you some insight into your prospect's behavioral style. It warms up a cold environment and has the side benefit of providing additional information about the prospect. If the prospect seems withdrawn or even hostile, this warm-up conversation helps you determine whether that is the prospect's real personality or whether you have arrived on an especially bad day.

People love to tell you what they do in their spare time, talk about their accomplishments, or tell you about their families. This non-selling conversation is important. An ideal topic for initial chit-chat is one that relaxes the prospect, is of interest, and relates – if possible – to your objective so that you can move easily into the attention getter and then into need discovery. [12]

People have no confidence in salespeople whose only interest is self-interest, who seek to use their clients instead of being of use to their clients.

Like snowflakes, people are unique, but they have commonalities. If you cultivate wide interests and make a sincere effort to be well-informed, you will always have a topic of conversation that will interest your prospect. Rex Russell, who represents Honeycombs Industries in Salt Lake City, subscribes to twelve magazines just to stay current on topics that may be of interest to his customers and prospects.

Use of the Prospect's Name

People do not like to have their names forgotten, misspelled, or mispronounced. Typically, when we are introduced to someone, we hear our own name, then we might hear the other person's name. In *How to Win Friends and Influence People*, Dale Carnegie says, "A person's name is to them [sic] the sweetest and most important sound in any language." If we forget a name or mispronounce it, we send out this message: "I care more about me and my name than I do about you and your name." Imagine how a prospect feels when you say, "So you see, Mr ... ah ... uh ..., excuse me (shuffle for prospect card or appointment calendar) uh ..., Mr. Danner, I mean, Tanner." The prospect probably stiffens, the environment turns a bit frosty, and you may well walk out without an order.[13] Now recall how pleased you were when someone remembered your name after just a casual meeting several weeks previously. You would stand in line to do business with such a person.

Improving your memory for names is not as difficult as it may seem.[14] Several books are available to help you devise a method to correct a careless memory for names. Table 9.2 gives some suggestions for remembering names.[15]

TABLE 9.2 - How to Remember Your Customers' Names

Five steps to remembering names:

1. **Pay attention.** Ask to have the name repeated (even spelled). It will impress the person.

2. **Concentrate.** Look for characteristics that distinguish this person from others.

3. **Associate.** Relate a characteristic with some gimmick to help you recall the name.

4. **Observe.** Study people regularly to strengthen your ability to see characteristics and practice your imagination.

5. **Repeat it.** Use the prospect's name several times during the interview.

The question of whether to use the prospect's first name or to be more formal and use the last name with the appropriate title (Mr., Miss, Mrs., or Ms.) creates a great deal of discussion and disagreement. Some salespeople feel that using the first name presumes that a relationship is more personal than business. Others feel that sticking exclusively to last names is so formal that rapport is difficult to establish. This question must be addressed by each individual salesperson on the basis of a number of factors:

- Relative ages of salesperson and prospect

- Prevailing custom in the geographic area or industry

- The type of product or service being sold

- The salesperson's conclusions about the prospect's behavioral style

If you are in doubt, you are wise to risk being too formal rather than risk being too informal. Some salespeople ask permission to use the prospect's first name. Others wait and follow the lead of the prospect. Whatever route you choose must be one that you can follow with respect for the prospect and sincerity of feeling on your part.

The professional salesperson should remember not only the names of prospects and clients but also the names of their secretaries, assistants, and associates. These people also have feelings and can be instrumental in helping you secure an order. Purchasing agents depend on their personnel to help evaluate you after you leave.

SUIT THE APPROACH TO THE PERSON

Most people today have more work than they can hope to complete during regular working hours. Individual consumers, purchasing agents, engineers—anyone a sales representative might contact—feel time pressure and quite naturally regard the salesperson as an intruder. Prospects may react with resentment toward anyone who appears intent upon "stealing" precious time to engage in "small talk." How much or how little time you give to small talk or chit-chat depends on the behavioral style of the prospect, the circumstances of the moment, and the nature of your visit. If you sense that the prospect wants to get on with the interview, then move on.

People are different, and you must communicate differently with them. Some are social, seek relationships, and love to talk to other people (*amiables*). Others are time-conscious, results-oriented, and strictly business and want to keep it that way (*drivers*). Others are creative and want to talk about ideas and concepts (*expressives*). Still others are extremely thorough, want all the details, are slow to make decisions, and do not want to establish personal relationships (*analyticals*).

Personal Data Assistant

Take Along Your Personal Data Assistant. The personal computer is a valuable partner to the professional salesperson. Rick Mahan is sales manager for Lowell Inc., a company that manufactures motion-control devices and electronic components. Mahan has a comprehensive software program for management of sales information in place that enables his sales team to maximize their individual productivity. The system is part of a database that can guide the sales force in every step of the sale. Qualified prospects are entered into a database. Prior to calling on a prospect, the salesperson asks the database via his *Personal Data Assistant* (computer) for the best approaches to use. Mr. Mahan and his salespeople have developed more than a hundred possible approaches; the choice of approach to utilize in a particular situation is left up to the individual salesperson.[16]

Developing Partnerships Using Technology looks at two types of Personal Data Assistants (PDAs) available to today's relationship-building salesperson: the palm-top computer and the hand-held computer. Both of these portable computers synchronize with a desktop or laptop system's contact management program. This synchronizing feature of palm-tops and hand-helds is very important.

Developing Partnerships Using Technology
The Salesperson and his Personal Data Assistant (PDA)

Portable Computers: Like taking a member of the sales team with you. The laptop is sometimes "too much" to take along. To solve this problem, there are two other types of PDAs. Both operate on Windows CE (a special version of Windows for smaller devices).

Palm-Top Computers. These mini-computers have considerable memory and storage capacity. They fold out like laptops into a keyboard with monitor. Most palm-tops have LCD color screens. The keyboard can have as many as 61 keys. They also offer a pointing device, like a pen, to navigate on the screen. It's like having a smaller version of Windows 95 in your hand. There is a full range of programs available:

a. Contact management
b. E-mail, faxing, word processor
c. Spreadsheets
d. Expenses manager
e. Modem card or external modem hookup
f. Planner/scheduler
g. Calculator
h. Presentation software
i. Mapping programs

Hand-Held Computers. Normally the size of a notepad that fits in the pocket of a shirt. There is no keyboard. These systems are totally "pen"-driven. Instead of using typing, they actually "learn" your handwriting style, enabling you to write information in a blank space on the bottom of the screen. Hand-helds use menu buttons or voice commands to perform specific functions. These computers have the following features:

a. Contact management
b. E-mail
c. Calendar/appointment scheduler
d. Voice recorder for personal memos
e. To-do/task lists
f. Calculator
g. Modem

With specialized software, salespeople can combine new contacts from the field with what they already have stored in their full contact management program. You can also update your traveling contact database with newer information that may have been added by other salespeople in the home office. The same procedure can be done for presentations, word processing documents, e-mail, spreadsheets, and calendar/task lists.

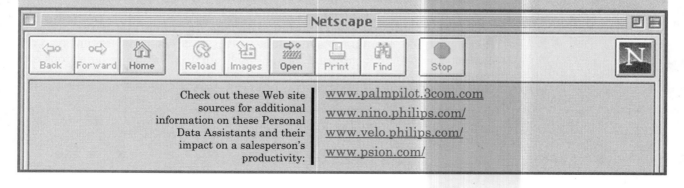

| Netscape |
| Back | Forward | Home | Reload | Images | Open | Print | Find | Stop |

Check out these Web site sources for additional information on these Personal Data Assistants and their impact on a salesperson's productivity:

www.palmpilot.3com.com
www.nino.philips.com/
www.velo.philips.com/
www.psion.com/

GAINING ATTENTION AND CAPTURING INTEREST

As the cartoon says, first you've got to get their attention! Develop a carefully constructed, attention-getting statement that focuses the prospect's attention solely on you and your proposition. Remember that prospects are thinking, "What does this person want with me? Why should I allow my work to be interrupted?" Unless prospects *want* to listen, they won't. Give them a reason. Just as the newspaper uses a headline to make you take notice, the salesperson must have an attention-getting opening statement that breaks through preoccupation and focuses attention on the selling situation.

"First you've got to get their attention!"

The two basic methods of getting attention are through an appeal to the senses and through the introduction of a benefit. An appeal to the senses gets the prospect involved in the presentation. Use a little dramatization. Show something the prospect can see; hand the prospect something to hold. Introduce a benefit by a statement that relates to the prospect's need for your product or service. Highlight the value of the product or service. The prospect always wants to know, "What's in it for me?" Phillip Proctor, vice president of sales and marketing for Associated Printing in Ft. Lauderdale, certainly knows how to get a prospect's attention. He routinely uses a corny but effective prop: a simple bag of bread with a note that reads, "Our clients say we're the greatest thing since...sliced bread."[17]

An effective attention-getting statement requires preparation. If you have done your homework in gathering preapproach information, you already know enough to have some idea about both the needs and the behavioral style of the prospect. If you spend a few minutes in small talk—chit-chat with a purpose—you gain further clues to confirm or adjust your preapproach information. Use what you know to plan an effective attention-getting device to introduce the heart of your presentation. Exhibit 9.5 suggests ways to gain prospects' attention by appealing to their behavioral styles during your initial exchange.[18]

EXHIBIT 9.5 - Using Behavioral Styles to Choose an Attention-Getting Approach

Expressive

Open in terms of long-range goals or implications

Example:

Mr. Crowe, I would like to show you how our innovative service will help your department reach its long-term potential.

Analytical

Open in very specific terms.

Example:

Mr. Crowe, I would like to give you the background on our service and then list the ways in which I think it will reduce your overhead, increase your production, and improve your profit margin by ten percent. (Be prepared to do so.)

Amiable

Open in supportive, people-oriented terms.

Example:

Mr. Crowe, I am aware of some of the pressing concerns you must be facing at this time, and I feel our service will help you and your people overcome some of these problems.

Driver

Open in results-oriented terms.

Example:

Mr. Crowe, our service will help you increase your sales by fifteen percent in just six months. Are you interested? (Be prepared to prove your statement.)

TYPES OF APPROACHES

Because every prospect and every selling situation is different, you ought to have several approach methods available and use the one that best fits the particular circumstance. Learn the principles of each of the different types of approaches so that you can use whichever one is appropriate for a particular situation. How many approach techniques are enough? You cannot have too many. The personality style of prospects, the mood they're in as you greet them, and your own feelings and mood that particular day suggest the need to have an opening for every occasion and every situation. You may have to deviate 180 degrees from the opening and presentation you had planned.

Self-Introduction Approach

This approach is commonly used but is probably the weakest approach to use alone. A smile, a firm handshake, and a relaxed but professional manner should accompany the introduction. Address the prospect by name, pronouncing it correctly, state your name and company, and present your business card. Although the business card is optional, it is a useful reminder of your name, and the prospect is not embarrassed by finding it necessary to ask you to repeat your name. Here is an example of a typical self-introduction:

Good morning, Mrs. Fritts. I am Heath Smith, representing the Xerox Corporation.

To increase the effectiveness of the self-introduction approach, follow it immediately with one of the other approaches. The consumer-benefit approach, for instance, is generally a good fit.

Consumer-Benefit Approach

Give the prospect a reason for listening and suggest a risk for failure to listen. The benefit statement should be unique and appeal to the prospect's dominant buying motive. It should be sincere and must not sound like a gimmick. Something new and different about your product or service that paves the way for the rest of the interview is a good choice.

Good morning, Mr. Carter. I am Kevin Davis with McLee and Associates. I stopped by to see if I might take fifteen minutes to introduce you to a concept that will, first of all, keep your name in front of your customers for ... maybe a year; second, it will allow you to provide each and every one of your customers with a value of up to $85 just as a way of expressing your appreciation that they are doing business with you; and third—and probably the best part of all—is that it should end up costing you not one cent.
Do you have fifteen minutes?

This example combines the self-introduction and the consumer-benefit approaches. Because most business people want to offer value to their customers, presenting this benefit statement may cause the prospect to seek more information about the concept. Such a statement often sparks questions from the prospect that lead directly into the presentation.

Curiosity Approach

The curiosity approach works best when you know something about the prospect. Used sensibly, this approach is an effective opener. Suppose you are selling a telecommuting software package so a sales force can get up to date information on their laptops when they are out in the field selling. You might say something like this:

Mr. Wanke, have you ever been in a meeting when a written report analyzing a new competitive product is brought to your attention for the first time, and you want to share parts of it with your salespeople immediately? Do you know how much time you are losing by having to edit the report manually?

People with certain behavioral styles, particularly analyticals and drivers, may find this approach offensive, especially if it sounds gimmicky.

Question Approach

The question approach quickly establishes two-way communication. It enables you to investigate the prospect's needs and apply the benefits of your product or service to those expressed needs. This type of approach suggests your interest in the prospect's problems and draws attention to the need to identify problems. You may frame a leading question designed to obtain mental commitment from the prospect and at the same time show a major benefit. Here are two examples of how this might be done:

1. *Mr. Fisher, you do want to have distinctive-looking, quality-driven reports and the most up-to-date pricing information to share with your customers, don't you?*

2. *Do you feel you could get more accomplished in meetings if you had complete and current information at your fingertips? Wouldn't you also like the capability to easily edit that information, thus enabling you to provide your customers the best support possible?*

Qualifying Question Approach

A variation of the question approach seeks a commitment from the prospect. This *qualifying question approach* asks the prospect to consider buying the product; it can help determine whether you have a prospect who is cold, lukewarm, or red hot toward your opportunity. Here are two illustrations of how this technique could be used:

1. *Mr. Armstrong, if I can satisfactorily demonstrate to you that the long-distance service provided by LDS will save you at least $1,000 within the next three months, would you be willing to do business with us?*

2. *Mrs. Woods, I am looking for individuals who have the discretionary funds to invest in an opportunity that will produce a return on their investment of at least 50 percent. If I can show you the evidence to support this claim, would you be willing to invest $125,000?*

If the prospect says yes, you have a sale, provided you can back up your statement with valid proof.

Compliment Approach

Opening with a compliment is like walking on eggshells, but the compliment opening is highly effective if used properly. Follow the same guidelines you would use in any situation: Offer compliments with empathy, warmth, and sincerity. The purpose of the compliment is to signal your sincere interest in the prospect. Sources for information upon which the compliment is based vary. Information from a person who provided a referral or from an item you saw in a newspaper or trade journal about the prospect can tell you about significant accomplishments that you genuinely admire. You can also see hints in the company offices as you come in or in the prospect's private office that suggest items that can be the basis for compliments.

Camco Inc., with international headquarters in Houston, sells gas-lift equipment, well-completion systems, safety systems, and wireline tools and units to the oil industry. At a time when the oil industry is experiencing a recession, a Camco salesperson would be out of line to compliment a prospect on the company's "obvious prosperity." Instead, a compliment should center on some other commendable factor:

I have been impressed with your continuous emphasis on safety on your offshore drilling rigs. I noticed the recent announcement that your company ranked first in safety ratings last year. You must be proud of that achievement.

This type of compliment not only builds rapport but also directs the prospect's train of thought toward safety and the related products that Camco has to sell. Whenever a compliment is used as an opening, it must be *specific*, of *genuine interest* to the prospect, and *sincere*.

Referral Approach

The referral approach is especially useful because it helps the salesperson establish leverage by borrowing the influence of someone the prospect trusts and respects. If you use a referral card signed by the person who provided the prospect's name, you can give it to the prospect to introduce yourself and your company. This approach enhances your credibility and increases the likelihood that the prospect will give you full attention. Here are two good examples:

1. *Miss Reid, your neighbor Ray Thornton has recently completed one of our courses in personal leadership. He told me that you are also interested in growing as a person and in becoming a better leader, and suggested that you would like to hear about what our company has to offer. (Give the referral card to the prospect.)*

2. *Mr. Carpenter, I am Don Edwards with MC Designs. Melanie Jacobs, for whom we just completed a large order, suggested that I contact you. She thought you would like to have an opportunity to consider whether our T-shirt products and prices also could be of benefit to you.*

Shock Approach

This approach must be used carefully. It must fit your personality and type of selling, and it must fit your product or service. Here are a few examples:

Product or Service	The Shock Approach
Time-Management Program	Mr. Stark, do you realize that if one employee earning $20,000 annually could, through using effective time management techniques, save an hour's time every day that could be used to increase productivity, your company would save over $2,500 each year?
Smoke Detection System	Mrs. Evans, do you realize that every two hours someone in the United States dies in a fire? The vast majority of these deaths occur in homes, usually after people have gone to bed. This fact is even more disturbing when you consider these deaths could have been avoided with a state-of-the-art smoke detection system.
Slow Train Coming (Public Awareness)	Every 90 minutes, despite warning lights and barriers, a train hits a car at one of 270,000 railroad crossings. Last year, 500 people were killed in cars illegally crossing railroad tracks.

Product Approach

This approach consists of actually handing the product, or some physical representation of it, to a prospect to produce a positive reaction. The product approach provides a visible image of the product or service. This approach should focus on the uniqueness of the product and, as far as possible, allow the product to tell its own story. Exhibit 9.6 tells how Bill Blake used a bit of showmanship to produce tangible evidence of product benefit to make a key sale.[19]

Bringing the product to the prospect stirs interest, permits a demonstration, makes a multiple sense appeal, and usually creates in the prospect a feeling of commitment to listen and to participate actively in the presentation. For example, a Norand sales representative might say,

"Mrs. Wampler, chances are, your busy field reps rarely have time to sit down. So why give them a computer that needs a lap? Our new lightweight, pen-based computer helps them work better anywhere. Here, catch."

Sometimes you cannot bring the actual product with you because of size or other constraints, but you can use other devices to simulate the actual product. A piece of literature, a sample of the output of the machine, a small working model, a picture—any visual tool that the prospect can hold and look at helps to focus and hold attention. If you are selling a service, such as a time-management program, hand the prospect a letter from a satisfied client that identifies specific benefits of the program. Statistical data that shows the return on investment earned by satisfied clients can accomplish the same purpose.

EXHIBIT 9.6 - It's Only a Paper Boon

Bill Blake, former vice-president, sales planning and development, Sweetheart Cup

"I was selling paper napkins to supermarkets for Hudson Pulp and Paper. This was back in 1951, and in those days, four big chains—A & P, Jewel, Kroger, and National Tea—controlled roughly 80 percent of the market. If you didn't get into these chains, you were out of business. Back then, paper napkins were not taken very seriously. They were thought of as a summer picnic item, and not for the winter months.

"For two years, I had called on the buyer at Jewel in Chicago every week. But every time I went to see him, he'd have something different to say about why he wouldn't buy from me. He had a terrific mental block against napkins.

"One day, I got an idea. We ran manufacturer's coupons on every box of napkins we sold. People had to bring them to the store to redeem them for a free box, and the coupons eventually came back to us. So I got hold of all the coupons, put them into big bags, and dumped hundreds of them on his desk one day in the middle of winter. Needless to say, he was convinced.

"Selling those napkins had to be the biggest sale of my life, because, after selling to Jewel, we went from nothing to 50 percent of the market in Chicago."

TRANSITION FROM THE APPROACH

Once you have met the prospect, exchanged the small talk needed to establish a comfortable selling climate, and attracted the attention and interest of the prospect, the next step in the selling process is to uncover the prospect's specific needs or problems that can be addressed by your product or service; that is, the time has come to move from the approach into the need-discovery phase of the sales process. A smooth transition from the opening approach into the need-discovery step that begins the main body of the presentation makes the rest of the interview easier. If your opening has involved "chit-chat with a purpose," the transition is fairly simple. Whatever approach device you decide to use, it should be directly related to your plan for beginning the need-discovery phase of the presentation. Any compliment you offer should relate to the general area of your product or service so that the presentation grows naturally from the opening. A consumer-benefit opening obviously leads directly into need discovery. A product approach immediately gets the prospect involved in examining your offering. The referral approach focuses upon your product or service the approval of someone whom the prospect respects; it emphasizes the referring person's belief that the prospect will be interested.

The exchange of conversation in the approach phase allows you to move smoothly into the questions you plan to ask to discover the needs of the prospect. Because the actual presentation of benefits cannot begin until the prospect agrees to having a need for what you have to offer, whatever you can do to make need discovery seem a natural process will be helpful. Chapter 10 deals with the critical task of discovering needs by asking questions and listening. The degree of rapport established between you and the prospect during the approach determines how willing the prospect will be to answer your questions and accept your buying recommendation.

SUMMARY

What you do and say in the initial moments of the face-to-face interview has a profound effect on whether you will achieve a successful close. The approach you use in those initial moments must be as carefully planned as all the other portions of the selling process.

Salespeople need to be aware of the power of first impressions and the effect they have on the selling process. Because first impressions are so lasting, salespeople must plan for them and take advantage of them. Proper dress and grooming give the prospect the feeling that you are competent. Appropriate choices in dress and grooming let the prospect focus on your sales message instead of on your physical appearance. Dress to enhance or play down physical characteristics as necessary.

The choice of greeting is important in creating a favorable first impression. Avoid trite phrases and trivial questions that might lead the conversation far from your desired purpose. Accompany the greeting with a firm, confident handshake and deliver it in a voice that reflects confidence and good taste. Use the prospect's name and pronounce it properly. Begin the approach with some "chit-chat with a purpose" to feel out the mood and behavioral style of the prospect and to lead naturally into your presentation.

Use your knowledge of behavioral styles to choose an effective approach to a prospect. During the approach, confirm or modify your earlier impressions of the prospect's behavioral style and adapt your plans for the presentation accordingly. By appealing appropriately to the behavioral style of the prospect, you can gain attention and capture interest that can sustain your presentation until the product benefits you present have time to appeal to the prospect as viable tactics for satisfying needs or solving problems.

A number of different types of approach tactics are available: (1) the self-introduction, (2) consumer-benefit, (3) curiosity, (4) question, (5) qualifying question (6) compliment, (7) referral, (8) shock, and (9) product. Although these approaches are different in their specific content, they share the purpose of gaining the prospect's attention. A good approach forms a natural transition into the need-discovery segment of the selling process.

QUESTIONS FOR THOUGHT AND DISCUSSION

1. What are the four objectives of an effective approach?

2. What are components of surface language? Why are these items called *surface* language?

3. What would you consider appropriate dress for calling on an insurance executive? A manager of a health and fitness facility?

4. What is the purpose of small talk? How can you use it to best advantage? For what kind of situation is small talk a negative?

5. Name and explain the nine types of approaches discussed in the chapter. Why does a salesperson need to master several approaches?

6. What are the advantages of bringing a product to the prospect? What are alternatives if bringing the product is not feasible?

7. Should the greeting you use be planned ahead of time, or should you depend largely on the inspiration of the moment? Justify your choice.

8. Under what conditions would you change the approach you had planned when you arrive for an interview?

9. In the selling situations below, what would be an appropriate compliment you might pay to the prospect? How would that help you move into need discovery?

   - You are calling on a physician who heads a group practice of seven physicians to propose a medical insurance plan for the employees of their clinic.

   - You are calling on the purchasing agent of a large school district to sell school buses to the district.

   - You are calling on a middle-income, blue-collar worker in his home to sell homeowner's insurance.

10. List some guidelines for making a good first impression.

11. What are some weaknesses of evaluating a prospect totally on your first impression?

12. What can you learn about a prospect from a handshake?

ACTIVITIES

1. Tour a local bank. Take notes about the dress of the men and women employees (other than guards). What similarities did you notice? What differences?

2. Interview a purchasing agent. Ask for some observations about the strengths and weaknesses of salespeople's approaches. Ask for the same observations from a retail shop owner. Ask them the best times for salespeople to call on them and why.

3. Assume you are a sales representative who sells a number of paper products. Today you are calling on the owner of a large soda fountain to sell paper cups. Assume also that paper cups are not now in use at this facility. How would you begin your presentation?

4. "I know the first few minutes in a sales presentation are important to most folks, but not to me. I never call on people I haven't already met." Evaluate this statement.

Case Study

CASE 9.1

Milt Beck has good days and bad days. On the good days, everything goes smoothly and orders come easily. Some days he wonders if he should find a nice nine-to-five clerical job. But coming out of a tough interview with an order makes him realize he wouldn't trade selling for anything. Milt had one of the bad days recently. His sales manager, Allen Merton, had insisted he call on a prospect. "Milt," Al said, "I ran into a guy on the plane from St. Louis the other day who is a prime prospect for our degreaser. He's in the electrical business making armatures and windings. Our degreaser is ideal for removing grease and dirt from those items. His name is Walter Prince, and his company is Ideal Electric Products. Here's his card."

"Oh," Milt exclaimed, "he's the president of the company."

"That's the best kind of prospect," Al said. "When the top man says, 'I'll take it,' you know the order will stick. Let me warn you, though. He's a real talker."

So Milt drove the twenty-five miles to the Ideal plant. When he told the receptionist he had been referred to Mr. Prince by Allen Merton, he was asked to go right in.

"Say, that sales manager of yours is some live wire. He didn't waste any time sending you, did he? How's he doing?" the president said, as soon as Milt introduced himself.

"He's fine," Milt assured him. "You're right, he's a dynamic person."

"We had quite a conversation during the flight," Walter said, and then he was off. He covered sports, politics, foreign affairs, and then taxes. He hardly paused for breath. Several times, Milt tried to turn the conversation to the degreaser, but every attempt just seemed to remind Walter of something else to talk about. Before long, Milt began to tell himself, "The chief will be some upset if I don't bring back an order. After all, he thinks he set it up for me. How can I get this talker to give me a chance?"

1. How would you deal with this type of prospect? Would you try to break in and insist that you get to business?

2. How long would you continue with this kind of talk with a prospect?

3. Give some suggestions for turning the conversation to business without alienating the prospect.

Identifying Needs by Questioning and Listening

LEARNING OBJECTIVES

- To understand the purpose of asking questions in selling.

- To learn how to select questioning tactics appropriate for the sales situation.

- To study specific questioning techniques.

- To examine *SPIN*® Selling and its applications.

- To understand the functions served by various types of questions.

- To become more aware of the importance of listening in the sales situation.

- To become acquainted with techniques for improving listening skills.

THE PURPOSE OF ASKING QUESTIONS

Telling isn't selling; asking is! For many years, salespeople were told that selling is talking. The message seemed to be to tell the prospect everything you know in hopes that something you say will touch the right spot and the prospect will buy. The result of this kind of thinking was a salesperson who kept the prospect pinned down with constant chatter that resembled oral machine-gun fire.[1] The problem created by that theory of selling lies in its assumption that every prospect uses the product or service for identical purposes and in the same manner.

Actually, each prospect has unique needs. Of the many benefits you have to offer, only a few will be key motivators to a particular prospect.[2] The challenge is to determine their buying criteria before beginning your presentation and then use only the specific benefits that address their particular situation. When Andy Callen, vice president of sales at Quaero, a technology consulting firm, was vying for a $350,000 account with Alltel, a telecommunications company, he took this approach: "The presentation was based on their business requirements. We didn't talk about Quaero at all. Instead, we based everything we said on their needs and issues, not on what we do." He had to convince Alltel that it was worth the extra investment to them in order to reduce the risk of buying the wrong CRM products. They won the account because the competition didn't bother to ask questions to figure out Alltel's specific technology needs before presenting their solutions.[3]

Salespeople are diagnosticians. If you went to your family doctor complaining of severe back pain, and the doctor—without asking any questions—wrote a prescription for a medicine to be taken three times a day for the next month, would you take it? Of course not! You would not believe the doctor could make an accurate diagnosis and prescribe the appropriate medicine without making a thorough examination and asking a number of probing questions about the problem. You would expect the doctor to understand *your* problem—not the problem of back pain in general—before prescribing for you. Your prospect has the right to expect the same professional attention from you.[4]

Need Discovery and the Sales Cycle

The evolution of consultative selling has reached the point where the need discovery step in the sales cycle is more important than making the presentation, handling objections, and closing.[5] Figure 10.1 shows the relationship between need discovery and the other basic steps in the face-to-face sales process. At this point of need discovery—not in the close—the sale is most often lost. The dotted line around *need discovery* in Figure 10.1 is a reminder that this step is often skipped or given inadequate attention by the traditional or transactional salesperson. In reality, more time should be spent in the approach and in discovering needs than in any other steps of the process.

Need discovery is the foundation upon which a successful sale is built. Telling prospects what they need is a mistake.[6] Asking questions that allow prospects to discover their own needs and share them with you sets you up as a sounding board for the solutions they "discover" while considering your proposal. Prospects are more receptive when they feel that the solution is their own idea. A study conducted by Willett and Pennington found that

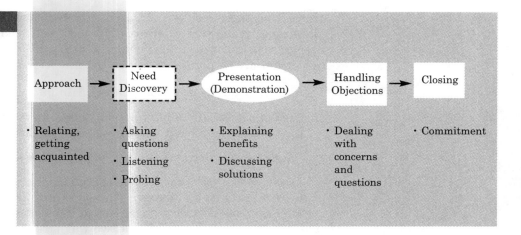

FIGURE 10.1

Relationship Between
Need Discovery and
Other Steps in the Sales
Process

successful sales interviews contained more requests for opinions and suggestions by the salesperson and fewer statements of disagreement and tension than unsuccessful interviews. More significantly, in the successful interviews the salespeople controlled the direction of the interview by the way they asked questions. Additional studies have found that the more questions salespeople ask, the more successful they are in closing.[7]

People are often unaware of a problem until they are questioned about it. Here is a case in point: A professor at a community college in Arizona conveyed an interesting story to the author of how an insurance agent sold him a policy by asking one simple question followed by an observation. The agent asked, "How much life insurance coverage do you have as protection for your family?" When the professor replied that he had $75,000, the insurance agent shrugged his shoulders and remarked, "I guess you don't plan to be dead very long, then, do you!" This strong statement could easily offend some people. However, it caused him to realize for the first time the substantial disparity between what he had and the actual amount needed that would enable his family to maintain their current lifestyle, should something unexpected happen to him. The professor has continued to buy additional protection from this same agent as his family's needs changed.

Specific Planning of Questions

As a salesperson, you must retain control of the questioning phase of the interview so that you obtain the required information and are not sidetracked into irrelevant areas. The old standbys – who, what, when, where, why, and how – are a vital part of the sales interview. Decide in advance what you need to know, and then plan what types of questions will elicit that information in the quickest and most efficient manner consistent with the prospect's social style and situation.

Because the *sale is made in the mind of the buyer and not in the mind of the salesperson*, using the questioning process to gain agreement on key issues is paramount. Then you must assist the prospect in

Focus your attention on the prospect's needs.

prioritizing those issues and agree that those are, indeed, the problems or concerns that must be addressed before a decision to buy can be made. Research points out that prospects are more likely to buy if points of agreement are established early in the interview.[8] To accomplish this...

Plan your questions in *sequence* to gain information in a logical order.

Predict beforehand all the possible answers to each question so that you are never left wondering what to do next.

Prepare a smooth transition from every possible answer into the next question.

Some salespeople hesitate to ask questions because they are afraid the prospect will refuse to answer. However, prospects that refuse to cooperate during the need-discovery phase are unlikely to cooperate at the end of the sale either. Communication is a two-way street that demands participation by both prospect and salesperson. If you are to involve prospects in the sales process, you must be prepared to ask the questions that maximize participation. The right questions never materialize out of thin air. Your questions should attempt to achieve four objectives:

1. To discover the prospect's "hot button" or dominant buying motives.

2. To establish the purchase criteria or specifications.

3. To agree on a time frame for completion of negotiations.

4. To gain prospect agreement on the problem(s) before making the presentation.

Army Recruiters Ask Questions

No standardized set of questions is universally applicable for salespeople in all selling situations. Your questions must be yours – not somebody else's.[9] For example, an army recruiter never asks, "Do you want to join the army?" Instead, his approach is to get the prospective recruits to *think about*, *visualize*, and *verbalize* their wants and desires. The questions used by the recruiter might be something like these:

* What kind of work do you see yourself doing in the future?
* If you could live and work anywhere in the world, where would you choose to be?
* You may want to go to college in the future. Where would you get the money?
* What would you do right now if you were given a $5,000 grant?

All of these questions are geared to specific benefits—variety of work, location preference, college assistance, and enlistment bonus. By asking a series of need-discovery questions and then *listening* both verbally and nonverbally, the recruiter begins to discover what the potential recruit is looking for in a career. The presentation of army opportunities (the benefits or selling points) can be tailored to appeal to that particular person's needs— the buying motives that make the "sale" possible.[10]

John Zavitz understands the value of asking the right questions

John Zavitz is one of just four business development managers for WilTel Communications Systems. John works out of the Chicago office. He devotes a large portion of his time to discovering customers' needs, determining those individuals who influence the purchase decision, the actual decision-maker, and the buyers' stated requirements, a process that involves asking questions, listening, observing, and building rapport.

As a business development manager, John's role is to seek out new prospects and manage a very small group of customers. John works with companies that require a major telecommunications system to meet their needs. As a result, the *sales cycle* can be anywhere from six months to 1½ years. The *number of calls* required to complete such a sale varies from four to 25 meetings. If at all possible, John meets first with the president of the company. He also meets early on with the vice-presidents of finance and MIS, and the senior vice-president of business development in charge of *outsourcing*. John learns about the business itself and discovers how he can help them solve their communications problems. By the time he is ready to recommend a particular system, he has met with vice-presidents, managers, and department heads in finance, legal, maintenance, and accounting. He considers each meeting as a minicontract negotiation. John carefully plans every question, always listening and watching for things that could affect his ability to win the business.

For John, the questioning phase is the most time-consuming step in the sales cycle. John and his company are really in the *outsourcing* business. They are providing their clients with a telephone system and the people and knowledge to manage that system. In John's words, "We become their telecommunications expert. Our contractual agreement is established for a five- to 10-year period." John's ability to diagnose each client's individual needs and recommend the correct solution is vital for this *partnership* to work.

STRATEGIC RECOMMENDATIONS

As you select specific questioning methods, keep these tactics in mind:[11]

Avoid Technical Language That Might Confuse the Prospect. An account executive selling ad space to a small business owner should avoid terms such as *kerning, bodoni extra bold, mistral fonts,* or *bleed page* unless certain that the prospect is technically sophisticated and would expect to use such terms. In the same way, using company stock numbers, codes, or abbreviations confuses the client. Your goal is to promote understanding and not to demonstrate your personal erudition.

Transition from the Approach. Chapter nine presented four specific objectives of the approach: to make a favorable first impression, to gain attention, to create interest, and to serve as a logical transition into need discovery. This transition into need discovery requires that you tell the prospect exactly what you intend to accomplish during the interview session. You are to provide a *clear agenda* for the sales interview. Always let the prospect know what you want to accomplish. When you and the prospect agree on an agenda, the prospect knows that valuable time will not be wasted. Your goal is to create an environment within which the prospect feels comfortable answering your questions. You can set up the desired atmosphere by <u>requesting permission</u> to ask questions. Here are two practical *permissive questions*:

1. *I believe I can offer you a service that will be of considerable value to you, but in order for me to be sure, and to know a little more about your particular situation, would it be OK if I ask you a few questions?*

2. *The only way for us to know how my company can best serve your needs is for you to give me permission to ask a few personal questions. Will that be all right with you? Oh, and may I make some notes while we talk?*

Phrase Each Question So That It Has One Clear Purpose. An ambiguous question or one with multiple meanings creates misunderstanding between you and the prospect. Proceed logically, one topic at a time. Murphy's law operates here: Anything that can be misunderstood will be misunderstood. A corollary to this principle is equally important: Phrase each question to produce the maximum amount of information so that the number of questions needed to elicit the needed information is as small as possible. Exhibit 10.1 gives a good example of how not to do it.[12]

EXHIBIT 10.1 - Focusing the Questioning Process

A real estate agent wants to find out how many children the prospect has, their ages and gender. Poor planning produces a scenario like this:

AGENT:	<u>Do you have any children?</u>
PROSPECT:	Yes.
AGENT:	<u>How many?</u>
PROSPECT:	Three.
AGENT:	<u>How old are they?</u>
PROSPECT:	11, 9, and 7.
AGENT:	<u>Are they all boys or all girls?</u>
PROSPECT:	Two boys and one girl.
AGENT:	<u>What age is the girl?</u>
PROSPECT:	She's the 7 year-old.

At this rate, the agent will be asking questions all day. Why not simplify the process with one straightforward question:

AGENT:	<u>What are the ages and gender of your children?</u>

THE SPIN TECHNIQUE

Neil Rackham is president and founder of Huthwaite Inc. and the author of the book *SPIN SELLING*. His corporation's 12-year, $1 million research into effective sales performance resulted in the unique sales strategy, the **SPIN®** method—**S**ituation, **P**roblem, **I**mplication and **N**eed-payoff questions. Successful salespeople don't ask random questions. This model represents how consultative salespeople probe. These are guidelines, not a rigid formula. There is a distinct pattern in the successful call. The answers you get will be used during the presentation to help underscore how the benefits you give support, reinforce, and solve the answers to the questions you have asked during need discovery. Its questioning sequence taps directly into the psychology of the buying process. The questions provide a road map for the seller, guiding the call through the steps of need development until explicit needs have been agreed upon. You want to allow customers to discover for themselves the problems they have. People don't like to think, and certainly don't want to admit, their problems are that obvious.[13]

SPIN® Selling in Action

Let's take a specific example of a company and demonstrate the **SPIN®** method just as they might use it. A business with overdue accounts receivables has three options: It can hire a conventional percentage-based agency, a flat-fee agency, or do the collecting internally. Transworld Systems Inc. (TSI) is one of the largest collection agencies in the country. TSI works with over 40,000 clients helping them to recover their slow-paying and delinquent accounts without having to pay up to 50 percent of the collection as charged by a conventional agency. Many clients with a wide range of account balances have found the TSI system to be the only economical method of obtaining professional third-party collection results. TSI pays the money they collect directly to the client, the client maintains control of their accounts, and they do not have to pay a percentage. TSI has a low flat fee that enables clients to assign their accounts in the early stages of delinquency, thus providing the best opportunity for successful recovery. Here is the **SPIN®** technique in action:

Situation Questions: These questions are designed to find out about the customer's situation. These are data-gathering questions. They ask about the prospect's general state of affairs or circumstances as it relates to the services TSI has to offer. They help the TSI sales rep get to know the prospects and obtain initial information about their background and situation. You are looking for a general understanding of the prospect's needs. The following questions have an important fact-finding role, are non-threatening, and help to build an atmosphere of trust and cooperation:

— Do you make the purchasing decision?

— How many active accounts do you bill each month?

— Do you do all the collection of overdue accounts internally?

— About what percentage of your customers do not pay their bills on time?

— Do you have out-of-state accounts?

— Is the billing and follow-up done in this office?

— Do you currently use a collection agency?

Problem Questions: Once the TSI sales reps feel comfortable about the buyer's situation, they move on to a second type of questioning technique. These questions explore needs, any difficulties they may be having, and dissatisfactions in areas where TSI's service could be the solution. The goal in this step is to have the prospect say, "I really do have a problem with the collection of my accounts receivables." Which ones are really most important to them? TSI wants to determine explicit needs or uncover the prospect's "hot button." Remember: *The sale is made in the mind of the buyer, not in the mind of the TSI salesperson.* Customers don't want to be told they have a problem; allow them to discover it for themselves. Whatever they say is true; when you say it, they doubt it!! You're searching for areas where the services TSI offers can solve their specific problem. If you can uncover problems your service can solve, then you're providing the buyer with something useful. Ask these kinds of problem questions:

- Do you know how much it costs to do your collecting internally?

- Do you ever get mail back? Wrong address? No longer at the address?

- When do you consider an account to be a concern or problem?

- Do you ever get checks back NSF or ACCOUNT CLOSED?

- Do you have a service to help recover these checks?
  If yes, is it a guarantee service?

Implication Questions: Implication questions build up the magnitude of the problem so that it's seen as serious in the mind of the prospect, and then the sales rep uses need-payoff questions to build up the value of the solution. Implication questions are the language of decision-makers, and if you can talk their language, you'll influence them. In larger sales you need to ask this third type of question. The phrasing of implication questions is critical because you want the prospect to discuss the problem and how it might be improved. Attach a bottom-line figure to the implication questions. The TSI sales rep wants the prospect to agree that the implications of the problem are causing such things as loss of revenue; ill-will with some of its customer base; prohibitive cost of time and money in trying to do the collection themselves; percentage-based collection agencies are too expensive. The prospects must see that the problem is serious enough that it outweighs the cost of the solution, namely, using the services of TSI. The TSI sales rep might ask these questions:

Plan these SPIN® questions in advance with your colleagues.

- Would it help if the money was paid directly to you? Last year we collected over $500 million for our clients and the money was paid directly to them.

- Do you know most collection agencies deposit the money they collect into their own bank account and hold it up to 60 days?

- Would it be important to you to recover a larger share of delinquent accounts and bad checks faster than a conventional collection agency and put the money directly into your hands and let it work for you?

- Is it safe to say that you would like to collect delinquent accounts quickly, without disturbing ongoing relationships with those customers?

Need-Payoff Questions: How would that help? What benefits do you see? Why is it important to solve this problem? Is it useful to solve this problem? These questions get the customer to tell you the benefits that your solution offers. These types of questions actually get prospects to name benefits and tell you why they should buy. These questions help you build up the value of your proposed solution in the customer's mind. You want to focus the customer's attention on the solution rather than on the problem. This creates a positive problem-solving atmosphere. In the words of an 8 year-old named Quincy, "Implication questions are always sad; need-payoff questions are always happy." That's because implication questions are problem-centered, while the following need-payoff questions are solution-centered: [14]

- Would it be useful to speed up the rate of collection, and at the same time be guaranteed that you will recover at least twice as much as you pay for our service?

- If you could create the perfect agency, what would you want them to do for you?

- If I can show you how TSI has been able to help others in your industry, and we can determine what kind of results you might expect, can we get started today? Let's take a look at your aging report.

- We automatically send out a report detailing the status of each account assigned for collection. Does this sound like something that would interest you?

- Do you want the account handled diplomatically or intensively? We have another division that handles the hard-core collection problems. Would you like to have that option?

- Would you like us to send a "thank you" card to the debtor after the account has been paid?

- Do you feel that a system that has a flat fee rate rather than a percentage-based system would really be of value to you?

SPECIFIC QUESTIONING TECHNIQUES

General Types of Questions

The major types of questioning techniques are summarized in Exhibit 10.2. Questions are generally classified by the type of answers required and by the purpose they are intended to serve. Begin the questioning process with closed-end questions or fact-finding questions that are easy to answer and therefore not threatening to the prospect. If the first few questions are reasonable, the prospect begins to gain confidence and feel comfortable with the questioning process. The next questions then, although progressively more challenging, seem easier to handle.

Closed-End Questions: These questions provide structured alternatives for the prospect. They ask an either-or question or request a choice from a series of suggested responses. Closed-end questions are usually answered with a very brief response, often a single word. They often ask for a yes or no response or a choice between two alternatives. They are direct, fact-finding questions designed to reveal background information about the prospect's business and/or family. They are *directive* questions for which you want specific answers:

- How many employees do you have working the day shift?

- What interconnect companies are you familiar with?

- Is a rear-window defogger important to you?

- Does your company pay the full cost of employee health insurance, or do the employees pay part of the cost?

EXHIBIT 10.2 - Types of Questions and Probing Techniques

General types of questions

1. *Closed-end questions.* Provide a series of responses from which the prospect selects one, are easy to answer, used to get feedback, and can be used to get prospect commitment.

2. *Open-end questions.* Identify a topic but do not provide structured alternatives for responses, usually begin with "how" or "what", cannot be answered "yes" or "no", and are designed to stimulate the prospect's thinking.

Classification of questioning techniques

1. *Amplification questions.* Ask prospect to expand on an answer; do not direct thoughts but encourage prospect to continue talking. (Double-check, nonverbal gestures, silence, and continuation questions)

2. *Internal summary questions.* Assimilate information presented, put it in perspective, and ask if the interpretation is correct; may repeat all of prospect's last response in the form of a question. (Reflective or internal summary question)

3. *Getting agreement on the problem.* Make a formal statement of the problem, get prospect to agree, and attempt to get commitment. (Formal statement of the problem)

Closed-end questions can also be phrased to get feedback or to gain commitment.

- Would you like delivery Friday, or is Monday of next week all right?

- Who else are you talking to about solving this problem?

- Who will be involved in deciding whether to purchase from us or a competitor?

- Do you know what your customers do with your product after buying it?

- Do you prefer to pay cash, or would you like to arrange a monthly payment plan?

Closed-end questions may be used as a substitute for telling the prospect something. A question can sometimes make a point in a more telling manner than a statement because the prospect must think to answer it, and thinking makes a stronger impression than hearing. Consider these two ways to impart the same message:

1. *Our procedure will completely eliminate waste in your welding operations.*

2. *How much cost savings would you have if you used a procedure that completely eliminates waste from your welding operations?*

The first method tells the prospect something. The salesperson hopes the prospect is impressed, but that may not happen. Unless the prospect reacts strongly enough to the statement to break in with a comment, any skepticism is buried until some later point, where it emerges as a vague objection or stall like, "Well, we're not thinking of making any changes just now." The question method, however, gains attention because the prospect has to think about an answer. Disbelief surfaces immediately where it can be dealt with instead of being postponed until later when the salesperson is trying to close. Exhibit 10.3 lists the various purposes served by asking closed-end questions.

EXHIBIT 10.3 - Purposes of Closed-End Questions

- Uncover specific facts.

- Reduce prospect tension because they are easy to answer.

- Check understanding and receive feedback.

- Maintain control by directing the flow of conversation.

- Reinforce prospect commitment to a specific position.

Open-End Questions. These broadly phrased questions allow prospects plenty of room to answer as they wish. They are evaluative questions designed to draw out a wide range of responses on broad topics. They call for explanations. Open-end questions encourage prospects to explain their needs by explaining their preferences, expectations, or judgments. Open-end questions tend to be *general* rather than *specific*. Use them when you want the prospect to talk freely. You can encourage the prospect to verbalize feelings by asking questions that begin with "What do you think?" or "How do you feel?" Talking out loud often helps people clarify and organize their thoughts. Real feelings are often not in the conscious awareness until they are verbalized.[15] Open-end questions help both the prospect and the salesperson sort out ideas and begin to make decisions. Here are some examples of questions that give prospects the freedom and responsibility to express their own thoughts and use their own information in the decision-making process:

- What options would you want on your new Mercedes?
- How do you think I might be able to help you?
- In a perfect world, what would you like to see us deliver?
- What are five unique characteristics of your business?
- What benefits would you expect from our ten-week, self-paced time-management program?

Open-end questions reveal attitudes that the salesperson must know if the sale is to be closed. You cannot easily ask a prospect, "Are you motivated by pride?" but you can ask open-end questions designed to detect this emotion, and you then have the answer to the direct question you cannot ask.

Generally, the best way to discover an answer to a question you do not want to ask is to make a statement and then tie an open-end question to the end of it. For example, an automobile salesperson knows on the one hand that the LX model has terrific appeal for people who are motivated by pride and eager to make a good impression. On the other hand, the smaller car is more convenient for driving around the city. The sale depends on knowing which appeal is greater for the particular prospect.

Uncover the necessary information by using a statement followed by an open-end question: "Many Beverly Hills residents find that our LX model is just what they need, although some of them prefer the maneuverability of a smaller car." This appeals to both attitudes—pride and utility—and is then followed by an invitation for the prospect to comment: "I don't know whether you do a lot of driving in traffic....?"

The delivery of an open-end question is vital. It should never sound like a straight-from-the-shoulder question like "How many people do you employ in your plant?" It may not even seem to be asking anything, but the prospect feels compelled to respond. Because it is low-pressure, the question prompts the prospect to tell you what you want to know (for example, whether the prospect is motivated by pride or convenience) and give you other important hints about how to close the sale. Exhibit 10.4 lists the properties of open-end questions.

EXHIBIT 10.4 - The Properties of Open-End Questions

- Allow the prospect to move in any direction.
- Cannot be answered with "yes" or "no".
- Ordinarily begin with "how" or "what".
- Designed to stimulate the prospect's thinking and increase dialogue.
- Help determine dominant buying motives (rational or emotional).
- Uncover the social or behavioral style of the prospect.

CLASSIFICATION OF QUESTIONING TECHNIQUES

The questions salespeople ask can be classified by the purpose they are intended to perform. Three basic classes of questions can be used: *amplification, internal summary* or *reflective,* and *questions to gain agreement on the problem.* Either open-end or closed-end questions may be asked for any of these purposes, depending upon the situation. If one type of question does not provide all the information needed, another type can be used to get a more specific response or to elicit a better sense of the prospect's point of view.

Consultative selling is more than a process in which two people sit together in a room and take turns talking. As the salesperson, you must be certain that the prospect knows what you are talking about and understands it. You must also be sure that you understand the prospect, know that person's needs and desires, and be certain you can satisfy them. You need feedback, and asking questions is the method for receiving feedback.

Be careful how you phrase the questions you ask. Place responsibility for not understanding on yourself rather than on the prospect. "Do you understand what I said?" or "Did you get that?" or "Are you with me?" seems to imply that the prospect may not be too bright. You must take responsibility for any possible misunderstanding by asking, "Have I explained this clearly enough? Is there some part I need to clarify or go over again?"

Amplification Questions

Ask probing questions and listen to your customer.[16] These questioning techniques encourage prospects to continue to provide enlightening information and encourage them to explain the meaning of a statement made. Amplification questions help both salespeople and prospects. At times prospects may not make themselves clear; they may wander off the subject or may stop talking before the salesperson can fully understand their

Ask probing questions and listen to your customer.

position. In a subtle manner, these techniques ask the prospect to expand on or clarify the meaning of a statement or help identify the frame of reference being used.

Double-Check Question. A double-check question is a means of giving feedback to the prospect. It involves taking the information the prospect has provided, rephrasing it, and handing it right back. A prospect might tell a motor freight salesperson, "Every Tuesday and Thursday the whole yard is backed up with trucks for the entire afternoon." The salesperson might offer feedback by saying, "Now as I understand it, you find that your loading platforms get badly jammed at peak hours." This statement is actually a question because it evokes an answer. It serves the dual purpose of clarifying the salesperson's impression of the situation and solidifying the prospect's opinion. They have agreed on the heart of the problem.

Nonverbal Gestures. *Visual cues* such as nodding the head or leaning forward show that the salesperson is listening, believes the prospect is on the right track, and is understanding what the prospect is saying. You may also *inject appropriate words* or phrases to encourage the prospect to continue: "You don't say?" "Is that right?" "That's interesting!" A question may be implied by the nonverbal choice of silence accompanied by a slightly raised eyebrow or furrowed brow. This tactic is especially good when a prospect has given a noncommittal answer to what you consider a key question. Just use an inquiring look as if you expect further response. Chances are, the prospect will go on to tell you what you need to know.

Silence. *Silence* is a powerful sales tool. When prospects avoid telling you the whole truth, the knowledge that they are being less than honest makes them uncomfortable. Your silence convinces them to go ahead and tell you the whole story. If they have been honest and open, they interpret your look as an indication that you do not understand and they will explain. This tactic backfires, however, and becomes an insult if you overuse it to the extent that you seem to be challenging the prospect's truthfulness.

Silence allows you to slow down and relax the pace of asking questions. Some prospects want to think and contemplate longer than others before responding to your questions. Give people time to reply at their own pace. Silence also gives you valuable time to formulate your own next question or comment.

Continuation Questions. *Continuation* questions encourage prospects to continue talking by making a positive request for more information. Such questions do not push for a particular response or for agreement; they just encourage more communication from the prospect. Here are three examples:

• What additional thoughts do you have on that topic?

- That's just the kind of information we must have to help pinpoint your needs. Please go on.

- Could you tell me in a bit more detail why you feel that way?

EXHIBIT 10.5 - Advantages of Using Amplification Questions

- Encourages the prospect to continue to provide revealing information.

- Allows the salesperson to rephrase what the prospect appears to have intended.

- Invites the prospect to expand or clarify any point of disagreement.

- Narrows down generalizations and clears ambiguities.

Internal Summary Questions

Probes designed to get prospects to think, see, and consider your interpretation of the situation may be called *internal summary or reflective* questions. Summarize what you understood the prospect to mean. You want to assimilate the information provided, place it in the perspective that suits your purpose, and ask if the interpretation is correct. You achieve this by repeating all or part of the prospect's last response in the form of a question or by rephrasing the entire idea expressed by the prospect, feeding it back in a slightly different form, and asking for confirmation. Consider an example in which a company president explains why the firm may not be able to sponsor an in-house blood drive. Note how the salesperson empathizes and rewords or echoes the president's remarks but suggests the process can be accomplished without disruption.

<u>**Prospect**</u> (company president): My company has always felt the need to support the charitable activities of organizations like yours. But where do we draw the line? I am constantly besieged with requests for my company's time. We have only so many hours a day.

<u>**Salesperson**</u> (donor consultant): I certainly understand how you feel. If I were in your position, I'd probably feel the same. I sense that the blood donor program is something you wholeheartedly endorse. But with only so many hours in the working day, humanitarian concerns take a back seat to the realities of the business world. However, if you thought this could be accomplished with a minimum of time lost, and you felt your employees really wanted to do it, it could be done. May I tell you how we manage it?

These types of questions are useful throughout the interview. Every salesperson knows about summarizing the key benefits just before asking for the order: "Now, as I see it, we've agreed that a complete line, with these particular items featured, will move for you with the proper promotion. Am I right about that?" Such summary techniques are especially useful during the close.

The summary question may be used to underscore points on which you already agree. An occasional summary of the points to which the prospect has already agreed will fix them firmly in the mind of the prospect and demonstrate just how wide an area of agreement there is between the two of you.

**Getting
Agreement on
the Problem**

In *Open the Mind, Close the Sale,* John Wilson says that the salesperson's failure to confirm the problem is one of the biggest mistakes in selling.[17] The whole purpose of asking questions is to determine whether the prospect has a problem or need that you are capable of solving. State the problem in your own words and get the prospect to agree, "Yes, that's it." Never begin the actual presentation phase of the sales interview until the problem has been clearly established in the minds of both you and the prospect. Begin the *formal statement of the problem* by using such phrases as these:

- Let me attempt to summarize what we have been saying.
- As I understand it, here is (are) the problem(s) we must solve.
- Based on your answers to my questions, I see the problem as ...

After you pinpoint the problem, you must seek confirmation. Get the prospect to agree by following your summary of the problem with questions like these:

- If I show you some comparisons demonstrating that my company can save you money without sacrificing quality, would you commit to our program?[18]
- Is that a fair statement of the way things stand?
- If I can satisfactorily demonstrate a solution to these concerns of yours, would it be enough to earn your business?

If the prospect agrees with the problem statement, you are ready to present the specific benefits of your product or service that can solve the problem. Even if the prospect disagrees with your summary of the problem, you have both learned by sharing information.

LISTENING

About 80 percent of waking hours is spent communicating, about half of that listening. Nevertheless, a school's communication training usually concentrates on reading, writing, and speaking. Was Listening 101 in your school catalog? Effective listening is not just hearing what the prospect is saying. Faulty listening results in misunderstanding and lost opportunities.[19] Research indicates that 60 percent of misunderstandings in business are due to poor listening.[20] Fortunately, improved listening skills can be learned.

The first step to listening.

To succeed in professional selling, you must be able to offer a product or service that satisfies the buyer's needs. Presenting features and benefits is not always enough. How they are presented may be as important as what is presented. Listening is the key to finding ways to present benefits that enhance the possibility of a close.

Effective listening helps sales professionals catch verbal and nonverbal signals indicating a prospect is interested in buying their product or service. "Unfortunately, good listening skills usually require a change in our behavior," says Barry Elms, CEO of Strategic Negotiations International.[21] Psychologists claim that listening uses only about 25 percent of our brain. The other 75 percent either thinks about what to say next or stops listening if the conversation is boring or of no interest. Exhibit 10.6 is an example of the kind of listening that destroys any credibility you have or ever hope to establish.[22]

Improving Listening Skills

To improve your listening skills, practice these mental activities as you listen:

Be Patient. Listen more and give "verbal nods" of encouragement. This allows speakers plenty of time to answer questions and encourages them to express their ideas. Speak at the same speed as the other person: Matching speed is a rapport builder. In addition, find the person's *mental rate of speed* and then adjust or modify your thinking to that rate. Even though the speaker is saying something exciting, wait until the message is complete and you are sure that you understand it all before you jump in with your own thoughts.

Take Notes. Remembering everything a person says is difficult. Use the pencil-and-paper approach to selling. Divide your notepad into two columns. On one side note what the prospect says. Then in the other column sketch out your proposal to meet those expressions of needs, requirements, or desires. Find the happy medium between trying to record everything you hear and recording nothing. The mere physical action of writing down a few key words reinforces your memory and understanding. You can go back to the prospect's own words to help you show your product's applicability to the problem. Taking notes means you

EXHIBIT 10.6 - The Way We Practice Listening

Are you listening?

Ed Milligan called on the drugstore every week to fill inventories and check new items. He always greeted the owner with a big smile and the question, "Good to see you. How's the family?"

The store owner answered, "Fine," and Ed always replied, "Terrific. Let me show you what we have for you this week."

Wondering if Ed really cared about his family, the owner decided to give a new answer to Ed's standard question. When Ed showed up on schedule the following week and said, "Good to see you. How's the family?" the owner said, "Well, my mother-in-law jumped off the cliff, the children are lost in a forest, and my wife had to go to a leper colony."

Without missing a beat, good old Ed answered, "Terrific. Let me show you what we have for you this week."

consider people's words important. The technology of computers with their ease of use and portability make them a realistic note-taking option. It may be impolite to open up a laptop computer and start banging away on the keyboard during a sales call, but the pen-based computer system allows you to discreetly take notes. You might want to consider doing away with the "old" pad-and-pencil routine. You write your notes directly onto the screen with the stylus, or pen, that comes with the system.[23]

Avoid Prejudgment. Not only should you allow the speaker to complete a message before you comment or respond, but you should also wait until you have heard the entire message before judging it. Making value judgments colors your thinking and creates *emotional blind spots* that block your ability to make a buying recommendation. Jumping to conclusions is a common fault of poor listeners. As the cartoon indicates, assuming you know what is coming next can seriously damage your understanding of the actual meaning intended.

Reinforce. Anchor—in your mind and in the prospect's—the points made by the prospect. Use your own reinforcing responses to achieve this purpose. If the prospect says the mileage per gallon a car gets is important, respond, "Yes, that is very important." Later, tell what mileage the prospect could get with your car. If the prospect says, "Our secretaries spend too much time making copies," respond, "That has to be a problem." Then later emphasize how your copier cuts secretaries' time by copying on both sides of the paper in one operation and by running more copies per minute.

Capitalize on Speed of Thought. We can process about 600 words a minute, but even a fast talker gets out only 100 to 150 words in that time.[24] Thus you can think about four times as fast as the average prospect talks. All that spare time is valuable. The poor listener uses it to fidget impatiently, to think about what happened earlier in the day or what will happen later, or to plan what to say as soon as the prospect takes a breath. Successful salespeople have a plan to follow for using this time profitably:

1. *Anticipate* where the prospect is going. If you guess right, your thinking is reinforced. If you are wrong, compare your thoughts with the prospect's; look for the main point the prospect is making.
2. *Mentally summarize* the message. Pinpoint problems, misconceptions, attitudes, objections, or misunderstandings. What you learn can be an excellent guide to the items that should be stressed in the presentation and at the close.

3. *Formulate a response,* but not before you hear everything the prospect wants to say. Listen, understand, and then turn the prospect's words to your advantage.

4. *Listen between the lines.* Nonverbal messages are as important as verbal ones. Watch facial expressions, body movement, and position; listen to the tone of voice and volume changes.

5. *Silence* speaks quite as eloquently as words. You do not need to speak the split second the prospect completes a sentence. Give yourself time to formulate an effective reply. If you need a little time, say something like this: "That was a thought-provoking statement. Let me think about it for a few minutes." You then project the image of a problem solver.

Just as speech habits may be irritating and distracting, some listening habits may cause prospects to reject the salesperson. Table 10.1 shows some of these habits and their results.

TABLE 10.1 - Irritating Listening Habits That Lose Sales

What the salesperson does	What the prospect thinks about the salesperson
Disagrees and interrupts.	Disagrees with everything I say even before I can finish saying it.
Invades prospect's personal space by sitting too close.	Crowding me; trying to take over.
Plays with pen, eyes wander, doodles.	Not really listening to me.
Overdoes acknowledgments: too many nods, too many tie-downs.	Must think I am stupid.
Attempts to show off personal knowledge.	Know-it-all! The hero type. Brag, brag, brag.
Tops everything prospect says.	Has to be one up. Can't let anyone else look good.

SUMMARY

Salespeople are diagnosticians. Asking questions is the primary tool for identifying problems or needs. Need discovery lays the groundwork for the presentation and close. Without it, the salesperson has no road map to follow in choosing the quickest and easiest route to a successful close. When the salesperson asks the right questions, prospects can clarify problems in their own minds as well as for the salesperson. Once a problem is recognized, the salesperson can choose the features and benefits of the product or service that apply to its solution.

A specific plan for asking questions may be developed for each prospect and each selling situation. No standard set of questions is universally applicable. The questions a salesperson should ask are determined by the product or service, the preapproach information available, the salesperson's assessment of the prospect's behavioral style, and any other factor that affects the salesperson's presentation.

Asking questions is useful as a transition from the approach. The process of asking questions creates an atmosphere in which the prospect is comfortable and willing to participate. The salesperson must be careful to retain control of the interview during the questioning phase so that the conversation is not sidetracked into irrelevant areas.

Questions may be either closed-end or open-end. A closed-end question asks for an either-or answer, a yes-no response, or a choice between alternatives. It may also ask for a specific fact. Open-end questions ask for opinions, reasoning, explanations, or judgments. They are more general in nature and are useful to learn what the prospect thinks and feels. Open-end questions get the prospect involved in the presentation, a necessary condition for discovering the dominant buying motive.

Questions may also be classified according to structure: clarification probes, amplification probes, internal summary or reflective probes, and probes to gain agreement. Each of these may be open-end or closed-end, depending upon the situation.

When you ask a question, you must listen to the answer, but listening is one of the most neglected skills in education and in any type of training program. The salesperson must learn patience to allow the prospect plenty of time to answer questions and express ideas. Taking notes focuses attention on what the prospect is saying and avoids prejudgment of ideas. Reinforce what you hear by comparing the prospect's ideas with your own. Review major points as you listen to fix them in your memory. Because people think much faster than they talk, listening occupies only a small portion of the power of the mind. The time not needed to listen can be profitably used in anticipating where the prospect might be going, summarizing the message, forming a tentative response and refining it as listening continues, and interpreting the message to gain full understanding.

QUESTIONS FOR THOUGHT AND DISCUSSION

1. A salesperson calls on a CEO after ascertaining that the CEO does not own a cellular telephone. Entering the CEO's office, the salesperson says, "Good morning, Mr. Jesse. I am Dale Peters, representing the A-1 Cellular Telephone Company. No one in your position should be without a cellular telephone. You need one because you lose a lot of valuable time when you are in your car." Comment on this scenario.

2. What factors determine a salesperson's ability to formulate the right questions?

3. What is the difference between manipulation and consultation? Which is most useful to the successful salesperson? Why?

4. What kinds of questions allow the salesperson to discover the prospect's behavioral style? How does this information aid the salesperson?

5. What tactic is useful as a transition from the approach into need discovery?

6. Who should control the needs-assessment phase of the interview? How is control maintained?

7. What is the purpose of the open-end question? Formulate an open-end question that might be used to sell investment property.

8. Describe in detail all the instruction you have had in school, at home, or elsewhere in listening skills.

9. In what situations do you find it hardest to listen? Easiest? What makes the difference?

10. Is listening easier if a visual factor is added? For example, do you prefer to talk to someone in person or on the phone when you have something serious to discuss?

11. Educators say learning that involves more than one of the senses is faster. Explain how this applies to listening and taking notes, to listening and looking at visual aids of some kind simultaneously, and to listening to radio versus watching television.

ACTIVITIES

1. Pair up in male-female teams of two. Assume that you want to ask your partner for a dinner date at a restaurant and list some questions that you could ask to find out what kind of restaurant to suggest to make the best impression. Avoid closed-end questions like "Would you rather go for pizza or eat at a fancy restaurant?"

2. Suppose you are selling lawn mowers in a retail store. List questions you could ask to determine what type of mower a particular customer needs.

3. You sell automatic garage-door openers. Your prospect has never had an automatic garage-door opener. Prepare a dialogue asking questions that would lead this customer to recognize a need for an automatic opener and create a desire to own one.

Case Study

CASE STUDY 10.1

Ken Simpson was elated. He called his sales manager and gleefully reported, "I have an appointment tomorrow with the head buyer for the Pilot Company, the largest department store chain in this area—you know, the one with the big garden centers in their suburban branches. If I get the contract for our power mowers, snow blowers, and garden tractors, you'll have to tell the plant to go on overtime!"

The sales manager congratulated Ken but warned him to spend some time preparing his presentation. This opportunity was not the time to go in poorly prepared. Ken assured his sales manager that he would be ready. No way did he intend to muff this chance!

The next morning, Ken was confident he could make the biggest sale of his career. He started by mentioning his company's excellent reputation for high-quality products. Then he told about the performance record of their power equipment, their high manufacturing standards, and their rigid specifications for raw materials and parts. And on and on and on. He finally asked his first question: "With your reputation for selling only high-quality merchandise, don't you agree that our outstanding line of lawn and garden equipment would fit right in with your image in the high-income, suburban area?"

The answer left Ken almost speechless. The buyer said, "Your company's promotional campaign has made me quite familiar with your line. But while you were gushing about how good your outfit is from your point of view, I was never able to get a word in edgewise. I want to know about markup and service centers. I don't want to hear about quality-control procedures; I want to know about the result of your procedures. You know, I see a lot of salespeople like you. You know your product, and I admit we want to handle the best line we can get. I still have two weeks before I have to choose a line of power mowers, tractors, and snow-removal equipment to recommend to the buying committee. If you can come back and will promise to answer my questions, I'll give you another appointment."

1. Ken's mistake is obvious. Correcting it, however, may not be as simple as it seems. What would you suggest he say to the buyer right now?

2. If he makes another appointment, how should Ken prepare?

3. What should Ken tell his sales manager about this interview?

CASE 10.2

Della King sells custom business forms as well as a complete line of stock forms applicable to almost any firm with large-volume paperwork. Her first call on Harry Thompson, purchasing agent for a large community college, was frustrating. He was the silent type. Della thought to herself, "This guy must have adopted that old slogan that says even a fish would stay out of trouble if he kept his mouth shut."

Della was sure the college could benefit from using the custom design service her company offered for printing all sorts of student information forms: invoices and bills, grade records, and transcript forms, as well as administrative forms like requisitions and purchase orders. After she completed her standard presentation, Della asked for an order. Harry spoke for the first time, "We've got enough inventory of forms to last through next semester. Call on me next time you're in town. If you'll excuse me, I have a meeting in the president's office in two minutes."

All Della could do was say good-bye and leave. Back at her car, she noted on Harry's prospect card: "A real clam. Find a way to get him to talk." A month later, she was back again. She checked over the points she could make about the service her company offered and thought to herself, "He's the purchasing agent; he can at least suggest some problem that we could address. I've got to get him to talk." As she approached his desk, he silently waved her to a chair. "It's good to see you again, Mr. Thompson," Della began. His only reply was a grunt. Determined to get him to talk, she asked, "Mr. Thompson, do people in your organization ever complain about the difficulty of reading the last copy in your multiple forms?" His only answer was a shrug.

1. What might happen if Della tried the silent treatment by asking a question and then just waiting until Harry actually said something? Is he likely to be uncomfortable with a protracted silence?

2. What other option can you suggest for Della to use in getting Harry to talk enough to reveal some need or buying motive?

THE SALES EDGE

CHECKLIST OF SUCCESS FUNDAMENTALS

		Yes	No
I.	**Goals:**		
	1. Increase size of existing accounts	_____	_____
	2. Contacts and networking daily	_____	_____
	3. New appointments daily	_____	_____
	4. New prospects daily	_____	_____
II.	**Closing Interviews**		
	1. Three today	_____	_____
	2. Three yesterday	_____	_____
	3. A minimum of *12* last week	_____	_____
III.	**Prospecting**		
	1. New qualified prospects each day	_____	_____
	2. *Five* referrals on every sale	_____	_____
	3. Adequate information on those referrals	_____	_____
	4. *Three* methods of prospecting	_____	_____
IV.	**Appointment Getting**		
	1. Call from same place and at same time everyday	_____	_____
	2. Prepare names and numbers to call before phone time	_____	_____
	3. Use the *MARC* approach daily	_____	_____
	4. Make at least 3 new appointments a day	_____	_____
	5. Use the <u>Six-Step Telephone Track</u>	_____	_____
V.	**Presentation:**		
	1. Complete the sales presentation in 30 minutes	_____	_____
	2. Close a minimum of *four* times	_____	_____
	3. <u>Use</u> an organizer or visual aid presentation	_____	_____
VI.	**Attitude Adjustment**		
	1. Use a personal program daily to help acheive my goals	_____	_____
	2. Work on <u>two</u> of the *Ports of Life* this week	_____	_____
VII.	**Personal Organization and Self-Management**		
	1. Use a *daily* and *weekly* plan sheet	_____	_____
	2. Use a *monthly* **goal** calendar	_____	_____
	3. Know how much an hour of your time is worth	_____	_____
	4. Schedule appointments geographically	_____	_____

C H A P T E R   1 1

Chapter 11

Making the Presentation

DEVELOPING A PERSUASIVE PRESENTATION

Some experts are predicting that salespeople are soon to be corporate relics on the road to extinction. Not true! Consultative salespeople will prosper in the future if they understand this: There are big differences between data, information, knowledge, and wisdom. In the past, traditional or transactional sales reps simply presented data. How "data dense" are most sales presentations? The typical salesperson presents six to eight features or benefits during the sales presentation. Twenty-four hours later the average prospect remembers one, and in 39 percent of the cases they remember it incorrectly. In 49 percent of the cases they remember something that wasn't mentioned at all. Prospects want a product that does what they want it to do, explained in a language they understand.[1] The future of professional, consultative selling is going to be based on real-time agilities and how well sales professionals become trusted advisors in guiding clients to a solution to their problems. Salespeople must become better knowledge managers and not just people who are trying to close a deal. There is a need for consultative salespeople that can do more than simply share data and dispense information. The future belongs to those sales pros that can present and share their knowledge, offer wisdom, and create value in a way that benefits the prospect.[2]

More often than not, customers buy because of the rapport building established over time. "Selling is all about relationship building. There are hundreds of competitors chomping at the bit," says Diane DiResta. It all comes down to the way you present yourself and your product or service, and the value you create for the customer. Sales presentations must be listener-centered. People want to have their problems solved. People-reading skills help salespeople adapt to their prospect's social styles. Mark McCormack in his book *What They Don't Teach You at the Harvard Business School* says there are three fundamental selling truths: 1. If you don't know your product, people will resent your efforts to sell it. 2. If you don't believe in your product, no amount of personality or technique will cover that fact. 3. If you can't sell your product with enthusiasm, the absence of it will be infectious. Nobody buys from a dispassionate seller. If you don't believe in the product, no one else will. The more options a sales rep creates for the prospect, the greater the chance for a sale.[3] Don't worry about making the perfect presentation. It probably will not happen! Besides, the prospects are looking to you for knowledge of what you're selling and how it can help them solve a problem or become more successful. You must truly believe in what you're selling and show some passion when doing it – that is far more important than perfection.

Planning: Begin with Planning

Does everything begin with planning? Yes, everything important begins with planning. Exhibit 11.1 is one man's account of the results he suffered from his failure to plan his immediate future. Random, haphazard action never leads to success in any worthwhile endeavor, and in this respect, selling is no different from any other undertaking. How well you plan what takes place during the sales interview plays a major role in the success you achieve when closing time arrives.

In reality, planning and preparing for the sales presentation begin when a name is first recorded in your prospect files. As information is gathered

EXHIBIT 11.1 - Failing to Plan My Immediate Future

I am writing in response to your request for additional information. In block #3 of the accident form I listed "not planning my immediate future" as the cause of my accident. I trust the following details will be sufficient.

I am a bricklayer. On the date of the accident I was working alone on the roof of a new six-story building. At the end of the day, I discovered about 500 pounds of bricks left over. Rather than carry them down by hand, I decided to lower them in a barrel by using a pulley that was fortunately attached to the building at the sixth floor..

Securing the rope at ground level, I went to the roof, swung the barrel out, and loaded the bricks. Then I went back to the ground and untied the rope, holding it tightly to ensure a slow descent of the 500 pounds of bricks. Block #11 of the accident report shows that I weigh 135 pounds. Due to my surprise of being jerked off the ground so suddenly, I forgot to let go of the rope. Needless to say, I proceeded at a rapid rate up the side of the building. In the vicinity of the third floor, I met the barrel coming down. This explains the fractured skull and broken collarbone.

Slowed only slightly, I continued my rapid ascent, not stopping until the fingers of my right hand were two knuckles deep into the pulley. Fortunately, I had regained my presence of mind enough to hold tightly to the rope in spite of my pain.

At approximately the same time, however, the barrel of bricks hit the ground and the bottom fell out of the barrel. Devoid of the weight of the bricks, the barrel now weighed approximately 50 pounds. I refer you again to block #11. As you can imagine, I began a rapid descent down the side of the building.

In the vicinity of the third floor I met the barrel coming up. This accounts for the two fractured ankles and the lacerations of my legs and lower body. The encounter with the barrel slowed my descent enough to lessen my injuries when I fell onto the pile of bricks. Fortunately only three vertebrae were cracked.

I am sorry to report, however, that as I lay there on the bricks, in pain, unable to stand and watching the empty barrel six stories above me, I lost my presence of mind again and let go of the rope. Now the empty barrel weighed more than the rope, so it came back down on me and broke both of my legs.

I hope these details explain sufficiently that my accident was caused by failure to plan my immediate future.

about the prospect, you are subconsciously planning how to approach this person, what features and benefits are most appropriate, and what kind of close is likely to be most effective. The final step of preparing for the sales interview is to crystallize all your plans and decide exactly how to proceed with making the presentation. You really need a clear, focused objective for your message, and that's partly determined by the type of individual or company you are calling on. According to Katherine Luckett-Watson, sales manager of Unibar Maintenance Services Inc., "Many salespeople think that a presentation is an end-all and fail to actually set realistic objectives." Of course, you want to earn their business, but often it's not a matter of closing on the very first call. It's a matter of moving a proposal forward to a higher level.[4]

Call Objective

The most successful salespeople have specific objectives for each sales interview. In many instances, the call objective is to present your product or service and secure an order. In others, your objective is to discover the prospect's needs so that you may prepare a proposal for later consideration or to persuade the prospect to set up a presentation to a group of people who are jointly charged with the responsibility for a buying decision. In these latter instances, you will probably plan several interviews that, taken together, contain all the elements that may be considered parts of "the presentation." The difference is that you accomplish the various steps in *successive* interviews rather than in a *single* meeting with the prospect. Whether you intend to complete the presentation and the close in a single call or in a series of calls depends upon the type of product or service you sell and the size of the expected order. The single-call close is appropriate for selling items that can be ordered upon the decision of one person; if a *buying center* is involved, multiple calls are usually necessary. Expendable products are more likely to be purchased at the first call, but capital investment items are usually purchased only after intensive study and several meetings.

Thomas Scott, a regional sales manager for WorldCom, usually works on a four-interview system. The sale may be closed on any one of the four calls, and sometimes it requires many more than four calls. Here is his system:

1. Initial call.

Develop rapport and establish a need. Judge how far to go by how quickly a relationship is established. Take notes all along to help build a trust level.

2. Survey call.

Interview all key decision makers to get information. The decision is ultimately based on three factors: cost, quality, and service. Discover which one is most important to this client. Begin using trial closes.

3. Proposal call.

Present a buying recommendation. Recognize the fact that this is a joint or buying center decision, and give each person what that individual needs to reach a decision. Use trial closes.

4. Closing call.

Get verbal and/or written commitment.

Calling on Regular Customers

If you are calling on the same person or dealer on a regular basis, you may tend to give the same old presentation over and over or even skip the presentation entirely and merely ask, "What do you need today?" If you are unwilling to put some real work into your selling and are content just to "take orders" all your life, your best opportunity to become rich is to win the Publishers Clearing House Sweepstakes! Vary your presentation. Provide new ideas to help your customer make money, save time, or increase efficiency. Plan to use ideas like these:

1. Give the customer a new advertising or merchandising idea.

2. Help the customer develop an overall marketing plan for improving the business.

3. Tell some new product fact that the customer needs to know.

4. Share a piece of industry or trade news of personal interest to the customer.

Sales Call Planning Sheet

Many companies, especially those whose product or service entails extensive research into customer needs, require salespeople to prepare a presentation plan in written form. The plan reveals the need for any additional information, makes it possible to check needs and goals against suggested solutions, and makes sure the salesperson has a clear picture of the entire situation before arriving for the personal interview. Exhibit 11.2 is an example of a sales call planning sheet that may be used for this purpose.

EXHIBIT 11.2 - Sales Call Planner

1. Company Name _____
2. Type of Company _____
3. Address _____
4. Individual(s) to contact
   _____ (position) _____
   _____ (position) _____
5. Background and profile of buyers _____
   _____
6. Major competitors to be aware of
   _____ (sales rep) _____
   _____ (sales rep) _____
7. Objective for this particular call _____
8. Best time to see buyer _____
9. Expressed needs or problems _____
   _____
10. Strategies and tactics useful for this situation
    a. Best approach to use _____
    b. Specific fact-finding questions _____
       _____
    c. Features and benefits to stress _____
    d. Anticipated objections _____
       (techniques to answer them)_____
    e. Closing techniques to be used _____
       _____
11. Sales tools to take (audiovisual, flip-chart presentation, etc.) _____
    _____
12. Results of this sales call _____
    _____

STYLE OF THE PRESENTATION

As long as people have been attempting to analyze the selling process, a running controversy has raged over the use of "canned" presentations. Opponents point to presentations that are obviously memorized, and delivered in a hypnotic manner likely to produce a mesmerized listener in the shortest possible time. Supporters of memorized presentations point to the many advantages of knowing exactly what to say and when. The question is not likely to be settled once and for all because the difference lies more with the salesperson than with the method of delivery itself. In deciding how you will deliver the message you want the prospect to receive, consider the advantages and disadvantages of three basic choices: the memorized presentation, the outline presentation, and the extemporaneous presentation.

Memorized Presentation

Some companies supply their salespeople with a printed presentation and require them to memorize it. A few words of caution are in order when considering the use of a memorized presentation. Even though it is memorized, the presentation should never sound memorized. A memorized presentation should be practiced and its delivery polished until it becomes natural. It should be internalized to the point that it is a normal, personal message. The memorized presentation must be used as a framework or guide to lead salesperson and prospect through the sales process. Most companies that make use of a standardized presentation provide a list of suggested questions to help discover buying motives, suggest options to use in different types of circumstances, and caution the salesperson to remain flexible.

A well-prepared, memorized presentation offers a number of important advantages, especially to inexperienced salespeople.

Quick Productivity. The salesperson who is new to the company or to the selling profession can memorize a good presentation in much less time than one can be developed. Using a standardized presentation gets the salesperson into production quickly. Enough sales can be made during the initial learning period to supply basic income needs while the salesperson gains knowledge and experience.

Reliable and Proven Effectiveness. The memorized presentation makes sure the salesperson gives the right information to the prospect. Nothing vital is omitted, and nothing erroneous is inserted. The presentation a company supplies to salespeople has usually been tested and refined over a period of years in actual selling situations.

Confidence Building. Using it is a confidence builder for the inexperienced salesperson. When you know the presentation has worked for others with no more experience than you have, you feel capable of using it successfully. When you succeed in closing a sale with the presentation, you gain even more confidence. Each success builds on the previous one, and you are earning and learning at the same time.

Outline Presentation

The outline presentation takes a great deal of thought and preparation. With this presentation technique, exact words are not planned in full detail. The salesperson knows what content will be presented at each stage of the presentation but is confident enough of both knowledge and skill to believe that the right words will be available as needed. This is the same process that most experienced public speakers use.

Using an outline presentation successfully depends upon the development of numerous *units of conviction* that are thoroughly internalized. The outline is built by considering all the information available about the prospect. Most salespeople who use an outline method follow the same general outline for most presentations. They may, however, have several approaches or openings from which to choose, numerous features and benefits to present, and all sorts of evidence to present—all of which can be combined and recombined to meet the needs of the specific situation. Ideally, the salesperson makes the choice in advance and knows which pieces of material will be used. The use of the outline presentation is appropriate for a salesperson who has gained a measure of experience and success. It calls for more judgment about people and broader product knowledge than the memorized presentation.

Many companies, especially those whose product or service entails extensive research into customer needs, require salespeople to prepare an outline presentation in written form. Any type of written plan you use reveals any existing need for additional information, enables you to check needs and goals against suggested solutions, and makes sure you have a clear picture of the entire situation before arriving for the interview. Procter & Gamble is one company that recommends its sales reps follow an outline plan for presentations. Exhibit 11.3 is an outline for a presentation written by one of its sales managers in Dallas, Texas.

EXHIBIT 11.3 - A Procter & Gamble Sales Plan

Purpose of the Sales Call

Sell 40 cases of Folger's one-pound for display.

Background of Account

Chain store with $100,000 weekly volume. Store is allowed to select displays in addition to headquarters' displays. Store's current need is to increase dollar volume per customer transaction. Manager has also expressed concern with labor cost.

This particular store has a backstock of eight cases of canister creamers.

Summarize the Situation

The store manager said several weeks ago that they want to increase dollar volume 7 percent in the next three months by increasing the average amount of each customer transaction. I want to suggest a way to sell more Folger's coffee to help achieve this goal.

State the Idea

My idea is for the store to display 40 cases of one-pound Folger's coffee with eight cases of canister creamers from the store's backstock.

Explain How It Works

Last year's records show that the store displayed 30 cases of Folger's one-pound coffee during this time, and it sold out quickly at regular shelf price. Now in the cold months, coffee consumption is the number one dry grocery item. Capitalize on customer appeal of Folger's, which has proved popular in the past, and enhance it with an appealing display with the canister creamers.

Store now moves 10 cases weekly, and a special display will move 40 cases easily.

I'll help build the display and save time and labor for the store.

Reinforce Key Benefits

Show calculations of contribution this display can make to help reach the 7 percent increase desired. $2,678.40 in sales on coffee. Add the quality image created by Folger's TV advertising. The related item display will increase movement on creamers that are now sitting in backstock. The result is an increase in the average per-customer sale, which is the goal.

Suggest an Easy Next Step

Ask for a decision on which truck to send the 40 cases of Folger's and suggest Tuesday.

Extemporaneous Presentation

Some highly successful salespeople, particularly those who have many years of experience, may be heard to say that they "don't prepare" for a sales presentation. Actually, their preparation time is distributed in a different way than that of the less experienced salesperson, but they do prepare. The extemporaneous presentation follows the same principles that any other presentation incorporates, but experienced salespeople who use the extemporaneous approach are master people watchers. They understand people; they ask questions and listen. They are experts in discovering problems and identifying dominant buying motives. They know their product so thoroughly that they can seize almost magically upon the one feature or benefit that will best appeal to the prospect. They possess such charisma that the air of trust and credibility they create makes objections nonexistent and painlessly places the client's name on the order form. People love to buy from them. As a result, these master salespeople spend most of their "preparation time" in gathering additional information about the prospect rather than spending time in *consciously* matching features and benefits to prospect qualification information. This step is almost automatic and subconscious as a result of their long experience.

You can use the extemporaneous presentation when you have paid your dues over a period of time. It takes up-to-the-minute product knowledge, intensive prospecting, thorough preapproach qualifying of prospects, and a full background of selling experience upon which to draw. Although salespeople who use the extemporaneous method sometimes claim not to prepare, listening closely to presentations made by these masters shows that they have, over time, developed some uniquely personal tactics for conducting a sales interview. Many of the same phrases and sentences appear over and over—because they work! Conscious preparation, for these people, consists of learning about the particular prospect. Then automatically the tactics, the procedures, and words themselves surface from the well of experience and provide the "extemporaneous" inspiration that accomplishes the goal.

PRODUCT-ANALYSIS WORKSHEET

Prospects have neither the product knowledge you have nor an understanding of the type of service you are prepared to render. You must not only know all the facts about your product but also be able to relate your knowledge directly to the specific needs of the prospect. If you can quote prices, catalog numbers, shipping dates, delivery schedules, and credit terms but have no solid, convincing evidence of the product's value to offer upon which the prospect can base a buying decision, you are afflicted with what has been called the *salesman's curse:* "You know your product better than you know how your client's business can use it."[5] A salesperson who suffers from the "salesman's curse" is in the same league as a math student who can recite all the formulas in the algebra book but never knows which one to use to solve the problem. Before you can expect a signed order form, you must determine what kind of buying decision to recommend to the prospect and then find a way to persuade the prospect that the solution you offer is the best possible. You can do this by preparing *units of conviction.*

Units of Conviction

Units of conviction are concise, carefully prepared "mini-presentations" used as building blocks to construct the information the salesperson presents. When the individual units of conviction are combined, they form what many sales professionals refer to as a *product-analysis worksheet*. A single unit of conviction consists of five elements:

1. A feature of your product or service
2. A transitional phrase
3. The benefits the feature provides
4. Evidence to support your claims
5. A tie-down question to gain the prospect's agreement

Preparing a written product-analysis worksheet helps you evaluate the various characteristics of your product so that you are better able to present it to your prospects. When you prepare units of conviction and add them to your store of available options, they become a permanent part of your selling arsenal. As you ask questions to discover and define the needs and goals of the prospect, you are learning how to *personalize* these units of conviction and recall them in an order that helps the prospect see them as clearly as you do. If you have not made this preliminary preparation, you may waste valuable time trying to figure out just what to say during the presentation and when to say it.

Features and Benefits. *Features* are the tangible and intangible qualities of the product or service you sell. Features are facts that are the same no matter who uses the product or service. The tangible features of a product include observable factors such as color, size, capacity, speed of performance, material from which it is made—anything that can be detected through one of the five senses. Intangible features are also important: the service given by the company, price, delivery, availability of service, and even the service and support that you promise. *Benefits,* however, are the value or worth that the user derives from the product or service. For example, thousands of l/4-inch drill bits are sold every year, but do buyers actually want l/4-inch bits, or do they want l/4-inch holes? Remember that a smooth hole of exact diameter and desired depth is what the customer wants. Which features and benefits of your drill bit will best produce that hole within the limits of the customer's desire for performance, reliability, long life, or price? These are the ones to describe.

Of the numerous benefits a product or service has to offer, only four or five will be key motivators to a prospect, and these will be different for each prospect. Your task as a salesperson is to find out which criteria are the key motivators.[6] The alert salesperson studies, observes, and listens to the prospect, and then stresses the applicable benefits of each feature. Every feature of your product has numerous benefits. Remember, *one feature does not equal one benefit*. Examine the insert that follows and challenge your mind to perform some mental gymnastics to prove this point.

Features and Benefits

Every feature of your product has numerous benefits. Here's an exercise to give your mind a healthy benefit workout: What are the benefits of a 270-horsepower engine in a luxury car? They could include a smoother ride, power to spare when passing a slower car, quick acceleration away from a hazard, the feeling of being in charge, less wear and tear, higher resale value, etc.

The point is, one feature does not equal one benefit. List your product's top 10 features, then come up with at least five different benefits for each feature. Remember, features only justify the price; benefits justify the purchase. This gives you 50 new ways to close more sales.

Transitional Phrase. The ability to translate features into benefits is one of the marks of a professional consultative salesperson. Even if you know which feature can fulfill the buying motive, you cannot expect the prospect to make the connection automatically. You must make the verbal transition. The prospect does not know your product as well as you know it and has to have features and benefits connected by transitional phrases; expressions like "because," "this lets you," "this heads off all the problems of," or "what this means to you" are examples of transitional phrases. Some salespeople call these *bridges*.[7] While the actual words may vary, they are all designed to accomplish the same purpose: to connect, in the prospect's thinking, features and benefits. These phrases all serve the purpose of answering the prospect's question, "What's in it for me?" Here are some examples:

- Your daughter will love this sweater *because* it's what all the girls are wearing this year. You'll love it *because* it's washable and *that means* no dry-cleaning bills for you.

- The premiums on this policy begin at a low rate while you are in your 20s and increase later when you can expect to be well-established in your career and earning more. *What this gives you* is the ability to provide full protection for your family now at a price you can afford.

- Our newspaper delivers 92 percent of daily readers in this SMSA. *This means* that new readers in the market looking for a place to shop or find services will identify immediately with your business and you will benefit from the increased traffic.

Begin preparation of units of conviction by listing in writing all the features of your product or service. If you sell more than one major product, make separate lists for each one. Then go back and list all the ways the first feature can benefit your prospect. If you neglect this preparatory step, you will find yourself confronting prospects who listen to the features you describe and ask, "So what?" and you will have no appealing answers. When you have prepared units of conviction in advance, finding the right one is just like reaching into your briefcase and pulling out a sample; you know what is there and all of it is at your fingertips for instant use when you need it.

Exhibit 11.4 shows a features and benefits card prepared by the Hartmann Luggage Company of Lebanon, Tennessee, for their carry-ons and carry-on totes. These cards are distributed by the company's marketing managers to retail salespeople to help them sell the product.

Evidence (Proof) to Support Claims. Just as you present benefits to head off the prospect's question "So what?" about the features of your product or service, you must present evidence to support the claims you make to head off the questions "Can you prove it?" and "Who says so?" Even if you have been unusually successful in establishing a high degree of credibility and trust with the prospect, you are unlikely to be looked upon as an all-knowing sage with all the answers whose statements are to be accepted without question. You must be prepared to back up what you say with: <u>1.</u> demonstrations, <u>2.</u> testimonials, <u>3.</u> facts and statistics, <u>4.</u> samples, and <u>5.</u> examples or case histories.

EXHIBIT 11.4 - Unique Features and Benefits of Hartmann Carry-on Totes

Features	Benefits
1. Seven pockets or compartments.	Lots of places for all those "extra" items when you need the space (organize your packing).
2. Two-way carry.	Comfortable strap that adjusts to hand-carry or shoulder strap. Lets you decide how to carry the bag most comfortably for YOU.
3. Full-opening front pocket.	Easy access and even has room for an umbrella or newspaper/magazine.
4. Carry it on a plane.	You know you will have it, AND your clothing/contents will arrive, AND you won't have to wait for baggage.
5. Easy-access large center compartment.	Makes packing and unpacking easy and fast.
6. Waterproof pocket on inside of center compartment.	Can be used as a cosmetic/toilet bag. Keeps inside dry and separates "spillables" from the rest of the contents.
7. Large outside back pocket. PLUS a zipper pocket.	Large pocket allows you to put in those last-minute items for easy access, and the zipper pocket gives you a secure place for your keys, passport, etc.
8. Lightweight—yet strong.	Light weight permits you to carry more clothing, and strength of bag protects the clothing and contents.
9. Teflon-coated fabrics.	Stays good-looking. Easy to clean.

1. Demonstrations. Show the product in use. The demonstration is especially effective for some types of prospects if they have hands-on use in the demonstration. Automobile salespeople urge the prospect to drive the car a few blocks. Furniture salespeople suggest that prospects sit on the furniture and experience its comfort. Some office machines are even left with the prospect for several days' trial.

Demonstrations showing the product in use are effective.

2. Testimonials. The best possible testimonial is for one of your satisfied customers to call the prospect ahead of time and suggest that you be given an appointment. At this time, your customer expresses satisfaction with the product or service; this predisposes the prospect to accept what you say. Other types of testimonials are also effective with the right type of prospect. Use customers' letters expressing their pleasure with your product and the service you have provided. Such letters are easy to get. Just ask for them! You may even write the testimonial yourself and ask the prospect to read and sign it to save the client's time and make sure the letter is worded to fit your needs. When a client thanks you for some help, just say you would appreciate a letter saying the same thing. This kind of testimonial is especially helpful when it comes from a person who has influence in the community or with the particular prospect or when it is written on the letterhead of a respected company. You may have pictures of your clients using your product, with their signatures on the back. All of these are excellent testimonials.

3. Facts and Statistics. Call attention to manufacturer's ratings, such as the energy ratings of air-conditioning and heating units and the estimated mpg ratings of automobiles. Show earnings of stocks or other investment vehicles over the past five years. Consider these facts and statistics: The U.S. Census Bureau is projecting that the 65-and-older age group will grow 75 percent by the year 2050. The Hispanics aged 65-plus will increase by more than 147 percent, faster than any other ethnic group in that age bracket. Information contained in Table 11.1 illustrates the percentage changes in various age categories.[8]

TABLE 11.1 - Aging Americans Percent Distribution of the Population by Age: 2000 to 2050					
Age Group	2000	2010	2030	2040	2050
14 to 17	5.6	5.9	5.3	5.3	5.2
18 to 24	9.5	9.8	9.1	9.2	9.0
25 to 34	15.5	12.7	12.4	12.4	12.5
35 to 44	16.2	14.8	12.9	12.9	12.2
45 to 64	19.9	24.9	22.1	22.1	22.5
65 & Over	12.8	12.7	20.2	20.2	20.6
85 & Over	1.4	1.7	2.4	3.6	4.6

Train your sales staff to show facts and statistics.

If a life insurance salesperson is looking for a market in which needs are clearly understood, daylight appointments are the norm, cross-selling is a natural, and personal gratification is high, then the 65-plus market is one to consider. One of three seniors will need some care; the average stay in a nursing home is three years, with a cost of over $30,000 a year. Patrick Maude, of Arlington Heights, Illinois, makes 95 percent of his income from the senior market. About 80 percent of his business is long-term care. Pyramid Life Insurance Company has developed a "Senior Solutions Operations Manual" from which salespeople can take their presentations. The concentration of wealth and prospects in the senior market makes it a market to explore. This type of niche marketing lends itself to a wide variety of companies in various industries, not just insurance.[9]

4. Samples. A sample of the product itself or of the material from which it is made gives the prospect something concrete to use as the basis of decision making. Supermarkets offer customers a taste of a featured food: cheese, sausage, pizza—anything that can be served from a small table, cooked in an electric frying pan, or stuck on the end of a toothpick. The demonstrator then indicates the display of the food item and asks the customer to try it. Publishers give samples of textbooks to college professors to entice them to adopt the new texts for their classes. A salesperson for operating room scrubs for hospitals might give the purchasing agent a swatch of the material from which they are made to feel as the quality is described. Samples are intended to provide an appeal to one or more of the five senses through which people gain information.

5. Examples or Case Histories. The use of examples or case histories is another way to present the satisfaction of other clients and customers. The salesperson may tell the prospect about other people whose circumstances are similar and how they were able to solve their problems or enjoy some benefit from using the product. Use these guidelines when planning this type of evidence:

1. The case history must be *authentic*. It should be about someone the prospect knows or can contact for verification.

2. Use *many details* to let the prospect know you are intimately familiar with the situation.

3. Back up the example with pictures, personal letters, newspaper articles, and other evidence.

4. Tie it directly to the prospect's circumstances.

The evidence used to back up the features and benefits you present must be as carefully tailored to the needs, problems, and personality of the prospect as the features and benefits themselves. For example, use cost-saving evidence for a prospect who is especially interested in economy; but use testimonials from prominent people for a prospect who is largely motivated by the desire for status. Use everything you know about the prospect as input for every step in the sales process.

The Tie-Down. Your goal as a salesperson is to translate features into benefits for the prospect, to provide the necessary evidence to prove your points, and to gain a commitment to act. Before you can gain the prospect's commitment to act, however, you must gain willing agreement with your solution for solving the problem the two of you identified earlier. Agreement is the key. People like to agree; they hate to be told. The "tie-down" is an essential step in building units of conviction, although it usually consists of no more than a single question that asks for the prospect's agreement. Here are some examples of tie-down questions:

• Considering these facts, you agree with me that this is a safe tire, don't you, Ms. Craft?

• I believe you will agree with me, Mr. Sanders, that this is a better way for handling this process than your present method, won't you?

The tie-down is important throughout the presentation to check on understanding and agreement and to make sure the prospect is ready to proceed to the next point. One of the functions of the tie-down is to ask a series of questions, all of which the prospect can be expected to answer yes. Then when you attempt a close, the prospect more easily says yes again. Suppose, however, that you ask, "You agree with me about this, don't you?" and the prospect says, "No, I don't." Where are you now? You are in a better position than you were before you asked the question because you now know you have a problem. Had you not asked this question and found out about the lack of agreement, you would have pushed on to the close and to failure. Now you are warned about the existence of a problem and can go back to find its source and correct it, ask another tie-down question, and move forward again when agreement is reached.

Exhibit 11.5 is a complete unit of conviction developed by a long-distance telephone service for their sales force to use. Notice the tie-down at the end—the question that leads the prospect into agreement.

EXHIBIT 11.5 - Unit of Conviction: Long-Distance Telephone Service

Feature	We offer one-tenth of a minute billing on your long-distance telephone service. A lot of other companies bill in full minute increments.
Transitional phrase	What this means is...
Benefit	On a call of 3 minutes and 6 seconds, for example, other companies would bill you for 4 minutes. We would bill you for only 3.1 minutes. This will provide you with a significant cost savings on your monthly telephone bill or will give you the luxury of increased service at the same cost.
Evidence (Facts and Statistics)	Here's an illustration of the extra savings you could receive: If a call is billed at the rate of 25¢ per minute, our charge would be approximately 78¢ for 3.1 minutes. The same call, when billed at 4 minutes, would cost you $1.00—an increase of 22¢. Of course, not all calls would save you this much because some would save you only three-tenths or one-tenth of a minute instead of nine-tenths of a minute. But for someone whose business relies as heavily on long-distance telephone service as yours, the savings could be enormous. Even a few cents saved per call would be a sizable amount.
Tie-down	I think you can get an idea of the enormous advantage you will have with one-tenth of a minute billing, can't you, Mr. Blackmon?

EFFECTIVE TACTICS FOR PRESENTATIONS

Professional selling is an exciting career because it provides such a variety of opportunities that work never becomes routine or dull. Even though you may be selling only one product or service, every prospect is different. Moreover, you are different each day. What is going on in your own emotional life, the success you are enjoying, the problems you are facing—all of these make every day different. In addition, you have the option of approaching the task of telling your story to the prospect using a variety of sales tactics. Which tactics you choose depend upon what you have learned about the prospect during preapproach qualification, what you observe in the opening minutes of the interview, what you personally want to do, and what kind of environment you find in the interview location. The only limit to the number of different presentation tactics is your own creative imagination.

The most common tactics are presented here; you will probably use all of them at one point or another as they fit into your sales activity. You will probably find yourself developing your own personal mixture of tactics—a blend that fits your personality, your product, and the needs of your prospects.

Participation

Every presentation—no matter how it is organized or what other method is used—must get the prospect involved in the selling process. When prospects are shut out of the presentation process or choose to remain aloof, say nothing, and contribute nothing, they also buy nothing. The prime tactic for gaining the participation of the prospect is asking questions and then listening to the answers. Plan the questions to be asked during the presentation to gain maximum participation by the prospect.

Beyond asking questions yourself, you should encourage prospects to ask questions about any benefit of the product you present or any factor involved in its application or use. Their questions prevent misunderstanding and give you the opportunity to direct your presentation to the problem or need that is most important to them.

Demonstration

Showmanship sells if it is more than mere carnival hoopla. There is a big difference between showmanship and *show-off-manship*. A well-timed dramatic touch seizes and holds the prospect's attention. A demonstration is an effective method of adding showmanship to the presentation while achieving the purpose of the presentation. A good demonstration provides you with these benefits:

1. Catches the buyer's interest
2. Fortifies your points
3. Helps the prospect understand the proposition
4. Stimulates your own interest
5. Cuts down on the number of objections
6. Helps you close the sale[10]

PERSONAL TOUCH PERKS UP SALES

Program: Hills Bros. Coffee Inc. sought to establish relationships with grocery store food buyers, and convince them to carry a new product. When visiting buyers, the sales reps arrived with a colorful, custom-designed briefcase-style kit.

Inside the kit were a sampler jar and a can of the promoted coffee, along with a graphically coordinated set of imprinted promotional products—a napkin, coffee cups, and thermos that contained freshly brewed coffee.

Results: After the buyers sampled and discussed the product, the salesperson presented the kit and promotional products to them. Orders were signed by over 80 percent of the grocers reached using this technique.

The value of a demonstration is that it involves more than one of the physical senses in the selling process. If you rely solely on "telling" the prospect about your product, only the auditory sense is involved. If you add a demonstration, you add the visual sense. If, in addition, you involve the prospect in the demonstration, you add the sense of touch. The more of the senses you can involve, the more quickly the prospect absorbs the information that leads to a sale. People remember 20 percent of what they hear and 20 percent of what they see. But they remember *50 percent* of what they see and hear. By mapping your information out visually, you unquestionably increase how much your clients retain.[11] A great example of multiple appeal to the senses through a demonstration is the Hills Bros. Coffee Inc. example. You can see how the innovative idea and personal touch really *perked* up coffee sales.[12]

Here are four principles to follow in using a demonstration as a part of your sales presentation:[13]

Principles For Planning a Demonstration

Concentrate the Prospect's Attention on You. The CEO of a large corporation once called a meeting of his associates in his office. When they came in, he was juggling several tennis balls. Finally, he tossed aside all but one and said, "We all have many things on our minds—like these tennis balls. But we must put them aside and concentrate on one problem at a time or we'll waste time trying to juggle them all." This demonstration illustrates the situation when you go to call on a prospect. You must focus the prospect's attention on one thing—what you are saying. A planned demonstration is an excellent tool for accomplishing this purpose.

Use Virtual Reality to Get Your Prospect Hooked. In this age of information technology, a number of companies offer a type of virtual reality demonstration for potential customers to use on their Web sites. Lands' End has developed what it calls *My Virtual Model*, which uses virtual reality to allow you to try on clothes according to your body size and characteristics. A series of questions allows you to pick your hairstyle, skin color, height, weight, etc. This simulated likeness of you can then model their clothes online. You can modify the look of "your" model and even e-mail your model to a friend. Go to www.landsend.com and click on *My Virtual Model*. You can have a lot of fun with this and may end up buying something. So have your credit card ready just in case!

Get Your Prospect Into the Act. Invite the prospect to operate your device, taste your food, smell the fragrance, feel the depth of the tread on the tires, or listen to the quiet sound of your machine in operation. If you are selling an intangible, hand the prospect photos, charts, or a prospectus. Get as many senses as possible involved. The Gulf Coast Regional Blood Center in Houston asks a prospect to put a thirty-letter word puzzle together. The sales representative hands the prospect a small box full of letters that, when properly arranged, spell: *WILL YOU HAVE BLOOD WHEN YOU NEED IT?* This demonstration dramatically illustrates how crucial a company-sponsored blood drive is to the community and to individuals.

Paint a Mind Picture Using Metaphors. Metaphors imply comparisons between otherwise dissimilar things without using the words "like" or "as", often creating a dramatic visual image. Remember, "facts tell, stories sell." Painting a mind picture is a hook that grabs prospects and reels them in. Steve Becker, west regional manager for Amersham Life Science, has used this creative metaphor with prospects: *Picture yourself in a desert without a canteen. In the distance you see a water well. There's a bucket with a rope nearby. Now, would you jump into the well headfirst or would you use the bucket and rope? What my firm can do for you is supply you with the bucket and rope—the tools you need to succeed.* Metaphors, analogies and similes can bring special life to sales presentations. These are effective ways to reinforce concepts, while building rapport and winning people over to your way of thinking.[14]

PRESENTATION SALES TOOLS AND VISUAL AIDS

Sales aids fall mainly into the categories of audio, visual, or audiovisual. Many people are visually oriented. That's why exciting, illustrative slides, overheads, and computer-driven programs are effective presentation tools. Sales aids are used primarily to help the prospect visualize or otherwise experience the benefits of the product or service or to help the salesperson organize the presentation so that the prospect receives an ordered, logical message that is easily remembered.

The Organizer or Flip Chart

Many companies provide salespeople with standard visual sales kits in the form of a small flip chart suitable for standing on a desk or in the form of a ring binder. When such an organizer is provided, a planned sales presentation usually accompanies the visual and is coordinated with it. The presentation and visual, used together, help the salesperson cover features and benefits and overcome objections. The organizer not only provides additional input for the prospect but also prompts the salesperson's memory about what to cover next and keeps the interview on track. Company visuals are almost always the result of long experience with selling the product or service and can be expected to be effective in the majority of cases.

A well-designed organizer has these characteristics:

1. It is built around user benefits.

2. It fosters two-way communication because the salesperson can concentrate on listening attentively to the prospect rather than worry about what to say next.

3. It increases the closing rate by leading naturally to that point.

4. It helps the salesperson tell the complete story in less time.

5. It helps the interview get back on track after an interruption by reminding both salesperson and prospect what was going on.

Although the company-prepared organizer is a good beginning tool, most successful salespeople develop additional visuals that are useful for their personal style and type of selling. Here are some of the visuals salespeople prepare for themselves:

1. Letters from existing customers expressing satisfaction with the product, the company's responsiveness, and/or the salesperson's personal service.

2. Business cards of existing clients, preferably with a note thanking the salesperson for service.

3. Pictures of clients actually using the product.

4. Pictures of product installations in customers' plants or offices.

Items of this nature that are included in the standard organizer should be neatly mounted in clear plastic covers that fit into the visual at the spot where they are likely to be used during the presentation. The kinds of visuals to use depend heavily upon preapproach qualification information. If you are truly professional in your approach to the development of visuals, you will have many different kinds prepared. As you plan for a particular sales interview, you can choose which ones are likely to appeal to the prospect you plan to see. Consider the product you plan to recommend, the personality of the prospect, what is going on in the industry at the moment, and anything else you know that might affect the selling climate. Select the items you want to use and insert them into the visual where they can be used as needed.

The number of people who will be present for the presentation determines the type of visual aids that can be used effectively. A visual in a ring binder is seldom effective for a presentation to more than two people. A tabletop flipchart is also limited in the number of people who can see it easily. If the sales situation involves presenting to a group, a large easel flipchart, overhead projector, or slides must be used. Exhibit 11.6 gives guidelines for preparing visuals.[15]

EXHIBIT 11.6 - Guidelines for Preparing Visuals

1. Visuals should be kept simple.
2. Don't use complete sentences. Text should be in phrases.
3. Leave plenty of white space and place text in similar location on each slide or overhead.
4. Use colors that are functional, not decorative. Colors should be easy on the eyes; hence, use red sparingly.
5. Never put the whole presentation on a visual and then read it to the prospect.
6. Tables, charts, or graphs with complex data must only be used for groups that intend to study the information closely.
7. Each chart or graph should present only one idea to ensure clear understanding.
8. Line charts are used to show how several variables change over time.
9. Bar charts show relationships between two or more variables.
10. Pie charts are used to show relationships among parts of a whole at a given point in time.

Audiovisual Presentations

For presenting complicated equipment or processes and for presenting to a group instead of a single prospect, audiovisual aids are especially helpful. However, they may also be effective with one-on-one sales presentations. Some of the most common audiovisual presentations involve computers, video, or slides. Computers can be used to produce multimedia presentations on a laptop screen or a portable video projector.

Current technology is rapidly producing hardware that enables salespeople to use audiovisual aids under almost any conditions. Presentation software gives professional salespeople the ability to create, modify, and customize their presentations easily and inexpensively. Numerous software packages produce graphs, charts, or other artistic renderings of data. Salespeople find such graphics useful in sales presentations. For instance, sales reps for ABC's TV stations now use laptop computers and the Internet to generate charts and graphs showing up-to-the-minute demographics, Nielsen ratings, and product-usage data. They can put together a thirty-chart presentation in less than two hours. A salesperson can communicate a message quickly, accurately, and dramatically with graphics like these.[16]

Developing Partnerships Using Technology illustrates several options for computer-based presentations. Just a few years ago, the only tools a marketer had to prepare a visual-aid presentation were flip charts, slides, and overheads. Today, salespeople have a variety of presentation tools at their disposal.

Developing Partnerships Using Technology
Customizing Graphical Presentations With Your Laptop Computer

Presentation Software. Echo 3 has a presentation manager and media library management system that makes every video, slide, overhead, brochure, electronic presentation, and audio file created by a sales organization available with a few keystrokes. Instead of reinventing the wheel each time they present to a prospect or client, salespeople can access existing presentations done by their peers and customize them for a particular opportunity.

Smart Phones. Cell phones that can decipher Internet data and handheld computers are a must for consultative salespeople. They are using these tools to get an edge on the competition by communicating with clients more effectively, accessing product and order status information, and staying on top of their schedules.

Pen-based Computers. These are especially effective for individual presentations. It works much like a pen and paper, except it's a computer LCD screen with a pen-shaped stylus stored inside a compartment. With the touch of the pen, the salesperson can bring up any information the prospect may need. The system reads your handwriting and translates it into text that can be edited, manipulated, and saved.

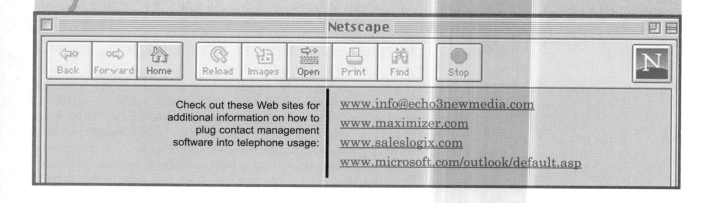

Netscape

| Back | Forward | Home | Reload | Images | Open | Print | Find | Stop |

Check out these Web sites for additional information on how to plug contact management software into telephone usage:

www.info@echo3newmedia.com
www.maximizer.com
www.saleslogix.com
www.microsoft.com/outlook/default.asp

Computers, Portable Projectors, and Whiteboards. According to studies by Texas Instruments, ultraportable and microportable projectors are the fastest-growing segment of the video projector industry. Epson and Sanyo have introduced projectors in which users can insert a card preloaded with their presentations—no laptop required. This new technology lets users transfer their presentation files to a PC card using Epson's conversion software, then insert the card into a slot on the projector and run the presentation. JPEG or bitmap images can be advanced automatically or with a few mouse clicks. Special effects, including slide transitions in such programs as PowerPoint, are preserved.[17]

Mimio is a new portable tool produced by Virtual Ink Corporation. What is it? It's a durable plastic arm that, when attached via suction cups to any regular whiteboard, turns it into an electronic whiteboard. Hook up your computer and flip on your projector, and the whiteboard basically becomes a large computer screen where you can run a PowerPoint presentation, access the Internet, or take notes that are automatically saved onto your computer. Need to do some computations for your clients? Simply pull up an Excel spreadsheet, tap on an empty cell, jot a number on the board, and the moment you stop writing the number will pop into the cell as if you've just typed it there.[18]

Liven Up Your PowerPoint Presentation. Salespeople should try to put some sparkle in their presentations, but avoid turning them into a three-ring circus. Use some bells and whistles without going overboard. A little color and some type-font changes can spruce up a presentation. There are a lot of electronic devices and special effects available today to create what is anything but a boring slide show. For example, liven up your PowerPoint presentations with PowerPlugs from Crystal Graphics. Spinning titles, TV-style transitions, and animated photographs are just some of the tools you can use to grab your client's attention.[19] Try to make the presentation interactive, fun, and as concise as possible without eliminating main points. Exhibit 11.7 discusses another new and innovative idea for your presentations.

EXHIBIT 11.7 - Voice on the Internet

A new technology called *Brainshark* uses the power of voice mail with the convenience of a PowerPoint presentation. It works this way: You upload your PowerPoint slides onto the Web site. Then you call a special telephone number and record your message to be delivered in synch with each slide. You use your telephone keypad as the record, play, rewind, and erase buttons. Once the slides are narrated, you can forward the presentation to a prospect or targeted audience. Tony Swierkot, marketing manager for Ricoh Company Ltd. in Canada, used it to send a presentation to Ricoh's sales force. The sales reps were delighted because *Brainshark* allowed them to actually hear the presentation from one of their own sales managers.[20]

The Tonight Show Starring Jay Leno! A presentation is a salesperson's opportunity to impress an all-important prospect or client. It's a chance to showcase what you know about the client's business, where it's headed, and how your company can help get it there. The example that follows illustrates how you can win a major account using showmanship, creativity, intense preparation, digital video, and your presentation skills.

Vari-Lite, a designer and distributor of lighting systems, had never used an outside agency for advertising to expand its customer base. They had done a good job internally. But now it was time for a change. James Florenz, vice president of M/C/C's client services, wanted to win the Vari-Lite account but knew his agency would have to do something special to secure the new client. And their final presentation was indeed very special. Florenz knew that Vari-Lite worked in a very creative industry so his team would have to work on the same level.

Florenz and his 12-person team created a *Tonight Show* atmosphere more suitable for Jay Leno, with all 50 of the agency's employees playing the parts of everyone from production assistants to Edd Hall and Kevin Eubanks. The conference room where the presentation took place had risers where the audience sat facing the standard talk show desk and chairs. Florenz, as host, went into M/C/C's business pitch, using digital video as an aid.

When Clay Powers, president of Vari-Lite, stepped off the elevator to attend what he thought was just another meeting, he was greeted by security guards, who hurried him past reporters and photographers, into the green room, where Elvis Presley was waiting to go on the show. Powers said, "It seemed like a nightmare at the time, but we turned down the other two companies that gave us the standard PowerPoint show and babbled about all the stuff they'd do for us. These guys actually thought about what we do."21

New technology allows for smarter selling utilizing creativity .

ADJUST THE PRESENTATION TO UNIQUE CIRCUMSTANCES

Situational Selling

Master salespeople have a specific plan for every sales interview, but they never feel slavishly bound by that plan. Consultative selling requires flexibility. No matter how much you learn about a prospect before you appear for the interview, you can never be absolutely sure what kind of situation to expect when you arrive. Instead of finding a calm, receptive prospect ready to listen and evaluate your product, you may find one who is angry, resentful, or emotionally keyed up—one who is being pressed to take quick action to meet a crisis situation. If planning has been adequate, the salesperson can shift gears and make a different kind of presentation, switch to another purpose for the interview, or even delay the presentation until a better time. Bill Hamilton finds his Palmtop computer ideal when making sales calls. This way he doesn't walk into a buyer's office "lugging equipment" during the initial call. Instead, he can reach in his pocket and be prepared to take an order, calculate it, offer "what ifs," and make any changes right on the spot.[22] The ability to exercise this type of flexibility is called *situational selling*—fitting yourself to the situation and making each contact with the prospect beneficial to your ultimate purpose of closing a sale.

The Setting

Where the sales interview takes place is often a vital factor in determining its success. The prospect's own office is usually the best place if interruptions can be controlled. If the prospect has a private office, the door can be closed and calls can be held. The prospect feels at ease and in control in familiar surroundings and is not required to put forth effort or travel time to accommodate the salesperson. You are a guest and automatically a person to be treated politely and with respect. If your information tells you that this prospect customarily tries to control every interview and every person, however, you might decide that meeting at a place where you are the host or even on neutral turf would give you more potency. Some salespeople make effective use of what is called a *power lunch*. Inviting the prospect to lunch at a carefully selected restaurant gives you an opportunity to present your product or service with several distinct advantages:

1. You are away from an office where interruptions may occur.

2. You are the host, and the prospect, as your guest, feels obligated to listen politely.

3. The atmosphere is nonthreatening.

4. Relaxing over the meal relieves some of the stress of making a decision.

Interruptions

No matter how carefully you schedule an interview, your best-laid plans often go astray. Many interruptions can be prevented by asking the prospect at the beginning of the interview if the secretary might hold all routine calls until later. This tells the prospect that you believe the interview is more important than routine matters, but that you know some important duties could take precedence over the interview. When preapproach information indicates that a particular prospect's duties involve continuous supervision of a work group's activities or that the prospect does not have a private office, consider arranging the interview away from that environment. When an interruption does occur, your sense of timing will tell you whether the discussion can be resumed or whether scheduling a later interview would be better.

If you decide to continue, summarize what has been said up to the point of the interruption. If a problem or need has been identified, state it again and ask a question designed to gain the prospect's agreement. Review in more detail the last major point made in your presentation, and again check for agreement or commitment by asking a question. Be sure the prospect is back on track and is following your planned path of reasoning. If you decide to come back later, attempt to set a time for the interview. If the interruption is caused by some real crisis that demands the prospect's immediate attention, say you will come again later and leave so that the prospect may give full attention to the urgent problem. When you do come back, begin the presentation all over. You can safely assume that the interruption has probably completely erased the effect you had built. Preface points with phrases like these: "You will remember that we discussed," "As I told you the other day," or "I believe you told me that." Intersperse your remarks with questions that check on what the prospect remembers, and you can quickly discover what needs to be repeated in depth and what can be quickly reviewed.

SUMMARY

You may memorize a presentation provided by the company or one that you prepare based on the planning you do. You may use an outline that keeps you on track to present each item in an effective order. You fix the outline firmly in your memory as a guide, but you do not memorize every word you will say. You may also use the extemporaneous presentation, the approach of the highly experienced salesperson who knows exactly what must be accomplished in the interview.

To personalize each presentation to the needs of the prospect, choose among the various strategies available for achieving your objective for the presentation. One of the most important tactics available is prospect participation. Demonstration of the actual working of the product or some component of it gains the prospect's interest and offers convincing evidence that the product is a good buy.

The actual presentation of your product as the solution to the prospect's defined problem or the fulfillment of the prospect's need consists of the information the client needs to make a buying decision. One way to choose what you will present is to develop units of conviction. A written series of these units of conviction is called a product-analysis worksheet.

Sales aids include all sorts of visuals and audiovisuals. Visuals are designed either to illustrate points in the presentation or to organize the presentation and keep it moving toward the goal of a successful close. Many people are visually oriented. That's why exciting, illustrative slides, overheads, and computer-driven programs are effective presentation tools.

A master salesperson knows how to handle all sorts of special situations. The setting in which the sales interview is held and the situational aspects of selling require that you are prepared to take advantage of situations as they come up. Interruptions are a problem that distract the prospect's attention. A professional salesperson learns to control these factors or transform them into advantages.

QUESTIONS FOR THOUGHT AND DISCUSSION

1. Describe the types of evidence that may be used to back up a claim.

2. Define "salesman's curse." Why is it a problem?

3. How does a salesperson learn to personalize units of conviction? Why is this important?

4. Distinguish between a feature and a benefit. Why is it important to know both?

5. What is a tie-down and why is it an important part of the sales presentation?

6. How can a novice salesperson prevent a memorized sales presentation from sounding memorized?

7. Why must the prospect become involved in the selling process?

8. What are the pros and cons of using a well-designed organizer as an integral part of your sales presentation?

9. What self-prepared visuals could be used by a salesperson selling a landscaping service?

10. How can a salesperson get back on track after an interruption?

ACTIVITIES

1. Choose three products advertised in a magazine you read. Name two features with corresponding benefits for each product.

2. Prepare a short demonstration of some product to share with the class. Suggestions: food items, cleaning products, laptop computer, small appliance or tool.

3. Visit several stores to shop for a compact disc player, some new make-up, a water bed, or some other product that could be demonstrated. Report on the demonstration techniques used by the salesperson and evaluate them.

Case Study

CASE 11.1

Anita Watson is a designer-salesperson for a leading manufacturer of office furniture. She tells how a personal shopping experience early in her sales career showed her why she seemed to be floundering and put her on the road to success.

When her old black-and-white TV set quit, Anita and her husband decided the time had come to get color. They went first to a store that carried a well-known brand. They knew it would be expensive, but they were quality -oriented and more interested in value than in price. Right away, Anita saw a console model in modern styling that would fit perfectly into the decor of their den. They hunted up a clerk (notice she didn't say salesperson) and here was the entire sales pitch: "This is a very good set. It has a good picture and good color. A good solid cabinet, too. It's a good buy." Both Anita and her husband reacted the same way. Almost in unison, they said, "Let's look around some more."

The next store they visited also handled a top brand. They saw a beautiful set with a bigger screen than the first set they had liked. Anita's husband — a rabid football fan — said, "Boy, the Cleveland Browns and their dog pound will really look great on that big screen." Anita watched the salesperson approach and hoped he would be wishy-washy, too. The set was obviously the most expensive in the place, and she had forgotten they would need a new antenna. "There goes our budget," she thought to herself.

However, this salesperson's approach was different. "I can't blame you for admiring that handsome cabinet. It's Danish modern and will blend into any contemporary room. But I'm sure you are also interested in bright, true-to-life color and high-fidelity sound. XYZ's exclusive color-compatible picture tube gives clear pictures and true sound with just one adjustment. Here, let me show you." He turned on the set and let it do the rest of the selling job almost by itself. Then he added the final touch: "You may think that we have a special antenna or booster here at the store, so I want to assure you that if you don't get the same performance with a regular color antenna, we'll take the set back and refund your money." That evening, Anita thought about the two salespeople they had met. Her sales had not been very good lately, and if the old TV had not conked out, they probably would not have considered spending money on a new one. So Anita tried a little trick that had worked for her before. She sat down in front of her dressing table and talked to herself in the mirror. "OK," she lectured herself, "you heard with your own ears what a terrible sales talk does even when the customer wants to buy. Then you heard a top-notch professional use a few colorful words and demonstration. And you bought! What have you been saying to your prospects?"

Anita replayed her interview with a real estate agent who was moving to a larger, plusher office in the new bank building. Anita had looked at the plans for the office space and figured she could concentrate on the top of the line. She recalled saying, "Obviously, Mr. Keller, you believe in doing things right. I have just the right furniture for this fine office. Not only is it stylish, but all pieces are made from quality material. It's not only comfortable, but it's practical, too. I can do the whole job for you, including sales offices, secretarial and filing needs, and an attractive reception area. Take a look at this catalog and tell me which style you prefer."

Anita looked herself straight in the eye. "And which did he prefer? None, of course. So what are you going to do about it?" Obviously, Anita found a good answer because she is now one of the top salespeople in her company. In fact, prospects sometimes call the company and ask for her to come talk about furniture for a redecorating project because they have heard from business acquaintances what a good job she did for them.

1. What kinds of measures do you think Anita took to transform her sales performance? Name several ways she could have solved her problem.

2. Suggest some resources a salesperson in Anita's position could use to improve her ability to make a good presentation.

CASE 11.2

A common problem of salespeople is dealing with a person who acts as a buffer to keep them from seeing the real decision maker who can buy their product or service. The buffer is usually pleasant, listens politely, asks a few questions, accepts brochures, and then says good-bye in a friendly manner. You could visit with the buffer a dozen times and be no closer to an order.

Pam Davis, a veteran salesperson of graphic arts services, seems to meet a lot of these buffers. For some reason, advertising executives, the prime prospects for graphic arts services, seem to be among the foremost users of buffers. Just last week, Davis called on the Mercury Manufacturing Company, a firm that does a large volume of advertising. She asked for Mr. Warner, the advertising manager. The receptionist called his office and then said, "Mr. Warner is not available, but his assistant, Mr. Bailey, will be right down."

"Here we go again," Pam groaned inwardly. The assistant was an affable young man with a firm handshake. He listened politely as Pam explained the services her firm provided: engraving, retouching, illustrations, and finished artwork. He agreed that Mercury's extensive ad program called for such services, but said they were satisfied with their current suppliers. Pam showed him her portfolio of samples of her company's work, but he said again that they really didn't need another supplier but would be glad to take her card and call her if they need anything.

"The old brush-off again," Pam said to herself. "I'd really like to have a slice of their business. They do more advertising than any other manufacturer in the area."

1. What is the major problem, and what options does Pam have?

2. Could Pam have had a better result with better planning prior to making this call?

Handling The Crunch Technique

In a recent issue of *Purchasing Magazine*, a leading expert on negotiation explained that there are seven magic words that drive salespeople crazy. They are: **"You've got to do better than that."**

The author, Dr. Chester L. Karras, says that the uninhibited use of this crunch technique ultimately results in false economy because sellers soon learn to add 10 percent to bids in order to have something to shave later when the crunch comes.

Selling Power Magazine collected responses from selected readers who have handled the crunch technique with success. They used answers like:

1. "I understand that you want a lower price, and we will be more than happy to lower it to the level you have in mind. Let's review the options that you'd like to cut from our proposal, so we can meet your needs."

2. "We are building a product up to a quality, not down to a price. A lower price would prevent us from staying in business and serving your needs later on."

3. "Yes, we can do better than that if you agree to give us a larger order."

4. "It is my understanding that we were discussing the sale of our product and not the sale of our business."

5. "I appreciate your sense of humor—how much better can you get than rock bottom? You see, our policy is to quote the best price first. We have built our reputation on high quality and integrity—and it's the best policy."

6. "I'd be glad to give you the names of two customers so you can find out how much they paid for our product. And you'll see it's exactly the same as we are asking you to pay. We could not develop our reputation without being fair to everyone."

7. "I appreciate the opportunity to do a better selling job. Obviously, you must have a reason for looking exclusively on the dollar side of the proposal. Let's review the value that you'll be receiving..."

Why We Build Them The Way We Do...

"It's unwise to pay too much, but it's worse to pay too little. When you pay too much, you lose a little money. When you pay too little, you sometimes lose everything, because the thing you bought was incapable of doing the thing it was bought to do. The common law of business balance prohibits paying a little and getting a lot—it can't be done. If you deal with the lowest bidder, it is well to add something for the risk you run. And if you do that, you will have enough to pay for something better."

CHAPTER 12

Negotiating Sales Resistance

NEGOTIATION AND THE CONSULTATIVE SALES CYCLE

Roger Dawson was president of a large real estate operation in California. His firm was writing $500 million in business annually but closing only $400 million, a typical fallout ratio in the industry. Roger quickly decided that the easiest way to improve the company's income was to improve that closing ratio. He began a concentrated study of negotiating techniques and created a training course for salespeople to teach them what to know to overcome buyer resistance and close a larger percentage of their sales. His firm was soon bringing in an additional $50 million annually. Before very long, Roger began to receive requests from outside his own firm to make presentations and conduct seminars on the subject of negotiating. Today, Roger is one of the country's top experts in the art of negotiating. His program "Secrets of Negotiating," published by Nightingale-Conant Corporation, is the best-selling program of its kind in the history of audio publishing. He is now a full-time speaker on the topic, and conducts "Power Negotiating" seminars throughout the world.

Most people think of negotiating as an activity that takes place between labor and management or between two high-powered corporations contemplating a merger, but Roger shows salespeople that negotiating* is just one of the communicating skills we all use every day. When salespeople use negotiating skills, they enhance their abilities in discovering needs, overcoming sales resistance, and gaining buyer commitment. Without negotiation, the whole concept of consultative selling reaches a stalemate.

NEGOTIATION IN SELLING

The **process of negotiation** is nothing more than seeking to reach an agreement based on mutual interest. It is a totally different concept from the win-lose concept of negotiation when one side – by sheer stubbornness, force of will, or trickery – hopes to beat the other side into submission. It is win-win negotiating that fits into the model of consultative selling, a process by which both parties seek solutions that bring mutual gain. For a salesperson, this type of negotiating is beneficial because neither salesperson nor prospect feels like a loser; they can both continue a mutually satisfying relationship.

Negotiation often suggests a picture of a formal confrontation between two nations attempting to avert a war or of law enforcement officers coping with a terrorist/hostage situation. Actually, we are involved in negotiations almost every day. Roommates negotiate about whose turn it is to cook, students negotiate with parents about an appropriate allowance for college expenses, and couples negotiate about where to go for an evening's entertainment. Skill in negotiating is essential for salespeople in closing a single sale and in maintaining a beneficial long-term relationship with clients.

Both sides must reach a satisfactory comfort level before the actual negotiations begin.[1] Building a level of trust and establishing credibility are important. In negotiation, as in selling, need discovery is crucial. Learning the real interests of the other party is more important than rattling off the selling

---

Material in this section on negotiation was modified and adapted from Roger Dawson's best-selling program "Secrets of Negotiating" and used with his permission.

points of your own proposal. When both sides are looking for creative ways to solve problems, finding some areas of agreement is helpful, even if they are not the primary issues. This helps build momentum toward reaching an agreement because the parties are emotionally involved in a solution. The side with the most information is in the stronger position; therefore, getting as much information as possible is advantageous. The best way to get information is to ask questions and listen. You may be surprised to find out that the buyer wants something you can give without causing you to lose anything of substance.

Making the presentation, overcoming objections, and getting commitment may be treated as one unit in the negotiation process. This phase is a matter of finding mutual interests that form the basis of an agreement. Never make the mistake of assuming others want the same things you do. The salesperson does not assume that one cake has to be divided; rather, the salesperson assumes that a complete cake can be found for everyone involved. During this creative, inventive phase, both parties look for solutions to solve a problem. If, for example, a buyer and a seller were having difficulty agreeing on the selling price of a house, they might agree to abide by the decision of an appraiser or compare the house to similar ones that recently sold in the neighborhood. If the parties can satisfy their real interests, the commitment is a natural outcome.[2] A final word of caution: *"No" does not necessarily mean the negotiation is over.* To a good negotiator, "no" is simply an opening negotiating position. Figure 12.1 is a visual presentation of several potential buyer concerns or problems in which negotiating skills are important.

FIGURE 12.1

Negotiating Situations in Selling

PROPER ATTITUDE CONCERNING OBJECTIONS OR SALES RESISTANCE

There have been hundreds of articles written discussing the topic of how to handle objections. In addition, sales managers have devoted countless hours in sales meetings discussing the topic. The problem with the word "objection" is that it conjures up an adversarial relationship between the salesperson and prospect – where someone must win, and someone must lose. The consultative sales cycle is a win-win process that produces a mutually satisfying long-term relationship. So we must look at the word "objection" a bit differently. Professional salespeople look positively at the objections prospects offer. Objections move prospects nearer to the close and reveal what they are concerned about. An objection often reveals the key to a successful sale.

If the prospect has been properly qualified as a Class "A" prospect, objections are really *buying signals*. Offering an objection is another way for the prospect to say, "Here are my conditions for buying," or "I want to buy as soon as you answer a few more questions or reassure me that buying is the smart thing to do." Welcome all objections! They are the verbal and nonverbal signs of *sales resistance* that give you the chance to discover what the prospect is thinking. These *objections or sales resistance* become leverage for closing the sale.[3] An objection is anything the prospect says or does that presents an *obstacle* to the smooth completion of the sale.[4] Objections are a normal and natural part of almost every conversation, not just in sale-situations, but whenever people discuss any current topic. A purchasing decision usually involves some risk. To ease the fear of risk, people object, raise concerns, or ask questions in hopes of getting answers that will convince them that the buying decision is in their best interest.

Objections actually indicate that the prospect is interested in your proposal. Statistics show that successful sales presentations, those that end in a sale, have 58 percent more objections than those presentations that are unsuccessful.[5] Most qualified prospects raise no objections to a proposal in which they have no interest. They just wait and say no. Adopt the attitude described by Ana Barber, a top sales representative for Sportswear International in San Jose, California. When she hears an objection, she says to herself, "Hot dog, another sale!" She knows that she has the necessary knowledge to answer every legitimate objection. Prior preparation and a servant's heart allow professional salespeople like Ana Barber to adopt such positive attitudes toward objections.

Throughout this chapter we will use the words "objections", "questions" and "concerns" to represent the broad term we categorize as sales resistance. However, it is strongly recommended that you avoid using the word "objection" in your actual sales presentations to prospects and clients. It is a very negative word! But it is perfectly all right for consultative salespeople to negotiate and resolve any concerns, questions, problems or sales resistance mentioned by prospects during the sales interview.

Disagree Without Being Disagreeable

Getting into an argument with a prospect, particularly in response to objections, is one of the easiest and most disastrous mistakes a salesperson can make. Your purpose is to remove the objection without being objectionable. Remember that selling is a win-win proposition. The negotiation process is not a battle that you win and the prospect loses; rather it is a situation of mutual cooperation and mutual benefit. You may well win the argument and prove you are right but lose the sale in the process. People who are forced to agree seldom actually change their minds.

Patricia Bender is a master at negotiation

Patricia Bender is in the people development business. Pat operates a training and consulting firm located in Silver Spring, Maryland. She works with major corporations to help improve the overall performance of their people through an in-depth understanding of themselves and what others bring to the organization. This is done through *Awareness Is Power—Career Choices,* a software tool that helps people make the most of their future. It matches an individual's behavioral style with jobs that are the most suitable and rewarding for them.

One of Pat's strengths as a negotiator is her persistence. She can persist in asking for an appointment, in closing, and in answering objections because she knows her product and has faith in it and because she has qualified her prospects so that she knows they need what she is recommending. Pat's attitude is that "emotionally" she does not "hear" stalls or objections. She hears only a need to continue negotiating by asking more questions to resolve all possible misunderstandings and to

reassure the prospect that a buying decision is wise. If the prospect says, "I need to think about it," for example, Pat counters with questions such as, "What part do you need to think about? How can I help you? When will you have the answer?"

When she encounters a price concern like "We have a tight budget," Pat displays her negotiating skills by showing that using the product will actually save money by making people more productive. If the price concern is based on the total cost compared to some other product or training method, Pat breaks the price down into some unit such as cost per month or percentage of expected savings from using the new skills. She also makes good use of the excellent service her company provides after the sale to show that the price pays for more than the assessment tools; it also includes a great deal of practical assistance that enhances the basic value of the product.

"I never ask for an order until the third call," Pat says. "I really care about my customers, and they trust me." Because she uses at least the first two calls to build rapport and learn as much as possible about the prospect's needs, when she is ready to ask for the order, the prospect is also ready.

Never force a prospect into making a decision. Prospects are more likely to stay sold and be resold for repeat business if the decision to buy was their idea.

Sales resistance contains elements of both logic and emotion. When people really want something, logic goes out the window and emotion takes control. The heart tends to rule the head.[6] The first task in answering an objection is to calm the prospect's emotions by proving that you are open to reason. Pause before responding; then acknowledge that you respect the prospect's opinion and find the views expressed worthy of consideration. Show a measure of empathy. People are open to changing their opinions and attitudes when they are convinced that others value their opinions, understand how they can feel that way, and grant them the right to those opinions.[7] If you must challenge a person's ideas, question the idea directly rather than the thinking process behind it. In his book *The Psychology of Dealing With People,* Wendell White offers an interesting way to challenge a prospect's idea without offending the person:

Remove any blame from the prospect for expressing an objection by saying: "I see I have not made that point clear," or "You may feel differently with this additional information."

This technique may not overcome the objection itself, but it is vital in paving the way for a rational discussion with the prospect. Nothing hurts a negotiation more than trying to prove that a prospect is thinking wrong. Thus, the key to maintaining a positive sales environment is to *disagree without being disagreeable.*[8]

TYPES OF OBJECTIONS OR SALES RESISTANCE

When the prospect objects, you must understand what type of sales resistance is being offered before you can handle it effectively. Sales resistance may be separated into four general types: the *stopper*, the *searcher*, the *stall* or *put-off,* and the *hidden* objection.

The Stopper

Prospects often have legitimate reasons why they feel unable to buy. One type of valid objection is what might be called a *stopper*.[9] Even Harry Houdini could not solve this one. The stopper is an objection to which no satisfactory solution can be found. For instance, if you can promise delivery no sooner than six months from now and the prospect absolutely must have the product in three months, you cannot—or at least, you should not—make that sale.

The difficulty with objections is that they all sound like obstacles that will stop the sale.

The Searcher

Some prospects object simply to get more information, even though they have already mentally decided that they want to buy. The customer just wants to be convinced that buying your product or service is the right thing to do. A second type is called a *searcher,* a request for additional information.[10]

HANDLE VALID SEARCHER CONCERNS WITH FINESSE

How Negotiators Might Respond to Four Common Searcher Objections:

1. I'm not interested.

There is no reason why you should be interested until I show you how my service can help you make money and solve your problems. May I show you how the product can do that for you?

Do you mean you are not interested at this time, or at all? I'll call back in four weeks; hopefully, things will be less hectic for you.

2. I don't have any money for this.

I can certainly respect that. If I could show you two ways the product will pay for itself, would you be interested?

If you did have the money, would you want it? Good! Allow me to present some facts and statistics illustrating just how affordable our product really is.

3. We are satisfied with what we have now.

What do you like most about the product you are using now? Then demonstrate how your product is better.

You don't like to change without a good reason, right? I certainly can understand that. Here are five reasons why more and more managers are switching to our online sales training material.

4. I really like the competitor's product.

I am not surprised to hear you say that. Their product does have some interesting features. I know some of my happiest customers are people who used to own that other company's product.

The Stall or Put-Off

When the prospect offers a *stall* or *put-off* objection, look for the true meaning. Frequently, the prospect is simply avoiding a decision. "Salespeople should never experience a stall if they properly qualified a prospect at the beginning," says Myers Barnes, author of *Closing Strong: The Super Sales Handbook*.[11] The stall could mean that you have not presented a compelling enough reason to buy. A stall is a classic sales killer unless the salesperson can create a sense of urgency to buy *NOW*.[12] The stall is actually the prospect's way of saying, "I really don't want to think about your proposition right now because I would then be forced to make a decision." Here are some examples of how *stalls* are phrased:

1. "I have to leave in fifteen minutes; I have an important meeting."

2. "Just leave your literature with my secretary. I will look it over in the next day or so and then call you."

3. "I must talk this over with my partner."

Handling a stall is a test of your attitude. If you believe you have a qualified prospect whose needs will be satisfied by your product, then you do not allow a *"put-off"* to put *you* off. Here are some suggestions for responding to the stalls given above:

1. "We are both busy people. Can I have five minutes to show you something that would save you hundreds, perhaps thousands of dollars?"

2. "Mr. Ray, I thought that I had adequately covered the points summarized in the literature. Obviously, I have not made myself clear at some point. Would you tell me what I have not explained to your satisfaction?"

3. "I certainly understand wanting to involve your partner in a decision like this. Can we ask him to join us now, or may I drop by his office this afternoon?"

The Hidden Objection

A fourth type of sales resistance is the *hidden objection*. This kind of resistance is more difficult to overcome. John Utter, regional sales manager for Motion Technology, defines hidden problems as "unspoken hesitations which, if not addressed, can delay or prevent a sale."[13] The prospect refuses to let the salesperson know the real concern. Many times the reason is quite personal, and the prospect prefers not to reveal it or has a vague feeling that cannot be easily articulated. Figure 12.2 pictures the hidden objection as an iceberg lurking below the surface. Just the tip is revealed. You know the prospect has a hidden objection when the answers fail to make sense. The reasons for not buying are not logical based on the interview up to that point. For example, a prospect may dislike revealing these real concerns:

1. "Circumstances have changed since you first qualified me. Recent family problems have caused severe financial hardships, and I do not have the ability to pay for your product."

2. "I find this whole situation distasteful, and I don't want to deal with you. I don't like you, but social convention prevents my being blunt enough to tell you so."

3. "I really don't know what my objection is. It just doesn't feel right. Quite frankly, the product looks like a cheap imitation to me."

The consultative salesperson must get to the heart of the prospect's objection before it can be negotiated successfully. Before you can marshal the appropriate facts, logic, and evidence to resolve a vaguely stated objection, you must know the basis for the prospect's point of view.[14]   To make intelligent responses to customer resistance, you must know the underlying circumstances.

FIGURE 12.2
The Hidden Objection

SPECIFIC CATEGORIES OF BUYER OBJECTIONS OR SALES RESISTANCE

Most objections that an experienced salesperson hears are not original. If you have been selling for any length of time, your chance of encountering an objection you have not heard before is remote. "Eighty percent of buyers will give you the same five or six objections. You should therefore be ready to handle each one in advance, and have practiced them in a training course or sales meeting first."[15] To deal effectively with the objections you hear, develop a worksheet to categorize them and the responses you use to answer them effectively. Write out your responses word for word, commit them to memory, and practice delivering each one so that it becomes a reflex action. Polish and

EXHIBIT 12.1 - The Basic Categories of Buyer Objections or Sales Resistance

Product Objection

- The materials are not up to industry standards.
- The product is poor quality.
- The product won't hold up over time.

Objection to Salesperson (Hidden)

- You are poorly prepared.
- I don't like you.
- You have tried to dominate me from the moment you arrived.

Company Objections

- Your company is not very well known; I prefer to deal with a large, established company.
- Wasn't your company charged with some unethical sales practices?

Don't Want to Make a Decision

- See me on your next trip.
- I want to think it over.
- We don't have room for your line.

Service Objection

- I can't live with your delivery schedule.
- We need same-day response on all service calls.
- Your maintenance contract doesn't meet our needs.

Price Objection (Possibly Hiding Real Objection)

- I can't afford it.
- Your pricing structure is out of line.
- I'm going to wait until prices come back down.

refine your responses; keep a record of how they are received. You will soon be able to choose the best possible response from your prepared list for each situation you encounter. Exhibit 12.1 lists six basic categories of buyer resistance with examples of what the prospect might say or, in the case of hidden objections, might think.

DECIDING WHEN TO ANSWER SALES RESISTANCE

A lot more has been said about *how* to overcome sales resistance than about *when* to answer them,[16] but choosing the proper time to answer an objection is just as crucial as the answer itself. In determining when to answer an objection, you must consider the type, why it has been raised, the mood of the prospect, and in what phase of the interview it is raised. Timing is important in any negotiation. Prospects introduce an objection at a time that favors their position. Why shouldn't you choose to handle it when the timing favors your position? Normally, there are four logical times for responding to the buyer's concerns:

1. Answer them *before* they arise.
2. Postpone the *answer* until *later* in the presentation.
3. Answer it *immediately* when it is raised.
4. Do not *answer an excuse.*

Anticipate and Forestall Objections

Every product or service has both strengths and weaknesses. Because no product is perfect, a prospect may well identify a negative feature or shortcoming in what you sell. Hoping that the prospect will fail to notice a negative feature is futile. Instead of waiting for the prospect to raise a specific objection, *anticipate* the objection and *forestall* or *answer* it in the presentation before the prospect can ask. You are thus able to make a more orderly presentation of benefits and maintain better control of the entire interview.[17]

Anticipating objections allows you to prepare a better presentation.

Weave into your presentation factual answers to anticipated objections so they are answered before the prospect verbalizes them. Anticipating objections requires a well-thought out, planned presentation delivered from the prospect's point of view and focusing on value. As an example of how you might *forestall* objections that come up over and over again, consider the two objections Fred Bass, a venture capitalist in Phoenix, was constantly hearing from prospects: "I don't have the money" and "I have to talk this over with my (partner, wife, agent, etc.)." After the opening, get-acquainted chit-chat, Fred gets down to business by saying:

> *Mr. Goode, I am working with professional athletes who have enough discretionary income that they can invest at least $75,000 in a business venture they are convinced is sound and who can also make their own investment decisions without consulting someone else first. Do you fit into these conditions?*

This opener is admittedly forceful, but Fred prefers not to spend forty-five minutes presenting his proposition and then hear one of these familiar objections. Of course, dealing with an objection early in the presentation does not guarantee that it will not be raised again. However, the salesperson is at an advantage in such a situation for two reasons:

1. The objection has much less impact the second time.

2. The salesperson may recall the original answer, expand upon it, and then move on into a close or back into the presentation if necessary.

Postpone the Answer

Some objections are better *postponed*. This tactic is logical when you are planning to cover that very point further along and the prospect has simply jumped ahead. To answer early might disrupt the flow of the presentation and make the answer less effective. For example, the prospect may ask about price—"How much is this going to cost me?"—before you have established the value of your product. If you answer immediately, the price may seem too high because the prospect has not yet learned enough about the product to make a value judgment. The price may depend upon options selected; in that case, you cannot quote an accurate price. You may need to build a better foundation before risking a confrontation with the prospect.[18]

You can postpone answering an objection by saying something like this:

That's an excellent question, and I can certainly understand why you want to ask it. Let me write it down so I won't forget to answer it. And if you don't mind, let's postpone the answer until later. I have some information we need to consider first. Is that all right?

Salespeople often get price questions early in the interview. Here are two ways to postpone the premature price question:

1. *I can appreciate that you would be interested in the price, and I assure you we will discuss it completely, but before we even consider the price, I want to be sure that my service can satisfy your needs. Will that be all right?*

2. *Mr. Osmond, your concern for price is quite understandable. The actual amount paid for the product, however, will depend upon the options you ultimately select. Let's consider the price for the system after we establish the specific features you will require. Is that fair enough?*

The price question should be answered near the end of the presentation, after need, value, and benefits have been discussed. Should the prospect *absolutely insist* that you answer immediately, then by all means do so. You do not want to risk the question remaining in his mind to block out everything else that follows.

Answer Immediately

Most valid objections should be answered when they are raised unless you have a logical reason to postpone them. If you feel the objection is valid and postponing an answer could cause problems, by all means handle it *immediately*. Answering an objection right away prevents it from festering in your prospect's mind and blocking out the more important information you are presenting. "Never answer until you are sure of the real concern, and once it is discovered, answer in 30 seconds or less."[19] A sincere and immediate response conveys professionalism, respect for the prospect's point of view, empathy, and listening skill. The right answer removes the resistance and promotes the sale.

Do Not Answer an Excuse

A final alternative is to simply not answer an excuse. Some issues don't have a worthwhile answer. On some sales calls, prospects raise concerns that have nothing to do with your discussion. They say things that have no relevance to the point you are trying to make. In reality, they are offering excuses for not buying rather than valid resistance. Never try to answer an excuse. By acknowledging excuses, you may actually turn them into real objections in the prospect's mind. If you must reply to excuses, suggest to the prospect that you will answer them at the end of the presentation. If the question is a serious objection, the prospect will repeat it later.

Exhibit 12.2 summarizes the factors to consider in choosing the best time to deal with objections.

EXHIBIT 12.2 - Timing Answers to Objections: Points to Consider

Anticipate the Objection and Answer It Before It Arises

- This option should be considered only when you are fairly certain that the prospect will bring up the objection.
- Anticipating the objection prevents a future confrontation and shows your objectivity.

Postpone an Answer Until Later

- Postponing an answer allows you to present many more benefits that have the effect of reducing the significance of the objection.
- Postponing an answer allows you to maintain control of the interview by keeping to your agenda rather than to that of the prospect.
- Postponing an answer gives you time to think about how you will answer the question. Better a good answer later than a poor one now.

Answer the Objection Immediately

- Answer immediately so the prospect can concentrate on the rest of the sales story.
- Answering immediately shows the prospect your sincerity.
- An immediate answer prevents prospects from inferring your inability to answer.

Do Not Answer an Excuse

- Not acknowledging an objection is one way to separate it from an excuse. The serious prospect will repeat the objection.
- By not answering, the salesperson suggests that the excuse is not relevant and implies that bringing it up again is not necessary.

A NEGOTIATION STRATEGY FOR DEALING WITH BUYERS' CONCERNS

Professional salespeople handle prospects' objections successfully by placing them in the proper perspective. They realize that well-handled objections become powerful aids. To handle them skillfully, you need a definite negotiation strategy so that you react naturally to buyers' concerns. Knowing that you have a strategy gives you confidence. Then you can welcome objections instead of shuddering at the very thought that the prospect may not go along with your proposition. The six-step plan presented in Exhibit 12.3 should be internalized so that you use it instinctively and automatically.

Listen Carefully, Hear the Prospect Out

The consultative salesperson is happy when the prospect raises an objection because it provides the information needed to complete the negotiation. Never interrupt a prospect who is expressing an opinion. Listen carefully to what the prospect says. Observe the prospect's verbal and nonverbal behavior, and listen to what is *not* being said. Recognize the prospect's right to express opinions and concerns. The prospect is telling you what to do: "Give me more information," "Go over that service agreement again; it wasn't clear," or simply "Reassure me one more time that this is a good decision."

Confirm Your Understanding of the Objection

Restate the prospect's objection to make sure you understand just what it is. This is a critical negotiation tactic. Use your own words and repeat what the prospect was saying to *clarify* and *classify* the real objection, and to tell the prospect that you understood what was said. In addition, you give yourself time to formulate your answer. Restating the objection in a sympathetic manner dissolves the prospect's defensiveness and helps you avoid the temptation to argue. Say, "Now as I understand it, your position is ... ," and then explain the prospect's position in your own words. When you prove you understand, the prospect is ready to listen to you.

Your purpose here is to *evaluate* and *isolate* the stated concern. Determine whether the reason given for not buying is the *real* reason, simply an *excuse,* or a statement *hiding* the actual objection. You may decide to answer immediately, not answer an excuse, or seek more information. If you need more information before you can answer, ask questions until you have the information you need. There are a number of questions you might ask the prospect that can help you isolate the real issue and confirm your understanding.[20] They include:

1. Other than that, is there any other reason that would prevent you from purchasing?

2. I am glad you brought that out into the open. Is this your only concern?

3. If we can work together to find a solution to this important concern, would that be enough to earn your business?

EXHIBIT 12.3 - A Strategic Negotiating Plan for Overcoming Buyers' Concerns

1. Listen carefully; hear the prospect out.

Learning to listen is not difficult, just unusual. We were born with two ears and one tongue. Listen twice as much as you talk. The buyer will tell you what you need to know. Just listen!

2. Confirm your understanding of the objection.

The key is to clarify and classify the objection. What type of objection is it and into what category does it fall?

3. Acknowledge the prospect's point of view.

Prepare the prospect for your answer. Don't just tear into your answer. After all, the buyer has a reason for stating the objection. Show concern for the their feelings. Practice empathy.

4. Select a specific technique.

No one technique works best for all prospects. It must fit your behavioral style as well as that of the prospect.

5. Answer the objection.

The answer must satisfy the buyer if a sale is to result, and it must be complete and prompt. Get a commitment from the prospect.

6. Attempt to close; if the close is not completed, continue the presentation.

After answering a major objection, ask for the order. The worst that can happen is that the buyer will say no. If that happens, continue with the presentation.

Acknowledge the Prospect's Point of View

All successful negotiations find points of agreement with the prospect before beginning to answer an objection. Agree as far as possible before answering, and take responsibility for any misunderstanding. If the prospect indicates a bad experience with your company or your predecessor, believe it. Find a way to cushion your response so that it has a chance of convincing the prospect. After all, prospects believe they have good reasons for not buying and give you those reasons. Instead of arguing directly, soften your answer and say something like this:

I can certainly understand how you feel, Mr. Maloney. Others have had much the same feeling when I first presented the concept to them. (Then provide a plausible explanation.)

I appreciate your concern, Mr. Maloney, and you do have a relevant point. Thank you for bringing it to my attention. (And the salesperson should appreciate it.)

Select a Specific Technique

In the next two sections of this chapter, nine techniques are detailed for use in formulating answers to the types of sales resistance a professional salesperson encounters. Not all of them work all the time. In deciding which of the techniques to use, take these factors into consideration:

1. The prospect's *behavioral* style
2. The *stage* of the negotiation process in which the objection is raised
3. The *mood* (argumentative or receptive) of the prospect
4. How *many times* the objection has come up
5. The *type* of sales resistance (searcher, excuse, stall, product or service)

You must decide quickly on the technique you will use and avoid showing that an objection has upset you. Keep in mind that far too many variables operate in a given selling situation to guarantee that every objection can be answered satisfactorily.

Answer the Objection

Negotiation is persuasion, not manipulation. Avoid explanations that merely cloud the issue and cause prospects to feel that you are trying to pressure them. The answer, however, must be conclusive; don't close off your answer with the question still up in the air. Present only as much information as required to gain the prospect's cooperation and commitment. Minimize the objection by not dwelling on it. Say just enough to dispose of it to the prospect's satisfaction. Be honest and factual, and do not promise anything that you, your company, or your product or service cannot deliver.

Prospects have their own needs, viewpoints, and ways of looking at things. Be sure to consider the prospect's ego and help the prospect to win. Your answer should include a benefit and should be shaped to fit the behavioral style of that prospect. Finally, confirm that your answer satisfied the prospect. Gain agreement by suggesting, "Am I correct in assuming that I have completely satisfied you regarding ...?"

Attempt to Close   Closing opportunities exist at various times throughout the entire negotiation process. Recognizing those times and capitalizing upon them is up to you. When you have successfully answered a major objection, you have created an opportunity to close, especially if you are near the end of the presentation. Attempt a *trial close* before continuing with the presentation. The trial close gets a prospect's reaction without exerting any pressure for making a definite decision. It may be used at any point in the sales presentation to test the water to see whether you have presented enough information for the prospect to make a decision. Typical trial closes start with "If you were to buy," "In your opinion," or "How do you feel about..."

If you receive positive buying signals from the prospect at this point, you can attempt to close. If the close proves unsuccessful, get back on track and *continue the presentation* until another opportunity presents itself.

FIVE TECHNIQUES FOR NEGOTIATING OBJECTIONS

Keep in mind that with any technique you must produce evidence to *prove* the validity of what you say. Techniques do not establish belief and credibility; that is your job. Techniques are merely vehicles for organizing your answer and your support for it. Exhibit 12.4 presents five ways to strengthen the impact of these techniques for handling objections.

After an objection has been clarified and classified, the salesperson is in an excellent position to respond by using one or more of the following techniques.

EXHIBIT 12.4 - Support Your Answers to Objections With Concrete Evidence

1. **Product comparison—** When the prospect is mentally comparing the present product or a competing product with your product, you may make a complete comparison of the two. List the advantages and disadvantages of each, taking care to see that the prospect follows the comparison.

2. **Relating a case history or showing testimonial letters—** Describe the experience of a customer whose situation is similar to that of the prospect.

3. **Demonstration—** A demonstration gives a convincing answer to a product objection because you let the product itself overcome the prospect's opposition.

4. **Guarantees or warranty—** A guarantee often removes resistance by reassuring the prospect that the purchase will not result in a loss. Guarantees must be meaningful and must provide for recourse on the part of the customer if the product does not live up to the guarantee.

5. **Showing the cost of delaying—** A common experience of salespeople is to obtain seemingly sincere agreement to the buying decisions concerning need, product, and price, only to find that the prospect wants to wait a while before making a final decision. Sometimes you can use pencil and paper to show conclusively that delaying the purchase is expensive.

Feel, Felt, Found   This practical technique overcomes a stall or a very personal concern. It can counter prospect hostility, pacify an unhappy customer, or inform someone who does not yet clearly understand the value of the product or service. Answer the prospect with this language:

I can understand how you *feel*.... I have had other customers who *felt* the same way until they *found* out....

This approach serves several purposes. It shows prospects that the salesperson understands their concerns, and it reassures the prospect that having this kind of objection is normal. Now the stage is set to introduce information that can change the prospect's way of thinking. This technique says that other people who are now customers had similar misgivings but changed their minds after they *found* out some new information. These new facts allow the prospect to reevaluate your proposition. The following example illustrates how a bank executive in a sales role might use this negotiation technique with an unhappy client:

Use negotiation techniques with unhappy clients.

BANKER: Good afternoon, Mr. Waugh. I am Don Edwards with Third National Bank. I have been assigned to your account and would like to ... (suddenly interrupted!)

CLIENT: So Third National is playing musical chairs with its loan officers again. It took Susan O'Malley six months just to learn about my business needs and now I have to train someone new. Why can't you people give me a banker who will stay with me?

BANKER: I can certainly understand how you might *feel* that way. Some of Susan's other clients have indicated that they *felt* the same way. However, the bank has *found* that someone with Susan's experience is an invaluable asset to our Problem Loan Division. I have previously worked with firms in your line of business (mention them and provide testimonial letters) and from my review of your account, I *feel* I have a pretty good understanding of your operation. (By the way, here are my credentials.)

The banker's tone is neither critical nor condescending. The comments are made in an empathetic manner. Evidence is presented as reinforcement.

Compensation or Counterbalance Method

At times, a prospect may buy in spite of certain valid objections. The prospect may be partly right or may have misunderstood a portion of what you said. Accept and admit any truth in the objection. Admit that your product does have the disadvantage that the prospect has noticed and then immediately point out how the objection is overshadowed by other specific benefits of the product. The salesperson's job is to convince the prospect that the compensating benefits provide enough value that the disadvantage should not prevent the prospect from buying. By admitting the objection, you impress the prospect with your sincerity and sense of fair dealing. Then you can select the real strengths of your offering to offset the prospect's negative feelings. A good way to deal with this situation is to provide documentation such as *statistical evidence, a third-party endorsement*, or the *case history* of someone who faced a similar situation. This method works because the prospect is approached positively with an acknowledgment of expressed concerns, and then given a series of logical, compensating benefits to counterbalance the stated objection.

Ask "Why?" or Ask a Specific Question

This method is helpful not only for separating excuses from real objections but also for overcoming objections. You can use questions to narrow a major, generalized objection to specific points that are easier to handle. If the prospect says, "I don't like to do business with your company," ask, "What is it that you don't like about our firm?" The answer may show a past misunderstanding that can be cleared up. If the prospect complains, "I don't like the looks of your product," ask, "Why do you object to its appearance?" The objection may be based on a relatively minor aspect that can be changed or is not true of all models.

Another value of this method is that some objections sound flimsy once they are put into words. The prospect may conclude that the objection is of little consequence and write it off without your needing to do anything.

Deny the Objection

One way to answer buyer resistance is simply to assert that the prospect is wrong. This technique must be used with caution or it will antagonize prospects. You can sometimes tell prospects they are wrong but you have to be careful how you do it. You could *win the argument but lose the sale.* Your ego may feel better, but losing the sale is a big price to pay for a soothed ego. Focus on why the prospect is resisting and try to see things from the prospect's point of view.

The denial technique is useful when the prospect clearly has the wrong information. Either a portion of the presentation was misunderstood or someone else has supplied incorrect information. In an *indirect denial*, point out that the prospect's information is wrong, but not by means of a direct, frontal assault. Present the denial sympathetically, thoughtfully, and with dignity.

After listening attentively to the buyer's concern, begin by saying, "I don't believe I quite understand what you are saying." (This response allows the buyer time to cool down emotionally and perhaps to soften the statement. It also gives you the opportunity to regain your composure).

After the prospect repeats the incorrect information, respond in this manner: "I don't know how you could have gotten that impression. I really must have stated my position poorly; please let me correct it for you." A bit more forceful statement would be, "Fortunately for me, that is not the real situation. I have some other information that does not support what you just told me."

Your attitude is crucial. Your goal is to earn the prospect's respect and, at the same time, avoid an angry reaction. You do want the prospect to know that you will not be intimidated and that you want to continue the presentation.

Sometimes a *direct denial* is your only recourse. You cannot let the prospect bully you. There are times when you must fight fire with fire. If the prospect questions your integrity or that of your company, you cannot answer that type of objection with arguments or mere talk. A direct denial is a high-risk method of dealing with any objection, but it is necessary at times, even if you lose a sale.

Boomerang Method

The boomerang method allows the salesperson to agree with prospects yet show them that their objections need not prevent a purchase. This method is often used in a situation where the point to which the prospect is objecting is actually a sales point in favor of buying the particular product or service. The boomerang method involves agreeing with the objection and then making another statement that *translates the objection into a reason for buying*. For example:

- A sales representative for *Blue Bell Inc., Brenham, Texas*, might hear this type of objection: "Blue Bell ice cream is too new to this area. My customers will not buy something they have never heard of before." Turn the objection into a sales point: "There is no question that our ice

A successful salesperson can agree with the prospect while still showing them that their concerns need not prevent a purchase.

cream is new to your area; that's why we are eager to build consumer awareness for the product. We intend to spend over $100,000 to tell your potential customers about our ice cream. Blue Bell uses its advertising messages to presell the product for you. If you agree to carry the product, we will generate a great deal of customer demand (and increase store traffic) for you."

The *boomerang method* works well when the prospect lacks complete information or perceives a drawback that actually may not exist. Be careful of the image you project when using this technique. If prospects feel that you are directly challenging them or perhaps patronizing them, then you could be in for a real battle. In that case, you might as well pull out your boxing gloves because you will have more use for them than you will for your order book.

The *tongue-in-cheek method* is an adaptation of the boomerang method. It uses a bit of humor that may soften up the prospects and turn away their anger. A salesperson for Strickfaden's Nursery in Sandusky, Ohio, used the technique this way: The prospect said, "I'm not going to buy any more shade trees from you; every time I plant one I have too much dirt left over!" Her reply was, "Yes, that is a concern. But the way to solve your problem is to dig your holes a little deeper."

Developing Partnerships Using Technology demonstrates how the virtual office can be virtually anywhere. Now you can input objections you hear and share them with other members of the sales force before you pull away from the prospect's office.

Developing Partnerships Using Technology
Virtual Private Networks link the Virtual Office to the Home Office

Virtual Private Networks (VPNs). This advance in technology has provided telecommuters with the ability to connect to the home office over the Internet instead of having to make a long-distance telephone call. This is far less expensive and provides a secure method of communication that can be encrypted.

Telecommuting is at the core of the virtual office and the road warrior approach to selling in the 21st century. Telecommuting is a "catch" phrase for the process of a salesperson using his or her computer to hook into the central office to retrieve e-mail and work on important database records. This technology, in conjunction with wireless modems, permits salespeople to work on the road or at home as if they were sitting at the office.

Add new objections to your database, but not while driving!

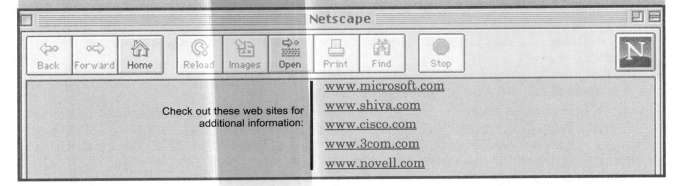

Check out these web sites for additional information:

www.microsoft.com

www.shiva.com

www.cisco.com

www.3com.com

www.novell.com

A MINDSET FOR NEGOTIATING PRICE RESISTANCE

One type of objection surfaces so frequently that it requires additional examination. Your prospects and customers want as much for their money as they can get. While that's not unexpected, you can't provide value-added service at reasonable prices if you give up too much at the negotiating table. How many times each week do you suppose a salesperson hears "I just think your price is too high." To succeed in selling, you must see this type of sales resistance for what it is and overcome it.

The price objection is more difficult to pin down because it can mean so many different things. The final price paid for a product or service depends upon the type of discounts available, advertising and promotional allowances paid by the seller, service after the sale, free trial periods, warranties or money-back guarantees, sales support service and training, delivery charges, and myriad other price-related variables. Then, too, the prospect may not really be objecting to the price but may just be hiding the real reason for not buying. When prospects says, "I can't afford it" or "Your prices are just too high," they may just be saying, "You have not convinced me that the value I will receive is worth the price I have to pay to get it." Often the buyer's concerns or questions about price represent an incomplete sales job!

Your company priced the product or service so it would sell. Never be afraid to ask the full value for your offering, but be prepared with *solid evidence* to support the price you are asking. Do not be defensive or *apologetic*. You must believe that the price you are quoting is actually much less than the value your product will give the prospect.

For a truly qualified prospect, price is seldom the main consideration. For example, the prospect should be reminded that buying a cheap suit can turn out to be an expensive purchase. The initial price may seem low, but the suit is likely to look cheap, fit poorly, and wear out quickly. A more expensive suit gives a better appearance and may wear up to three times as long. What matters most for your customers isn't what they pay for the product, but what they get for their money.

If your product has exclusive features that are not readily apparent, convert them to benefits and sell those benefits[21] as this classic example of Ma McGuire in Exhibit 12.5 illustrates.

EXHIBIT 12.5 - Sell Benefits to Overcome the Question of Price

Two farm wagons stood in a public market. Both were loaded with potatoes in bags. A customer stopped before the first wagon.

"How much are potatoes today?" she asked the farmer's wife, who was selling them.

"A dollar and a quarter a bag," replied the farmer's wife.

"Oh, my," protested the woman, "that is pretty high, isn't it? I gave one dollar for the last bag I bought."

"Taters has gone up," was the only information the farmer's wife gave. The housewife went to the next wagon and asked the same question. But Ma McGuire "knew her potatoes," as the saying goes. Instead of treating her customer with indifference, she replied:

"These are specially fine white potatoes, madam. They are the best potatoes grown. In the first place, you see, we only raise the kind with small eyes so that there will be no waste in peeling. Then we sort them to grade out culls so you get only full-sized, good potatoes. Then we wash all our potatoes clean before sacking them, as you see. You can put one of these bags in your parlor without soiling your carpet—you don't pay for a lot of dirt. I'm getting $1.50 a bag for them—shall I have them put in your car or will you take them now?"

Ma McGuire sold two bags, at a higher price than her competitor asked, in spite of the fact that the customer had refused to buy because she thought the price was too high!

Ma McGuire certainly understood how to sell value. People have a perceived price-quality relationship. They do not mind spending money when the quality and value of the purchase have been successfully established.

SPECIFIC METHODS FOR OVERCOMING THE QUESTION OF PRICE

Face the fact that you will not always have the lowest-priced product or service to sell. Be prepared to justify your asking price and show that it is fair. Understand and be able to apply the differential competitive advantages you have in product, source, people, or service superiority.[22] There are a number of negotiation tactics that can help you overcome the price obstacle. The consultative salesperson may respond to the question of price by using one or a combination of the following methods.

Break Price Down

The price that sounds huge in its entirety often sounds much smaller when you break it down into weekly or monthly payments and compare it to how the customer normally spends extra money. If the prospect is really objecting to the absolute magnitude of the price, then a logical response is to *break the total cost down* over a period of time. Here is an example of how you might use this technique:

I am glad you mentioned price, and I can certainly appreciate your concern. The $3,000.00 does seem like an awful lot of money for a Bose car stereo system. But just imagine, for the price of a daily cup of coffee and a newspaper, you will enjoy your terrific new sound system during that hour-long commute you said you make to and from work every day. What a small price to pay for the increased enjoyment and relaxation that comes from owning such a magnificent system. You may just decide to take the long way home on some evenings!!

Compare the one-time price of your product to the amount of money the prospect will save after years of using it. The clearer you make the distinction between what your prospects pay and what they get, the easier for them to recognize your product's great value.[23] Talk about the initial and ultimate costs. Look at the *price-cost-value* comparison from two perspectives: *Price* represents the initial amount paid for the product; *cost* is the amount the buyer pays as the product is used over time.

The Towering Inferno

All other things being equal, the customer may be looking for the lowest price. However, in sales, all other things are seldom, if ever, equal. Tom Peters, the management guru, said, "Nothing need be a commodity." Customers use price as a decision-making point because it is the easiest way to compare two completely different offerings. However, if you differentiate your offering, then what customers really want is not the lowest price. Rather, they want the lowest total cost solution.[24] The lowest total cost model of selling tells the customer that every decision has implications. As the insert below clearly demonstrates, if you buy substandard electrical wiring, you may have a fire. Our job, as consultative sales professionals, is to raise the visibility of these implications.

The Towering Inferno

The only way to respond to a price differential is to raise the visibility of the value of the ideas contained in your offer. Customers will always buy on price until we show them that the price of the product is only one element of the total cost of ownership. An extreme example of this point is contained in the movie, *The Towering Inferno*. The plot of the movie involved a firm building a spectacular, new skyscraper. The cost of the construction project was over budget, so the firm decided to cut costs by installing substandard electrical wiring. Unfortunately, the wiring was unable to handle the electrical load and a fire started. The fire became so insidious that the building was consumed by the flames – certainly demonstrates that "you get what you pay for." Yes, the customer received the lowest price on the electrical wiring; however, they paid much more for the total project cost since they had to rebuild the skyscraper after the fire.

You can be confident when your firm does quality work.

Employ the Presumption of Exclusivity

What can you do when the price for your company's product is higher than that being asked by a competitor? Stress those features that are *exclusively* yours. What does your product have that the competition cannot offer? No two products are exactly alike. You will find strengths and weaknesses in any offering. Analyze your competitor's offering to see why the same product has a lower price. If your analysis indicates that you are offering more, then your task as a professional salesperson is to drive home those exclusive features. You may have to show more interest in the prospect than the competition that concentrates only on price. Go out of your way to isolate other needs of the prospect for which you can provide assistance.

If your company has a higher price, then it must be because you offer more to your customers. Identify your superior advantages and convince the prospect that the extras can be obtained only from you. In other words, justify the price with facts. Determine what the prospect wants more than anything else from your product and then identify the features that satisfy those wants. This is what Mack Hannan calls the *presumption of exclusivity*.[25] Concentrate on those features until the prospect feels that only with you can his or her needs be completely satisfied.

If a prospect gives you a hard time about price, stop selling price. Show what the money buys. Make the price seem unimportant in comparison to the value received. You may proceed something like this:

Mrs. Harvey, allow me to share some information with you. The lower price of our competitor may not be the best buy for you. Let's look at the quality of our product and why we are more expensive. We pay our employees a fair wage, purchase superior-grade raw materials, and have a multimillion-dollar advertising program that has made our product nationally known. Our price includes training for your people; our staff is skilled at maintaining and upgrading the product over time. You will have easy availability of parts and a one hundred percent guarantee. We stand behind our product. We don't fight your complaints; we settle them promptly and equitably. The price paid for a solution to your problem should be based on what gives you the best solution. Don't you agree?

Draw the picture clearly and convincingly. Sell quality and exclusivity when the prospect argues price. If the consultative salesperson sells the exclusive features properly, the prospect is not even thinking about price by the end of the presentation. Most buyers are fair-minded if you show why your company must get the price it does.

Use Comparison

Be prepared to present logical reasons for the price you are asking. One way you can do this is to compare the quality of your product to that of the prospect's company. For example, you could stress that both are selling superior products:

Mr. Becker, your own company makes a high-grade product that commands an exceptionally high price, and deservedly so. Your tool-and-die products warrant their outstanding reputation because of the top-quality materials used to make them. Our high-viscosity, high-grade motor oil is naturally suited for your machines. Oh, you can buy less expensive brands than ours, but you would not be satisfied with their performance.

Acknowledging the superior nature of your prospect's product and suggesting that the prospect's company and your company are two of a kind makes considerable sense. This approach elevates your product to the same level of pride the prospect's company has in its products.

If you choose to make comparisons, be sure you have facts to substantiate your claims. Case histories and testimonials are useful for this purpose. For example, Dick Randolph sells X-ray equipment to hospitals and clinics by focusing on company performance and referrals to build trust. "My customers are more concerned about what happens after they sign a purchase order than the actual price," says Randolph, account manager at NXC Imaging. He provides prospects with current customers and a referral list encouraging them to contact any or all of them. Randolph uses his company's reputation to build trust and justify the higher price.[26] A demonstration could also work effectively to show a comparison. Let the prospect see personally how your product compares to other alternatives. Visual evidence and verifiable case histories produce powerful comparisons, regardless of what you are selling.

Negotiate a Winning Deal*

Nibbling. The relief and good feelings that accompany the end of a negotiation can leave you vulnerable to nibbling—a buyer's last-ditch effort to get a final concession from you. Don't give in. Justify your position by reminding your prospects and

The six tactics discussed in this section on Negotiating a Winning Deal were also modified and adapted from Roger Dawson's best-selling program "Secrets of Negotiation" and used with his permission.

yourself that they're already getting a great product and unparalleled service at a reasonable price. Be prepared to feel generous when your negotiations come to a close, but stand firm. Use competitor product and pricing information to show buyers they're already getting a great deal. You might say, "I really feel the terms we've agreed on are fair, and I'm going to personally see to it that you get more than your money's worth out of this product."

Hot Potato. Some buyers start negotiating by saying they can't spend more than a specified amount for your product or service. Given an exceptional deal, however, they might drop their insistence on that dollar amount like a hot potato and consider spending more. Find out if they're really serious about their professed price limitations by making them an offer. If your buyer only wants to pay $100 for a CD player, say, "If I could show you a $200 compact disc player that has the quality usually found in a $400 one, would you be willing to look at it?" You don't have to be pushy about persuading customers to spend more, but it never hurts to ask.

Bad Guy, Good Guy. In team negotiating situations, you may find that those you negotiate with take on roles to manipulate you into making concessions. One team member may pretend to be so disgusted with the terms you suggest that he walks out. The one left behind may act friendly and understanding, then ask for a break because his partner is being so difficult. You might respond by asking, "You wouldn't play 'bad guy, good guy' with me, would you?" Or simply say, "I'm sorry your friend is upset with these terms. You seem to think they're fair. Perhaps we should bring him back in to go over once again the benefits you'll both enjoy."

Higher Authority. You need to know early in the negotiating process if you're negotiating with people who have to consult with a loan committee, board of directors, or partner before closing the deal. Before you start, ask, "When we reach an agreement, you will have the final authority to sign the contract, won't you?" If they can't make the decision on their own, ask them to recommend the terms you agree on to those who can.

Ideally, make every effort to negotiate only with those who can make a decision. You know best how to present your product, so you and no one else should be the one selling it to the decision makers.

Flinching. When the terms you have in mind are much different from your buyer's, your buyer may flinch when you make your proposal. Instead of assuming your buyer is truly horrified at your offer, reserve judgment until you find out what's behind the objection. Ask open-ended questions. Be able to justify the terms you suggest and ask your buyer for specific reasons why he or she think they are unreasonable. If the buyer claims your price is too high, ask if they know of a similar-quality product at a lower price that comes with all the benefits of yours. Even if your buyer isn't acting, they may be objecting because they don't know the going rate of products like yours.

Red Herring or Decoy. Like the Uncle Remus story of Br'er Rabbit, who pleaded not to be thrown into the briar patch when that was what he wanted

---

COMING TO TERMS

Learn to handle these special negotiating circumstances for more harmonious and profitable negotiations.

1 ULTIMATUMS

Set ultimatums aside temporarily without making an issue of them. Then find points you both can agree on to build positive negotiating momentum. Your buyer may forget the original ultimatum if you can agree on enough other points.

2 TRADE-OFFS

Negotiations are usually a series of trade-offs or concessions made by both sides. Keep track of what you're giving up and what your buyer is getting, and when you make a concession, immediately ask for one in return.

3 DEADLOCKS

In the event of an impasse, both parties should agree to ask for advice or mediation from a neutral third party, or to abide by some fair standard such as legal or ethical considerations or fair market value.

most of all, some buyers may feign interest in a specific area of negotiation only to get what they really want in a different area. A car buyer may claim to want only a specific color and model of a car in order to get a completely different model. Thorough questioning, careful needs analysis, and attentive listening should tell you when buyers aren't being totally honest about their interests. When you detect a mysterious change of mind in your prospects, ask why their interests suddenly changed and remind them of the benefits of their original choice.

SUMMARY

Learning to handle sales resistance and stay in control is one of the greatest challenges in professional selling. Success in handling objections depends in large measure upon your attitude. If you assume that the sale is over when you hear an objection, it will be. If you regard an objection as an invitation to continue negotiating, you are more likely to enjoy a successful close.

Buyers offer objections for a number of reasons, most of which are psychological. People resist making decisions. Objecting to something in the sales presentation enables them to avoid the risk of making a decision that has potentially unpleasant consequences.

Some objections are valid and indicate either a logical reason for not buying or a need for additional information before a buying decision can be made. Other objections are invalid. Sometimes they hide the real objection; sometimes the prospect does not realize what the real objection is. The objection must be classified as to its type and the appropriate plan for overcoming it can be applied. Because salespeople encounter only six basic types of objections, preparing to overcome objections is not an overwhelming task.

The six-step strategic negotiating plan for overcoming buyer's concerns enables salespeople to become expert at overcoming whatever objection or stall they encounter. This six-step process should be internalized to the extent that it becomes automatic. Within the scope of the four broad strategies for overcoming objections, a number of specific techniques may be used. The choice of technique depends upon the situation, the type of objection, and the behavioral style of the prospect. Professional salespeople who become experts in countering objections take the time to record the objections they hear during each sales presentation, study them to determine which ones they hear most often, and then develop several scenarios they can use when these objections arise.

Every salesperson needs negotiation skills. Few purchase decisions are made by the either/or approach. Salespeople and prospects negotiate about what features are important to fill needs and what terms can be arranged for delivery, service, price, and payment schedules. Both parties establish criteria for solution of the problem. These criteria are used as a guide for exploring options that will be acceptable to both sides.

QUESTIONS FOR THOUGHT AND DISCUSSION

1. How does a salesperson sometimes cause a specific objection to be raised? What can be done to prevent this?

2. Who is responsible if prospects misunderstand part of the presentation or are not convinced that the product is applicable to their needs? Give examples of how objections reflecting these conditions are likely to be stated.

3. If you were selling homes in the price range of $200,000 to $250,000, how would you anticipate and forestall price objections?

4. In deciding when to answer objections, what factors would lead you to choose to answer them before they arise, postpone the answer until later in the presentation, answer them immediately, or ignore answering at all?

5. List the six steps in the strategic plan for handling objections.

6. List and discuss several strategies for coping with price objections.

7. How can an objection be considered a buying signal?

8. What are some underlying causes for psychological sales resistance?

9. Why might a prospect raise objections even when that prospect has already mentally decided to buy?

10. In what phases of the consultative sales cycle does negotiation play a part? Describe its purpose in each.

11. In the course of negotiation, how should you handle an ultimatum? trade-offs? deadlocks?

ACTIVITIES

1. Visualize a situation in which a student is asking a parent for permission to get her own apartment. Make three columns and list in the first the objections the parent might raise; in the second, note a technique that might be used to overcome each objection; in the third column, write out the specific answer the student might give using that technique.

2. Go to three car dealers and attempt to get the price of an automobile near the beginning of the sales encounter. What techniques did the salesperson use to postpone the question of price? Were they effective?

Case Study

CASE 12.1

Bob Hawkes woke at the first shrill ring of the telephone. He groped for the light switch in his motel room and grumbled, "Who could be calling at this time of night?" It was his sales manager.

Bob's sales manager had called to say that he had learned that the chance of selling the new Faxmatic Total Copy System to the Sullivant Broadcasting Company was about to evaporate. Sullivant was about to sign with a competitor. "You'd better get there fast," the sales manager warned Hawkes.

"Chief, I've already seen Sullivant and shown him slides of the Faxmatic System. He liked it and asked me to come back early tomorrow."

"Yes, but did you research ...?"

"It's all done. They now have their Monthly Program Guide printed outside. I found out it's Sullivant's pet project and he writes the program notes. Why are you so uptight about this guy? You've called me four or five times about him. Don't worry, I'll do the best I can."

"Okay, but remember, no special price deals without consulting me first."

Early the next morning, Bob, briefcase in one hand and a copy of Sullivant's Monthly Program Guide in the other, walked into Sullivant's office. Sullivant was absorbed in a stack of financial reports. "Why the gloomy frown?" Bob wondered. "Something's wrong."

"Didn't you get my message?" Sullivant growled.

"What message?" Bob asked.

"I had my secretary call your home office a few days ago and cancel our appointment. "

"But why?" Bob was bewildered.

"After you were here last week, I discussed your copy system with two of my key people. One says we should sit tight and not spend any more money we don't have to. There's a point there, especially in this unstable economy. The other prefers another product. It's an import, but it costs less."

"And what is your opinion, Mr. Sullivant?"

"Well, I'll be frank with you. Of all the products we've seen, I'm inclined to agree that the import does offer more quality features for less money."

Bob could see his sale going down the drain. "But, Mr. Sullivant, the last time I saw you, you liked our Faxmatic System and admitted that it can save you money, didn't you?"

"I know," Sullivant agreed hesitantly. "But now I'm not so sure, considering its price. That's why I've decided to think it over."

1. As Bob doesn't know what competing system Sullivant is considering, how can he effectively counter Sullivant's objection that it offers more than the Faxmatic System?

2. What should Bob's next move be?

CASE 12.2

Karen Burgess sells a line of computer terminals that are compatible with most mainframe computers. She was certain that Ed Sommes, manager of a regional insurance office, was sold on the purchase of a dozen new terminals that the accounting clerks would need because the company was adding new software to replace their old batch system that had used only two data entry clerks to enter all documents. Now, all the accounting people would be entering data directly instead of preparing written documents to be entered by someone else.

Karen summarized the benefits she had presented. "Our terminals are especially adapted to accounting needs. One of their best features is that the ten-key pad is designed in two models: one for right-handed operators and one for left-handed. Because the pad plugs into either side instead of being part of the keyboard, you can order the kind you need. When you have a new clerk who needs the other kind, you replace only the ten-key pad and you are ready to move. You could even stock a right-hand and left-hand pad as spares and have instant flexibility. The non-glare screen is easy on the eyes, yet sharp and clear for ease of reading. The special tilt adjustment gives people of different heights just the angle they need. And our service people are on 24-hour call with radio dispatching whenever you have a problem."

But before Karen could ask the closing question, Ed broke in. "I've got to admit your units look attractive, but with the capital outlay for the new software, I need to hold down my cost for terminals to the minimum. Just how much would a dozen new terminals set my budget back?" When Karen quoted the unit figure, Ed sighed. "That's almost ten percent more per unit than the price your competitor offers. I don't see how I can justify that much at this time."

1. Put yourself in Karen's situation. Your prospect has just told you that your price is too high. How would you handle it?

2. Would knowing the competitor's line help to give you a clue about how to handle the objection?

CHAPTER 13

Closing the Sale

Success in the End is What Counts—Not Failure in the Beginning

His failures far exceeded his successes:

- 1832 lost his job
- 1832 defeated in the race for the legislature
- 1833 failed in business
- 1834 *elected to legislature*
- 1835 sweetheart died
- 1836 suffered a nervous breakdown
- 1838 defeated for speaker in the legislature
- 1843 defeated for nomination for Congress
- 1846 *elected to Congress*
- 1848 lost renomination
- 1849 rejected for job as land officer
- 1854 defeated for Senate
- 1856 defeated for nomination for vice-president
- 1858 defeated for Senate
- 1860 *elected sixteenth president of the United States*

ABRAHAM LINCOLN

WHAT IS A CLOSE?

A *close* can be defined as a question asked or an action taken by a salesperson designed to elicit a favorable buying decision from the prospect.[1] It is always related to the specific objective you identified for the interview. Suppose, for example, you are selling advertising space for a local consumer magazine. You have just asked the prospect to run an ad, and the prospect replies, "Yes, I'll run a half-page ad for three months beginning September 28." You have closed a sale. You have a new client. If your sales call is one in a series of contacts you are making on a tough prospect, however, your objective might be to establish that the profile of your magazine's readership is a good match with the prospect's target audience. On this trip, then, you provide evidence to support your claim: circulation figures, a map showing coverage, selected demographic and psychographic data, and geographic reach and penetration figures. Your close consists of asking for the prospect's agreement that the evidence is acceptable. When you have received this agreement, you have achieved a successful close by satisfying the objective for this particular call. A consultative salesperson, then, may *close a sale or close a call.*

PERSPECTIVES ON CLOSING

Closing the sale is not really difficult for the salesperson who is conducting a professional sales interview held under favorable conditions, including the presence of a qualified prospect. Although closing a sale is actually quite natural, far too many salespeople have adopted such a distorted view of the close that they dread trying, even though the close is their only reason for being there. In fact, according to Chris Hegarty, in sixty-three percent of all sales interviews, salespeople fail to ask for the prospect's business.[2] The usual scenario goes like this:

Well, Dr. Bickley, that's about all I have to tell you. Is there anything else you would like to ask me? No? Okay, I guess I'll call you again in a few weeks. Have a good day. I enjoyed talking with you.

Then the salesperson is standing outside the prospect's office wondering, "What happened? I thought sure I had that order. What did I do wrong?" The usual answer is the salesperson did not do anything *wrong*. The salesperson just did not do *anything*.

The sale has actually been made or lost long before the time arrives to sign the agreement. The final step should be just a formality – a necessary step, but not one that requires making weighty decisions. Jeff Sharpe is sales manager of CK Worldwide, a welding supply manufacturer that sells through independent manufacturer's sales reps throughout the country. Training these salespeople to close effectively is one of his biggest challenges. Many of his sales reps don't get sales because they don't ask for the orders. Sharpe advises his reps to focus on listening rather than talking. Then, "don't be afraid to ask for the order," he advises them.[3] Unless you complete the selling process by asking for the order, the only title you deserve is *conversationalist*.

Closing is not a separate event tacked onto the end of a sales interview. It is something that happens all along during the course of the presentation. Closing would probably be easier to understand if someone had devised a better name for it. Because the word *close* suggests something that occurs at the end of a process, salespeople seem to feel that it is an isolated segment of the selling process that must be approached in some exact manner to produce success, but the opportunity to close may occur at any time during the sales interview. The wise professional watches for and takes advantage of every closing opportunity. Take the order as soon as you can get it! Instead of regarding the close as a separate segment of the interview inflexibly located at the end of all you planned to say in the presentation, consider the close in the context of the entire sales cycle. Closing begins the moment you speak the first word to the prospect and continues throughout the whole process until the order is signed, sealed, and delivered. You *close* on many points: the prospect's agreement to grant an interview, confirming the existence of a need, permission to make a survey or an on-site visit, permission for a trial installation, and acceptance of your explanation of product benefits.

Failure at the close is the result of inadequate completion of the prior steps in the sales process: inadequate prospecting, incomplete qualifying of the prospect, or too little probing to determine the prospect's real needs. As a

When each step in the sales process is handled correctly, the close is the natural conclusion to a successful sales interview.

result, the presentation has focused on the wrong features and benefits, or the wrong evidence has been supplied to support claims for the product. A prospect's failure to buy, then, does not automatically brand you as a poor closer. Studying your entire performance to find the weak link in the chain is necessary. Focusing only on closing as an indicator of sales skill is like expecting to hear Tiger Woods say that putting is all that matters in golf. Of course, that final putt that wins the championship is the most obvious success moment, but if your approach shots always leave you with ninety-foot putts, you will lose most of the time.

FUNCTIONS OF THE CLOSE

The Need for a Close

Even when all the steps leading to the close have gone well, the prospect may still hesitate. Logically, the prospect would gladly sign the agreement when a professional salesperson has a good product or service to offer, has presented meaningful benefits, has a carefully planned strategy for servicing the prospect's account, makes an impressive sales presentation, and successfully answers all of the buyer's concerns. However, the *moment of decision* is difficult for most people. Buyers take many risks: They must live with the purchase and pay for it; they may be forced to justify the buying decision to someone else; they may be responsible for an important impact on the company's productivity or profitability as a result of the purchase. Risks are threatening to most people. Of course, the salesperson is also feeling some strain at the moment of decision. You may be asking yourself, "Have I told the prospect enough? Did I find the real need? Did I read the verbal and nonverbal clues correctly? Is this the best moment to close? What if the answer is *no*?"

The close, therefore, is the moment of truth for both the prospect and salesperson. The buyer knows that an affirmative decision involves a change in attitude and/or behavior, and change can be painful and threatening. If, for example, a company president agrees to purchase a ten-week, self-paced time management program for twenty people in the organization at $600 per person, a major commitment is required, not only of a significant amount of company money but also to persuading those twenty executives that using these materials will benefit both the company and them personally. The buyer must also make the personal commitment to monitor the use of the program and the results it produces. Refusing to buy, in contrast, leaves the prospect and the situation unchanged. Because the present situation is bearable even though it is not ideal, saying no is easier than saying yes.

The salesperson-prospect relationship is much like the doctor-patient relationship. The patient knows something is wrong and looks to the doctor for advice about diagnosis and treatment. The doctor guides the patient to a course of action to which the patient gladly agrees. Closing a sale requires a similar guidance of the prospect by the salesperson. Just as a doctor urges the patient to follow the treatment closely, a salesperson must make wise decisions about the prospect's needs.[4] If you believe that the decisions you recommend are in your prospects' best interests, then you must support buyers and help them make the decisions that will solve their problems.

> The art of closing sales is not the process of persuading people to make decisions, but the art of making decisions with which people will agree.

Reassure and Close. Consider how the prospective buyer is probably feeling and thinking. Do you remember the first time you jumped off a diving board? You thought, "the board is too high; I can't swim that far; I'll choke on some water; I think I see sharks." You thought about all the possible bad consequences. Perhaps a friend in the water encouraged you to try. When you finally jumped, you discovered that the water was fine, just as your friend had said. In the sales situation, you are the friend in the water, you know how the prospect feels and you offer the needed reassurance: "Come on in; you'll be glad you took that first dive; I'm here to help if you need me." Your attitude as a salesperson must be that you respect prospects and their decisions, whether or not they decide to jump in. You continue to reassure them until they finally make a decision. When prospects jump in, they find the experience is exhilarating. They learn for themselves that everything you promised them about your product or service is true. The next time you advise them to make a buying decision, they will trust your recommendation more readily.

> **WIFE:** Dear, Do You Have Difficulty Making Decisions?
>
> **HUSBAND:** Well, Yes and No.

Once prospects agree that they can benefit from using your product or service, your responsibility is to guide them to a close. You must never be discouraged by no. If you honestly believe that a sale is an exchange of mutual benefits, then a no should set up this train of reasoning: The prospect is asking me to explain once more that this decision will work, so I will continue to reassure and close. The consultative salesperson is not dissuaded when the buyer hesitates. People do not like to make decisions; without assistance and reassurance, some simply cannot make decisions at all. *There is no agony like that of indecision.*

A CLOSING CONSCIOUSNESS

The Salesperson's Attitude

The most important factor in successfully closing a sale is not having the lowest price or the best product. *Your attitude* is the crucial factor. You must have an absolute belief in what you are selling, and you must *expect* to be successful. According to Gary Karrass, author of *Negotiate to Close*, salespeople's negative attitude and reluctance to negotiate stem from their reactions to the multitude of criticisms and complaints they hear each day from buyers—remarks that are usually unconnected to the presentation they are making. "If you have a feeling you're not going to make the sale, you listen and store information that validates that feeling."[5] That feeling is, in turn, sensed by prospects, who increase their negative input in reaction to your attitude. If you assume that you will successfully close the sale, the prospect interprets your confidence as reassurance that the product will provide the needed benefits. Your positive attitude makes the difficult decision, "Yes, I'll buy" much easier. All they have to do is say, "Yes, you're right" when you recommend that they buy. Confidence is contagious; it infects prospects and draws them to your side. Confidence at the close allows you to ask for the order in a straightforward manner.

Mr. Evert, we have agreed on the capacity of the printer, its speed capabilities, and the cost of supplying paper, and we have clarified your questions regarding the service contract. We could significantly speed up the process if we could settle now on a delivery date. Is Friday okay with you?

Closing is only frustrating if you haven't identified customer needs, shown the right attitude, made a memorable presentation, and were perceived as a genuine help.[6] If you and the prospect have together defined the problem and worked out a solution, then the final question, the close, is nothing more than the last step in a sequence. After all, you have provided a quantity of solid information and helped the prospect study the existing situation and work out solutions to personal and/or business problems. You have been working for the prospect as a—so far—unpaid business consultant. The close is payday.

When you maintain a positive mental attitude, a high level of self-confidence, and belief in your product, you create an atmosphere within which you can handle the day-to-day rejections that are inevitable in the world of selling. Steve Simms, noted author and speaker, reveals how to *shake off the shackles of rejection.* When prospects fail to follow your buying advice, you know that the rejection is seldom directed toward you personally but is instead a reflection of their own differing opinion about what will best fill their needs or a result of their personal hesitancy to make a decision that they perceive as a risk. In other words, you have lost nothing except a little of your time, but the prospects who say no have lost the opportunity to benefit from using your product or service and of being your personal customer. The bigger loss is theirs.

SHAKE THE SHACKLES OF REJECTION

First of all, you can disassociate yourself from the rejection by pretending you're watching the disappointing sales encounter from a distance. In your imagination, pretend to step out and away from your body, then turn around and watch yourself and the prospect. From that perspective, the pain and discouragement of rejection are greatly diminished. You can add humor by pretending you're watching your sales manager get rejected instead of yourself.

Second, try delaying judgement of the call. When you finish a sales call that ends in rejection, refuse to evaluate your situation in a negative way. Disagree with any feelings that tell you things are awful, and instead say to yourself, "It's too soon to tell. Maybe this is awful, maybe it isn't. I'll decide later." Then, like Scarlett O'Hara, say to yourself, "I'll think about that tomorrow."

Steve Simms is president of Attitude-Lifter Enterprises and author of *Mindrobotics: How To Be Happy For The Rest Of Your Life.*

Persistence

Diana Smith, a representative for Jim Stephenson and Associates, Inc., says, "You should push, but never be pushy." Smith calls on Houston home builders to convince them to use her company's line of plumbing supplies in their construction projects. She suggests that "making repeat, *meaningful* calls demonstrates to prospects that you are not going to give up. The idea is to be graciously tenacious—without being obnoxious."[7] Focused persistence involves asking whether doing *this* today will get you *that* tomorrow.[8] Successful salespeople like Diana Smith never take no for an answer unless it is in everyone's interest to do so. If the business is worth having, it is worth going after repeatedly—with repeated calls or repeated attempts to close during a single call. The extra effort often makes the difference between success and failure.

By permission of Syndication International Ltd., London.

How often do you ask a prospect for the business? The answer often given is "one more time." Realistically, you should be prepared to ask *at least* four or five times. A research study of several thousand salespeople demonstrates just how important the persistence factor really is:

1. Forty-eight percent of those interviewed quit after the first contact with a prospect.

2. Seventy-three percent give up after the second contact.

3. Eighty-five percent quit after the third contact.

4. Ninety percent give up after the fourth contact.

The most dramatic statistic from the study shows that the *ten percent* of salespeople who continue past the fourth contact, end up with *eighty percent* of the business.[9]

Selling should be a side-by-side, step-by-step process, involving both prospect and salesperson, in which the salesperson *earns the right to close*. When you understand the problems faced by prospects, stay with them through the problem-solving process, watch for buying signals, and time the close to fit the prospect's behavioral style, your chances of a successful close skyrocket. Opportunities to close occur a number of times during the sales process; recognize them, persist, and ask for the order. Exhibit 13.1 describes the kind of persistence needed for success in sales.

EXHIBIT 13.1 - Persistence

One of the best examples of persistence is a story you probably loved as a child: *Green Eggs and Ham*. This Dr. Seuss classic describes the attempt of the "salesman," Sam I Am, to induce a wary "prospect" to try a meal of green eggs and ham. When his first straightforward offer is rejected, Sam I Am tries one assumptive close after another: "Do you want them here or there? Would you like them in a box or with a fox? Do you want them in a house or with a mouse?" Finally, the prospect tries green eggs and ham and is surprised to find them quite delicious. His no's seemingly never registered with the persistent Sam I Am. If you have not read *Green Eggs and Ham* lately, visit the children's section of the library and learn the story's important lesson about persistence.

Dr. Seuss, *Green Eggs and Ham* (New York: Random House, 1960)

Dealing With Rejection

So many salespeople leave the profession because of their inability to cope with the day-to-day sense of rejection they experience. They interpret a prospect's refusal to buy as a message that says, "You are personally worthless." Mary Crowley, founder of Dallas-based Home Interiors Inc., would tell her salespeople what Eleanor Roosevelt said: "No one can make you feel inferior without your permission." She feels that this concept is especially important for her people to internalize. Sales professionals must learn to deal with rejection by keeping a positive attitude about themselves and how they make their living. True, they feel disappointment if they fail to close, but successful salespeople focus in on the sense of accomplishment they feel when they do close a sale.[10] To keep from being overwhelmed, accept the fact that rejection exists, see it for what it really is, and never make the mistake of allowing it to serve as a measure of your own self-worth.

What is a good batting average in selling? Professional baseball players who average .300 (three hits for every ten times at bat) or more for a full season are a small minority of players in the major leagues. Imagine failing to get a base hit 70 percent of the time. Consider some of the great names in baseball history:

"The number of failures salespeople have is not important. What counts is the number of times they succeed, and this is directly related to the number of times they can fail and keep trying."
-Tom Hopkins

- Babe Ruth hit 714 career home runs, but struck out 1,330 times.

- Cy Young won 515 games, but lost 313.

- Ty Cobb stole 96 bases one year but was caught stealing 38 times.

Baseball fans ignore the failures and concentrate on the successes of their favorite players. The attitude of all professionals is, "I may have *failed,* but that does not mean *I am a failure.*"

A salesperson who never hears a 'no' is no salesperson, only an *order taker*. Rejection is as much a part of sales as getting dressed in the morning, and salespeople who can't or won't deal with it had better find another career.

"The first thing to remember when handling rejection is that you just can't take it personally," says Gavin McIntyre, senior consulting engineer for Bryan Research and Engineering.[11] Refuse to permit anyone else to *make you* feel bad about yourself. Exhibit 13.2 describes seven specific strategies for coping with rejection.[12]

EXHIBIT 13.2 - Seven Tactics for Dealing with Rejection

1. Remind yourself of exceptional salespeople and how many hundreds or thousands of rejections they had to face on their journey to success. You see, you are not alone!

2. When you make mistakes, forgive yourself. Mistakes are great learning experiences, but to benefit from them you have to keep moving forward. Continue to generate, gather and harvest prospects. The more prospects you have, the better you feel.

3. Give yourself a pep talk. Replace negative thoughts with positive ones such as, "I'm a great salesperson, and after they hear what I have to say, they'll want to buy from me."

4. Remind yourself constantly that persistence is key to success, and that rejection may not be pleasant but you won't let it stop you. Stubbornly refuse to let it get to you!

5. Remind yourself of the difference between self-worth and performance. Never equate your worth as a human being with your success or failure as a salesperson.

6. Engage in positive self-talk. Separate your ego from the sale. The prospect is not attacking you personally. Say to yourself, "This prospect doesn't even know me; the refusal to buy cannot have anything to do with me as a person."

7. Positively anticipate rejection and it will not overwhelm you. Expect it, but don't create it. Think in advance what your response to rejection will be.

WHEN TO CLOSE

Most of the sales you make will not close themselves. The "Sales Competency Research Report," compiled by the Forum North America Company, studied hundreds of top salespeople in six major industries and found that the few *true superstars* did not find it necessary to ask overtly for the order. The good salespeople openly asked for the order approximately ninety percent of the time before the sale was closed.[13] The closing curve shown in Figure 13.1 illustrates how the closing process works. The *will-buy line* (WBL) shows that some sales will be closed almost at once, others are easy sales, and that most can be closed with an interest-building presentation. A few can never be closed. The key is recognizing the spots at which a close can be made—when the buyer gives a buying signal. The appearance of a buying signal is the critical moment during the presentation when a successful close is more likely. When you sense the psychological moment to close do so immediately. A delay of even a few seconds may give prospects a chance to change their mind.[14] If you fail to recognize these critical moments at which the prospect is most nearly ready to make a buying decision and continue to talk past them, the close becomes steadily more difficult. After a critical point is passed, you must *buy back* the prospect's readiness to decide. In other words, you must once again convince the prospect that buying is the proper decision. Talking too much and *overselling* is a much greater danger than *underselling*. Your attempts to close early and often eliminate the possibility of going past the point at which the prospect is ready to buy.

FIGURE 13.1
The Closing Curve

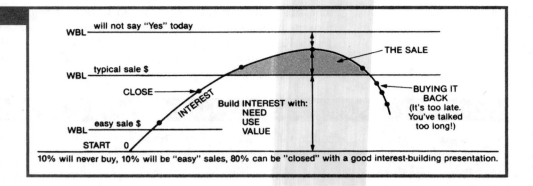

The professional salesperson guides and directs the prospect's behavior. As you reach the point where the final decision is to be made, it's just as important for you to know *when to ask* for the order as it is for you to know *how to ask*.[15] Instead of just watching passively for signs of interest, you must create situations in which interest can be generated and revealed. Every creature sends out signals about its feelings. A cat purrs contentedly while lying in your lap; a dog growls if it senses danger; a baby cries when wet or hungry. The best psychological moment for closing may occur at any time during the presentation. When it comes, prospects *signal* in some way that you have convinced them and they are ready to buy.[16] You never have only one possible moment to close. You may be in the early stages of the presentation, you may have completely exhausted all the selling points you planned to present, or you may be somewhere in between.

RECOGNIZING BUYING SIGNALS

A buying signal is anything the prospect does or says that indicates readiness to buy. "Buying signals are all around us if we learn to recognize them," says John Pendley, sales manager for the Hampton Inn in Casper, Wyoming.[17] Unfortunately, it's all too easy to become focused on your presentation that you overlook these signals even if they are obvious. Buying signals occur quickly and may be verbal, nonverbal, or both. Genuine buying signals show that the prospect has moved from evaluating your proposal to an appraisal of it. A buying signal may come in the form of a question. A prospect may ask you to repeat some point or benefit previously discussed or stop you right in the middle of the presentation to ask how long delivery will take. However a buying signal comes, take advantage of it and close immediately. Always remember that when the prospect is ready to buy, you will receive a signal.

The CHEF Technique

Just as the experienced chef in a fine restaurant knows precisely the right ingredients to blend to produce exquisite cuisine, similarly professional salespeople can exhibit chef like characteristics as they try to translate the combination of gestures fed to them by their prospects. Use the CHEF method to identify prospects' verbal and nonverbal buying signals.[18]

Cheek Or Chin. When prospects touch or stroke their chin or cheek they are signaling satisfaction and gratification. Leaning forward and nodding the head in agreement says, I'm almost persuaded. In this instance, ask if you've answered all their questions, move quickly and ask for their business. Prospects that tighten their jaw muscles or cover their mouths suggest that they are not receptive to what you have to say. This is a critical time to ask questions to open them up.

Hands. Open and relaxed hands, especially with palms facing upward, are a sign that prospects may be ready to buy. Rubbing their palms together signals that they are already assuming ownership. Those individuals who steeple (like a church steeple) their hands together are indicating confidence or superiority. When the prospect's hands are fidgeting or forming a fist, they're more than likely skeptical, or worse yet, irritated. You must stop talking and find out what is wrong!

Eye contact, or the lack of, can signal to the salesperson a prospect's level of interest.

Eye contact. Maintaining consistent eye contact with the salesperson indicates the prospect is probably paying attention to what is being said, and the handling and examination of any visuals shows the intensity of that commitment. This is a good time to request a buying decision. When the pupils of the prospect's eyes are dilated this signals relaxation, and you are on the right track. However, rolling or squinting of the eyes often means irritation or confusion. In addition, the rate at which a prospect blinks can indicate anger or excitement. A raised eyebrow can mean the prospect doesn't believe what you are saying.[19] Something is wrong and you had better find out what that something is. If you sense this you might say, "You seem a bit uneasy with this. Please tell me what concerns or questions you have."

Friendly prospects. Prospects who are smiling, relaxed, or engaging you in conversation are telling you that you've earned their trust. A prospect indicates readiness to purchase by saying, "It sounds good, but I ought not to buy." Give this prospect another reason to buy. Reassure and ask for a decision. When prospects turn unfriendly, be sensitive and empathetic. After all, the basic reason for becoming experts at relationship selling is to create an atmosphere within which an act of trust can take place! *People like to buy from people who are like them.*

The Trial Close

A *trial close* asks for an *opinion;* a *closing question* asks for a *decision.* A trial close, by asking for an opinion, serves as a thermometer that tells you whether the prospect is warm, hot, or cold to your proposition. It is designed to help you read the prospect's feelings and predict probable reactions. In Chapter 11, the tie-down question was discussed as one element in a *unit of conviction.* The tie-down and the trial close are used for basically the same purpose. When you get the prospects agreeing with you throughout the presentation they are much more likely to agree with you when you ask the closing question, that is, when you make the formal request for their business. You want to be careful not to talk past the sale. Close when the prospect wants to buy.

Many salespeople think of closing as the last phase of a sales call. If they do, they may not get all the sales that they should. During every sales call there will be a number of opportunities to close the sale. How do you know the proper time? When in doubt, test the prospect with trial closes such as, Is this what you're looking for? Can you imagine how this will boost your productivity? Do you have the necessary budget for this? What else do you need to make a decision? Does this sound like something you would like to do?[20]

Although it resembles a definite attempt to close, the trial close is used primarily to probe and to reveal how far along the prospect has gone in the decision-making process. You do not need to ask a closing question if you know the prospect is not ready to buy. The time to ask for the order is when the prospect is fully ready to buy. You can, however, ask for an *opinion* at any time.

A Closing Question

A *closing question*, in contrast to the trial close, is designed to produce an answer that confirms the fact that the prospect has bought. Look at these two examples:

1. Would it be better for you to receive shipment of a full month's supply immediately, or would you prefer to receive half at the end of this week and the other half in about ten days?

2. We can have the product on your dock next Monday. Is Monday a convenient delivery day for you?

When you ask a closing question, say *nothing* else until the prospect gives an answer. The pressure of silence is enormous. Silence is golden because of what it brings you in terms of the information you need. *Never miss the opportunity not to say something.*[21] If you can remain silent after asking the closing question, only two outcomes are possible: 1) the prospect says yes or 2) the prospect gives a reason for not wanting to buy. In either instance, you are better off than you were before you asked the question. If the answer is yes, you have a sale. If the prospect gives you a reason for not buying, a concern has surfaced that you can convert into another opportunity to close.

COMPUTERS AND CLOSING

Computer technology can make closing the sale quicker for salespeople. It may eliminate the need to return to the office for price approvals or price calculations. Saving time is also possible when several individuals must approve a price or bid before the salesperson can close. For instance, the Falconite company sells cranes and lift equipment to industrial and commercial users. In the past, days or weeks might pass before all the individuals involved study, make corrections, and approve a bid on a large purchase. Today, the bid is sent to each person's electronic mailbox. Each one makes changes and returns the bid to the salesperson with applicable comments or notes. The changes are incorporated and the bid is sent back for final approval. Less than a day may be required for complex bids even though all those whose approval is required are at widely separated locations in the field.

Developing Partnerships Using Technology examines how computer networks shorten the selling cycle and facilitate the purchasing function. Computer-to-computer systems link customers and suppliers, providing a one-stop communication tool for the salesperson. These systems are referred to as Electronic Data Interchanges.

Developing Partnerships Using Technology

The Closer with a member of his sales team, the *Electronic Data Interchange*

Electronic Data Interchanges (EDI). It's like having your own personal sales team member. The EDI system provides a one-stop communication tool for the ordering, production, delivery, and billing of a product. Simply put, it is a large, complex e-mail system that can connect salespeople to their own company and to their customers. This automatic communication frees up salespeople to provide quality customer service and keep track of any order and its status. EDI provides a quick, paperless solution to the age-old problem of transaction processing and product delivery. Here is just a sampling of what this electronic EDI tool can do:

1. Shorten the selling cycle and simplify the purchasing function between the salesperson and his clients.

2. Allow automatic replenishment of inventory on a just-in-time (JIT) basis.

3. Recording of all production, ordering, and delivery communication.

4. Automatic processing of information through computers without human interference.

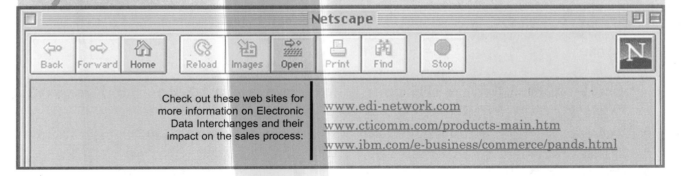

Check out these web sites for more information on Electronic Data Interchanges and their impact on the sales process:

www.edi-network.com

www.cticomm.com/products-main.htm

www.ibm.com/e-business/commerce/pands.html

TYPES OF CLOSES

Become familiar with as many types of closing techniques as possible. One or two standard closes are not enough in the competitive selling arena that is filled with many different kinds of buyers, all with varying needs and personalities. You need a specific close for every occasion and for every type of prospect. If you attempt to use the same close for every prospect, you will walk away from much of the business that should be yours. The sales plan for each interview calls for a specific type of presentation strategy; your plan should also extend to the type of close you use. Just as circumstances often dictate some changes in your presentation, however, they also point up the need for shifts in your closing plans. Your *sales call plan* should provide the preferred closing routine to fit with the presentation you expect to deliver. Be sure to plan some alternative closing routines you can use in the event you find it is necessary to modify your presentation to fit into some special situation you encounter when you arrive for the appointment.

For example, an insurance agent who had prepared a comprehensive insurance program to present to a particular client might arrive at the interview to find an excited prospect who shares the information that he and his wife have just been told that the baby they were expecting will actually be triplets. This prospect's needs have changed dramatically in just twenty-four hours. As a result, the presentation becomes a work session to devise a new insurance program, and the expected close may not fit. A master salesperson with a full repertoire of closing techniques merely chooses one that fits the revised situation and moves on as though nothing unusual is occurring. The various closing methods shown in Exhibit 13.3 and described here are not the only methods available. Most of them are subject to combination with other methods to fit your unique personality, your product, and your market. Learn the principles upon which these techniques rest and adapt them to your needs.

EXHIBIT 13.3 - Successful Closing Techniques

1. *Assumptive closes*— Throughout the presentation, assuming that the prospect will buy allows the prospect to make the decision more easily by presenting opportunities to make smaller or easier choices. Common assumptive closes include the continuous-yes close, the minor-point close, the physical-action close, the order-blank close, and the alternate of choice close.

2. *Impending-event close*— Stress the urgency to make a decision because something is about to happen that means the opportunity to buy with the present advantages may be lost.

3. *Balance-sheet close*— The salesperson takes an active part in the decision-making process to help the prospect understand that the reasons for buying heavily outweigh the reasons opposed to buying.

4. *Direct close*— Make a straightforward request for the order. Many buyers appreciate a no-nonsense approach, but be mindful of each prospect's behavioral style and use this approach only with those who welcome such tactics.

5. *Summary close*— Review the features and benefits of the offering with particular emphasis on selling points that generated the most prospect interest earlier in the presentation.

6. *Call-back close*— Most sales are not closed on the first attempt. Offer to call back on a prospect with a specific purpose in mind and with new information.

7. *Trial-order close*— Either guarantee the prospect's money back or offer to absorb all expenses if the prospect tries the product or service and decides not to keep it.

Assumptive Closes

In a sense, every close is assumptive. You do not attempt to close until you have received one or more buying signals from the prospect and have reason to believe you have a better than even chance of success. When you enter every sales interview with a positive expectation of success, you are assuming that the prospect will buy at the close. Your attitude throughout the interview is assumptive. Say, *"When* you use this product" and *"As your* program progresses." Avoid words like *if* and *should* because they are conditional and block closing action. The assumptive approach to closing establishes a positive environment in which the prospect can more easily say yes. These closes work well with indecisive buyers who tend to be nervous about making a final decision. Present them with minor decisions that give them the opportunity to appear decisive in a small matter while they are actually painlessly making the big decision at the same time. Prospects with the *driver* behavioral style may resent these closes as manipulative; measure the prospect before choosing the type of close. The closes described below are common assumptive closes.

Continuous-Yes Close. By asking a series of questions throughout the sales presentation, all of which are designed to be answered in the affirmative, it becomes more difficult for buyers to say no when they've already said yes a number of times. That is why consultative salespeople get agreement on small things before they ask for the order.

These questions begin in need discovery. For example: "I'd like to ask you a few questions that help me understand your particular needs. Would that be okay with you?" *Yes.* Continue them during the presentation: "Do you like the idea of our billing in six-second increments on all your long distance calls?" *Yes.* During the closing phase the salesperson may ask: "Are you satisfied with the comprehensive service contract that we offer?" *Yes.* "Does the financing of this telecommunications system seem fair to you?" *Yes.* "Then it seems we can go ahead with our plans to begin the installation process." *Yes.* These are all closed-end type questions, so you must be confident that you will receive an affirmative response before you ask them. When the final closing question is asked, the prospect is inclined to keep on agreeing with you. You have a sale.

Minor-Point Close. Ask the prospect to make a decision about a small, relatively minor detail related to the product or service. A salesperson who is selling a communication training course for employees might ask, "Do you want to send your people to the meeting room in our offices for their training, or do you have a conference room available that would be convenient?" If an answer is given to this question, the decision to buy has been made.

Physical-Action Close. The physical-action close is quite simple, but can be most effective. Without directly asking for the prospect's order, begin taking some action that assumes the sale is completed. For example, you can begin filling out the order form and ask the prospect for a signature when you finish. A retail salesperson may simply begin wrapping the merchandise or move to the cash register to ring up the order. If the prospect does not object or stop your action, the sale is made.

Order-Blank Close. Begin to ask the prospect a series of questions and write the answers on the contract or agreement form. You might ask, "Do you use your complete middle name or just an initial?" Continue to fill out the information and then ask for a signature. "Now that we have reached agreement, I know you will want to expedite delivery. Just indicate your approval by placing your name right here."

Alternate of Choice Close. In general, people like to exercise their freedom of choice and salespeople like to lead their buyers toward an easy agreement. This well-known close consists of giving the prospect a choice between two positive alternatives. Here are some suggestions:

1. *Would delivery be convenient on Thursday, or would you prefer Friday?*
2. *Do you prefer to pay cash or is our monthly payment plan more convenient for you?*
3. *Where would you like the order sent — directly to your warehouse or to the main office?*
4. *When would you like to have the new system installed — by the end of your fiscal year or at the end of the calendar year?*

The idea behind the alternate of choice close is to offer the prospect a choice between buying *A* and buying *B* instead of a choice between buying or not buying. The question is not "Will you buy?" but "When?" or "Which one?"

Impending Event Close

This close uses the sense of urgency that is suggested by some impending event that will affect the terms or the effectiveness of the buying decision. Use this close with discretion. It must be based on truth and must not seem manipulative. The most common inducements are concerns that prices are going up or that resources will be in short supply.

My company has announced that prices on this product will go up about five percent next month because of an increase in supplier costs. If I can call your order in now, you can stock up before the price increase becomes effective.

Never use this close deceptively! Whatever the impending event is, it must be real and in the prospect's best interests to take advantage of an order placed now. Because this close is often abused by unscrupulous salespeople, prospects are likely to be skeptical of it. A conscientious salesperson working with good information who can prevent a customer from running short of inventory or from facing an unexpected price increase acquires appreciation and the loyalty of the customer. Properly applied, this close can work wonders for your long-term credibility.

The Balance-Sheet Close

This practical, decision-making format is familiar to most prospects, and they will feel comfortable as you use it. The procedure involves using a blank sheet of paper with a line drawn down the center to form two columns. In the first column, list all the reasons for making an affirmative decision in favor of your buying recommendation. These are the *assets*. In the second column, list all the questions or concerns about a buying decision—the *liabilities* involved in saying yes. The closing process is an analysis of the two columns to show the prospect that the reasons for buying heavily outweigh the reasons for not buying. Give the prospect the opportunity to express agreement with your conclusions. The prospect must take an active part in the decision-making process.

Do not shy away from stating all the concerns about buying along with the reasons for not buying. Many prospects, particularly those who are *analytical* in behavior style, are already thinking of all the reasons not to buy. You cannot keep those reasons a secret. If you try to cover up negatives, they act like a boiling pot with a too-tight lid; they build up into an explosive situation. Allow the negatives to surface and let the steam evaporate harmlessly. Negative thoughts left unchallenged in the prospect's mind cause problems. Get them out into the open and show how the positives outweigh them. Then the prospect has nothing to think over that can delay a decision. If your approach is that of an advisor or consultant who presents every alternative, prospects feel free to make up their own minds.

As you build the balance sheet, resist the temptation to hurry. As you list each advantage for buying, pause and allow time for the prospect to absorb the idea. Be sure that you have many more ideas in favor of buying than opposed to it so that the *number* of reasons will be so impressive that you won't have to deal with the relative weights of individual reasons.[22] To use the balance-sheet method, you can begin like this:

Mrs. Hillman, the decision you are about to make is important. I know you want to be sure you are making a sensible choice. So that we will be sure to make the decision that is best for you, let's look at all the reasons in favor of buying this product and any questions or concerns about it. We can then determine which side weighs more and make your decision accordingly. Let's begin with the ideas that favor a positive decision today. Is that fair enough?

Take out a sheet of paper and begin to list the reasons for buying. Be sure to avoid the word *objection*. Instead of talking about the prospect's objections to buying, state them as concerns or questions to be answered: "You expressed concern about delivery schedules." When you use the word *objection* out loud, you are setting up the prospect and yourself as adversaries; if you are adversaries, one of you must win and the other must lose. You are looking for a win-win solution to the buying decision. Table 13.1 shows a partial balance sheet for selling a mutual fund.

TABLE 13.1 - The Mutual Fund Decision

Reasons for buying	Questions or concerns
1. This fund has grown faster than savings accounts.	1. Higher risk than a savings account.
2. Diversification lowers risk.	2. Less liquidity than a savings account.
3. Professional management lowers risk.	
4. Blue chip portfolio lowers risk.	
5. Stocks are a hedge against inflation.	
6. You can quickly redeem or borrow on shares.	

You may use the balance-sheet close by actually writing down the reasons for a buying decision and the concerns or questions about buying, or you may review them verbally. Your choice depends upon what you observe about the prospect's behavioral style. For a slow, meticulous *analytical* who takes a great deal of time to decide, you surely want to write out the balance sheet. The prospect would do this kind of examination if left to think it over. An *expressive* is probably too impatient for a written balance sheet to work. Either talk through the reasons or sketch them only briefly. Once the balance sheet is complete, you must still use one of the other closes to ask for the order.

The Direct Close

The direct close is a straightforward request for an order. Once you have covered all the necessary features and benefits of your product and matched them with the buyer's dominant buying motives, you can ask with confidence, "May I have your business?" This type of close is quite common when selling to industrial buyers. Many buyers appreciate a no-nonsense approach. Of course, be mindful of the buyer's behavioral style. *Amiables*, for example, could find this approach threatening. Be sure to keep the direct close positive. Avoid the word *don't*. "Why don't we begin next week?" and "Why don't you try the product for a while and see what happens?" are open invitations to additional objections. Insertion of a negative into the close may implant doubt where none existed, and the prospect may try to tell you why not. Use positive statements like these:

1. *May I schedule delivery for next Tuesday?*
2. *It comes in five-pound, ten-pound, and twenty-pound bags. I suggest you take five of each to begin.*
3. *Let's run your first ad beginning Friday of this week.*

When you use this type of closing statement, then you and your customer can make positive plans together.

The Summary Close

One of the best closing tactics is to summarize the major selling points made during the presentation. This method is especially good when the prospect must defend a purchase to someone else. The repetition of benefits at this point overcomes the prospect's tendency to forget or overlook points previously identified as important to satisfying existing needs. Go over the buyer's requirements and how you, your company, and the product or service meet those requirements. Review the benefits and ask the prospect to confirm again that they are important. Avoid mentioning any new benefits during this close. Bring up additional points only if the summary fails and you need additional ammunition to answer new objections.

Concentrate in the summary close on those items that were of most interest to the prospect and that related directly to the dominant buying motives.[23] For example, the sales representative selling advertising space in a consumer magazine might use the summary close like this:

Mr. Longacre, let's review the major points on which we have agreed:

1. *An ad in our magazine will give you maximum effective circulation coverage.*
2. *Your ads will enjoy high readership.*

3. *We saw that businesses similar to yours have had a great deal of success advertising with us (indicate testimonials or case histories used during presentation).*

4. *Our marketing staff will help you develop ads for all the media you use, not just our magazine.*

5. *You'll receive free artwork and layout help. These services are included in our basic price.*

6. *Your advertising will be based on a total campaign concept rather than being just a series of unrelated messages.*

This summary puts into capsule form the highlights of your sales story. It gives both you and the prospect an opportunity to reconsider what was covered throughout the sales interview.

Give the prospect an opportunity to agree that the summary is correct. Once agreement has been expressed, the prospect is in a positive frame of mind, and the time is ripe to get some sort of formal commitment. The summary close must be combined with some other closing technique to complete the sale. For example, you might use *the alternate of choice close* like this:

Mr. Hicks, with all of these major benefits available, you can see that advertising with us is a sound investment. Do you want to run your first ad on October fifteenth, or would November first be better for you?

With another prospect you might prefer a more direct close:

Mrs. Duerr, we've worked together to identify your needs, and I've shown you how my service will meet those needs. You have agreed that the items just reviewed are important to you. At this point, I need your permission to process your order. How would you like to handle the financial terms?

Call-Back Close

Many sales opportunities are lost every day because salespeople take the prospect's decision not to buy as permanent. Studies show that many accounts are won by salespeople who call five or more times on the same prospect. Each time you return, you must present new information or ideas that will stimulate the prospect to buy. If you have the same old story told in the same old way, you probably will not make a new impression. If you walk into the prospect's office and say, "Well, have you thought it over?" the prospect's natural tendency is to restate the original objection: "Yes, and I still feel it is not a good time to spend that much money." In other words, "No deal." Here is an effective plan for a call-back situation:

1. *Approach.* Begin by giving a reason for calling back: "Coach Blevins, after I left the other day, I realized that there is some information I did not give you that has real bearing on your situation." Be sure you do have something different to present—new data, additional proof material in the form of testimonials, or whatever. Be sure it is pertinent and logical.

2. *Review.* Next, review the whole presentation. Begin with, "Let me review briefly the items we talked about last time." The last meeting may be

fresh in your mind, but the prospect will not remember ten percent of what you presented. Throughout the review, use phrases like *as you remember, you will recall, and we said that* to suggest points of agreement from the previous meeting.

This approach may not always work, but you *know* that you cannot sell to someone without face-to-face contact. Being there gives you the only opportunity you will ever have to sell this prospect.

The Trial Order Close

This technique involves asking the prospect for a trial order with no obligation. You either guarantee the money back if not completely satisfied or absorb all expenses and make the offer free . Prospects like it because they can simply refuse to pay for any unsatisfactory merchandise. Their risk is low and yours is minimal because only a small quantity is shipped with the possible result of establishing a satisfied customer who will give you repeat orders. Sometimes salespeople call this the *puppy dog* close. How could you ever return a puppy to the pet store and get your money back after the children have played with it for a week? By then, everyone is in love with it.

One company that suggests that its sales representatives use the trial order is Christian Resources, a company located in Washington, D.C. One of their products, the Audio-Visual Bible Handbook, is especially suited to ministers or preachers. The handbooks are multimedia resources consisting of filmstrips, matching audio cassettes, teacher's guides, and student materials. Often a pastor tells a sales representative something like this: "I have never used aids like these in my teaching or counseling activities. Let me think about it before I decide." The company suggests this kind of response:

> *Pastor, I can certainly appreciate that. One thing we do that might be helpful to you is to make the program available on a fifteen-day, satisfaction-guaranteed basis. This enables you to work with the material firsthand and see if it is something that would be useful in your ministry. We encourage you to listen to some of the tapes, go through the manual, and try it out in some actual counseling situations. After you have done that, if you find that you can use it in your library, then just hang on to it and we will bill you next month. In fact, you can even spread the payments out over six months; that would mean just $43 per payment. But if you find that you can't use the material or that it's not suitable for your situation, we'll understand. All we ask is that you return it to us. Is that fair enough?*

Follow this statement with one of the assumptive closes to get the prospect to take action that will allow you to actually enter the order.

After the Close

Once you have closed the sale and have completed any necessary paperwork, you have no further business with the prospect at this time. Learn to leave gracefully. Don't become afflicted with "lingeritis." You may be tempted to stay and enjoy the company of a new customer you especially like. You feel like celebrating a successful sale. However, the customer has other work to do, and so do you! If you linger, you invite second thoughts and perhaps even regret. Leave while the client still has good thoughts about you and your efficient, professional manner. Thank the client for the order, say you are looking forward to meeting again, and leave.

SUMMARY

Closing the sale is a natural conclusion to a carefully prepared and well-conducted presentation to a qualified prospect. Failure to get the order is more often a matter of attitude than of skill. Mastering the basic types of closing techniques is a relatively simple task; adopting winning attitudes about closing seems more difficult for many salespeople. When regarded as a natural part of the sales process, the close loses the formidable qualities it often has for salespeople. Learning to understand dominant buying motives and to recognize buying signals enables salespeople to close at the earliest possible point in the presentation. When a sense of timing is added to adequate preparation for the interview, closing is easier.

The close is the moment of truth for both salesperson and prospect. Because making an affirmative buying decision involves both taking a risk and making a change, the process is both painful and threatening for the prospect. The close is also a time of concern for the salesperson because the result is an evaluation of the job the salesperson has done in preparing for and making the presentation—and it also determines the salesperson's income! The most threatening element in the situation for many salespeople is the looming fear of rejection.

Successful closing is easier for those who learn to recognize buying signals. Both verbal and nonverbal clues point to the prospect's readiness for the close. The buying signal often suggests the type of close that would be appropriate. One effective tactic for responding to buying signals is a *trial close* that asks for an *opinion* rather than a *commitment;* this allows the salesperson to determine just how ready the prospect is for a close.

Different types of closing techniques are available to assist the salesperson in leading the prospect into a decision. Assumptive closes are based on leading the prospect through one or more decisions, each of which adds to the previous one so that the buying decision can be assumed to be only the final one of these small decisions. When the earlier decisions are all affirmative, the salesperson can rightly assume that the final decision is automatically made. Other closing techniques include a direct request for the business and various types of procedures designed to aid decision making or to reduce the threat connected with commitment.

QUESTIONS FOR THOUGHT AND DISCUSSION

1. Discuss some strategies for handling the feeling of rejection that salespeople tend to experience from missing a sale.

2. Why do many prospects naturally say no when a close is attempted?

3. Why do many salesperson dread the close? Why is this fear unfounded?

4. When should the salesperson decide what kind of close to use? Why?

5. Should the planned close ever be changed in the course of the interview? Why or why not?

6. Timing is crucial in closing. Is attempting a close before the prospect is ready more harmful than trying to close past the critical point? Why or why not?

7. Distinguish between a trial close and a closing question. When is each appropriate ?

8. What is the purpose of reassurance in connection with the close?

9. How many times in one interview should a salesperson ask for the order? How many times should you call on the same prospect to ask for an order?

10. What is the difference between persistence and pushiness?

11. Describe some typical verbal and nonverbal buying signals.

ACTIVITIES

1. Assume you are making a sales presentation to a prospect about the purchase of a big-screen television. Write a possible trial close and a closing question that you could use.

2. Visit a furniture showroom or store that sells exercise equipment. What sorts of attempts to close the sale were made? Could they have been improved? If so, why, and how?

Case Study

CASE 13.1

Linda Parker, representative for a leading cosmetic maker, leafed through a business magazine directed to retail drug stores. She noticed an ad for a new, low-priced home-permanent kit being introduced by one of her company's competitors. "Here we go again," she thought. "These prices are going to look good to stores who love to advertise low prices on popular items to build up store traffic." So Linda was not surprised to meet a price objection the very next day from the proprietor of a leading independent store who was in fierce competition with cut-rate stores in the neighborhood.

"I can't understand you big outfits," the druggist said. "There's no reason to keep prices so high on home permanents. You're probably making a huge profit on them by now; you should have recovered your research cost long ago."

"I can assure you there's no inflation in our prices," Linda said. "We use only the very best and therefore the most expensive ingredients. Our formulas are more expensive to put together, but that's why they produce a faster, longer-lasting permanent for the customer. And we're continually improving the product; so research is still important. I doubt if we'll ever stop research on this type of product because perfection isn't possible, and current hair styles call for new techniques all along."

"But those less expensive brands are all right," the druggist complained. "With this type of product, an appealing price brings people into the store, and we sell a lot of impulse items that are real profit makers. If we could feature a well-known brand like yours at a low price, we'd get better results. So if you'll give me a break on the price, I'll reorder. Otherwise, we'll just have to go with the new product. I'll still want some of your other products, but at present prices, you'll have to forget about permanents in this store from now on. My competition is giving me fits with price cuts as it is."

1. If Linda's company has a strict policy against special deals, a special price offer to this customer is not an option. Can you suggest other concessions or special help Linda might offer to convince this customer to continue to buy the more expensive item she offers?

2. Can Linda convince this customer that price is not the primary consideration for all customers?

PART V

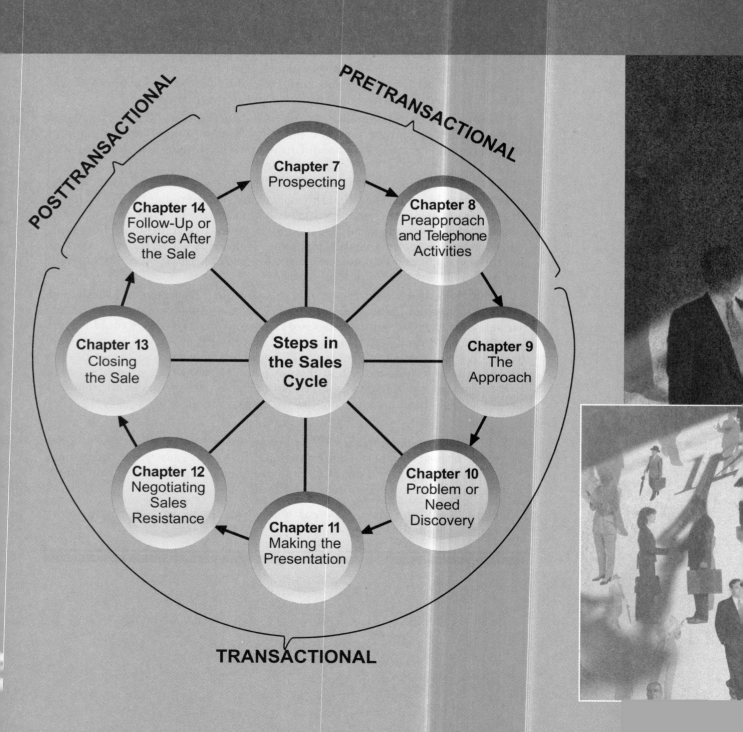

POSTTRANSACTIONAL

PRETRANSACTIONAL

Chapter 7
Prospecting

Chapter 8
Preapproach
and Telephone
Activities

Chapter 14
Follow-Up or
Service After
the Sale

**Steps in
the Sales
Cycle**

Chapter 9
The
Approach

Chapter 13
Closing
the Sale

Chapter 10
Problem or
Need
Discovery

Chapter 12
Negotiating
Sales
Resistance

Chapter 11
Making the
Presentation

TRANSACTIONAL

Management Aspects—
Personal and Organizational

The service you give the customer after the sale has been completed can be as important, or even more important than the sale itself. Keeping current customers happy and regaining lost clients is the focus of chapter 14. Professional, consultative selling requires that you possess an ample amount of personal organization and self-management skills and habits.

Chapter 15 shows you how to get better control of your time and your activities. Administrative ability on the part of the salesperson is fundamental to success. Statistics indicate that only about 20 percent of their time during a typical day is spent in face-to-face interviews with prospects. Finally, chapter 16 details the job responsibilities of sales managers, and provides a useful introduction for more advanced sales management courses.

TWELVE COMMANDMENTS OF TOTAL CUSTOMER SERVICE ....

1. CUSTOMERS ...
are the life-blood of every business—satisfying them is an income-producing endeavor.

2. CUSTOMERS ...
are the most important people in any business.

3. CUSTOMERS ...
are not dependent on us—we are dependent on them.

4. CUSTOMERS ...
are not cold, hard, lifeless statistics—they are flesh and blood human beings with feelings and emotions just like our own.

5. CUSTOMERS ...
do us a favor when they call with a complaint or service request—customer retention is the bottom line.

6. CUSTOMERS ...
are not an interruption of our work—they are the purpose of everything we do.

7. CUSTOMERS ...
are the key components of our business—they are not outsiders.

8. CUSTOMERS ...
deserve the most courteous and attentive service we can give them—develop a servant's heart.

9. CUSTOMERS ...
are people who bring us their wants and needs—it is our job to thrill *them.*

10. CUSTOMERS ...
are not someone to argue or match wits with—why win a battle and lose the war.

11. CUSTOMERS ...
should be considered economic assets—manage them to maximize your return on investment.

12. CUSTOMERS ...
make it possible for a company to pay your salary whether you are a secretary, production employee, office staff, salesperson or sales manager.

Customer Service and Follow-up After the Sale

LEARNING OBJECTIVES

- To examine the purpose of *total customer* service.

- To determine what constitutes service quality.

- To know when *and how* to service.

- To understand the salesperson's role in servicing.

- To recognize the value of systematic tracking of service activities.

- To understand how to upgrade and cross-sell current customers.

- To see the impact of technology within the channel of distribution.

- To develop a systematic plan for follow-up activities.

BUILDING PARTNERSHIPS WITH TOTAL CUSTOMER SERVICE

Increased Expectations

How do you sell your products or services and keep them sold when there are so many others fighting to do the same thing? Total customer service is the answer. More and more companies are turning to *service quality* as a strategy to acquire and maintain customers. The value of customer service is not lost on Luis Martinez, manager of Daimler-Chrysler's Five Star program, a multimillion-dollar process to change the *sales culture* within the company's 4,500 dealerships. His job is to make the salespeople and support personnel look at their jobs differently. That is, not just get people in the door and sell them a car, *but to do what is best for the customer no matter what.* The customer absolutely defines quality in every transaction. Don't *talk* customer service – *live* perfect service.[1]

Because meeting and exceeding customer expectations is so vital to success, companies must develop customer service strategies. This usually involves segmenting customers because they generally have different service needs. You can go out of business if you provide too much service to the wrong people, or if you fail to deliver adequate service to the right people. So you must inform specific customers what kind of service they can expect, and the key to success is exceeding what you promise. Keeping customers happy, and coming back, takes more than smiles and thank-yous. It takes *outrageous service.* Allen Endres of the Juran Institute, which conducts quality improvement seminars, explains that "customers have an increasing rate of expectation for services and a decreasing tolerance for poor service, and as a result are more likely to migrate to the vendors who provide the highest-quality service."[2] To effectively use service as a competitive weapon, the salesperson must exceed customers' expectations.

> *"A lot of people have fancy things to say about customer service, including me, but it's just a day-in, day-out, ongoing, never-ending, unremitting, persevering, compassionate type of activity."*
>
> -Leon Gorman, L.L. Bean

Second-mile Action

Be willing to give your customers more than they demand, more than they expect, even more than they deserve. Exhibit 14.1 depicts a salesperson with such an attitude. Act from the desire to serve–not the desire to gain. When this is your policy, you will do whatever you must to be of service to your client. That means you sometimes deliver an order in your own car to get it to the customer sooner than the company truck could deliver it. Going the second mile may involve a service for the customer that is unrelated to the business. "Big Jack" Frazier, who sells industrial chemicals, had a regular client in Waco, Texas, whose son was a student at San Angelo State University. The student's mother had typed a term paper for the son. Because Jack was leaving Waco for his regular trip through West Texas, he offered to take the paper to the student so it would be sure to arrive on time. Going through San Angelo was a bit out of his way, but he was happy to do it. Paul J. Meyer, founder of SMI International, once had a client who made a hobby of collecting rocks containing fossils. When Meyer was on a vacation trip one year, he found a rock with a particularly interesting fossil on it. He packed the rock carefully and mailed it to his client. That kind of extra service, when given from sincere interest, pays rich dividends.

Here are a few additional ideas that could be seen as going the extra mile in the eyes of the customer:[3]

1. *Offer to pick up or deliver goods to be replaced or repaired.* Lexus got a lot of mileage out of offering to pick up the recalled car rather than have the customer bring it in.

2. *Give a gift of merchandise to repay for the inconvenience.* The gift may be small but the thought will be appreciated. Things like a free dessert for a restaurant customer who endures slow service or extra copies of a print job to offset a minor delay are examples. It's really the thought that counts.

3. *Reimburse for costs of returning merchandise* such as parking fees or gas. A mail-order retailer may pay all return postage fees to help reduce customer frustration.

4. *Acknowledge the customer's inconvenience and thank him* for giving you the opportunity to make it right. Make the wording of the apology sincere and personal. Say, "I'm sorry you had to wait," rather than "The company regrets the delay."

5. *Follow up to see that the problem was taken care of.* Don't assume the problem has been fixed unless you handled it yourself. Check to make sure that the problem has stayed fixed.

EXHIBIT 14.1 - Second-mile Service

Moments of Truth

Awareness of *quality service* by your customers and prospects can be a great advantage. Salespeople are far more likely to make a sale when they can truthfully say, "If you buy from me, I will never let you down. Servicing your account is my top priority." Jan Carlzon, president of Scandinavian Airlines (SAS), writes in his book *Moments of Truth*, "Each of our 10 million customers come in contact with five SAS employees. Each contact lasts about 15 seconds. Thus, SAS is *created* in the minds of our customers 50 million times per year, 15 seconds at a time."[4]

Customer service is like a daily election and customers vote with their feet.

Those 50 million "moments of truth," when customers are made aware of service quality, are the moments that ultimately determine the success of SAS. All employees must realize and care that their work affects customers' perception of service quality and even product quality, no matter how far they are removed from the "front line" or from direct communication with customers. Customer satisfaction is measured as moments in time. Plenty of customers do not come back unless the service you provide is consistently better than service provided by competitors. You must create a trust-bond relationship. Sixty-five percent of a typical firm's sales volume is done by loyal customers who return to buy again and again because of the service quality provided.

There are many ways a service organization can determine when service recovery efforts are likely to be needed. For instance, one simple method is to provide customers with an opportunity to voice their dissatisfaction by providing customer response cards, or supplying a toll-free telephone line, e-mail address, or Web site. Such means make it easy for an unhappy customer to express a complaint. For example, Holiday Inn posts a toll-free number in its rooms for travelers to use if they wish to complain to company executives rather than to the hotel property. Many organizations, such as Scandinavian Airlines, routinely provide the Web site address of their central office to allow angry or happy customers to communicate their complaints or positive comments with ease.[5]

CUSTOMER SERVICE TECHNIQUES THAT SUPPORT THE RELATIONSHIP

Value Added

Jim Jewett, author of *Discovering Fast Track Success* and founder of Telco, an international telecommunications company, attributes much of his company's success to the ability of his salespeople to engage in value-added thinking. He defines this concept as "seeking out every possible opportunity to add customer value."[6] Recognizing value added is much easier than defining it. When you are in the position of the customer, you recognize value added when you receive it – and you remember it!

• A customer service representative for an audiovisual aids company was setting up a training seminar to show your sales force how to use her company's products in sales presentations. She stayed after the session to help one of your sales reps rehearse for a presentation that he was going to be making the next day.

• Salespeople from Caterpillar Tractor promise that their customers will receive ordered parts within forty-eight hours anywhere in the world. This after-sale service is very appealing and is very successful. The promise is not an idle one; if the delivery is not made within the forty-eight hours, the part is free.

- The air conditioner in your car goes out, and you take it in to the service department of the car agency to be repaired. They find they must order a part that will not arrive for two days. You mention to the service manager that you really need to get the car fixed before the weekend because you are planning a trip. Two days later when you take the car in to have the new part installed, the mechanic finds that the wrong part was shipped and they will have to reorder. The service manager asks you to wait for a minute and returns with a set of keys and says, "Here, we want you to use one of our demonstrators for the weekend. The new part will be here early Monday morning, and you can pick up your car by noon."

When an automobile service department repairs your car's air conditioner, that isn't service. It's what you paid them to do. When you are provided with a car while they wait for a replacement part, that is service—and you remember it. The delay in getting the part was not their fault, but they knew the delay was not your fault either. Their concern was helping you have a comfortable trip. One weekend's use of a demonstrator was a small price for the agency to pay for the kind of goodwill that will bring you back to purchase a new car next year.

EXHIBIT 14.2 - A Friend in Need

At 9:00 p.m. one Christmas Eve, customer service agent Rachel Dyer was working the ticket counter at Southwest Airlines when a man with a cane approached her. In a faint voice he told her that he had to go to New Orleans. It seems that his sister-in-law had dropped him off with some cash and a plastic bag full of clothes, and told him to go to New Orleans where he had some relatives. Confused and worried, the man explained that he'd also recently undergone bypass surgery.

Dyer responded by reassuring him that they would work everything out. She booked him on the earliest flight to New Orleans the next morning, got him a hotel and a meal ticket for dinner and breakfast, and tipped a World Services employee to take the man to the airport shuttle. Dyer bent down to explain his itinerary to him and told him everything would be okay. He told her, "Thank you," then bowed his head and started to cry.

In Southwest's monthly employee newsletter, Dyer wrote, "I am so proud to work for a company that not only allows but encourages me to help people who really are in need. I truly believe the success of this company has to do with the fact that it was founded and is run by kind, honest and loving people."[8]

Another way to consider the importance of customers' loyalty is to take a long-term view of their value. Instead of considering the customer's worth in terms of a single transaction, you should factor in all of the possible purchases over his lifetime. The automobile industry estimates that a brand-loyal customer represents a lifetime average revenue of $140,000 to the manufacturer. Carl Sewell estimates the lifetime value to his Cadillac dealership in Dallas of one satisfied buyer at well over $300,000. Home improvement retailer Home Depot determined its typical shopper's lifetime value to the store to be $25,000.[7] The professional salesperson has numerous opportunities for follow-up activities that determine whether particular customers will reorder as well as whether they will tell others of their satisfaction or provide referrals to other prospects. The consultative sale rep is sincerely and unselfishly helpful to clients and prospects alike. Sometimes value-added service costs nothing except thoughtfulness and a few minutes of time.

Herb Kelleher founded Southwest Airlines to set itself apart from other airlines. Since inception the company has been known for its low fares and attention to customer service. Southwest has maintained a high level of customer satisfaction not just because of its flights, but also because of its value-added service. Exhibit 14.2 shows how Southwest Airlines is adding value to its service and developing a loyal customer base.

Get More From Current Customers

Managers are increasingly telling their sales forces to get out of the office and start building personal relationships with their customers. As-vice president of sales and marketing for Phillips Inc., a midsize steel manufacturer in Boise, David Schumacher has instructed his salespeople to focus on solidifying their current customer base. Just a short time ago he was telling them to go after new business and try to shift purchasers to do e-commerce. Schumacher says, "Now I have to quickly reverse my course, because there aren't as many new customers out there. We have to do our best to nail down our short-and long-term revenues by getting closer to current customers."[9]

Sell current customers more of what you're already selling to them. Other departments may have a need. Sell them upgrades, enhancements, or additional products. Needs change over time. Sell your current clients something new. Keep them up-to-date on new products. Sell customers on you. Strive to become a trusted member of their team and opportunities will present themselves.[10]

Upgrading or Up-selling. Upgrading, also known as up-selling, is the process of persuading the customer to purchase a better-quality product or, perhaps, a newer product. Upgrading is largely a matter of selling your company and pushing the quality factors of your product and customer image. The salesperson asks for the upgrade because the newer or higher-quality product will serve the needs of the client better than the less expensive version of the same product. Most firms have products that vary in quality and price. And most buyers like to have choices when making a purchase. The only way you can succeed in upgrading is to believe one hundred percent in what you're doing, think ahead, service your clients, and create win-win relationships. This is what partnership selling is all about.

The cornerstone of selling – especially when trying to upgrade a client – relies on continuously qualifying the prospect throughout the buying process. It's ultimately the customer's choice and you don't want to oversell, but giving them options is just logical. You want to sell to the real needs of the prospect. Salespeople need to remember they don't sell products – they sell results. Sadler Evans, account executive for Comcast Cable Advertising of Huntsville, Alabama, says he is "more of a consultant instead of just a salesperson scrambling to make his monthly numbers."[11] Evans attempts to upgrade his clients to the point where he thinks the advertising schedule will work. One of his clients wanted to start out at $600 per month, but Evans was convinced that at least $750 was needed for the advertising to be effective. The client took his recommendation. It worked, and now the company is a really solid account, spending about $2,500 per month.

Cross-selling. Cross-selling is the process of selling products that are not directly connected to the primary products being sold to new and/or established clients. For example, cross-selling occurs when in a conversation with your bank's loan officer *about a loan* for expanding your business, you casually mention how expensive it is to keep your two elementary school children in a private school. Several days later, you receive a note in the mail from that same loan officer with materials describing how a *limited trust fund* could be used to help pay college expenses and *offering* the bank's services to help set it up.

Here is a second example that is a bit more complex: Jan Hildebrant and John McCarthy — business and development managers with the 3M company — wanted to go after the storage systems market. The two executives represent 15 different technologies and divisions within 3M that have applications in the hard drive industry. Jan and John successfully negotiated with IBM and sold them a variety of products and new process applications. Prior to setting up the strategic account, 3M was doing less than $1 million worth of business with IBM Storage, McCarthy says. But as result of the program, 3M's business with IBM Storage "went up by at least a factor of ten," he adds. It had a significant impact, and it was just the beginning of a sustainable relationship. It's not a one-time deal.[12]

Cross-selling and upgrading have become increasingly important to many companies in this information age. Customers have to be convinced that what you have available is going to solve a problem or save them money before they're even willing to talk. "To be truly customer-focused you have to make as many channels available as your customers are demanding," says Ann Vezina, vice-president of customer relationship management (CRM) at systems integrator EDS. To do the best job of fostering lifetime loyalty, you need to know exactly what your customers are thinking. The ideal scenario goes like this: When a customer contacts our customer service hotline via e-mail, chat, or telephone, the agents in our call center can call up a comprehensive record of every interaction, no matter how, why, or when. And the most profitable callers are identified and directed to the most knowledgeable agents right away. Our agents get a view of our customers that is so granular they can *cross-sell* and *up-sell* products to our customer base.[13]

Selling to Retailers

The distributor salesperson's ability to service clients has been greatly enhanced due to the introduction of portable computers. The mobility of these computers allows you to track, record, and process information on site. This is especially important in a situation where inventory turnover is high, and the tracking of any trends can provide valuable information to the company or the customer. Information technology will enhance much of the communication that goes on between the buyer and seller in terms of service after the sale.

Marketing middlemen who deal with retail chain organizations are going high-tech. Because of the increased focus on customer relationships, food brokers must know what their customers currently sell and the trends in various product and individual brand categories. In the past, a food broker's computer system was merely a piece of office equipment. Today, it is not just an adjunct to his business, but the heart of it. The ability to computer-scan consumer purchases has truly revolutionized the grocery industry with respect to market analysis.

Developing Partnerships Using Technology describes how sales automation has increased efficiency in customer service for the 45 merchandising technologists (sales reps) who represent over 100 manufacturers on behalf of the Volunteer-Miller Sales Company to grocery chains, school systems, and restaurants statewide.

Developing Partnerships Using Technology
The Largest Food Broker in Tennessee Has Gone High-Tech

Ken Miller

Volunteer-Miller Sales Company represents over 100 manufacturers such as Del Monte, Borden, Keebler, Stouffer, Smuckers, Solo Cup, Johnson & Johnson, Ocean Spray, and many others to grocery chains, school systems, and restaurants statewide. Each of its 45 sales reps (or merchandising technologists) are equipped with laptop computer technology. According to Ken Miller, executive vice-president, "When you literally represent products in every aisle of a grocery store, you welcome any opportunity to automate and disseminate information." Computerizing their calls virtually eliminates the need to write up customer call reports. Plus, the most current account, manufacturer, store, and product information is always in the software system where the rep can access it. All this helps the home office coordinate the total sales effort.

At one time all sales reps had to fill out call reports by hand and turn them into the home office. The staff took the information, wrote reports, and sent them to each manufacturer, noting call frequency, products discussed, actual sales, and so on. The old system was very labor-intensive. Now field-activated computer tracking systems allow sales reps to simply answer questions on the computers' screen, download onto a disk, or transmit via modem directly to the home office. The computer takes all the information and breaks it up into separate reports for each manufacturer represented by the company. Each client will receive current data on product movement, shelf position, retail pricing, sales by store, and much more. The rep with a handheld wand can scan item UPC codes and do a complete audit of the marketplace. Various shelf schematic software programs can also be given "what if" situations and will set up or reconfigure an entire section of products on a grocer's shelf. In addition, sales reps can receive new product information, appointments, and electronic mail via their laptops.

RETAIN OR WIN BACK UNHAPPY CUSTOMERS

A customer calls and launches into a tirade, complaining and whining about everything. Who needs an account like this? But then you stop, catch your breath, and think – "When clients are rude it's usually because they are having a problem with some aspect of our product or service." No matter how badly clients behave, avoid responding angrily. You must learn not to take their rudeness personally. Maintain a positive attitude and an even tone of voice. This serves to disarm them and they will generally follow your lead.

Restate the client's concerns (not objections) to demonstrate that you were listening. Employ empathy by putting yourself in their shoes and seeing it from *their perspective*. Remember that this customer is reacting to a real or perceived problem with your product or service that they feel has let them down. Thank the customer for bringing the issue to your attention and then recommend a plan to solve it while the client is still on the phone. Make sure your proposed solution meets with the customer's approval. Lastly, follow up with a personal visit to ensure the issue has been resolved and the client is completely satisfied. This tends to build a stronger relationship and greater loyalty with clients.[14]

Service in Response to Needs

Service must be offered promptly when a complaint or a problem surfaces. Some salespeople are quick to respond to a complaint from a new customer. They want to be sure to retain new customers and to establish themselves and the company with these customers. However, the same salespeople sometimes neglect complaints or problems reported by long-standing accounts. The attitude seems to be that the account has been around so long that it will always be there.[15] The customer has not complained before, they reason, so this complaint will probably go away by itself. Actually, the long-standing customer is far more valuable than a new one who may or may not be ready to make a long-term commitment. Satisfying a long-time client solidifies the credibility of salesperson and company; it produces new respect and loyalty; it has the potential of providing a number of new referrals because the customer experiences a new level of security and importance in the salesperson-customer relationship.

When you are practicing ongoing service, you can anticipate complaints and handle them promptly before they become serious sources of customer dissatisfaction. A customer who is dissatisfied with a product or service tells an estimated nine or ten other people. Always respond immediately to the possibility of a complaint or to one that is actually expressed. The salesperson who assumes that a customer must be satisfied because he has voiced no gripes over an extended period, is living in an unreal world. "Unless those dream customers called me to order goods or praise my products or service, I wouldn't let too much time go by without visiting them. Complaints can be customer-saving opportunities," says Ray Dreyfack.[16]

Technical Assistance Research Programs Inc. (TARP), based in Washington, D.C., conducted research among manufacturing concerns that produced overwhelming evidence of the value not only of "handling" complaints but also of going out of the way to encourage and then remedy complaints. TARP's key findings include these:

1. Of unhappy customers, only four percent complain to company headquarters. For every complaint received, the average company has twenty-six customers with problems, six of which are "serious," who do *not* complain.

2. Among customers with problems, complainers are more likely than noncomplainers to do business with the company again, even if the problem isn't satisfactorily resolved.

3. Between fifty-four and seventy percent of complainers will give repeat business if their complaint is resolved, but a staggering ninety-five percent are repeat customers if they feel the complaint was resolved quickly.

4. Dissatisfied complainants tell nine or ten people about their experience. Thirteen percent recount the incident to more than twenty people.

5. Customers who have their complaints satisfactorily resolved tell an average of five people about the treatment they received.[17]

Retaining Existing Customers

Service after the sale is critical to retaining existing customers, particularly in technical selling. In many technical sales, up to fifty percent of the sale involves the follow-through stage of the selling cycle. More technical sales are lost through inadequate follow-up than from any other cause. When so much time is invested in making a sale, attempting to save time by neglecting follow-up is a costly mistake.

All the efforts to retain customers is certainly not without benefits. Customer retention results from customer satisfaction. The average business loses about 20 percent of its customer base a year, forcing them to put money and effort into attracting new customers. It has been estimated that reducing customer defections by as little as five percent can double a firm's profits.[18] A bad buying experience can be a bitter and enduring memory. Exhibit 14.3 illustrates one company's effort to provide top-notch customer service in an effort to retain its customer base. There is no substitute for salespeople asking their customer base how they feel about the service the company is providing.

EXHIBIT 14.3- Getting Personal With Customers

In an attempt to improve customer relations, Cabot (a Boston-based manufacturer of industrial chemicals) trained its salespeople to conduct face-to-face meetings in which customers rated the level of service they received. The objective here was to create an ongoing interview process in order to teach the sales force how to stay constantly informed of customers' needs. During interviews, salespeople try to generate specific suggestions and criticisms from their customers. Once the interviews are completed, the company acts on any and all suggestions it can. Georgia Wilkinson, Cabot's director of distributor relations, states, "Clients have been very receptive on the whole...it impresses customers that you're taking the time to do this...they feel that we're more focused on what their specific needs are."[19]

Win Back Those Angry Customers

No one enjoys losing a customer. Winning back a customer who has turned to a competitor helps your feelings as well as your sales records. The first step in regaining a customer is to discover why you lost the account. Almost 80 percent of former customers leave because they feel they've been badly treated.[20] It is the salesperson and the company's responsibility to mend this relationship. Exhibit 14.4 gives some of the most common "excuses" given by salespeople for losing accounts. If you put aside such excuse-making, then some real delving into reality can show you why the account was lost.

You will probably have to talk with the customer face to face, ask some blunt questions, and refuse to accept "polite" answers. Ask some questions like these:

"Those who enter to buy support me. Those who come to flatter please me. Those who complain teach me how I may please others so that more will come. Those only hurt me who are displeased but do not complain. They refuse me permission to correct my errors and thus improve my service."

-Marshall Field

1. Did I act angry when you placed a small order or said you didn't need anything?

2. Did I stay away too long between calls and make you feel I don't care about your business?

3. Did I fail to keep you informed about products and applications of interest to you?

4. Did I fail to keep some of my commitments to you?

5. Was our maintenance or repair service slow or ineffective?

6. Can I help in any way to make doing business with you again possible?

EXHIBIT 14.4- "Excuses" Salespeople Give for Losing Accounts

It's not my fault I lost that customer ...

- If it isn't price, then it's because the competition uses unfair or unethical tactics.

- My company fails to back me up; delivery is late, or quality deteriorates.

- That customer is just too difficult for anyone to get along with.

- The customer never cares about anything but price, so I was helpless.

- I just don't have time to make all the service calls I'd like to make.

- There can't be anything wrong with my sales techniques. I'm doing exactly what I've been doing for years.

You will find other questions to ask that relate directly to the product or service you sell. Listen carefully to what the customer tells you in answer to each question. Do not contradict what the customer has told you, argue, or become angry yourself, no matter how angry or unreasonable the customer may seem to you. *Listen!* Sometimes a customer will be so upset about something that you will face a barrage of irate criticism. When faced with an angry customer, you have two choices. One, you can walk away and consider the account lost; or two, you can resolve the conflict and further reinforce the relationship.[21] If you listen politely, ask additional questions, and probe for hidden feelings, the mere act of telling you what is wrong often defuses the negative feelings of the customer. Then get top management involved. Even the executives need to listen and take some responsibility by being a part of the recovery. The former satisfaction experienced in doing business with you surfaces and the customer may be quite happy to consider reestablishing your relationship.

Your Customers Just Might Explode
If You Don't Let Them Blow Off Some Steam

Do your best to glean every bit of current information you can regarding this angry customer, along with what you know of your relationship with the customer in the past, in order to decide what went wrong. Here are some possible reasons that a salesperson might lose an account.[22]

1. *Something the salesperson does*
    No one is at top effectiveness all the time. Without intending to do so, you may have said or done something that offended the customer or damaged your credibility in some way. Exhibit 14.5 illustrates a sure-fire way to offend a customer and destroy a relationship. The old slogan for Arpege perfume began, "Promise her anything, but...." For the consultative salesperson, the "but" must be followed by "don't promise what you can't deliver."

EXHIBIT 14.5 - Destroying Credibility With The Customer

YOU WANT IT WHEN?

2. *Something the salesperson fails to do*
    Failing to tell the full story about what the product can or cannot do, failure to keep the customer informed about product or delivery changes, failure to meet promises, failing to follow up or waiting too long to follow up—all these omissions destroy the customer's faith in you, your product, and your company.

3. *Something the company does*
    If the company delivers only a portion of an order, substitutes some items in the order without telling the customer or makes errors in billing, the customer may become dissatisfied enough to change suppliers.

4. *Something the company fails to do*
    The company may fail to meet the promised delivery schedule without warning, fail to provide necessary training and technical backup as promised, or fail to meet maintenance agreements.

Take some time for problem solving. Discover the real problem. Until you discover and acknowledge the real problem, you cannot solve it. Sometimes the answer is unpleasant. If the problem lies in your actions or attitudes, you must accept responsibility so that you are free to solve the problem and regain the account. If you deny your obvious responsibility, you escape into excuse making and are blinded to the options available for regaining the customer's goodwill. When you know what the problem is, you can plan strategies for rebuilding the account.

SYSTEMATIC PLAN FOR FOLLOW-UP ACTIVITIES

Your tracking system for servicing should be as well-organized as your prospecting system. Set up a rotating tickler file by dates of expected contact for each account. Use a card file or computer program. The file method chosen should list the customer's name (company and individual with whom you deal), the date of each service contact, and the form it took (telephone call, letter, visit). If possible, indicate in a word or two what happened on the last service call: new order entered, scheduled delivery or reorder, cleared up billing error. Whatever organizing system you choose, be sure to have a *specific, written* plan for servicing. Your plan should include at least these five elements:

Staying Informed

The process of buying and selling does not end with the purchase—unless you intend for the current purchase to be the only possible transaction you will ever have with this customer or with anyone this customer can influence. Service is the marketing concept in action. Service is the activities you do to keep customers sold permanently. The sale is not complete until the customer is satisfied.

Frequent service calls on existing customers help the salesperson to keep up with personnel changes in the client's company. If you meet new personnel early, a relationship can be developed and your credibility established before you ask for a new order. Make sure you do not continue to send mail addressed to a buyer's predecessor. Keeping up with personnel changes not only helps you solidify your presence with the existing company client but also gives you an additional prospect in the company to which the former employee has moved.

You also learn about anticipated changes in the company structure when you make frequent service calls. Perhaps a merger or an acquisition is about to take place. Your customers may be planning to introduce a new product line that will increase their need for your product or service, or they may be expanding their whole general operation as a result of increased sales. All of these conditions affect you as a salesperson, but you will not hear of them while the information can help you unless you are there. It takes days, weeks, even months to get a customer. Regaining a lost customer after poor service will be much more expensive than keeping a current customer satisfied.[23]

GAINING A NEW CUSTOMER COSTS FIVE TIMES MORE THAN KEEPING A CURRENT ONE.

Phone Calls

The telephone is one of your best service tools. It allows you to give the customer personalized attention with less investment of time for both you and the customer than would be required by a personal visit. Customers respond positively to the fact that you are interested in them and how the product is meeting their needs, and they are also pleased that they did not need to spend half an hour in a personal visit with you. Here are some of the items of service you can handle through phone calls:

- Verify delivery
- Check for problems
- Inform the customer of price changes or possible shortages
- Check customer's inventory level

The telephone's usefulness is not limited to the salesperson's calls. You can encourage customers to call with questions, requests for information, complaints, and other needs. The research by TARP cited previously in this chapter indicated that consumer behavior in regard to complaints holds true for both industrial and retail sales. That is why Procter & Gamble prints a toll-free number on all of its products. Annually, they are the nation's largest producer of consumer products (Ivory soap, Folger's coffee, Crest toothpaste, Pampers disposable diapers, Tide detergent, etc.), and answer more than 750,000 telephone calls and letters from customers. One-third of these deal with complaints of various kinds: about products, ads, and even the plots of soap operas sponsored by the company.

A variety of communication devices. "Make it possible for your customers to reach a live person—even when you aren't available," advises Eric Harris, sales manager at Benefit Partners in Roseville, California. His job is to offer independent insurance agents or brokers and their customers access to a wide selection of health insurance plans. The brokers need fast, accurate information when they call, and for that reason Harris' phone does not have voice mail. Callers always talk to a live person at Benefit Partners. If their specific rep is not available, brokers talk to another member of the sales rep's team who can answer their questions.

The telephone isn't always enough. Use a variety of communication media to make sure you reach your customer and that your customer can reach you. When you secure a new client, learn the person's schedule, best times to call, e-mail address, fax number, cell phone number, other office telephone numbers, and even his home telephone number. Also consider using the postal service or Federal Express. You want to find out – Does the customer answer the phone himself? Is the voice mail always on? How long does the person take to return calls? Exhibit 14.6 illustrates the value of having the necessary information and the trust of your client.[24]

EXHIBIT 14.6 - Telephoning a Client on a Sunday Afternoon

Robert Lowcher, national account manager of Time Distribution Services, called a customer at home on a Sunday, and it paid off for both of them. Lowcher said, "When John F. Kennedy Jr.'s plane went down, most people were uncertain if he was dead." However, *Time* magazine assumed he had died and planned a memorial issue in his honor. The buyer he called usually ordered 5,000 copies for his stores, but that would not be nearly enough because this issue would be a big seller if indeed their assumption proved correct. Lowcher talked to his buyer on Sunday afternoon and told him about the special issue and that the deadline for ordering extra issues was that evening. The customer ordered 25,000 copies and sold 90 percent of them that next week. Lowcher says, "If I hadn't been looking out for my customer and built a relationship based on trust, both of us would have lost out."

Call Frequency

Decide how often you will call on each customer. Base this on your experience with each customer and with customers in general in your business. Consider account penetration (current and potential volume) and customer need. Rate your accounts as A, B, and C, much as you rate prospects, according to how much business you can expect to develop with each one and how many referrals that customer can generate for you that will produce business in addition to what that account provides. Also consider the personality and needs of the customer and determine what care is needed to maintain goodwill and a solid relationship. Decide also whether calls will be by telephone, in person, or a combination.

Mail (Letter or Card)

When your customer has no specific problems or need to reorder, keep your name before the customer with direct-mail items like these:

- New promotional material your company produces that will help the customer use the product more successfully
- Information about new products from your company that might interest your customer
- Your company house organ that includes trade information, promotional articles, and stories that might interest your customer (Be sure to write a few words of greeting.)
- A letter with a self-addressed business reply card on which the customer can check the level of satisfaction (excellent, good, fair, poor) with your product.[25]

Give close attention to the effectiveness of each type of service contact you offer to your customers or clients. Discard methods that do not work, and repeat methods that do. Keep your service records as meticulously as you do your data on prospecting. Know what you have done for each customer, what you plan to do next, and when.

Hallmark keeps in touch with their customers by regularly sending personalized cards. They developed a division called Hallmark Business Expressions that caters specifically to businesses and consulting services. The salespeople send welcome cards to new customers, as reminders of their purchase and to begin the relationship. Scott Robinette, director of business development for Hallmark Business Expressions, says, "We don't attempt to get a sale. When we send a card to a customer we do so with the intent of developing a relationship." In the future, the company plans to send cards to clients marking their "anniversary" as customers. Exhibit 14.7 illustrates how a thank-you card and a follow-up phone call pay off for a creative salesperson.[26]

EXHIBIT 14.7- A Prompt Thank-You and a Follow-Up Phone Call

Thank each client you visit promptly! This is what Julie Puckett, a sales rep with Home Buyer Publications in Fairfax, Virginia, does. And it is something worth emulating. Before Julie travels on business she addresses an envelope to each customer she plans to visit. After each appointment, and while the details are still fresh in her mind, she immediately creates a handwritten card thanking them for their time and expressing how much she enjoyed the meeting. The note is mailed that day in their city! By the time she returns home to make follow-up phone calls, the clients have received the "thank you" cards. Puckett says, "It's surprising how often my customers refer to my note and express appreciation for its timeliness." It doesn't surprise me! It may seem like a no-brainer, but it certainly is effective for her.

Problem Solving

The consultative salesperson is a problem solver. The first application of problem-solving skill comes in the sales process at the point of need discovery and application of the product or service to the need. However, the salesperson also solves problems after the purchase decision and after the product or service is delivered. The salesperson's problem-solving function operates in at least two areas.

Coordination Within the Salesperson's Company. The salesperson is responsible for coordination of all internal company services necessary to deliver the product and see that the customer is satisfied. Any question regarding technical capacity, payment terms, delivery dates, shipping methods, or user training is the salesperson's concern. Because your customers buy from you, they expect you to provide the help they need to make the product continue to satisfy their needs.

Assistance With Training. What you sell determines the amount of time and the type of expertise required in training the client's personnel to use the product or to sell it to their customers. When the product is technical, client training may require the assistance of your company trainer or engineer. The salesperson's role, then, becomes training coordinator—notifying the proper individual that the service is needed and scheduling training sessions as appropriate. Customer education is an integral part of the marketing strategy of Foxboro, a manufacturer and marketer of process-measurement and control equipment worldwide. In this highly competitive industry, the complex equipment is only as good as its operator. At Foxboro, the sale is a long-term relationship that begins when the client makes a commitment to buy. Because they want clients to stay sold, Foxboro spent $10 million dollars to build an educational facility that became the standard for the rest of the industry. Clients sometimes spend several months being trained at the Foxboro educational center adjacent to the company's headquarters in Foxboro, Massachusetts.[27]

SUMMARY

The importance of service is its effect in bringing you repeat business from the same customers over a long period of time. A buying decision is a one-time action unless it is turned into a habit by continued satisfaction after the sale.

Service after the sale adds value to the product or service you sell by demonstrating to the customer that someone is available to take care of problems, complaints, repairs, or installation. In many instances, the service after the sale is more important to the client than the product itself. It also gives you an opportunity to keep up with personnel and other company changes so you will know who to contact for reorders and what additional opportunities you have for supplying this customer because of company reorganization or other changes in size, marketing, or location.

Service is an ongoing activity. It is never too soon or too long after the sale to provide service. If you truly attempted to establish a relationship with the client in the initial sales interview, service after the sale is a natural process both for you and for the client. Customers' needs vary from simple questions that can be answered in a phone call to complex technical situations that need expert attention.

Routine telephone calls and mailings to customers as part of the marketing strategy should be planned, executed, and tracked for effectiveness. The type of product you sell, as well as the type of customer you service, dictates many of the specific means of giving service.

Service is the key to winning back lost accounts. No matter what causes the loss of an account, that loss is a signal for renewed service activity. Attempt to discover the reason the account was lost and do what you can to remedy any problem caused by you personally or by your company. Continue to contact the former client with sincere concern and interest.

Servicing may require different types of activities at different levels in the marketing channel. Firms involved in selling complex technological equipment often maintain educational establishments to train their customers' employees. If you are selling consumer goods to a retail store, you can expect to work with customers in their own stores, perhaps to suggest display designs or to help salespeople become familiar with the features and benefits of the product.

QUESTIONS FOR THOUGHT AND DISCUSSION

1. List ten elements of service after the sale and give a concrete example of each.

2. What is meant by *value added* in connection with selling? Can you give an example of a time when you experienced value added as a customer?

3. Think of a situation in which failing to keep up with personnel changes could cause loss of sales for a salesperson.

4. List some types of problems a customer might have that you, as a salesperson, could solve before they become serious by following a regular servicing program.

5. What is the salesperson's responsibility if a piece of machinery or equipment is installed and then is found to be defective or has some part missing?

6. Discuss the importance of service as an ongoing activity.

7. Explain how you would go about setting up a systematic plan for follow-up activities.

8. Describe some of the particular services that are beneficial to buyers for a retail business.

9. Is prospecting for new customers or servicing existing ones more important? Justify your answer.

10. Describe some specific servicing activities that could be used to win back a lost client.

ACTIVITIES

1. Contact the manager of a major grocery store chain. Find out what services salespeople perform in the store. For example, do they build product displays, check inventories, or suggest price changes? Ask the manager what these salespeople do well and how they could improve.

2. Interview the purchasing agent of a local hospital. Ask what kinds of servicing needs arise during the course of a year. Find out if the agent has ever changed to a different supplier because of a servicing problem. With what kinds of salespeople does the agent prefer to form long-term relationships?

Case Study

CASE 14.1

Marty Silva sells a line of industrial fans in a large metropolitan area. Because he doesn't travel long distances, he is in his office the first thing every morning to make calls to set up sales interviews and to prepare for the day's sales activity. One morning just as he walked into the office, the receptionist stopped him. "There's a Mr. Morton on the phone and he sounds angry. Will you take the call?"

"Sure," Marty agreed, "he's my customer." Picking up the phone, he said, "Good morning, Mr. Morton. What can I do for you?"

"You can tell me how I'm supposed to install that circulating fan you sold me without mounting brackets. What kind of slipshod operation ships a thing like this without brackets?"

Marty was confident that the fan couldn't have been shipped without brackets, but he wisely didn't tell the customer his thoughts. "I certainly can't blame you for being upset, Mr. Morton. I'll check with our shipping department right now and I'll be in to see you this afternoon."

"Well, okay." The customer sounded a little less angry. "But maintenance had scheduled the installation for today. They're so busy that I'll probably have to wait awhile to get on their list again. I still think it was stupid on someone's part. Do what you can, Silva. Come in anytime you can get here today."

After hanging up, Marty looked at his appointment schedule. At 2:00 he was supposed to be in Westdale, all the way on the other side of the city. He didn't see how he could get to Morton's shop before closing time. He decided to check with shipping right away, though. The traffic manager, Carl Todd, suggested looking at the receiving slip. Sure enough, Morton's receiving clerk had checked off the items—including *brackets, mounting* (2)—and signed the receiving slip. "They must have lost them over there," Carl suggested. "Tell them to look around."

1. Marty now has proof that the brackets were delivered. Should he call the customer and tell him that his own operation is stupid and slipshod? Should he call and politely ask the customer to have his receiving people give another look for the brackets?

2. Does he have other options to consider?

3. Should he keep his promise to put in an appearance at Morton's shop today? What about his other appointment?

CASE 14.2

Sometimes salespeople who have built a good volume of business and a sound relationship with a customer forget to be as energetic in sustaining that business relationship as they were to establish it in the first place. Ron Beebe, who sells industrial safety equipment, tells about how he learned an important lesson.

"I suppose it's natural to gradually become complacent with a good customer and, as a result, lose a lot of good business you could have had by staying on the ball. I remember when I sold my first order of safety glasses to a large manufacturer I had been calling on for months. I followed that order through the factory, checking all along the line to be sure the customer got what was specified. As soon as the first batch was delivered, I made a special trip to the plant to be sure the order was right. Soon I was selling them hard hats, safety shoes, and ear protectors. Before long I was no longer giving such close attention to their orders. I just assumed everything was going fine. Even when I got a complaint, it seemed routine to me. But one day I learned a real lesson about keeping buyers informed.

"I had been selling ear protectors to this customer for two or three years. In the meantime, our company developed a new model that is adjustable to fit any shape or size of head. It can also be worn with various types of safety hats without discomfort. But as long as this buyer seemed satisfied with the old model, I figured I wouldn't rock the boat by showing him anything new. But my complacency backfired. One day I mentioned that they must be low on ear protectors since they hadn't ordered any for some time. That's when I got the big shock. He told me they were buying from another supplier whose product was adjustable and fit under safety hats. This cut the number of ear protectors they had to keep in inventory and solved the comfort problem when protectors had to be worn with hard hats.

"I guess I blew this one,' I admitted. 'We've had a model like that available for over a year. I didn't know you wanted to change styles,' I finished lamely.

"How could I know I wanted to change if I didn't know the model existed? We are always looking for better protective devices. And another thing, you haven't given me a new catalog for ages. Just because we've done a lot of business together doesn't mean we're married to you,' he told me in no uncertain terms. Now my problem was not only to regain the ear protector business, but to be sure I kept the business for other items, too. I won't ever forget that painful lesson!"

1. What suggestions can you give Ron about regaining the ear protector business ?

2. How should Ron apply this lesson to his overall selling strategy?

Time Saving Tips

To keep staff meetings short, I always try to sandwich them between two scheduled appointments.

Dan McNamee, president
McNamee Consulting Company

Simplify expense reports by keeping an envelope in your pocket. Write the date, city, and names of customers to be visited on the flap; note expenditures on the envelope; then put each day's receipts inside.

Merrill Douglas, chairman
Time Management Center, Inc.

I look for the kind of guy who says, "Forget that, it'll take ten years. Here's what we gotta do now."

Lee Iacocca
from "Iacocca: An Autobiography"

Be sure to handle each piece of paper only once.

Alan Lakein, author of
"How to Get Control of
Your Time and Your Life"

Put a dollar value on what you have to do; if it doesn't add up in dollars and cents, don't do it.

Edward J. Feeney, consultant
Edward J. Feeney Associates

Yesterday is a canceled check: forget it. Tomorrow is a promissory note: don't count on it. Today is ready cash: use it!

Edwin C. Bliss
from "Doing It Now"

CHAPTER 15

Time, Territory, and Personal Management

DEVELOPING A TIME MANAGEMENT ATTITUDE

Time is perhaps the most precious commodity. Although a continuous supply of time is available, it cannot be stored for future use, and it cannot be reclaimed if it is wasted. When you realize that life itself consists of time, the value of time becomes clear. We loudly denounce attitudes or practices that show a lack of respect for human life, but we seem not to notice when we throw away priceless hours—the fabric of life—in useless activity or idleness. How to manage time effectively has always been a problem for professional salespeople, but you can learn how to use this precious commodity for both profit and pleasure. There are more than one hundred new books and time management systems on the market, each offering a unique take on this topic.[1] Begin your program of managing time by asking yourself a question posed by Alan Lakein in his book *How to Get Control of Your Time and Your Life:* "What is the best use of my time right now?"

The term *time management* is a misnomer. Because *every* minute has sixty seconds and *every* hour has sixty minutes, time itself cannot be managed. It can only be used. What *can* be managed, however, are you and your activities. Time management, then, is actually personal organization as well as self-management. It involves three areas:

- self-management (self-discipline)

- planning and organizing

- systems and techniques to automate routine

Use your time instead of simply spending it. Time is made up of a series of events. The key to managing time is controlling these events to your advantage.[2] Time control and self-management can be learned. You have the ability to control your present thoughts and actions and to decide how to use your time. Benjamin Franklin said, "Dost thou love life? Then do not squander time; for that's the stuff life is made of."

Get a firm grip on the reality of the worth of time. Pretend that the president of your bank informs you that you have been chosen to receive a special prize: Every day for the rest of your life $86,400 will be deposited into your account. The only stipulation is that it must all be spent every day. Anything left at the end of the business day goes back to the bank. You can't hold anything over from one day to the next. Those first weeks are exhilarating. By the end of the first month, you have received over $2 million. After a while, however, you begin to have trouble spending that much

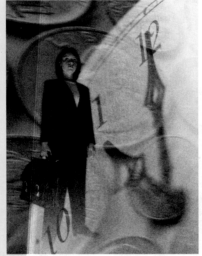

Manage your time as you would manage your money.

every day. Think how you would feel the first time $20,000 slipped away from you and went back to the bank because you failed to spend it all. You would quickly realize that using this much money every day calls for some serious planning.

This imaginary scenario is not entirely fantasy. The old adage is true: Time is money. Every day 86,400 seconds are deposited in your account and in that of everyone else. You cannot save any unused time for another day. How many—or how few—of your 86,400 seconds go back to the "bank" unused depends on your skill in planning and managing your time. The important questions are these:

1. How will you spend your time?

2. How will you invest your time?

3. How much time will go to business, to service for others, to family, to leisure?

4. How much time will be reserved just for yourself—for the things you want to do?

Your most important asset is time, and how you use it is crucial to your success. Noted speaker Ira Hayes says,

"The inability or lack of desire to become organized is responsible for the vast majority of failures. It is why otherwise bright people turn out to be only mediocre performers and achieve only a small degree of the success that they rightfully could achieve. A disorganized work plan or way of life leads to rushing around and confusion and generally results in a poor attitude which makes people around you question the advisability of doing business with you."

Nearly everybody has the *ability* to manage time. The *desire* is the variable that makes the difference, and taking charge of your life depends on your personal choice.

Nearly everything that we think, say or do is governed by patterns of behavior that we have developed over the years. We develop most of them early in life and rarely change them. The only way to lose a habit is to stop practicing it. Stop practicing negative habits and start practicing positive ones and your life will improve automatically.[3] Behaviorists tell us that over ninety percent of the results achieved in life come from the exercise of habit patterns. If you want to achieve good results in professional sales, establish good habit patterns. In sales, more than in many other professions, the management of time is a matter of personal choice and responsibility. Here's an idea for you to try: get to work by 5 a.m. three times a week, and you'll gain an extra day. You will realize a great feeling of satisfaction at 8 a.m. when you've already finished what would have taken you six hours to do after 8 a.m. because of the interruptions.[4]

Betty Levstik discusses her penchant for managing time

Success in sales? What about running a family business? What about managing a family at the same time? Betty Levstik can show you how! Betty and her husband, John, are in a family-run business. They wanted to find a business they could enjoy together. They decided on a T-SHIRTS PLUS franchise. They now sell T-shirts and sports wear in a large, regional shopping mall near Chicago. As a testimony to their success, 36 stores have opened and closed in the same mall since they opened theirs.

What makes this husband-and-wife team successful? *Hard* work of course, but they really work *smart*. Betty's affinity for management of time and resources is evident in her role as a small business owner. The large master planning calendar she uses is one indication of how her use of time management techniques pays off. She schedules everyone in two-week blocks. Betty allows employees off on the days they request. This flextime approach helps them with their own management of time. In the years she has used this scheduling method, only two people have missed work. In addition to Betty and John, the business has a full-time assistant manager and depending on the time of year anywhere from 4 to 12 part-time employees.

Betty and John each have specific responsibilities. This division of labor makes them a very efficient team. Betty takes care of the merchandising, display and promotional efforts. Her husband does all the ordering of inventory and supplies and takes care of the record keeping to ensure all bills are paid on time. John works at home on Monday so he will not be disturbed as he does the ordering.

Betty schedules it so one of them is at home in the evening to be with Sarah, their youngest daughter. They also schedule two nights a week when both are home together. When both of them are away from the store, Betty leaves a *list* of special assignments to be accomplished when employees are not waiting on customers. Betty knows from experience that employees will not automatically think about what else they could he doing. There is always something that needs to be done. Betty's *list* is a gentle reminder.

Attitudes Toward Time

Mental preparation is necessary to win the race against time. Developing a time management attitude helps to overcome life's obstacles. Just as Olympic champions practice diligently and relentlessly to perfect their athletic techniques, you can practice time management techniques and maximize the benefits to be enjoyed from both professional and personal pursuits.

You can let the whole subject of time management assume such proportions that the mere thought of attempting to master it becomes frustrating. You might even feel trapped and manipulated by the demands others make on your time. When you feel time pressures and believe you are working to your full capacity, you would probably be surprised to learn that a significant portion of each day is being wasted. According to William E. Edwards, the typical salesperson spends an average of only two hours a day in productive selling. However, just increasing the time spent with a customer doesn't do very much for you, it's what you do with the time that's important. As a salesperson focus your time so that it matches opportunity. Perhaps it is a better strategy to target five large accounts, rather than target 50 accounts and divide your time trying to get each one of them. You don't have enough time or enough protection, and competitors swoop in and take them away.[5]

Keep a positive perspective toward time and your use of it. Here are some suggestions for establishing the kind of time attitudes that will bring you success:

1. Make a list of the activities you want to complete during the next week to achieve the results you desire.

2. For an entire week, keep an hour-by-hour record of exactly what you do with your time. Summarize your record and compare what you actually do to the list you made of what you want to do to achieve your goals. (Exhibit 15.1 illustrates a form you can draw to use for this purpose.)

3. At the end of each day and at the end of each week, take a personal accounting of what you have accomplished compared to what you set out to do.

4. List the five habits or attitudes that were the biggest obstacles to the achievement of the results you wanted. Write out a plan for changing these habits or attitudes. Conduct another time analysis study three months from now and compare the two. Determine whether you are making progress in replacing these habits or attitudes with new ones.

EXHIBIT 15.1

Record time every hour or more frequently to ensure an accurate record. Keep the record for an entire week. Activities listed are typical for salespeople.

DAILY TIME SUMMARY

Time \ Activity	Prospecting	Telephone for Appointments	Sales Interviews	Travel	Reports and Paper work	Meetings	Sales Training	Servicing Accounts	Preparing for Interviews	Studying Product Info.		
6 a.m.												
7 a.m.												
8 a.m.												
9 a.m.												
10 a.m.												
11 a.m.												
12 noon												
1 p.m.												
2 p.m.												
3 p.m.												
4 p.m.												
5 p.m.												
6 p.m.												
7 p.m.												
8 p.m.												
9 p.m.												
10 p.m.												
Total												

Conducting a detailed personal time-analysis study at least twice a year is a good habit to establish. Just as you schedule a regular medical checkup, plan for a time management checkup to keep you aware of how well you are using your time resources.

PROCEDURE FOR GETTING ORGANIZED

Before you can gain any measure of control over your time, you must address your need for laying the groundwork to handle the onslaught of information you encounter every day. Several techniques can help you.

Remove the Clutter

Removing clutter allows you to think more clearly and creatively.

You can think more clearly and more creatively if you remove as much clutter as possible from your life and your living space. Remove unnecessary papers from your work area—your desk, your attaché case, your car. Even if the stacks of paper are neat and appear to be well organized, they promote a subconscious psychological tendency to review and think through the items in sight. In a very few seconds you can think through all of the tasks or incompletions that are represented by a sizable stack of paper. For all practical purposes, however, your mind does not differentiate between doing a task physically and doing it mentally. If you mentally review a big stack of paper a dozen times a day in the process of deciding which one to tackle next (or which one to avoid), you are exhausted long before the day is over.

Once you decide to dispense with clutter, tackle the job at once. Follow this plan:

1. **Collect the Clutter.** Gather up all the clutter that affects you and take it to one convenient work area. Empty your car, bedside table, pockets, and any other cubbyhole where you stick things that are waiting to be done. Dump all the clutter into one container. Hopefully, you won't need a dump truck.

2. **Sort the Clutter.** Divide the clutter into two categories: time-critical material (that is, items with a specific due date) and "someday" material (that is, items that need to be addressed but have no specific due date).

3. **Deal With Priorities.** Deal first with the time-critical items. Provide a series of thirty-one folders to represent the days of the month. (This is commonly called a *1-31 file.*) A computer master calendar is just as handy and can quickly retrieve each day's notes or retrieve items by subject. You may still need the 1-31 file to collect reports, memos, and other written items. Examine each of the items you have identified as time critical. If it involves a meeting or a specific hour of the day, write it on your calendar. Then put each item in the folder for the day that the first action must be taken to meet the due date. Each day check the appropriate folder as you make your daily to do list. Then each item will be accomplished on time.

4. **Set Up Working Categories for the Rest.** Now begin to organize the someday material. Set up two convenient files—the stacked "in-out file boxes" are handy. Label these files *reading* and *projects*. Go through your

someday items and sort them in the two files according to their nature. Pull out a reading item to take along when you are going somewhere that might involve a wait, and then use waiting time to catch up on reading. The material in the projects box may then be sorted into folders for each separate project.

Handle Interruptions

To handle them properly, you must first determine whether an occurrence is truly an interruption or part of your job. Only when you understand this difference are you able to control your attitude toward the people and the circumstances that threaten to get in your way as you are doing your job. Once you determine that an interruption is part of your job, decide whether it is more important than what you are currently doing or whether it should be postponed. This determination helps you keep your priorities straight and reduces procrastination.[6]

Interruptions typically fall into three categories, each of which you can handle with the right attitude. Table 15.1 lists the types of interruptions that most people experience.

TABLE 15.1 - Types of Interruptions

People	Paper	Environmental Factors
Superior	Notes	Telephone calls
Associate	Memos	Visual distractions
Subordinate	Correspondence	Comfort factors (e.g., temperature, light, clothing)
Client or customer	Periodicals	
	Messages	
	Projects	

People Interruptions. People interruptions are the most frustrating because they are the most difficult to solve. A piece of paper can be stuffed into a file or crumpled up and thrown into the wastebasket, but people represent relationships. They must be treated with the respect that preserves the relationship and recognizes the worth of the individual. Who the person is makes a difference in the way you respond. If you are interrupted by your superior, remember that that person probably has the right to interrupt you. If you are working on an item of extreme importance with a tight deadline or are due to leave for an appointment with a prospect, however, you can properly ask respectfully whether your superior might wait until your project or call is completed. As your work is presumably important to the success of the organization, and therefore to your superior as well, most bosses consider such a request to be a mark of both effectiveness and self-confidence on your part.

When a client interrupts you either by phone or in person, adopt the attitude that this contact is not an interruption. It is an opportunity. Clients make your job possible. You are there to serve them. You do not automatically put your full day at the disposal of a client's whim, but you do give full attention while the client is talking and then do whatever is necessary to take care of the situation.

Paper Interruptions.   People who work in a disorganized environment experience both confusion and frustration when confronted with necessary paperwork.   They feel confused because they have no automatic method for handling the item; they spend too long thinking about how to handle it.   Then, because they dislike feeling confused, they become frustrated with the repeated inroads made on their time by additional paperwork.   Before very long, disorganized people decide they just hate all paperwork.   Salespeople are often among those who say they hate paperwork because they realize that it is less important in producing their income than their direct selling activities. Howard Langejans, vice-president of Orion Research, equips all salespeople with laptop computers.   Using this equipment, they enter orders and call reports directly into the computer by phone from wherever they might be. They can also access the computer to find new leads that may have come in. The only paperwork left is the expense report, and Langejans adds, "Salespeople don't mind that kind of paperwork because it brings them money."[7]

Environmental Interruptions.   Salespeople usually work best by scheduling a specific telephone time each day to set up appointments for sales presentations and take care of other sales-related business. Then the remainder of the day is free for those vital selling contacts.   When you have a particularly important piece of work to complete, take everything you need to do the job and go to a place where you can work without any kind of interruption.   Cyndi Schrader, account development manager for Herman Miller, an office manufacturer, is in her car about 50 percent of the work week.   While in her car, she uses her laptop to answer email, check her schedule, and compose letters.   Schrader uses her cell phone to check and respond to voice mails, carries on phone conversations, and listens to books on tape as she travels.   There is also a mapping software program installed to save her time when traveling in a new territory.   Schrader certainly uses her "concentration hideaway" creatively.   It has had a dramatic impact on her personal productivity.[8]

AN ORGANIZING SYSTEM

Once you remove the clutter and the incompletions from your work area and get a firm grip on controlling interruptions, two simple tools will help you organize your activities.

The Master Calendar

Many salespeople prefer a pocket-sized book that is always available to note an appointment.   Whatever its size, the calendar should list only specific time commitments such as appointments with clients and meetings to attend. All the information needed for those specific commitments is collected in the 1-31 file folders or recorded on the computer master calendar until it is needed for the appointment or other commitment.

Daily To-Do List

The second time-organizational tool you will need is a daily to-do list.   Be sure to prioritize each item on your list.   Highlight those activities completed, and carry forward the uncompleted items.[9]   A familiar story about Charles

Schwab, former president of Bethlehem Steel, confirms the real impact of this simple tool. Schwab called in consultant Ivy Lee and proposed, "Show me a way to get more done with my time, and I'll pay you any fee within reason."

"Fine," said Lee, "I'll give you something in twenty minutes that will increase your output at least fifty percent." Lee then handed Schwab a blank sheet of paper and said, "Write down the six most important tasks that you have to do tomorrow and number them in order of their importance. Now put this paper in your pocket, and the first thing tomorrow morning look at item one. Work on it until you finish it. Then do item two, and so on. Do this until quitting time. Don't be concerned if you have finished only one or two. You'll be working on the most important items. If you can't finish them all by this method, you couldn't have finished them by any other method either; and without some system, you'd probably not even decide which was the most important."

Lee continued, "Use this system every working day. After you've convinced yourself of the value of the system, have your men try it. Try it as long as you wish and then send me a check for what you think it's worth." Several weeks later, Lee received Schwab's check for $10,000—a much more impressive sum around the turn of the 20th century than it sounds now.

Simple to-do lists become more valuable when they are prioritized.

Remember you can't alter time. The trick to managing your time is to manage not your time, but your activities. Keep a daily to-do list of what needs to be accomplished and use the list to make sure your moving the sale forward.[10] The value of a to-do list is apparent, but it becomes even more valuable when you use it not only to identify needed tasks but to establish priorities for them. Putting top priorities first is the only way to be sure that your activities are making a direct impact on your goals. Sales success depends on establishing and steadfastly pursuing a series of goals. A salesperson with specific and measurable *growth goals* is an individual with the determination and drive it takes to succeed.[11] Charles A. Coonradt, president of Western Leadership Group, says, "In the absence of clearly defined goals, we are forced to concentrate on activity and ultimately become enslaved by it." Using a to-do list helps you develop the automatic habit of attaching a *when* to every thought, idea, commitment, or promise. Your co-workers, your boss, and your clients soon become aware that when you promise to send a report, to return a call, or to deliver an order you will do as you promised. Your credibility soars. Figure 15.1 is an example of a format you can use for your to-do list. If you are using a computerized master calendar, you can print out your daily to-do list. The form is not nearly as important as the practice!

The Integrated System

The 1-31 reminder file, the master calendar, and the to-do list together constitute a place your mind can trust and a place where you can store all the reminders that must surface at a given time in the future. You can safely forget about incompletions until they surface in your system. Together these organizing tools form a system that makes organization of your daily activities an automatic process. At the close of each day's work, transfer any left-over items from today's to-do list to the new list for tomorrow. Then consult your 1-31 file and your master calendar to find all the items you have scheduled for tomorrow. Note any specific times associated with those items, such as the time for an appointment or meeting. Now you are ready to begin work tomorrow without even thinking about what to do first. You are ready to begin your day with the task of highest importance.[12]

FIGURE 15.1

A To-do List with a
Daily Plan to List
Appointments

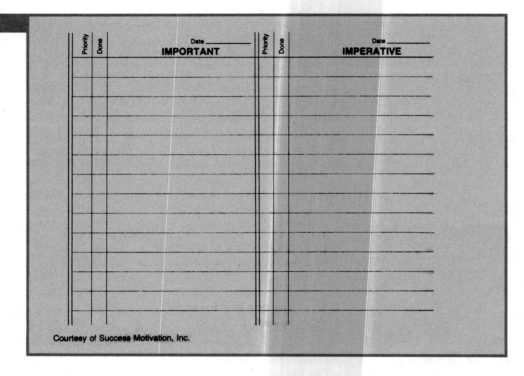

Courtesy of Success Motivation, Inc.

Identifying Priorities

An important concept for good time managers to understand is the Pareto principle. It states that 80 percent of the value (or the frustration) of any group of related items is generally concentrated in only 20 percent of them. The principle, named for the Italian economist who proposed it, holds true for many areas of today's experience. For example:

In Measuring Value, You Receive:

80% Of	Comes From 20% of
Sales	Customers
Productivity	Activity
Profit	Products
Referrals	Clients
Commisson Income	Orders

In Measuring Frustration, You Experience

80% Of	Comes From 20% of
Absenteeism	Employees
Errors	Workers
Servicing Problems	Customers

Likewise, 80 percent of your success comes through the achievement of the top 20 percent of your goals. In managing your time effectively, you must recognize that *which* items you complete, not *how* many items you complete, determine your success.[13]

To identify the special 20 percent of your activities that have the potential for producing the greatest success, practice establishing different categories of priorities. **"A" priorities** are the most pressing. They include the items that must be done by a specific date if you are to reach one of your major goals and items that would damage the reputation of your company or your personal credibility if you failed to accomplish them. A **"B" priority** item is any item that can be done at any time within the next week or month without causing any repercussions. A few items may be assigned **"C" priority**; they would be nice to do at some time when you have nothing else pressing to do, but you would suffer no real loss if you never got around to them. Obviously, you want to give first attention to your **"A" priorities** and carefully number them in the order of their importance. Your goal is to complete as many **"A" priorities** as you possibly can each day and then supplement them with any "B" items you can.[14]

Time Goals

Once you have established the habit of using a to-do list, begin to record next to each item your estimate of the amount of time you will need to complete it. Estimating the required time lets you judge whether you can complete everything. If you can't, you have the possibility of getting someone else to help before you fail to complete some vital item. Jeff DeRoux, manager for the SanMar Corporation, encourages his salespeople to delegate those things that they simply can't take care of because of workload. Selling is a cooperative effort, and the salespeople at SanMar are all geared to work together.[15] A second benefit of estimating completion times is to help in avoiding procrastination. A deadline – even an informal estimate of the time required – pushes you to complete the work in the allotted time. Northcote Parkinson is noted for his observation that *work expands to fill the time allowed for its completion.* Something about a stated time allotment seems to establish a mental set that causes you to use just that amount of time. If the time is short, you work efficiently and push for completion. If the time allowance is too generous, you procrastinate, spend extra time getting ready to work, and find a dozen small interruptions to make sure you don't finish too early. This behavior sounds foolish, but unfortunately an overly generous time allotment convinces your subconscious mind that you must fill that time, and you do just that.

Time studies have shown that even people who know which items are most important and set priorities still waste an average of fifteen minutes between items of work in simple procrastination or in trying to decide what to do next. When you make your daily to-do list and establish priorities, you then should logically add a sequence for each event. You may have three sales interviews scheduled for Monday, and these are your most important priorities. If they are scheduled for 10 a.m., 2 p.m., and 4 p.m., however, you cannot afford to sit around drinking coffee until 10 a.m. Your **"A" priorities** should be scheduled in a logical time sequence. You may want to use an hour earlier that same morning for making telephone calls to schedule sales interviews for the rest of the week. Your to-do list, along with setting priorities and sequencing the items on the list, should be done at the end of each working day. Alvin Perez, sales executive with Total Graphics in Norwalk, Connecticut, says, "It is important to spend an hour at the end of each day planning ahead for tomorrow."[16] Once the workday is in full swing, interruptions arise and circumstances begin to do your planning for you.

MAINTAINING A POSITIVE ATTITUDE TOWARD TIME

Anyone who expects sales success should also expect hard work and long hours. If you always seem to have more work than working hours, though, you may be due for a refresher course in time management. These techniques can't give you more time, but they can help you make the most of what you've got. Follow them to help you get—and keep—time on your side.

Set Deadlines—and Beat Them. When you've got a lot to do and not a lot of time to do it in, deadlines can help you to stay on schedule. Prioritize your tasks, then draw up a schedule for completing them. Think about what kinds of interruptions you can expect and how to prevent or limit them. Instead of trying to finish a task at the time of a deadline, make a game of trying to finish early. Don't make the mistake of waiting to start on a task just because the deadline seems far away. Chances are, something will come up to fill the extra time you think you have.

Place a Time Limit on Meetings. If you or your salespeople tend to dread meetings, maybe it's because they drag on too much and accomplish too little. Knowing your meeting lasts only an hour should help keep things moving. Before each meeting, decide on a limited number of topics to discuss and a limited time period for discussing them. Make sure you and all other attendees are well-prepared with any information you need or questions you'd like to ask. Start meetings on time and have latecomers ask their colleagues what they missed.

Take advantage of your peak time to be most efficient.

Take Advantage of Your Peak Time. To be most efficient at the jobs you like least, tackle them at the time of day when you feel most productive. Just as some of us are "morning people" and others are "night owls," not everyone hits their peak at the same time of day. Pay attention to your moods and work output throughout the day to find out when you're most productive, and save your worst jobs for when you're at your best.

Learn to Say "No". When it comes to time management, many of us are our own worst enemy. You'll never have enough time to finish your work if you're always biting off more than you can chew. Before you agree to take on someone else's responsibilities, make sure you have plenty of time for them. Ask what the person expects you to do and by when. Don't be afraid to politely refuse if your plate's already full. When people ask you to take on extra projects, they are *putting a monkey on your back*. If you agree to take on too many jobs for others, you are soon carrying an impossible load of monkeys and accomplish nothing.

Make Up Your Mind. When you have a choice to make, let the time you take to decide reflect the importance of the decision: Don't waste 30 minutes figuring out where to hold your next weekly sales meeting. To make important decisions promptly and wisely, know the pros and cons of each choice, then weigh all your options carefully. Accept the fact that decision making involves risk, and forgive yourself when you make a bad one.

Don't Overload on Overtime. If your work week consistently exceeds a reasonable number of hours, ask yourself why. Identify the tasks that take up the most time and look for ways to complete them more efficiently. Also, compare the number of hours you're working to what you're actually getting done. A too-small return on your time investment indicates a problem. Measure how long it takes you to do a time-consuming task (i.e., making 20 prospecting calls), then ask your co-workers how long it takes them. If they're consistently faster, compare your working methods with theirs for ideas on streamlining yours.

Decide to Delegate. Don't feel guilty about delegating responsibility—if you take on a job that someone else could handle more effectively, you're not making the best use of your company's resources. Ask yourself how the task compares in importance to what you'd be doing if you chose to give it to someone else. Or compare how long it would take you to complete with how long it would take someone else.

Put It in Writing. To remember phone numbers, important dates or anything else, write them down. Freeing your mind of clutter helps you think more clearly, and concentration is key to productivity. Carry a notepad and pencil with you so you can jot down ideas whenever you think of them. Keep a card or computer file of ideas from speeches, books, conversations or other sources.

Time is like talent—you can't create more of it, you just have to make the most of what you've got. You need self-discipline from the time you wake up in the morning until you go to bed that night.[17] Spending your time more wisely starts with paying attention to how you spend it. Once you decide to take control of your time, you'll have the power to stop squandering it.[18]

PLANNING TELEPHONE TIME

The telephone can become an ally if you use it to save time. Few salespeople can operate effectively without using the telephone to set up appointments for sales presentations. Unless an appointment is made ahead of time, precious hours are wasted traveling to prospects' offices only to find that they are not in or cannot be disturbed. Use the telephone not only to set up appointments but also to confirm them on the morning of the day the interview is scheduled. You can save a trip when a prospect has been called away on an emergency and was not able to contact you before leaving. Your call reminds the prospect of the appointment; not everyone is as well organized as you are, and your prospect may have failed to make a note of your coming. Confirming appointments is perceived as a professional technique and adds to your credibility.

Planning phone calls allows time to be used more productively.

Controlling Telephone Time

Once you designate a specific time period to use for telephone calls, your next concern is to see that the time is used profitably.[19] Three tactics will help you: get organized before you begin, set a time limit for completing your calls, and set a time limit for a group of calls.

Get Organized to Make Calls. Make a list of the people you plan to call. Below each name, list the topics to be covered in the order you wish to discuss them. Have any necessary reference material at hand. If you are calling prospects, have your prospect records at hand so you can see all information you have about the prospect. Add new facts you pick up during the call. Open your contact management calendar so you can check your schedule as you set up appointments or make other commitments in the course of your calling. If you make some of your calls to others in your company with whom you work closely, let one of the items on your list be to ask if they have some item they want to cover with you before you hang up. This practice saves answering later calls from these people.

Limit the Time for Making Calls. Time limits involve both planning and control. When you plan the content of each call before beginning, you do not spend time thinking about what else you want to say. Although a reasonable amount of friendly social exchange is necessary to establish a feeling of comfort between two people, minimize your small talk. If you feel uncomfortable when you try this, begin your conversations by saying, "I know you are busy, so I promise to keep this brief." This preface acknowledges the importance of the other person's time and is seen as a bigger compliment than social small talk.

Set a Time Goal for Your Calls. Another tactic for cutting telephone time is to set a time goal for a group of calls. Place a clock or your watch in sight and pace yourself as you call. In telephoning as in any other work activity, work expands to fill the time available. If you allow an hour for making ten telephone calls, you are likely to spend the entire hour. If you set a goal to complete the calls in forty minutes, your sense of urgency keeps you moving and you finish in the time you allotted. Table 15.2 summarizes seven tips for saving time on the telephone.

TABLE 15.2 - Techniques for Terrific Telephone Time

Time waster	Technique for elimination
Socializing	Save socializing for social occasions. Stick to your priorities. Distinguish between your desire for business availability and social availability.
Lack of awareness of time spent	Keep a time log of your calls and evaluate their contribution to profitability. Find a substitute for the types of calls that waste time.
Easy availability	Set up a quiet hour when you can work undisturbed. Set a time to make and take calls.
Facts not available	When you must look up facts for a caller, call back. Don't keep a caller hanging while you look. And don't be left hanging. If those you call need to look up facts for you, ask them to call back with the answers.
Fear of offending	Remember your priorities. Remember, also, that the other person may be as eager as you to end the conversation but doesn't know how to conclude it.
Lack of self-discipline	Practice makes perfect. Don't become someone else's time problem.

MANAGING TRAVEL TIME IN THE SALES TERRITORY

One of the most important considerations for field salespeople is protecting their time for making those vital sales presentations. Travel through a territory—small or large—is, in a sense, nonproductive although necessary time. Linda Meyer, sales director for Oakstone Publishing Company in Maineville, Ohio, says, "Organize your time before you hit the road, not while on the road."[20] She plans for time blocks – how long it will take her to write letters, do reports or recap a meeting. Look at your time as a 24-hour cycle of fragments. Travel time must be kept to a minimum. The Pareto principle says that 80 percent of your business will come from 20 percent of your customers. Thus, you must determine how much time and energy each account receives. Scott Gander, a sales rep for Geneal, a company selling restaurant supplies, divides all accounts into A, B, C and D accounts. He tries to spend 40 percent of his time helping A's, 30 percent with B's, 20 percent with C's, and 10 percent with the D's –the D accounts are only interested in price.[21] Be sure to categorize your accounts in a priority ranking such as:

"A"– High-volume, repeat customers.

"B"– Moderate sales volume, but reliable customers.

"C"– Lower-volume accounts.

"D"– Accounts that presently cost you more time and energy to service than you receive in sales and profits.

Field salespeople travel through time and space, so it will help if they set themselves in motion on the most efficient route between customers and prospects. Sales professionals pay close attention to the routing and scheduling of their calls. They take into consideration the proper mix of accounts on each trip. Prioritizing is useful for determining a profitable mix of account visitation and servicing. A common mistake is to call on **"D"** accounts simply because they are located near **"A"** accounts, and require little travel. These customers do not need to be called on with the same regularity as the **"A"** accounts. Instead use your time to prospect for new high volume, repeat customers.[22]

COMPUTER MAPPING SYSTEMS

It's probably a safe bet that most sales managers have spent time with magic markers and paper maps to plot where to position their sales reps. A category of software known as mapping systems, or Geographic Information Systems (GIS), is a rapidly growing market of sophisticated products which put numeric data into visual form, making the data easier to understand and digest. Simply put, this mapping software are programs designed to do the coloring and pasting for sales managers. These products create computer-generated maps of various geographic areas of interest to both sales managers and their salespeople. More and more of this software is being used to balance sales territories, optimize driving time, and target new markets and accounts. This desktop mapping software is letting managers do in minutes what used to take hours, or even days to complete.

Have Personal Data Assistance, Will Travel

Wherever your travels take you it helps to know where to eat, where to stay and what to see. Now all of this information is available in a handheld computer. Register with the AvantGo Internet Information Service (www.avantgo.com) and download the information to your Personal Data Assistant (PDA). Avantgo choices include a mapping program for getting you from point A to point B and RestaurantRow.com that organizes restaurants based on ZIP code. The maps that are generated are so precise that large buildings, tunnels, bridges, and even historic landmarks are indicated. And it will even phone or e-mail a reservation on your behalf through the channel's concierge service.[23]

Unless you have intimate knowledge of all the ZIP codes in every sales territory, it's impossible to know which areas border one another, and which don't. "You can look at a spreadsheet, but there's no substitute for looking at them nicely mapped," says Richard Bohn, president of Denali Group. "You can simply visualize the territory more easily that way."[24] Spreadsheets and databases tell you *how much* and *what kind*, while mapping software tells you *where*. Dave Delmonte, sales engineer for Steel Heddle, uses a product called *TripMaker* (from Rand McNally) that simplifies his trip planning. Delmonte types in his point of origin, his final destination, and any stopover points. In seconds, the digital atlas generates the appropriate map and compares alternate routes side-by-side. *TripMaker* can help track expenses and budget costs for hotel, gas and meals. The program also includes information on 2,800 restaurants and 12,000 hotels.[25]

Strategize Your Prospect Calls

The inability to get and stay organized is the biggest waste of time. Like a leaf in the wind, many salespeople leave home in the morning with no idea where they're going. They go where the wind blows and when the wind changes direction, so do they. The solution is a good contact management system coupled with a good mapping system.[26] The goal of all the various mapping programs is to minimize the salesperson's travel time and maximize his selling time. For example, Thom Frame, photo processing equipment salesman for Noritsu of Buena Vista, CA, uses a mapping system called *BusinessMap* to plan his road trips more efficiently. He covers a midwestern territory that spans seven states, requiring him to spend 70 percent of his time on the road. Frame says, "If I know that I will be visiting a customer in Milwaukee, I can map out my route so that I can call on customers on the drive out there as well as on the way back."

Automap, a type of automated map technology, calculates the shortest and fastest route for the field salesperson. Simply enter your starting point and destination and *Automap* will give you precise mileage, how long it will take to get there and gas consumption.

The uses of computer mapping systems are limited only by a salesperson's creative imagination. For example, when prospects ask Thom Frame for referrals he uses a variation of the *BusinessMap* system. He places the prospect on the map, then uses the mapping system to draw a circle that identifies every Noritsu customer in, say, a 50-mile radius. Proximity is important when providing referrals to potential customers. This mapping technology also enables a sales rep to get a list of every potential customer in a geographic area and map it against a display of the company's existing accounts. The result is an up-to-date analysis of how well you have penetrated your territory and the potential that remains. Maximizing travel time is an obvious and critical competitive advantage for today's *Road Warriors*.[27]

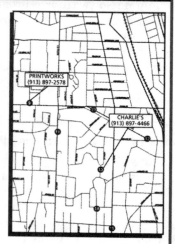

Developing Partnerships Using Technology examines mapping programs and GPS (Global Positioning Systems). Getting lost is no longer an option with salespeople. There is no longer a need to be flipping through an atlas on the side of the road. Just plug in your computer, and dial in for directions.

Developing Partnerships Using Technology
Mapping Programs Calculate the Most Efficient Route to Your Destination and Best of All, They Don't Get Mad At You Even if You Ignore Their Advice.

Here are some of the features found on most quality mapping programs:

a. Full-color maps with street names and geographic markings.

b. Zooming-in capability for more detail.

c. Suggested routing information: the shortest, fastest, or most scenic.

d. Hotel listings: by price range, pool, tennis courts, health club, etc.

e. Restaurant guides: searchable by cuisine, price range, credit cards accepted.

f. Toll-free numbers for car rentals and airlines, as well as information on toll roads.

g. Assistance in tracking expenses and budget costs for your hotel, gas, and meals.

h. Available printouts with written and picture directions.

Global Positioning System (GPS). GPS was developed by the Department of Defense. The system uses satellites to locate the position of anything with a GPS receiver, like a car. You always know where you are even in a bad storm or heavy fog. GPS will soon become standard equipment in new cars and installation kits will be available for older models. Lock your keys in your car? No problem: Use your cell phone to call a toll-free number and the satellite system will beam down a signal that will unlock your car door.

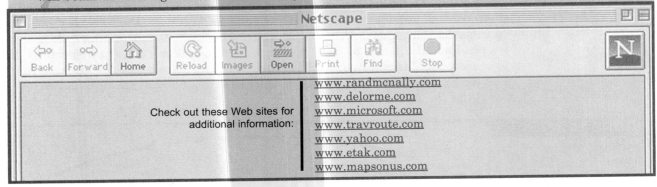

Check out these Web sites for additional information:
www.randmcnally.com
www.delorme.com
www.microsoft.com
www.travroute.com
www.yahoo.com
www.etak.com
www.mapsonus.com

Territory Routing Patterns

Two popular scheduling or routing patterns used by field salespeople to cut travel time in their territories and maximize face-to-face selling opportunities are:

1. *The Cloverleaf Pattern*—Figure 15.2 illustrates how this might look. The starting point may be the salesperson's home or the district or regional sales office location. One leaf is covered at a time. Each leaf or quadrant could take one day, a week or longer to complete. A new leaf is started on each subsequent trip, until the entire territory is covered.

FIGURE 15.2

The Cloverleaf Pattern

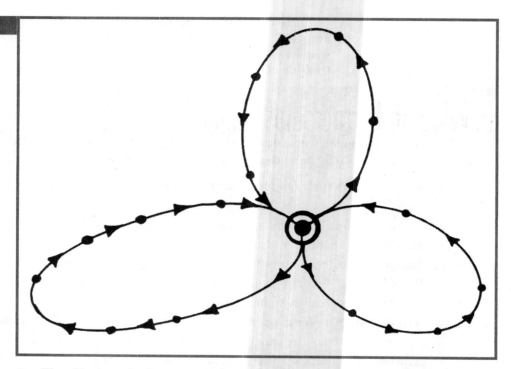

2. *The Hopscotch Pattern*—Figure 15.3 is a graphic illustration. The salesperson begins at the most distant point from the home base and makes prospect and client calls on the return trip. Depending on the size of the territory (and some sales reps have territories that encompass several states), you may fly out to the starting point and drive back. The field salespeople can vary this pattern and cover different directions on subsequent trips.

Two other routing patterns are the *Circular Pattern* and the *Straight-line Pattern*. Dividing the territory into several segments and scheduling appointments for a single day in one segment of the territory makes considerable sense. Controlling your schedule in this manner does not preclude flexibility to meet an important prospect or client regardless of location; occasionally, you will choose to readjust your plan for an important reason. Without a plan, however, you are so flexible that you are soon all bent out of shape.

FIGURE 15.3

The Hopscotch Pattern

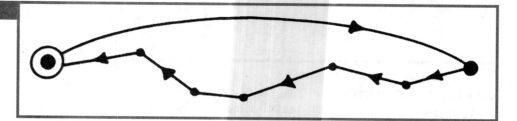

SUMMARY

The ability to manage time efficiently and effectively is largely a matter of attitudes. When you understand that time is life, and that you can control your life only by controlling time, the importance of good time management becomes apparent. Professionally, time is money; if you seek professional advancement and a good income, managing time properly is one of the best skills you can develop.

Developing the proper attitudes about time management involves knowing how you now spend your time, planning to spend it more effectively, and then working your plan consistently. When you know what you want to do with time, you can organize your schedule and all the clutter that passes through your hands daily to demand your attention.

Interruptions are time wasters that can be handled with planning and control. Interruptions arise from people, paper, and environmental factors. Appropriate planning keeps lost time at a minimum.

A workable system for time management includes at least three elements:

1. A master calendar for scheduling commitments

2. A daily to-do list to record activities to be done each day to meet commitments and reach goals

3. A 1-31 or other reminder file to hold items that will become important at a specific later date

Salespeople need time-effective telephone techniques. The telephone is an important tool, but you must control it by organizing ahead of time for its use by limiting the time spent making calls. Techniques include grouping calls, preparing beforehand to use the time for each call for maximum benefit, and setting time goals for handling necessary calls.

The time management system is an integrated whole that enables you to determine priorities, plan for meeting them, and be sure that nothing of importance is overlooked. Many salespeople are beginning to use contact management and mapping programs to manage their time commitments and find them to be excellent tools.

The most important tool for controlling time and getting the most benefit from how you spend each hour is to maintain positive attitudes toward time and your ability to manage it for achieving your personal goals.

QUESTIONS FOR THOUGHT AND DISCUSSION

1. Write a hundred-word statement giving your opinion about the importance of effective time management and its possible impact on your future in professional selling.

2. What three activities must your mind perform that affect how you use time? How does a system for time management make each of these tasks easier?

3. Describe an effective method for handling incompletions.

4. How does a cluttered desk or briefcase affect time use?

5. How does the appearance of a salesperson's car and briefcase affect professional credibility?

6. Describe the necessary elements of an effective organizing system.

7. Explain how a computer can be used to help with time management.

8. What three main sources of interruptions cause time problems? Give some strategies for handling each type.

9. How can a salesperson best get organized to set up appointments by telephone?

10. What can be done to limit the time needed for telephone calls?

11. How can the time needed for travel in the sales territory be kept to a minimum?

ACTIVITIES

1. Write a list of the six most important activities you perform every day. After each item, estimate the amount of time you spend on that activity each day. Now keep a detailed record of how you use your time for the next three days. (Use a form similar to Exhibit 15.1 and record your time usage at least every hour all day.) Compare your estimate with what you actually spent. Can you identify some ways you could improve the use of your time to increase your ability to reach your goals?

2. Select a product or service for which you might be a salesperson. Secure a map of a metropolitan area, a county, or a group of counties that could logically be an assigned territory for a salesperson. This may be your home area, where you are attending college, or some other area for which you can secure necessary information. Divide the map into segments to show how you would organize the territory for best time management. Write out a territory management plan giving attention to each of these considerations:

   • Where the best prospects are located in the territory.

   • How many segments are needed in the territory.

   • How the territory can best be divided to minimize travel.

   • How you determined where to draw segment lines.

   • How often each segment should be visited.

   • What percentage of total time should be given to each segment.

Case Study

CASE 15.1

Carol Puckett has had quite a wait in the reception room of the Seaboard Hardware Works. After about twenty-five minutes, she was thinking to herself, "I can't hang around here much longer. This is still a pretty small outfit, and they've never bought very much. Maybe I should cost this out. I might even be losing money. On top of that, they can be pretty demanding. Guess I'll cut out; I'll be around this way again in a few weeks, anyway. I've got a lot of miles to cover today."

Just then, the switchboard operator spoke up. "Ms. Puckett, Mr. Griffin can see you now. Do you know where his office is?"

"Yes, I do, thank you. I'll go right in."

"Sorry to keep you waiting," the manufacturing manager said, "but our production committee meeting took a little longer than usual. It's always that way when you're trying to get started on a new product."

"How is business these days?" Carol asked.

"Things are pretty hectic, but it's better that way than being too slow."

"I'll buy that," Carol replied. "Speaking of buying, you should be about ready for a reorder on those special fasteners, if they worked out as we thought they would."

"Haven't had any complaints from assembly so far."

"Good," said Carol. "Shall I just repeat the order?"

"Yes, that should do it," Griffin said.

"Okay, delivery will be four weeks."

"Let me see," Griffin replied. "We're getting a little low on these, according to our running inventory report. Could you make that three weeks?"

"As I was saying," Carol answered, "four weeks is normal. But I suppose that if you really need them sooner, I can give it a try."

"If I didn't need them, I wouldn't have asked," Griffin said with an edge on his voice. "If you can't deliver, say so. There are plenty of other fastener suppliers around."

"I assure you that I'll take your request right to the top if I have to. I'm going to be calling the office in a short while anyway. I'll have it checked out with our production control manager and call you back this afternoon," Carol promised.

"Well, okay. But you can certainly make a partial shipment earlier than four weeks, can't you?"

"Probably. However, these are a special design, and that means a completely different machine setup. Once the setup is made, production goes along pretty fast. The schedule for all of our other products and previous customer orders is really the determining factor in our lead time. But I'll try my best. What I mean to say is that if we can make any shipment at all in less than four weeks, it'll probably be a complete one," Carol explained.

When Carol phoned the plant, the sales manager, after agreeing to push Seaboard's order through in three weeks, asked Carol to come in to see him the next day.   The unusual request made Carol somewhat apprehensive. Field salespeople usually went into the main plant only for a full or district sales meeting.

The next day, after the handshake and the invitation to sit down, Carol asked, "Why did you ask me to come in? Is something the matter?"

"That's what I want to know," the sales manager said. "Just before you called I was checking your call reports. Contrary to what most of you bird dogs think, I do read the reports. Anyway, I noticed a strange sort of pattern. You seem to be doing very well with your major accounts. But what I can't find is any evidence that there's been any growth in the smaller ones. It just stands to reason that some of these must have grown since you hit the territory. There are some in the electronics field, for example. And, of course, the two that make safety equipment must be benefitting from the Occupational Safety and Health Act."

"I guess it's possible that some will grow," Carol replied. "But the way I figure it, and with the amount of business they're giving me now, I just can't give them the time it would take to build them up."

"Still, you should be thinking about their potential for the future. As a matter of fact, it is quite a coincidence that you should have called about that Seaboard order.   Did you know that they're taking over the Flatley Company?" the sales manager asked. "They're in your territory, too."

"No, I didn't," Puckett admitted. "And I was at Flatley last week, too. Neither of them gave any hint of anything in the works. How did you find out?"

"Just between you and me," the manager whispered, "I read it in the paper. But, seriously," he went on in a normal tone, "things like this can change a situation overnight. As I said before, you're doing fine in most areas. In fact, I consider you to be one of our top young salespeople. Have you any suggestions about how you can make your volume grow as some of your smaller accounts expand? Stay here and think about it for a few minutes. I've got to check a few things with production control, including how the Seaboard order is being scheduled. I'll be right back. You can tell me your ideas then."

1.   Is the sales manager nit-picking, or is Carol neglecting an opportunity to increase sales? Support your answer.

2.   Did Carol miss anything in her conversation with Griffin that should have given her a clue to the Flatley takeover? Was there a clue of any other kind she missed?

3.   What ideas can you suggest that Carol might list for the sales manager?

Chapter 16

Sales Force Management

LEARNING OBJECTIVES

- To examine the function of sales management in a company.

- To learn what is personally required of the sales manager.

- To discover the differences in qualifications between sales managers and salespeople.

- To understand the specific responsibilities of the sales manager.

- To examine the impact of various compensation plans.

- To discuss recruitment and selection of salespeople.

- To describe orientation, training and motivation practices.

THE SALES MANAGEMENT FUNCTION

Management of the sales force plays a vital part in the overall success of any company. If salespeople do not sell the company's products or services, no amount of effort in sales or marketing planning will produce success. Although the failure of an individual salesperson to sell may occasionally be attributed to lack of ability or unwillingness to work, the failure of an overall sales force is more likely to result from a basic sales management problem: The salespeople were improperly recruited, selected, trained, compensated, or motivated. The costs associated with managing a sales force are often the largest single operating expense item for a company. The hiring process is expensive.

Exhibit 16.1 shows the actual dollar investment 10 different companies make in every salesperson they hire.[1] The cost of hiring and training a single salesperson ranges from a low of $5,000 at Boise Cascade to a jolting $100,000 at ACDelco, Brown-Forman, and General Electric ICS. In addition, the time invested in training a new salesperson ranges from eight weeks to two years. You begin to get a very clear picture of just how expensive recruitment, selection, and then the actual training really is. And when you include the turnover factor, you begin to fully understand that companies must have a process in place that provides them with salespeople who are committed and loyal to the company.

EXHIBIT 16.1

Cost of hiring and turnover vary widely

Company	Number of salespeople	Cost of hiring and training per salesperson	Time invested in training a new salesperson	Average annual turnover
ACDelco	500	$100,000	24 mos.	3%
AT&T	10,000	$20,000	6 mos.	35%
Boise Cascade	1,400	$5,000	18 mos.	15%
Brown-Forman	435	$100,000	24 mos.	5%
General Electric ICS	12,800	$100,000	6 mos.	12%
Lucent Technologies	10,000	$30,000	6 mos.	6%
Mark IV Industries	282	$25,000	6 mos.	2%
Reynolds and Reynolds	1,200	$10,000	6 mos.	10%
UPS	3,038	NA	8 wks.	5%
Zellerbach	750	$50,000	6 mos.	14%

The sales function is the responsibility of the sales manager, who is involved with all aspects of selling, including planning, organizing, controlling, and evaluating the sales force. The sales manager is the link between individual salespeople and their customers and the organization's upper management. In a smaller firm, the sales management function may be assigned to the marketing manager. A larger, more diversified company may have several sales managers classified by geographic area, customer type, or product line, and each may report to a district or regional manager who, in turn, reports to the chief sales executive of the company.

Regardless of how broad or how limited the sales manager's job might be, both sales ability and management ability are required. The management ability required of a field salesperson is primarily applied in the area of personal time and activity management. The sales manager needs excellent management ability in addition to the basic sales abilities that everyone in sales needs. The amount of time spent in actual sales activity versus administrative activity changes at each level of management in the company. The manager who directly supervises field salespeople spends more time in actual selling activities than in administrative duties, but a chief sales executive who is separated from field salespeople by several levels of sales management may be almost completely involved in administrative activity.

MANAGING IN THE 21ST CENTURY

Historically, marketing and sales companies used the 4P's—Product, Price, Place, and Promotion to formulate strategy. Now, a fifth P is needed: People. A sales manager's job is no longer to ride herd over the sales force using the traditional authoritative management style. Individuals entering the sales world today have a different set of values. They have more education and sophistication, desiring managers who listen, encourage, teach, coach and give them a voice in how they are managed. If the sales environment does not meet these requirements, they will search for one that does. According to Dr. Ken Blanchard, co-author of the *One-Minute Manager*, younger sales professionals are foregoing other aspects of the job, including financial considerations, to work in a caring, supportive environment. In a recent study by the Families and Work Institute, 3400 randomly selected men and women ranked their three most important job considerations.

1. *Open Communication:* Information is power; do not withhold information as a way to abuse your management position. Tell your sales force everything you know that is pertinent to their job. Involve them in the decisions that affect them.

2. *Effect on Personal/Family Life:* The explosion of two-wage-earner families and the growing number of families with single parents makes it more stressful to juggle all the demands of work and home life. Problems that did not impact the work place a generation ago, such as sick children or scheduling a day-care provider, means managers must find new ways to allow for greater flexibility and autonomy in individual jobs.

3. *The Nature of the Work:* Workers want to feel their job is important to the success of the company. A wise sales manager takes every opportunity to let the sales force know how critical their efforts are in meeting company goals. Saying "thank you" frequently is easy and costs nothing.[2]

The sales manager's challenge is to walk the fine line between pleasing top management, and keeping the sales force motivated to produce. Sales managers must be coaches, facilitators, and cheerleaders for their people. Their main concerns must be how to shape a more supportive work environment and to find ways to help each salesperson be more productive.

TEAM SELLING

In companies that use team selling, the sales manager must possess the knowledge and skills needed to create effective teams.[3] There are few individuals who possess the personality characteristics that make them naturals at both opening and closing a sale. It has become very difficult for the salesperson without a technical background to know the product as intimately as clients demand. In an attempt to resolve this dilemma, many companies have turned to a strategy called *team selling*.[4] The team approach gains an advantage over *one-on-one selling*, because it utilizes the strengths of each individual on the team. Some professional salespeople may lack the patience and attention to detail required to eventually influence the prospect to commit. Yet, technical support people involved on the team may possess these very characteristics, as they tend to be detail-oriented by nature. Similarly, a personality that appears too brusque in the eyes of a client may be offset by a conservative personality who can energize the client with a sense of confidence.

Team Selling is a cooperative action by two or more professionals directed to selling a product or service. The sales team often consists of at least one salesperson, supported by technical specialists, a combination that utilizes the persuasive expertise of the salesperson as well as the technical competency of other personnel throughout the organization. Team selling involves not only several people from the seller's company but also a *buying center or purchasing team* from the prospect's company.

Benefits of Team Selling

A healthy team attitude begins with a solid commitment to help team members win. There is no room for prima donnas within the team. The only person who is allowed to be the prima donna is the customer.[5] One of the primary benefits of team selling is that it enables a company to improve its relationship with customers, by allowing direct communication between the buyer and product specialists before the sale is made. Thus, the seller can more accurately define the customer's needs, and the buyer can have questions answered by an individual who has an intimate knowledge of the product. This creates an aura of authority and trustworthiness for the company and the salesperson. Imagine the technical expertise required to sell satellite time to the telecommunications industry, a service of Satellite Corporation. The needs of each client are unique, and once the sale is made, the relationship has just begun. Buyers not only want to know what the service can do for their company, but also who will be working with them after the sale is made. For these reasons, Satellite Corporation requires that all 200 employees act as *informal partners* of the sales department and are expected to contribute their expertise in making all sales. Technical people, for instance, frequently accompany salespeople on calls, and the salespeople work closely with their marketing colleagues to produce the brochures, technical guides, and other materials used in setting up and closing a sale.

The Roles of Each Team Member

The sales manager should appoint the account's salesperson as the team leader, and the technical and creative experts assume supportive roles. The leader may begin, coordinate, and close the presentation, calling on specific personnel to use their expertise in amplifying certain points. Technical experts must know when to contribute and when to remain silent. Team members should reinforce the leader's presentation with body language and affirmation.

Nalco has a field sales force to be reckoned with.

Designating one team leader is vitally important, even when only two people will be making the call. This individual should be fully aware of the objectives of each call, and should communicate them to each member. All team members should agree on the objectives before the call, but the team leader is responsible for keeping the presentation on track, or signaling to switch to another objective when necessary. The team leader has the authority to tactfully intervene when another member begins to discuss topics that are not germane to a particular sales call. For example, an advertising executive may get into a detailed discussion with the client's marketing director about advertising strategies, or an engineer may get into a debate with a client's technical expert. These topics would be of little interest to the other members of the buying or selling teams, and better left to be discussed in private meetings between the two individuals.

Guidelines for Effective Team Selling

Nalco Chemical Company is accomplished at the art of team selling. Nalco is the world's largest supplier of specialty chemicals for water treatment. They service customers in the refining, steel, and metalworking industries; paper manufacturers; hospitals; universities; and food producers. Jim Scott, vice-president for corporate sales, says, "Our customers are buying applied technologies along with our chemicals, so we must also sell ourselves as experts on their businesses and manufacturing methods. Our reps have to be on-site consultants to the customers."[6] He goes on to suggest that personal agendas at customer sites are blurred into a team agenda. *If a team buys, a team must sell.*

Generally, the companies Nalco calls on have a *purchasing team* that includes the vice-president of operations or his staff, the purchasing director, and engineering reps from individual plants. Nalco counters with a team consisting of an account executive to facilitate negotiations, sales managers, general managers, marketing managers, and district sales representatives. Nalco is able to exclude technical support staff on its selling teams because its field reps are themselves engineers or technical consultants specializing in the customer's business. Exhibit 16.2 presents a number of guidelines gleaned from Nalco's approach to team selling.

EXHIBIT 16.2 - Team Selling at the Nalco Chemical Company

Their customer's decision-making process is more teamlike. So Nalco needs to have a team on its side. At Nalco, these guidelines are pertinent for effective team selling:

1. Know who needs to be part of the team by studying your customer's needs.

2. Provide the customer with the necessary details.

3. Make sure you have the right mix on the team to meet needs.

4. Look for a second opinion to help you assemble the team, especially if you are new to this process.

5. Develop good relationships with team members and keep up-to-date on what each one can offer to the process.

6. The lead salesperson should be on hand for the installation to represent the team.

7. Know your own limits and call for help when it is needed.

Combinations That Work

One very common sort of teamwork is the two-person sales call team, often made up of a sales rep and a sales manager or a sales rep and a technical expert. It is so common, many companies don't think of this as team selling.[7] There is so much to gain by pairing salespeople. Such partnerships can be productive both for the individual sales reps and their companies. Don't force people into a team approach unless you recognize a serious flaw in one sales rep that a partner can correct. To illustrate how this partnering could prove beneficial, consider this illustration:

Openers and Closers—For some salespeople, their greatest skill is the ability to capture the attention and interest of prospects. This is analogous to the carnival barker whose job it is to get you inside the circus tent. There is nothing wrong with this—bringing customers inside the tent is a valuable skill. We learned earlier that making a good first impression is critical to future sales success. The problem is, some salespeople lack substance and depth in subsequent meetings with a prospect, and hence can benefit by being teamed with a detail-oriented sales rep who knows how to close.

Major-league baseball managers have a similar situation to the one just described. A manager has starting pitchers (openers) and relief pitchers (closers) on his ball club. Many of baseball's best starting pitchers average six or seven strong innings each time out. The relief pitcher then comes in and shuts down the opposing team and saves the game for the starter. Neither player is complete on his own. Together, however, they produce a winning performance.

Using Technology

Sales managers have an increasing array of options to choose from as they communicate with their remote sales forces: cell phones, teleconferences, Internet Web processing, e-mail, videoconferencing, voice mail, chat, and the old standby, face-to-face.

Videoconferencing. In today's global marketing economy, the salesperson must sell to a more diversified and physically spread-out customer and prospect base then ever before. Finding the time and resources to have a "face-to-face" meeting can be difficult and expensive. One of the truly amazing technological innovations is the advent of videoconferencing.

Videoconferencing is the combination of a telephone call and a video camera. It allows the salesperson, sales manager, or customer to have a "face-to-face" meeting that is so critical to success in professional selling. Videoconferencing is far less expensive than flying to a business or sales meeting. A skilled sales manager can conduct an interactive meeting with sales reps in offices from New York City to Perth, Australia. No expensive plane tickets are necessary, and the sales reps never have to leave their territories.

Internet conferencing takes this process one step further. With videoconferencing you need a special room and equipment. For Internet conferencing all you need is an Internet account, computer, camera, and microphone. This enables the sales manager to conduct a meeting with his salespeople who might be anywhere in the world. And the salesperson can connect with customers no matter where they happen to be located.

Internet and videoconferencing enables companies to conduct sales meetings around the world.

One sales manager who attempted to use the technology had it flop so badly that he now uses the equipment as a plant stand. However, Eli Lilly and Company has had considerable success using it. Eight of their major sales offices keep in regular contact with headquarters using videoconferencing. For Christopher Roberts, manager of business communication technologies for Eli Lilly, this technology makes sense. He says, "You're able to keep people informed without taking them out of the field."[8]

Maximize Your Twin Investments. As you prepare for an all-important sales conference, here is one idea that has considerable merit. Suppose you are bringing in your salespeople from all over the country to one central facility for two days of meetings. Prior to the sales conference with your sales reps, use a tool called *Group Mind Express* from Catalyst Consulting. Here's how it could work: Send an e-mail to each salesperson that includes a link to a site that contains a survey instrument you constructed. When your salespeople go to the site, they answer the questions and the site immediately displays the results to date for the entire survey – showing them where they stand on the issues you raised compared to their colleagues. This allows you to quickly see the concerns that are most important to them. Using this type of tool for surveying your sales force prior to a critical two-day sales meeting will help you zero in on the topics that are of critical interest to them once you actually all come together. This is one way to maximize your twin investments of time and money.[9]

THE SALES MANAGER AS A LEADER

It's not just a good idea to push yourself to greater heights of leadership—it's crucial for your company's survival. It's not enough to just "keep up the good work." On top of that, managers must create a motivational culture that challenges and inspires positive change in their salespeople.[10] The pressure is on everybody in this economy, so managers should be ready to step up and lead a sales force toward success. One of the keys of leadership is motivating people. Sustained motivation comes from day-to-day motivation – and that has to come from sales managers who are leaders themselves. Elaine Harkins, associate vice-president of financial services sales at Dun & Bradstreet, credits a one-on-one talk she had with an employee for saving

Elaine Harkins believes one-on-one talks can help employees overcome problems.

a great salesperson. Managers like Harkins who get involved and are genuinely excited about helping others are the most effective in inspiring their associates and encouraging them to increase personal productivity. Bob Nelson, author of *1001 Ways to Energize Your Employees*, says, "For today's employees, you can't light a fire under them. You have to light a fire in them."[11]

A study conducted by Wilson Learning Corporation found that 69 percent of employee satisfaction stems from the leadership skills of managers. Research from the study points to five specific characteristics that turn a good sales manager into a great day-to-day leader:[12]

1. Provides employees with a sense of mission.

2. Creates a work environment where salespeople feel free to stretch their talents.

3. Gives immediate feedback on what salespeople need to improve on so they don't have to guess.

4. Offers praise and rewards in an appropriate way so that individual salespeople are recognized as well as the team as a whole.

5. Helps and supports employees in developing their talents and careers.

These characteristics are the basis for the sales manager's approach to the task of sales management. You must remember that leadership isn't an event; it is a process. Sales managers must be able to diagnose what their people need and remain flexible enough to provide for those needs.

Based on the characteristics brought to light in the study outlined above, Exhibit 16.3 recommends a new management style. To maximize a team's performance, sales managers must break away from the traditional management style and develop a winning style of management. The idea is to lead, not to simply tell people exactly what to do. You develop people and ask how they think a task should be handled. The winning manager takes the sales force to the next level, because it is very difficult for them to do it on their own. "The key to management lies in always providing value to the people who work under you."[13] This is the definition of strong leadership according to Edward Berube, president of Conseco Insurance Group in Indianapolis. Sales managers serve as champions to the people who report to them. The high from helping others achieve their goals is addictive.

The qualifications that produce success for an individual salesperson are not necessarily the same as those needed for success as a sales manager. On one hand, a salesperson must possess a strong sense of self-discipline coupled with a love of independence. A sales manager, on the other hand, is

EXHIBIT 16.3 - Becoming a Winning Manager

Traditional Managers	Winning Managers
1. Stick to their old ways. Resist change.	1. Thrive on, and relish, change.
2. See themselves as cops or bosses.	2. Think like a coach or team leader.
3. Make all the decisions on their own.	3. Believe in group decision making.
4. Are reluctant to share information.	4. Are eager to share news and information.
5. Demand action and effort. Long Hours.	5. Expect progress and results to occur.
6. Neglect any career-planning discussions. Assume company will do that for them.	6. Take initiative for planning own career and assist sales staff in planning theirs.
7. Consider sales staff to be their subordinates.	7. Consider their sales reps to be an integral part of the "team."

Adapted from: Dr. Wolf Rinke's book *Winning Management: Six Fail-Safe Strategies for Building High-Performance Organizations*

continuously involved in interaction with a diverse clientele both inside and outside the organization. The freedom enjoyed by salespeople to arrange and manage their own time and activities is not as likely to be available to the sales manager who is held accountable for the overall effectiveness of a number of salespeople. Managing yourself and your own time is not the same as directing and managing other people's time and energies. Choosing the best salesperson for promotion to sales manager does not always work. A manager's job is to do whatever is necessary to achieve consistent production and growth, both personally and in all members of the sales force, and to build top-performing producers while maintaining a profitable business.

SPECIFIC RESPONSIBILITIES PERFORMED BY THE SALES MANAGER

In building and maintaining an efficient sales force, the sales manager performs at least six distinct managerial functions, as shown in Figure 16.1. This model serves as a basis for the information presented next and illustrates the complexity of the sales management function.

Determine Sales Force Organization

Organizing the sales force within imposed budget constraints is one of the sales manager's major concerns. No precise rules apply for choosing the organizing strategy to follow. Figure 16.2 depicts the three basic types of sales force organization.

Product Organization. When this plan is used, salespeople specialize in the sale of a relatively narrow line of goods or services. This organization is effective in a company that sells expensive, complex, or technical products that require high levels of product knowledge. It is also effective when buying patterns vary greatly among the various parts of the product line. Product organization is expensive because of the time, effort, and human resources needed for specialization.

Recently, the Bertelsmann AG company reorganized along strict product lines. According to Michael Dornemann, head of the entertainment division, "If you have a decentralized corporate approach and have too many divisions, it becomes difficult to handle because there are so many overlapping strategic ideas." They now have four clearly differentiated divisions. The move has been enormously successful for them.[14]

FIGURE 16.2

Types of Sales Force Organization

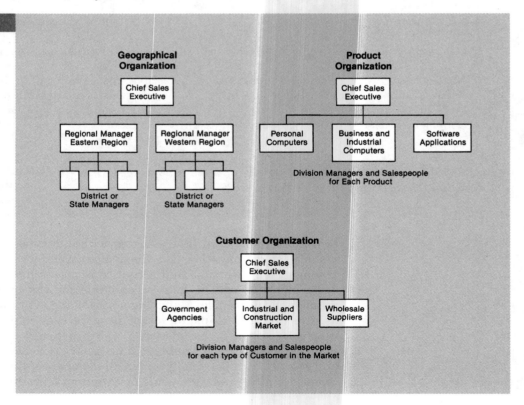

FIGURE 16.1

The Job of the Sales Manager

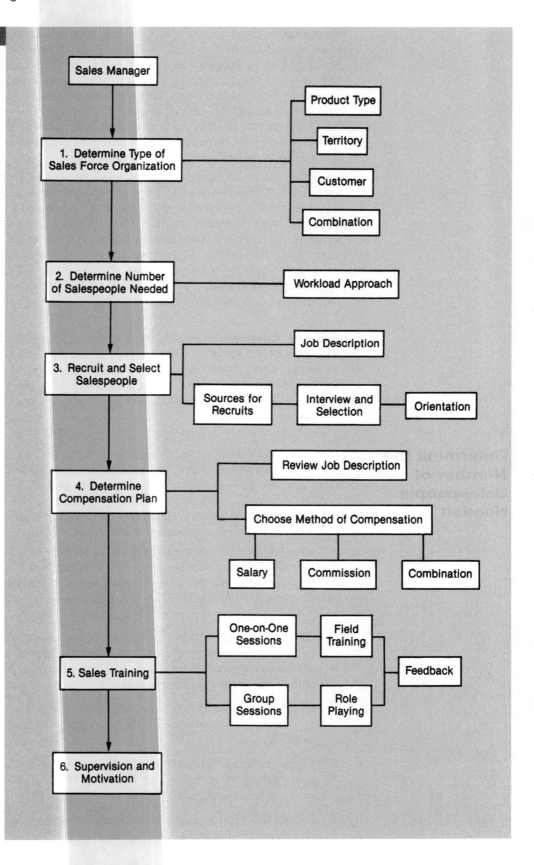

Geographic Organization. Salespeople assume responsibility for selling the entire product line within a defined geographical region. This type of organization is probably the most common. If the product line is extensive, this method of organization hampers the salesperson's ability to gain enough detailed product knowledge. If the territory is large, the number of customers and the amount of travel required may cut the amount of service the salesperson can give to each account. The risk exists that such salespeople will choose to concentrate only on the products or services with the highest demand or that are easiest for them to sell.

The Sentrol Company, located in Oregon, has a customer base of 17,000 distributors. However, its 15 field salespeople focus on the top 2,000 accounts. Sentrol sales reps meet with the larger customers up to eight times a year pitching their complex product lines. Each of the 15 reps have a specific geographic territory assigned to them. Within those territories they really zero in on the roughly 14 percent that furnish the company with most of its sales and profits. Reinforcing the efforts of the 15 field reps are 22 inside salespeople who contact the "premier" accounts every three weeks attempting to sell them the less complex products.[15]

Type of Customer. Organization on the basis of customer type assigns salespeople to serve a specific type of customer. Some call on industrial accounts, and others call on retail accounts. This method allows salespeople to become knowledgeable about the needs of a given industry or customer type. It also gives the salespeople time to employ personalized sales strategies.

Determine the Number of Salespeople Needed

The importance of determining how many salespeople to employ can hardly be overemphasized. An understaffed sales force produces sales levels that are too low; over-staffing, however, creates excessive costs and cuts profits. Although simple in theory, determining the appropriate number of people to hire may prove relatively difficult. The problem lies in estimating the impact on the marketplace of adding salespeople.

One frequently used method for determining how many salespeople to hire is called the *workload approach*. This method is based upon determining the total amount of sales work needed, estimating how much one salesperson can do, and then dividing. This method follows a four-step process:

1. Determine the number of calls needed. Companies may classify their customers into categories. Often these categories are based on the level of actual sales or potential sales to each customer. Not all accounts may get called on with equal frequency.

2. Determine the average time necessary per call and multiply this amount of time by the number of calls to be made to find the total working time needed.

3. Figure how much actual selling time (total hours per year) is available for each salesperson (allowing time for travel between appointments and other sales-related activities).

4. Divide the total working time by the working time per salesperson to find the number of salespeople needed.

The following formula (based on the four-step process) provides an estimate for the number of salespeople needed:

Sales force size = Total Number of Customers and Prospects x Call Frequency x Call Time Required ÷ Selling Time Available for One Salesperson

For example:

	Customers	150
	Prospects	+600
	Total =	750

- Call frequency = call on each customer once a month (or 12 times/year)
- Average call time per visit = 45 minutes (.75 hour)
- Actual selling time available per year = 4 hours/day x 250 days a year = 1,000 hours

Sales force size $\dfrac{750 \times 12 \times .75}{1,000} = \dfrac{6,750}{1,000} = 7$ salespeople

The more realistic the estimate for each factor, the more accurate the final determination. In addition to accurate estimates of these factors, other considerations include the quality of the people recruited: level of selling skill, personal motivation, experience and product knowledge, initiative, and work habits. All of these factors play a part in whether the estimated levels of sales activity and the estimated results will be reached.[16] The sales manager's ability to determine how many people are needed improves with experience and with knowledge of the people already in the work unit.

Recruit and Select Salespeople

Building a winning sales force depends in large measure upon the sales manager's effectiveness in recruiting and selecting the best salespeople. The process, like every other selling activity, requires planning and preparation, careful tracking, and efficient carrying out of plans. At least four phases are included in the total process.

Phase I: Determine Requirements for the Position. Finding the right person to fill a sales position is a major concern for every sales organization regardless of size or type. Finding the right person is impossible before you know what qualities are necessary. Develop a profile of the candidates who will stand the best chance of succeeding. *Make this profile realistic, not idealistic.* Planning begins with development of a job description that sets out in written form all of the requirements for a given sales position. The process of writing a job description forces the sales manager to be explicit about what the job requires. Once the activities are listed, the sales manager can more easily decide exactly what skills and experience a prospective salesperson must have to be considered as a viable applicant. All salespeople are not suited to all sales jobs. Some do an excellent job selling products with low unit value but are unable to close a sale on a big-ticket item. Others do well selling tangible products but have difficulty selling intangibles like insurance or mutual funds. A job description helps to avoid a mismatch between the job and the salesperson. In defining the qualifications for the job, the sales manager should consider these factors:

1. *Educational Requirements*

    A basic requirement (high school or college degree) and any special training (accounting, liberal arts, pharmacy, computer science, etc.) should be defined.

2. *Experience*

    Both the length and type of experience required or preferred must be identified. Must experience be in a particular line? What substitutes are acceptable? Will experience with a competitor be considered? *Dartnell's 29th Survey of Sales Force Compensation* of more than 800 companies in 30 industries reports that companies are increasingly preferring senior and experienced salespeople over entry-level recruits. According to Christen Heide, "They realize they are not in the training business and don't mind paying more for what they need."[17]

3. *Job Conditions*

    List any special conditions that affect the job: seasonal or cyclical demand for the product, low ratio of sales to calls, long absences from home. Make sure the prospective salesperson is able to deal with these conditions both physically and emotionally.

4. *Type of Customers*

    Determine whether the type of customers to be called on has any bearing on what type of salesperson is needed.

Thorough planning is as important in recruiting a sales force as in any other portion of the selling process. Without planning, the people you hire may fail to fit into the job you offer them. *You not only need good people—you need people who are good for a particular job.*

Phase 2: Sources for Recruiting. Each sales manager learns through experience the best sources for finding recruits for specific types of sales jobs. Here are six possible sources:

1. *Within the Organization*

    Occasionally an employee in the production or service portion of the business qualifies for a sales job. Students often take part-time jobs on the maintenance crew or in the office and are eager to enter sales when their education is complete.

2. *Competitors*

    A competing company is a possible source, but caution should be exercised as ethical problems may be involved. Be sure that the salesperson has a legitimate reason for wanting to leave present employment. Take care to evaluate the person's stability, work habits, experience, and attitude toward selling.

3. *The Internet*

Companies are using the Internet to locate potential candidates for various sales positions. More and more Web sites are being established for this explicit purpose. For example, *Monster.com* is one of the sites most of us are familiar with.

4. *Trade and Other Media Advertising*

A well-written classified ad in the newspaper produces good prospects. A blind ad asking for a written application to be sent to a post office box number saves time by letting you weed out obviously unqualified applicants without taking time for a personal interview.

5. *Schools*

Technical schools, night schools, colleges, and universities are potential sources of prospects. Use the placement service in the school for screening.

6. *Employment Agencies*

The state employment agency in many cities is valuable. Private agencies are also in the business to find prospects. When using any type of agency, be sure to make the job requirements clear and perhaps set them a little higher than actually required. Get to know the service representative in the agency and you will get better prospects referred to you.

Tips for Hiring Right

SKIP THE LEARNING CURVE. Hire someone with experience in the areas specific to your needs.

CHOOSE MARKETING SKILLS OVER SALES SKILLS. Some sales experience is beneficial, but marketing requires different abilities and approaches than does sales.

SEEK OUT CHARISMATIC TYPES. Look for someone with leadership abilities and strong communication skills.

RAID THE BIG GUNS. Some of the best training grounds are in companies such as Procter & Gamble. So try to entice their best.

Phase 3: Interview and Selection. The interview between the sales manager and the prospective salesperson accomplishes three objectives: to give information, to receive information, and to establish a friendly relationship. This applies whether the prospect qualifies for the position or not. The interview process may involve completion of an application form, check of references, personal interview(s), testing, physical examination, and the final decision to hire.

• One effective question that may be asked of former employers is, "Would you consider this person for further employment?" A similar question to put to other references is, "Why do you feel this person would be good in sales?" Some sales managers use the telephone exclusively for checking references. They feel that information may be given on the phone that might never be put into writing in a letter.

The Interview Itself. A personal interview can be designed to help the sales manager determine whether a prospect is right for the job. The interview process may require several meetings. One may be used to complete the application form and review it briefly; a second may be a more in-depth interview several days later when the sales manager has had time to check references. Depending on the organization of the company itself, several people other than the sales manager may also interview the applicant. Robert Head, president of Strategic Sales Services Inc., says, "Good hiring procedures for salespeople require a minimum of two interviews, preferably three."[18]

Asking the Right Questions. The session should be used to discover answers to these types of questions:

1. Is the individual actually qualified for the position?

2. How badly does the person want this sales position with our company?

3. Can the candidate demonstrate an understanding of our company's business?

4. Is this individual a problem-solver? Can this person think quickly on his feet?

"Most interviews are a waste of time because the candidate isn't prepared," says Mick Corcodilos, author of *Ask the Headhunter.* He suggests that sales managers ask the job candidates on the phone to come to the interview with solutions to two problems that their company is facing. This challenge stops most of the job seekers dead in their tracks. There is just too much work involved. What a way to reduce the pool of candidates and, at the same time, force those who do accept the challenge to demonstrate an understanding of the job's requirements.

It is essential that new salespeople be brought in as part of the team.

Phase 4: Orientation. All the time and expense of the selection procedure are lost if the new salesperson is not properly integrated into the organization. Of course, the size of the organization affects what is done and how, but in every case a definite program should bring each new salesperson into the company as part of the team and establish for that person a feeling of belonging. The process should include items such as these:

*   Introduction to fellow workers

*   Office practices

*   Company policies

*   Vertical communication

*   Company-sponsored recreation activities

*   Expense account procedures

In addition to these routine items, the new salesperson should be made aware of every facet of the job. The sales manager and the salesperson must agree on duties, work schedules, reports, and expected results.

Determine Compensation Plan

Compensation plans are usually either straight commission, straight salary, or a combination of the two.

Straight Commission. A commission is usually figured as a percentage of sales volume. The plan might call for a simple percentage of total gross sales, or it could be based on a percentage of the sales less variable costs. The benefit of the latter plan is that it offers the salesperson concrete incentives for helping to keep selling costs low and therefore emphasizes profit instead of mere volume. The main benefit of a commission plan is the motivation it offers to salespeople for productivity. The disadvantage is that some salespeople are tempted to neglect activities that do not bring in short-term dollars, including service after the sale, helping with installation, and completing needed reports and related paperwork. The straight-commission plan is the plan of choice when aggressive selling is desired.

Straight Salary. At the other extreme is a plan based on a fixed amount regardless of volume. About 15 percent of companies use straight salary as their sole means of compensation.[19] A straight-salary plan gives management the greatest ability to control the activities of salespeople. If the company has an unusual need for postsale activities, developing new territories, or continuing technical training, salespeople do not feel that they are cutting their own income by giving time to that work. However, a salary plan offers less motivation for intense sales effort than the commission plan. Therefore, a salary plan is the plan of choice when management needs to control salespeople's activities and when aggressive sales activity is not necessary.

Combination Plans. One method to exercise control over sales activities yet retain the incentive value of a commission is a combination of a base salary and a commission or bonus paid on sales above a set level. Another type of combination plan makes use of a commission plus a draw against future commissions earned. This plan protects salespeople in slow seasons or when some outside circumstance lowers productivity temporarily. The company sets a base amount that the salesperson is guaranteed to receive. If commissions earned fall below that figure, a draw is paid to bring income up to the base level. If the salesperson earns commissions above the base next month, the excess is used to repay the draw. Table 16.1 shows how the draw operates.

TABLE 16.1- How a Combination Commission-Draw Compensation Plan Works

Month	Commissions Earned	Commissions Paid	Draw* Paid (Repaid)	Total Income
January	$1,500	$1,500	$0	$1,500
February	900	900	300	1,200
March	1,400	1,400	(200)	1,200
April	1,500	1,500	(100)	1,400
May	1,700	1,700	0	1,700
June	1,200	1,200	0	1,200
Total	$8,200	$8,200	$0	$8,200

*Assumes company guarantees a base amount of $1,200 per month. Some companies do not require an actual payback as shown in this example. They use the draw as a yardstick for performance.

There aren't many other topics that a professional salesperson or a sales manager is more eager to talk to someone about than sales compensation. With all of the requirements and devices used, compensation plans can be quite complex. They can bring about unethical behavior. And in many cases they can be very difficult to administer. Exhibit 16.4 points out how much easier it is becoming for sales reps to keep track of the commissions they earn the moment a deal is closed, and the commissions they could earn on any deals that are pending.[20] The special challenge companies have is to keep themselves from cluttering up their incentive plan with everybody's favorite program "du jour." In the past, companies have failed because they end up with a sales plan where there are bonuses or a contest on just about every one of the products being sold.

EXHIBIT 16.4 - Computers to the Rescue – Clarifying the Compensation Plan

A new software tool makes it possible for companies to go way beyond the minimum in communicating their compensation plans to their field sales forces. *SalesOnline* is a software product developed by Oracle that allows companies to manage and control their compensation plans. "It handles the whole sales compensation cycle, from designing the model to aligning it with your strategic objectives to getting approvals before executing It, then implementing it," says Juliette Sultan, vice president of CRM Product Strategy at Oracle. One powerful advantage of *SalesOnline* is its clarity. Sales reps can see what's going on each time a transaction comes in, and exactly what commission they will be paid. This is all about visibility and tracking progress. It enables them to understand the commission structure and increases their satisfaction.

SalesOnline also features an Income Planner that reinforces company incentives for long-term selling efforts. It will calculate future commissions for sales that are pending. A salesperson can see that when he closes a deal, here is what he will make. If sales reps are working on multiple deals, it motivates them to devote the right amount of time to each to work toward maximizing their company's profit. This feature will become even more significant as companies develop compensation plans with many variables: revenue and activity, current and historical, and single and multi-channel sales. The software tool is quite flexible and enables the compensation plan to be as complex as a company wants it to be.

A TQM-Based Compensation Package

According to *Dartnell's 29th Survey of Sales Force Compensation*, the importance of profitability is increasing in sales compensation plans. Companies should reward salespeople not only for making sales, but also for achieving corporate sales objectives. Sales managers who do not carefully consider specific marketing and sales objectives almost by default choose dollar sales volume as the incentive criterion. A compensation plan based only on numbers can be detrimental. Rather than satisfy the customer, salespeople are tempted to spend their time focused on exceeding their numbers to maximize their *own* personal income. A reasonable base salary shows commitment to your sales force.

If the compensation plan is salary-based, it can be structured to reward company loyalty and longevity. Turnover is expensive to a company through training costs and lost sales. It takes a salesperson time to learn the company, its products, policies, and customers. A company with a lot of turnover causes clients to question its stability and may, and apparently does, result in business lost to the competition.

Today's consultative sales professionals should be listeners, information gatherers, educators, relationship builders, counselors, and the primary sources of customer input to the company. Cultivate a longer-term focus on adding customer value and integrating sales with all other people in the company who impact customers and products. Their pay needs to reflect these expectations. Some of the newer approaches involve paying differentiated awards based on strategies concerning customers and products.[21] A Total Quality Management (TQM)-based compensation plan includes:

Customer Retention Bonus. Reward the salesperson for maintaining long-term relationships. Retention is a good indication that customers are being satisfied. Hewlett Packard has instituted customer satisfaction into their sales force compensation as they move toward Total Quality Management. According to a survey of 300 top American companies by Handy HRM Corporation of New York, 54 percent of those surveyed tie pay directly to quality standards, including customer satisfaction.[22]

Penetration of Target Accounts Bonus. New, targeted accounts take longer to develop and often do not offer the immediate financial return of established customers. Some salespeople also fear the added rejection that invariably accompanies calling on new prospects. However, gaining the business of target accounts indicates a salesperson's ability better than traditional methods that focus only on volume. A bonus paid for securing the business of targeted individuals or companies will keep salespeople motivated to continue building their customer base and providing their company with expanded growth opportunities.

Company-Wide Performance Bonus. The success of the salesperson is tied to the overall performance of the company. Therefore, the bonus is based on company-wide goals. A national survey reported that 39 percent of companies have annual bonuses for salaried employees tied to company performance.[23] At Federal Express, Fredrick W. Smith, chairman and chief executive officer, has everyone, including himself, on the same company-wide bonus plan. If the company does poorly, everyone including himself makes less money. Marshall Industries has introduced a corporate-wide compensation system that pays everyone, including all 600 salespeople, on the same plan. Exhibit 16.5 discusses how a quality initiative inspired the plan and the positive results achieved.[24]

EXHIBIT 16.5 - Selling Without Commissions

Marshall Industries, an industrial electronics company based in El Monte, California, is evidence that a sales organization can work without commissions and incentives and that a company can grow its business without volume-based rewards.

As part of its quality effort inspired by W. Edwards Deming, Marshall introduced a corporate-wide compensation system that paid everyone—from secretaries to the president—on the same plan, a salary plus a bonus based on the company's quarterly profits. Marshall's 600 inside and outside salespeople are included in the plan.

Robert Rodin, Marshall's president and chief operating officer, stresses, however, that the change was not a compensation issue per se, but a quality issue aimed at "aligning our compensation to support customer service." Under the previous commission arrangement, says Rodin, salespeople were "too concerned with their own performance, as opposed to listening to the customer. Compensation was an obstacle to world-class quality."

Whereas, in the past, pay was determined by how much a salesperson had shipped the last quarter, now it is a base salary and profit-based bonus, same as everyone else. Base salaries are set on the basis of the internal value of a position to the company and external salary surveys, and factors like seniority, training, and education. Salary increases are tied to reviews that look at factors like customer satisfaction, designing new products, offering solutions, and training new employees.

To those who argue that you can't motivate salespeople without commissions, or some form of incentive program, Rodin responds, "You can get people to do anything by offering a reward, but can you get them to sustain it? Can you get them to look at both sides of the sale?" Rodin adds, however, that Marshall's changeover was carefully planned and constructed, and that the development process included input from salespeople and other employees affected.

And does it produce results? The company reports that salespeople are earning, on average, more than they made under the commission plan, and turnover among salespeople is down by 80 percent.

Provide Sales Training

Every authority agrees that ongoing sales training is necessary, but measuring the benefits of sales training is a difficult process. In addition, what sales training should accomplish is also not clear,[25] although almost everyone agrees that training is needed in product knowledge and in selling skills. Companies are interested in sales training because they want to increase sales productivity. The emphasis is largely on results. The chairman and chief executive officer of U.S. Steel expressed it this way:

"We support training and development activities to get results.... We're interested in the specific things that provide greater rewards to the employee, increased return to the stockholder, and enable reinvestment of sales revenue to meet the growing needs of the business. In other words, [we're interested in] those things which affect the "bottom line."[26]

Sales managers usually agree that company training programs should address the purpose of developing in salespeople the characteristics of success. These characteristics, though generally listed in a somewhat vague manner, usually include traits such as these:

1. Skill in listening
2. Enthusiasm
3. Empathy
4. Planning skills
5. Personal organization
6. Problem-solving ability
7. Time and territory management

Designing and implementing the sales training program is the sales manager's responsibility. An effective program includes these basic elements:

Field Training. It is a good idea to have both an experienced salesperson and a manager assist in training new sales reps. Traveling with a senior sales rep to observe selling skills, personality, and work habits is very revealing for novice sales reps. It is also a good idea to have the new reps accompany different sales managers to pick out the strengths and weaknesses of each manager, and eventually create their own style. Both managers and senior sales reps can impart more wisdom on a newcomer than many training courses might offer. At Interplane Glass in North Carolina, new reps learn the basics of selling by traveling with four regional sales managers, spending a week with each one. At Viking Freight, a shipping company in San Jose, field reps spend three days a week with a senior salesperson, one day with a local manager, and one day back in operations.[27]

Group Sessions. Sales training sessions that focus on a single topic (e.g., prospecting, closing, or product knowledge) are valuable in sharpening skills for all members of the sales group. The group training session provides valuable interaction between salespeople and allows individuals to learn from one another.

A common form of training in group sessions is *role playing*: One trainee assumes the role of salesperson and another trainee or the sales manager plays the role of a prospect. A third person may act as observer to critique the performance. They go through the various steps of the sales process to gain experience in using the sales aids, giving the presentation, asking questions, and handling objections. A session may cover the entire selling process or concentrate on one specific step in the process. Some role-playing sessions are either audiotaped or videotaped for later review.

One-on-One Sessions. The sales manager must be willing to spend time with individual salespeople to give specific feedback and encourage continuing development. One-on-one time can be used to pinpoint individual problems and help the salesperson to develop a program of personal growth to correct any problems discovered.

Interactive Sales Training. The rate of learning from an interactive electronic medium is 35 percent higher than from traditional classroom approaches. Interactive multimedia sales training has arrived. With the interactive format you get the benefits of sound, videos, slide shows, and self-tests, and the capability to determine what you want to learn, when you want to learn it. Salespeople using this new interactive format will have higher rates of retention, take less time to train, have easier access to information, and have a higher comfort level. Sales managers now have the opportunity to work with one, or one hundred, salespeople in front of a computer to watch and learn new techniques or practice what they do best.[28]

Feedback. The sales training program must provide for feedback on performance. When a skill is noticed in a training session, a method for tracking field improvement shows whether the training has been effective. When salespeople see that the training has made a direct impact on their performance and their incomes, they are eager to receive more training and give their best efforts to learning.

The amount of time spent in sales training for recruits and for experienced salespeople varies from industry to industry and also from company to company. Time for training is affected by the complexity of the industry, the commitment of the company to training, and the company's experience with past training programs. The exact procedure also varies as a result of the same factors. Some companies conduct concentrated training for new recruits before they are allowed to go into the field. Others use a mix of training and field experience to help recruits learn by doing. A few still hand the recruit a sales kit and follow the *sink-or-swim method*. On the whole, the training period for recruits tends to be shorter for manufacturers of consumer products than for manufacturers of industrial products. Service companies—including insurance, banking, public utilities, and transportation—companies, generally have longer sales training programs than manufacturers.

Supervise and Motivate

A sales manager must see that salespeople call on their accounts with sufficient frequency, prospect for new business, keep up to date on new developments in the general market, and receive continuous training in new product technology or advanced sales techniques. Guiding salespeople in setting realistic goals, offering appropriate incentives to trigger achievement of those goals, and rewarding them for success are the sales manager's responsibility. Motivation is at the heart of supervision. The sales manager's involvement in motivation is designed to provide an environment within which salespeople can develop the ability to motivate themselves.

A sales manager is much like a professional sports coach. John Madden, a former successful professional football coach, explained to a reporter his philosophy about motivating football players like this: "I don't motivate them. I find motivated men and teach them how to play football." The principle is clear: If the basic functions of recruiting and selection are successfully performed, training and motivation of the sales force become less of a problem.

SUMMARY

Although organizations often promote leading salespeople to positions in sales management, the functions of the sales manager differ considerably from those of salespeople. The sales manager must be both a skillful salesperson and an efficient manager. The sales manager stands between field salespeople and company management. The sales manager performs the usual managerial functions of translating the goals of the company into strategies and tactics that the members of the sales department can address through daily activities and seeing that those activities result in the achievement of the department's responsibilities to the company.

In addition, the sales manager is concerned with helping salespeople develop personally and professionally so that they can make the greatest possible contribution to achievement of the organization's goals. The specific tasks of the sales manager include: (1) organizing the sales force, (2) determining personnel needs, (3) recruiting and selecting salespeople, (4) designing a compensation plan that motivates salespeople and assures that sales activities will achieve desired goals, (5) training salespeople to sell the company's product or service effectively, and (6) supervising and motivating salespeople.

QUESTIONS FOR THOUGHT AND DISCUSSION

1. List the advantages and disadvantages for choosing a sales manager in each of the following ways:

    a.   Promoting the top-producing salesperson in the organization
    b.   Lateral transfer of an effective manager from another department (e.g., finance, advertising, manufacturing)
    c.   Hiring someone from outside the organization

2. Are top salespeople automatically likely to be good sales managers? Why or why not?

3. What are the six key functions of a sales manager?

4. How can a sales manager determine how large a sales force should be?

5. What are the most common components of sales training?

6. What does the sales manager need to learn through interviewing a prospective salesperson?

7. What do you consider the most important incentives for salesperson productivity that a sales manager could provide?

8. If a company wants to exercise a great deal of control over the time and activities of its salespeople and does not especially need aggressive selling, what kind of compensation package is most appropriate?

9. If the organization's goal is high-volume sales and management is willing to have salespeople structure their own time and activities, what type of compensation plan is most likely to result in achievement of that goal?

10. What are some of the most easily accessible sources of recruits for positions as salespeople? What are the advantages and the disadvantages of each of these sources?

ACTIVITIES

1. Check the Sunday paper classified advertisements for sales positions. Cut out three ads that include job descriptions and bring them to class.

2. Look in the employment section of *The Wall Street Journal*. Find several ads for sales management positions. What qualifications are listed and what compensation is offered for each?

3. Interview a sales manager in a local company. Ask about the sales manager's job responsibilities, what percentage of time is spent on each, and what is the biggest job frustration.

Case Study

CASE 16.1

Jesse Schavey had been appointed branch manager for the Lyantic Electrical Switch Company in its Mideast region just three weeks ago and already he had to deal with a problem salesperson.

A week ago, Clarence Brewster, the hotshot salesperson, had demanded that the branch service engineer ignore scheduled calls and rush out to one of his good accounts and leave the office clerk to make excuses to the bypassed customers.

This morning, another problem came up. The credit manager from the home office phoned: "Your man Brewster is trying to pull another fast one. He says that the Myard Company is temporarily strapped for cash and he wants us to extend their discount date for another fifteen days."

"As you know," Jesse said, "I'm new in this territory. How good a customer is this Myard outfit?"

"I'd say they're about medium size. Of course, Brewster claims that if we do relax our rules, it'll put him in line for a huge order. It seems that Myard is coming out with a new product that will be using solid-state switches. They seem to think that the market for their product is virtually unlimited."

"This sounds like a pie-in-the-sky deal to me," Jesse said, "but you know your business better than I do; so if you do sometimes grant extensions, this might be a chance to find out if Brewster's just talking through his hat."

The credit manager agreed to go along with the experiment. As he said, "If the order does turn out to be a good one, we won't mind waiting a few days for payment. If it turns out to be a dud, we haven't lost much and we'll have a good argument for sticking to our regular discount schedule."

Jesse told the office clerk to keep an eye out for an order from Myard. A few days later, one came through that was actually smaller than usual. This incident prompted Jesse to do some investigating. First, he dug out Clarence's call report files; no reports had been received for the past two weeks. Each salesperson was required to leave a weekly call schedule in the office, so Jesse tried to reach Clarence by telephone. However, the three customers on Clarence's call list hadn't seen him.

That Jesse has a maverick on his hands was becoming clear. Clarence is obviously a nonconformist who ignores the usual business practices as he sees fit. He's developed and follows his own pattern of work, even though company policy, office routine, and sales methods fall by the wayside. Before he took any action or made any judgments, however, Jesse decided that fairness required looking at the results. What sort of business was he producing with his do-it-yourself methods?

The year's records showed him second in branch standing. He kept the orders rolling in; he ranked highest in new accounts; he was resourceful in developing new uses for the product, which increased business with present customers.

In talking with the rest of the staff, Jesse learned that Clarence had a close identification with the company, obvious pride in its products, and respect for the selling profession.

Despite Clarence's record and pride in the company and its products, Jesse thought that all concerned would benefit if Clarence were brought into line, as long as he did not lose his enthusiasm for selling.

1. Is Jesse attaching too much importance to Clarence's style? As long as he produces, should Jesse care about Clarence's little idiosyncrasies?

2. If Jesse is justified in thinking he has a problem, how should he approach Clarence to gain his cooperation and yet not dampen his enthusiasm for the company and his job?

END NOTES

CHAPTER 1

1. Quote from the Conference Board: Found in *The Selling Advantage* (May 28, 1992), 2. A publication of *Progressive Business Publications.*
2. Jenny C. McCune, "The Sales Arsenal," *Success* (May 1994), 11.
3. Beth Brophy and Gordon Witkin, "Ordinary Millionaires," *U.S. News and World Report*, Vol. 100, No. 1 (January 13, 1984), 43-52.
4. Bob Alexander, "Picture Perfect: How Kodak Trains For Sales Success," *Personal Selling Power* (March 1994), 19-20.
5. "Do Commissions Equal High Turnover?" *Sales & Marketing Management* (January 1994), 40.
6. Charles W. Stephens, "Why is Training so Important?" *Industrial Distribution*, Vol. 89, No. 2 (February 2000), 4.
7. Roy Chitwood, "Web-based Technology Makes Sales Training Easier," *Puget Sound Business Journal*, Vol. 20, No 37, (January 14, 2000), 14.
8. Erika Rasmusson, "Training Goes Virtual," *Sales & Marketing Management* (September 2000), 108.
9. Michael E. Rega, "Professional Salesperson: You Have Got To Earn It," *The American Salesman* (February 2000), 7.
10. The information contained in Table 1.1 has been modified and adapted from the following sources: D.L. Thompson, "Stereotype of the Salesperson," *Harvard Business Review*, Vol. 50, No. 1, (January/February 1972), 20-29; Robert W. Cook and Timothy Hartman, "Female College Student Interest in a Sales Career: A Comparison," *Journal of Personal Selling & Sales Management*, Vol. 6, (May 1986), 29-34; Michael Swenson, William Swinyard, Frederick Langrehr, and Scott Smith, "The Appeal of Personal Selling as a Career: A Decade Later," *The Journal of Personal Selling & Sale Management*, Vol. 13, No. 1 (Winter 1993), 51; "Sales Strikes Out on Campus," *Sales & Marketing Management* (November 1997), 13; "Selling Sales to Students," *Sales & Marketing Management* (January 1998), 15; Harry Harmon, "An Examination of Students' Perceptions of a Situationally Described Career in Personal Selling," *Journal of Professional Services Mar-keting,* Vol. 19, No. 1 (Fall 1999), 119-136; Susan DelVecchio, "An Investigation of African-American Perceptions of Sales Careers," The *Journal of Personal Selling & Sales Management*, Vol. 29, No. 1 (Winter 2000), 43-52.
11. Audrey Bottjen, "The Benefits of College Recruiting," *Sales & Marketing Management* (April 2001), 12.
12. Melissa Campanelli, "Finding Top Reps On Campus," *Sales & Marketing Management* (March 1995), 38.
13. Andy Cohen, "Whiz Kid," *Sales & Marketing Management* (July 1994), 92; "Babes in Toyland: Donald Spector's Investors Hoped for an IPO," *Business Week Frontier,* (April 14, 1999); "Youngest Toy Company Leader Hasn't Forgotten How to Have Fun," *The Augusta Chronicle,* (February 28, 1999).
14. Adapted from Michael E. Riga, "The Five Biggest Myths of Professional Selling," *The American Salesman* (April 1998), 11-14; and Caroline Bollinger, "Do You Think Selling Can Be Taught," *Selling* (July/August 1994), 15.
15. Nick DiBari, "Compensation vs. Motivation," *Sales & Marketing Management*, Vol. 133, No. 5 (October 8, 1984), 48-49.
16. Abraham H. Maslow, *Motivation and Personality*, 2nd ed. (New York: Harper & Row Publishing, 1970).
17. Andy Cohen, "The Best Route to CEO," *Sales & Marketing Management* (May 2001), 14.
18. Heather Baldwin, "Sale to the Top," *Selling Power* (July/August 2000), 71-72.
19. Sherry Siegel, "Selling Your Way to the Top," *Success,* (January/February 1987), Vol. 34, No. 1, 44.
20. Derek Newton, *Sales Force Performance and Turnover* (Cambridge, MA: Marketing Science Institute, 1973), 3; Derek Newton, "Get the Most Out of Your Sales Force," *Harvard Business Review* (September/October 1969), 130-143.
21. For the person not familiar with Network marketing I encourage you to read: Richard Eisenberg, "The Mess Called Multilevel Marketing," *Money* (May 1987), 136-160; "Melaleuca: A Future to Bank On," *Inc.* (December 1991), 6-7; Mark Yarnell, "A Venture Expert's Advice," *Success* (July 1994), 26.
22. These traits were gleaned from the following sources: David McClelland, "Hiring Top Performers," *Success* (May 1994), Vol. 41, No. 4, 34; Brian Azar, "Are You a Master Salesperson," *Personal Selling Power* (April 1992), Vol. 12, No. 3, 27; "Top Ten Sales Reps Prove Their Worth," *Purchasing* (March 22, 1990), 27; and "Qualities to Look for When You're Hiring," *Sales & Marketing Management,* Vol. 135, No. 3 (August 13, 1995), 84-87.
23. Ralph Waldo Emerson, "Circles," in *Essays: First Series* (1841).
24. Stan Moss, "What Sales Executives Look For in New Salespeople," *Sales & Marketing Management,* Vol. 120, No. 4 (March 1978), 47.
25. Laird E. Landon, "Lessons from a 'Million-Dollar' Salesman," *Bank Marketing*, Vol. 15, No. 2 (February 1984), 6.
26. Joseph Jones, "Ten Sales Fundamentals," *Personal Selling Power,* Vol. 15, No. 2 (March 1995), 52.
27. Information Adapted from "How Salespeople Spend Their Time," The Fenemore Group. *Sales & Marketing Management* (March 1998), 96.
28. Betsy Cummings, "Retire? No Thanks," *Sales & Marketing Management* (December 2000), 29.
29. Geoffrey Brewer, "What Makes Great Salespeople?" *Sales & Marketing Management* (May 1994), 85.

CHAPTER 2

1. Neil Rackman, "The Other Revolution in Sales," *Sales & Marketing Management* (March 2000), 34.
2. Betsy Cummings, "Listen Don't Talk," *Sales & Marketing Management* (March 2001), 65; Judy Corwin, "Taking Sales Education Global," *Baylor Business Review* (Fall 1997), 16-17.
3. Cummings, "Listen Don't Talk," 65.
4. Edwin Rigsbee, "The Relationship You Build with Your Prospects and Customers is More Important Than the Close," *The American Salesman* (October 1997), 1-4; Robert P. Degroot, "An Overview of 12 Selling Models," *Personal Selling Power* (July/August 1994), 57; and John R. Graham, "Turn Added Value Into Added Sales," *Personal Selling Power* (January/February 1995), 62.

5. Joan Leotta, "How to Become a Business Asset to Your Customers," *Selling Power* (January/February 2000), 44.

6. William F. Kendy, "Buyers View Your Product or Service as a Commodity," *Selling Power* (September 2000), 53; Cliff Zalz, "Building Relationships," *Business Marketing* (August 1992), 34.

7. Figure 2.1 was created from ideas gleaned from the following sources: Nancy Arnott, "It's a Woman's World," *Sales & Marketing Management* (March 1995), 56; Larry Chambers, "Don't Let Fear Kill Your Sale," *Personal Selling Power*, Vol. 12, No.6 (September 1992), 36; "Top Sales Reps Prove Their Worth," *Purchasing* (March 22, 1990), 27; and Tony Alessandra, Phil Wexler, and Rick Barrera, *Non-Manipulative Selling*, 2nd. Ed. (1987).

8. Barbara Geraghty, *Visionary Selling* (New York: Simon & Schuster, 1998), 240.

9. Geoffrey Brewer, "Alive and Selling," *Sales & Marketing Management* (September 2000), 8.

10. Lisa Ferrari, "Sell Faster," *Selling Power* (January/February 2001), 96.

11. Robert McGarvey and Babs S. Harrison, "How Tech Hip are You?" *Selling Power* (March 2001), 77.

12. Elana Harris, "Maidenform Manages Its Supply Chain Online," *Sales & Marketing Management* (April 2001), 26.

13. Lois A. Mohr and Mary Jo Bitner, "The Role of Employee Effort in Satisfaction with Service Transactions," *Journal of Business Research,* Vol. 32, No. 3 (March 1995), 239-240.

14. Gabrielle Birkner, "Wired Executive," *Sales & Marketing Management* (June 2000), 42.

15. William C. Moncrief, Emin Babakus, David W. Cravens, and Mark W. Johnston, "Examining Gender Differences in Field Sales Organizations," *Journal of Business Research*, 49, 3 (September 2000), 245-257.

16. Nancy Arnott, "It's a Woman's World," *Sales & Marketing Management* (March 1995), 57; "1991 Sales Manager's Budget Planner," *Sales & Marketing Management* (July 17, 1991), 77.

17. Lucette B. Comer and Marvin A. Jolson, "Perceptions of Gender Stereotypic Behavior: An Exploratory Study of Women in Selling," *Journal of Personal Selling & Sales Management* (Winter 1991), 43-59.

18. Patrick Schul and Brent Wren, "The Emerging Role of Women in Industrial Selling: A Decade of Change," *Journal of Marketing*, 56 (July 1992), 38.

19. Fredrick A. Russ and Kevin A. McNeilly, "Links Among Satisfaction, Commitment, and Performance," *Journal of Business Research*, 34, 1 (September 1995), 57-61.

20. Judy A. Siguaw and Earl Honeycutt, Jr. "An Examination of Gender Differences in Selling Behaviors and Job Attitudes," *Industrial Marketing Management*, 24 (1995), 46; Robert Sharoff, "She Said, He Said," *Selling* (May 1994), 54-58.

21. Paula Zmudzinski, "Gender Mutters," *Selling Power* (March 2000), 8.

22. Gary Bachelor, "Selling Beyond Gender," *Selling Power* (January/February 1996), 66-67.

23. Ron Zemke, "TQM: Fatally Flawed or Simply Unfocused?" *Training* (October 1992), 8; Paul Mears, "How to Stop Talking About, and Begin the Process Toward TQM," *Business Horizons* (May/June 1993), 11-14.

24. Rose Knotts, "Rambo Doesn't Work Here Anymore," *Business Horizons* (January/February 1992), 44-46.

25. Geoffrey Brewer and Christine Galea, "America's Best Sales Forces," *Sales & Marketing Management* (October 1997), 63.

26. Philippe Hermel, "The New Faces of Total Quality in Europe and the US," *Total Quality Management* (August 1997), 131-143; James W. Cortada, *TQM for Sales & Marketing Management* (McGraw-Hill: New York, 1993), 17.

27. His classic work is W. Edwards Deming, *Out of the Crisis* (Cambridge, MA: MIT, 1986); also see M. Walton, *Deming Management at Work* (Putnam/Perigee: New York, 1990), 20.

28. John Tschohl, "Benefits of Customer Service," *The Selling Advantage*, Vol. 4, Issue 82 (June 12, 1992), 3.

29. Tom Peters, "Meeting the Dangers and Opportunities of Chaos," *Personal Selling Power*, Vol. 10., No. 6 (September 1990), 49.

30. The idea for this figure was adapted from a manuscript done by Dr. James C. Cotham, Belmont University, Nashville, TN. Author used it on March 23, 1995. Actual date of Dr. Cotham's work is unknown, "Principles and Concepts of Total Quality Management; Competing in the Marketing Wars of the 1990s: Get Better or Get Beaten."

CHAPTER 3

1. Stephen Koepp, "Having It All, Then Throwing It All Away," *Time* (May 25, 1987), 22.

2. Clarence Walton, ed., *The Ethics of Corporate Conduct* (Englewood Cliffs, NJ: Prentice-Hall, 1977), 10.

3. Thomas R. Wotruba, "A Framework for Teaching Ethical Decision-Making in Marketing," *Marketing Education Review*, Vol. 3, No. 2 (Summer 1994), 4.

4. Allan Bloom, *The Closing of the American Mind* (New York: Simon and Schuster, 1987), 61.

5. Charles Schwepker and Thomas Ingram, "Improving Sales Performance Through Ethics: The Relationship Between Salesperson Moral Judgement and Job Performance," *Journal of Business Ethics* (November 1996), 3.

6. Peta Penson, "Success Depends on Strong Ethics From the Top," *The Business Journal* (March 24, 2000), 20.

7. "Nice Guys Finish First," *Business Ethics*, Vol. 7, No. 3 (May/June 1993), 10.

8. Arthur Bragg, "Ethics in Selling, Honest," *Sales & Marketing Management*, Vol. 138, No. 7 (May 1987), 44.

9. Michele Marchetti, "Whatever it Takes," *Sales & Marketing Management*. (December 1997, 29-36.

10. Andy Cohen, "Slowdown Effect: Lack of Ethics," *Sales & Marketing Management* (June 2001), 13.

11. Charles Schwepker, O.C. Ferrell and Thomas Ingram, "The Influence of Ethical Climate and Ethical Conflict on Role Stress in the Sales Force," *Academy of Marketing Science Journal* (Spring 1997), 2-3.

12. Saul W. Gellerman, "Why 'Good' Managers Make Bad Ethical Choices," *Harvard Business Review*, Vol. 64 (July/August 1986), 89.

13. Karen Trent, "The Dangers of Groupthink," *Teamwork* (June 4, 1990), 1.

14. Erin Strout, "Doctoring Sales," *Sales & Marketing Management* (May 2001), 59.

15. Patrick Willard, *The Nashville Tennessean* (November 24, 1987), 1A.

16. Dale Buss, "Ways to Curtail Employee Theft," *Nation's Business* (April 1993), 36.

17. Kathleen O'Neill, "Firms Say Thank You with Business Gifts," *Public Relations Journal* (September 1991), 28.

18. "Ethical Eating," *U.S. News and World Report* (August 5, 1991), 11.

19. Bragg, "Ethics," 44.

20. Nancy R. Hauserman, "Whistle-Blowing: Individual Morality in a Society," *Business Horizons*, Vol. 29 (March/April 1986), 4.

21. Janet Bamford, "When Do You Blow the Whistle?" *Forbes* (October 21, 1985), 168.

22. "For Whom the Whistle Blows," *Business Ethics*, Vol. 7, No. 2 (March/April 1993), 10.

23. Philip Mulivor, "E-Mail Whistleblowers," *American Journalism Review*, Vol. 15 (December 1993), 10.

24. Glenn T. Wilson, "Ethics, Your Company or Your Conscience," *Working Woman* (June 1984), 67.

25. Robert Tucker, "Values: The Key To Winning in the New Millennium," *Sales Doctors.com* (November 22, 1999), 1. Excerpt taken from Robert Tucker's book, *Customer Service For The New Millennium*. The book tells

how America's most successful companies outsell their competitors by employing outstanding service.

26. Melinda Ligos, "Clicks and Misses," *Sales & Marketing Management* (June 2000), 74.

27. "Sexual Harassment: Injured at Work." [Online] Available http://www.lawguru.com/sexhara.html (April 22, 1998).

28. Herff Moore and Don Bradley III, "Sexual Harassment in Manufacturing: Seven Strategies Successful Companies Use to Curb it," *Industrial Management* (Nov/Dec 1997), 14-18.

29. Betsy Cummings, "Falling Stars," *Sales & Marketing Management* (December 2000), 62.

30. Robert Aalberts and Lorne Seidman, "Sexual-harassment Policies for the Workplace," *Cornell Hotel and Restaurant Administration Quarterly* (October 1996), 82.

31. Abby Brown, "Is Ethics Good Business?" *Personnel Administrator*, Vol. 32 (February 1987), 67.

32. David J. Lill, "Issue of Ethics Often Faces Professional Salespeople," *Nashville Business Journal* (April 22-26, 1991), 5.

33. "Selling and the Law," *Industrial Distribution*, Vol. 71 (October 1981), 38.

34. Ibid., 39.

35. Ibid., 40.

36. Modified and adapted from the following sources: Mike Elgan, "The War Over Windows," *WINDOWS* (June 1998), 17; "Microsoft Asks for it, but Lawsuits go too far," *USA TODAY* (Friday, May 22, 1998), 15A; "Why Nader is Taking on Gates," from an interview with the editor of *Sales & Marketing Management* magazine (January 1998), 82; Jay Greene, "Microsoft How It Became Stronger Than Ever," *Business Week* (June 4, 2001), 75-81; Additional information in an article by D. Ian Hopper, *Court Reverses Breakup of Microsoft*, newsroom.compuserve.com/nr/editori...slot.1 on June 28, 2001.

37. Robert Posch, "Antitrust is Back," *Direct Marketing* (February 1994), 46.

38. Steven M. Sack, "The High Risk of Dirty Tricks," *Sales & Marketing Management*, Vol. 135, No. 7 (November 11, 1985), 58.

39. Gellerman, "Why 'Good' Managers," 86.

CHAPTER 4

1. Chester R. Wasson, *Consumer Behavior: A Managerial Viewpoint* (Austin, TX: Austin Press, 1975), 9.

2. For an expanded description of the model, see James F. Engel, Roger D. Blackwell, and Paul W. Miniard, *Consumer Behavior* (Hinsdale, IL: Dryden Press, 1990).

3. Lorrie LiBrizzi, "What Makes Business-To-Business Marketing Unique," *Direct Marketing* (October 1999), 30-31.

4. A more thorough discussion is found in William O. Bearden, Thomas N. Ingram, and Raymond W. LaForge, *Marketing* (Boston: Irwin McGraw-Hill, 1998), 124-140.

5. *Statistical Abstract of the United States, 19th ed.,* US Department of Commerce (Washington, DC: U.S. Government Printing Office, 1999), 115; "The Biggest Customer: How to Sell State Governments on Buying Your Product or Service," *Selling Power* (October 1997), 33.

6. For an expanded analysis on the roles played see, Francy Blackwood, "Nowhere to Go But Up," *Selling* (April 1994), 16-19; William G. Zikmund and Michael d'Amico, *Effective Marketing* (St. Paul, MN: West Publishing Company, 2001), 165; and Frederick E. Webster, Jr. and Yoran Wind, "A General Model For Understanding Organizational Buying Behavior," *Journal of Marketing*, Vol. 36, No. 2 (April 1972).

7. There are 40 squares in the figure.

8. Tim Connor, *The Soft Sell* (Crofton, MD: TR Training Associates, 1981), 16.

9. Betsy Cummings, "Selling Around the World," *Sales & Marketing Management* (May 2001), 70.

10. "Solving Problems With Languages," Source: PR News, 127 E. 80th St., New York, NY 10021. Found in *Communication Briefings*, Vol. 9, No. 11 (November 1991), 6.

11. Nanci McCann, under "Protocol" in the Selling Solutions Section, *Selling* (June 1994), 79.

12. James C. Simmons, "A Matter of Interpretation," *American Way* (April 1983), 106-111.

13. Carolyn Dickson, "Learn the Business Culture Before Hitting Foreign Turf," *Crain's Cleveland Business* (February 14, 2000), 18-19; Lionel Laroche and Susan Morey, "Minding Your Manners," *CMA Management* (March 2000), 38-41; George Haber, "Use Cross Cultural Savvy and Patience," *Personal Selling Power* (January/February 1992), 43-52.

14. Tim Connor, "Effective Sales Communication Skills," *Salesdoctor.com* (September 20, 1999), 1-5.

15. Anthony J. Alessandra and Philip S. Wexler, *Non-Manipulative Selling* (Reston, VA: Reston Publishing Company, 1979), 43-45.

16. William F. Schoell and Joseph P. Guiltinan, *Marketing*, 6th. ed. (Englewood Cliffs, NJ: Prentice Hall, 1995), 441-447.

17. Albert Mehrabian, *Silent Messages* (Belmont, CA: 1971).

18. Robert Pryor, *A Dress for Success Seminar*, Baylor University, Waco, TX (October, 1986); and Matthew J. Culligan, "What It Takes to Succeed in Sales," *Nation's Business* (April 1982), 42-45.

19. Bob Ayrer and Ray Considine, "I Said, "Are You Listening To Me?" *Agency Sales Magazine* (January 2000), 58.

20. "Fine-Tuning Your Negotiating Skills," *Professional Selling*, Vol. 22, No. 4 (February 25, 1984), 2.

21. "The Perils of Miscommunication" *Professional Selling*, Vol. 27, No. 20 (October 25, 1989), 2.

22. Alessandra and Wexler, *Non-Manipulative Selling*, 48-51.

23. This section on the voice was adapted from: Jeffrey Jacobi, "Voice Power," *Selling Power* (October 2000), 66; Robert A. Peterson, Michael P. Cannito and Steven P. Brown, "An Exploratory Investigation of Voice Characteristics," *The Journal of Personal Selling & Sales Management* (Winter 1995), 1-16; John H. Melchinger, "Communication—One Key to Unlock Your Sales, " *Personal Selling Power*, Vol. 10, No. 3 (April 1990), 51.

24. This section was inspired by Alessandra and Wexler, *Non-Manipulative Selling*, 95-113; Gerhard Gschwandtner, *Non Verbal Selling Power* (Englewood Cliffs, NJ: Prentice-Hall, 1985), 3-80; and John T. Molloy, *Live for Success* (New York: Perigord Press, 1981).

25. T.R. Baron, "Using Gestures to Listen," *Personal Selling Power*, Vol. 3, No. 4 (May/June 1993), 45.

26. Kevin Daley, "See the Sale," *Selling Power* (May 1998), 42-44.

27. David J. Lill, James C. Cotham, and Jennie Carter Thomas, "Listen Up," *Optometric Economics*, Vol. 1, No. 4 (April 1991), 27. Contributed by Laurie Bergman, PEP Strategies Editor, *Optometric Economics*.

28. Tom Metcalf, "Communicating Your Message: The Hidden Dimension," *Life Association News* (April 1997), 18-21.

CHAPTER 5

1. Carl G. Jung, *Psychological Types* (New York: Harcourt Brace and Co., 1924).

2. I am indebted to these individuals and their companies for sharing this valuable information with me. For more detail, see David W. Merrill and Roger H. Reid, *Personal Styles and Effective Performance*, (Radnor, PA: Chilton Book Company, 1981); Paul Mok, *Communicating Styles Technology* (Dallas, TX: Training Associates Press, 1982); Larry Wilson, *Social Styles Sales*

Strategies (Eden Prairie, MN: Wilson Learning Corporation, 2000); Tony Alessandra, Phil Wexler, and Rick Barrera, *Non-Manipulative Selling* (Englewood Cliffs, NJ: Prentice-Hall, 1987).

3. John R. Graham, "Four Basic Categories of Prospects," *Personal Selling Power*, Vol. 13, No. 8 (November/December 1993), 56.

4. John L. Bledsoe, "How to Improve Your Relationships with Clients— and Your Staff, Too," *The Practical Accountant* (Institute for Continuing Professional Development, 1984).

5. *Interpretation Manual for Communicating Styles Technology* developed by Dr. Paul Mok, President of Training Associates Press of Richardson, Texas (Dallas: T A Press 1975) 5.

6. Robert F. Kantin and Mark W. Hardwick, *Quality Selling Through Quality Proposals* (Danvers, MA: Boyd and Fraser Publishing 1994), 28.

7. Hugh J. Ingrasci, "How to Reach Buyers in their Psychological 'Comfort Zones,'" *Industrial Marketing* (July 1981), 64; Merrill and Reid, *Personal Styles*, 88-117.

8. Todd Duncan, "Your Sales Style," *Incentive* (December 1999), 64-66.

9. Seth Godin, "The Dating Game," *Sales & Marketing Management* (May 2001), 34.

10. Tom Hoek, guest lecture at Belmont University, Nashville, TN, September 25, 2001. Mr. Hoek is president of Insurance Systems of Tennessee.

11. Tony Alessandra, Phil Wexler, and Rick Barrera, *Non-Manipulative Selling* (New York: Prentice Hall, 1987), 112.

12. Rod Nichols, "How to Sell to Different Personality Types," *Personal Selling Power**, Vol. 12, No. 8 (November/December 1992), 46; and Malcolm Fleschner, "The Microsoft Way," *Selling Power* (January/February 1998), 86.

13. Bruce Seidman, "The Psychology of the Sale, Part 1," *Salesdoctors.com* (February 14, 2000), 2.

14. Personal Communication with Roger H. Reid (July 21, 2001).

15. Vincent Alonzo, "Role Call: Defining Your Reps' Personality Types Can Open a Window to Motivate," *Sales & Marketing Management* (June 2001), 34-35; Helen Berman, "Selling to Different Personalities," *Folio: The Magazine for Magazine Management* (June 1999), 34-35.

16. Richard Jensen and Roy Spungin, "Analyze Your Prospects to a tee," *Selling Power* (July/August 1997), 80-81.

17. Flo Conway and Jim Siegelman, "The Awesome Power of the Mind-Probers," *Science Digest* (September 1983), 72-73.

18. Ed Rigsbee, "Explore the Benefits of Partnership Selling," *Personal Selling Power*, Vol. 12, No. 7 (October 1992), 46.

19. Conway, "The Awesome," 91.

20. William G. Nickels, Robert F. Everett, and Robert Klein, "Rapport Building for Salespeople: A Neuro-linguistic Approach," *Journal of Personal Selling & Sales Management* (November 1983), 2.

21. *Ibid* 1.

CHAPTER 6

1. Renee Houston Zemanski, "The Green Team," *Selling Power* (September 2000), 166.

2. Les Kiaschbaum, "How the Terms of Sale Can Impact Profits," *Personal Selling Power* (March 1990), 28.

3. James Mullen, "In (Name Here) We Trust," *Selling* (October 1995), 79.

4. George W. Colombo, "Need Info? Pick Up a Pen," *Selling* (May 1994), 24-26; and Malcolm K. Fleschner, "How to Automate Your Sales Force," *Personal Selling Power* (September 1991), 42.

5. Melinda Ligos, "Man on a Mission," *Sales & Marketing Management* (March 2001), 25.

6. Adapted from Ginger Trumfio, "On-Line at the Prudential," *Sales & Marketing Management* (June 1994), 42-44.

7. Malcolm Fleschner, "Easy Does It," *Selling Power* (March 2001), 120.

8. Modified and adapted from the following sources: Karen Starr, "The Socratic Method for The Next Millenium," *Selling Power* (June 2000), 21; Henry Canaday, "Know How," *Selling Power* (July/August 2000), 16; and Malcolm Fleschner, "In the Know-How Zone," *Selling Power* (September 2000), 32.

9. From a telephone interview with Paul Goldner on May 16, 2001; and adapted from Erika Rasmussan, "Training Goes Virtual," *Sales & Marketing Management* (September 2000), 108.

10. Adapted and modified from the following sources: James Kickie, "Lessons From An SFA Pioneer," *Sales & Field Automation* (March 1998), 31; and George Colombo, *Sales Force Automation: Using the Latest Technology to Make Your Sales Force More Competitive* (New York: McGraw-Hill, 1994).

11. Nelson King, "Contact Managers: Keep Your Sales Force in Touch," *Sales & Field Force Automation* (March 1998), 84.

12. Malcolm Fleschner, "Ooh, That Smarts!" *Selling Power* (January/February 2001), 30.

13. Adapted and modified from an article by Chad Kaydo, "A Position of Power, *Sales & Marketing Management* (June 2000), 105-112.

14. "Avon Rings Millions of New Bells," *Sales & Marketing Management* (October 1992), 25.

15. Don E. Schultz, "Objectives Drive Tactics in Integrated Marketing Communication Approach," *Marketing News* (May 9, 1994), 14; and Junu B. Kim, "Databases Open Doors For Retailers," *Advertising Age* (February 15, 1993).

16. Michael E. Cavanagh, "In Search of Motivation," *Personnel Journal*, Vol.63, No.3 (March 1984), 76.

17. Robert McGarvey and Babs S. Harrison, "Easy as Pie," *Selling Power* (March 2000), 116.

18. The sections of this chapter dealing with motivation and goal setting were taken largely from Paul J. Meyer's *Dynamics of Personal Goal Setting*, *Dynamics of Personal Leadership*, and *Dynamics of Personal Motivation* (Waco, TX: Success Motivation, 1991, 1992, and 1993, respectively).

19. Chris Glass, "Getting to Know You," *Sales & Marketing Management* (December 1997), 24-25.

20. Geoffrey Brewer, "Mind Reading," *Sales & Marketing Management* (May 1994), 85.

21. Harvey Mackay, "Life is a matter of perspective: It all depends on how you choose to see it," *JustSell.com* (May 1, 2000), 1.

22. Edwin Bobrow, "Goal-Oriented Selling," *The American Salesman* (January 2000), 14.

23. Gary Bachelor, "Map Your Goals," *Personal Selling Power*, Vol. 14, No. 1 (January/February 1994), 58.

24. Jack Cullen and Len D'Innocenzo, "How to Set and Communicate Goals," *Personal Selling Power*, Vol. 13, No. 8 (November/December 1993), 69.

25. Paul J. Meyer, *Dynamics of Personal Goal Setting*, Lesson 5 (Waco, TX: Success Motivation, Inc., 1984), 2.

CHAPTER 7

1. Barry Farber, "Get On Track." *Entrepreneur* (February 2000), 138.

2. Renee Zemanski, "Developing New Leads," *Selling Power* (March 2000), 34.

3. Dirk Beveridge, "Qualifying Your Prospects," *The American Salesman*, Vol. 36, No. 6 (June 1991), 6-9.

4. Paul J. Meyer, Sales Training Material for Distributors of SMI International, Inc. (Waco, TX).

5. "Fewer Than 10 Percent of Decision-Makers Contacted by Salespeople One-Month Period," *The American Salesman*, Vol. 33, No. 3 (March, 1988), 13-14.

6. Bill Cates, "Referrals 101," *Selling Power* (October 2000), 56.

7. Cliff Zalz, "Building Relationships,"

Business Marketing (August 1992), 34.

8. Michael Twining, "Million To Win," *Selling Power* (March 2000), 50.

9. Art Siegel, "Multiply Your Sales Through Referrals," *SalesDoctors magazine* (February 28, 2000), 1-6.

10. John R. Graham, "Stop Asking for Referrals," *The American Salesman* (October 2000), 9-13.

11. "Working with Distributor Salespeople," *Professional Selling*, Vol. 21, No. 19 (October 10, 1983), 4.

12. Irby F. Stewart, "Golden Opportunities," in power tips section of *Selling Power* (March 2001), 62.

13. Andrea J. Moses, "Taking the Stress Out of Cold Calling," *The Selling Advantage*, Vol. 4, Issue 1 (May 28, 1992), 1-2.

14. "The Medium and the Message," *Direct Marketing*, Vol. 56, No. 9 (January 1994), 27.

15. Behram J. Hansotia, "List Segmentation: How to Find Your Best Direct Marketing Prospects," *Business Marketing*, Vol. 71, No. 6 (August 1986), 64.

16. "Army Recruits Them by the Numbers," *Sales & Marketing Management*, Vol. 131, No. 8 (December 5, 1983), 12.

17. *USA Today* (March 8, 1988).

18. Richard Pluntron, "onthewebwith," *Sales & Marketing Management* (September 2000), 19.

19. Jeffrey Gitomer, "Networking Not Working? Try Smart-working," *Dallas Business Journal* (January 14, 2000), 43.

20. Tony Lee, "Networking; Only Connect," *Folio: the Magazine for Magazine Management,* Vol. 23, No. 2 (February 1, 1994), 33.

21. Al Urbanski, "Networking for Sales," *Sales & Marketing Management*, Vol. 130, No. 7 (May 16, 1983), 41.

22. "Bright Idea," *Personal Selling Power* (January/February 1993), 50.

23. John Greenwald, "Sorry, Right Number," *Time*, Vol. 142, No. 11 (September 13, 1993), 66.

24. M. L. Stein, "Telemarketing Tips: At the Houston Chronicle, Phone Sales Result in Nearly 40% of Ad Revenue," *Editor & Publisher*, Vol. 124, No. 35 (August 31, 1991), 16.

25. Robert J. Ayers, "Developing Incentives to Stimulate Sales," *Insurance Review*, Vol. 47, No. 3 (June, 1986), 57.

26. Karen Starr, "If the Shoe Fits, Make it Personal," *Selling Power* (January/February 2001), 26.

27. Eduardo Javier Canto, "Survey Says: Where the Sales Are," *Sales & Marketing Management* (June 2001), 18.

28. Jeff Tanner, *Curriculum Guide to Trade Show Marketing* (Bethesda, MD: Center for Exhibition Industry Research, 1995), T12.

29. Philip Gelman, "You have 20 seconds," *Personal Selling Power* (January/February 1994), 50-51; and "PepsiCo's Tradeshow Promotion Successfully Trades on 50s Nostalgia," *Imprint* (Winter 1996),14.

30. Ben Chapman, "The Trade Show Must Go On," *Sales & Marketing Management* (June 2001), 22.

31. Henry Canaday, "Virtual Exhibits Boost Trade Show Sales," *Selling Power* (January/February 2001), 22.

32. George Colombo, "E-Marketing: Target Your Market With Affiliates," *Sales & Marketing Management* (March 2001), 32.

33. Ginger Conton, *Sales & Marketing Management* (September 2000), 28; Karen E. Starr, "Web site Selling," *Selling Power* (May 1998), 18-21.

34. Robert McGarvey and Babs S. Harrison, "How Tech Are You," *Selling Power* (March 2001), 74; "The Sales Software Solution," *Personal Selling Power* (April 1990), 46-47.

CHAPTER 8

1. Sharon Parker, "Stand and Deliver," *Sales & Marketing Management* (January/February 2001), 18; Bryan Hysdu, "Surviving the Cold Call without Freezing," *The Journal of Commercial Bank Lending* (November 1986), 49.

2. Gabrielle Birkner, "Catapulting Sales," *Sales & Marketing Management* (June 2000), 17.

3. "Prime Preparation Makes the Grade," *Personal Selling*, Vol. 21, No. 16 (August 15, 1983), 3.

4. Linda Richardson, "Winning Strategies for Meeting Prospects," *Selling Power* (September 2000), 44.

5. Chad Kaydo, "Lights! Camera! Sales!," *Sales & Marketing Management* (February 1998), 111.

6. Rich Wilkins, "Visualize Your Success," *Professional Selling Power*, Vol. 13, No. 1 (January/February 1993), 69.

7. Kelly Immoor, "Copy That," *Selling Power* (March 2001), 61.

8. Robert E. Hite and Joseph A. Bellizzi, "Differences in the Importance of Selling Techniques between Consumer and Industrial Salespeople," *Journal of Personal Selling and Sales Management* (November 1985), 23.

9. Renee Zemanski, "Developing New Leads," *Selling Power* (March 2000), 34.

10. G. Berton Latamore, "Perfect Match," *Selling Power* (September 2000), 150-155.

11. John J. McCarthy, *Secrets of Super Selling* (Boardroom Books: New York, 1982), 91.

12. George N. Kahn, "Without Ammunition," *The Smooth Selling Series* (New York: George N. Kahn Co., 1976) 3.

13. Graham Roberts-Phelps, "How to Add Value to Every Sales Call," *Personal Selling Power*, Vol. 14, No. 1 (January/February 1994), 47.

14. Adapted from John J. Franco, "Ring Up More Telephone Sales with Well-Trained Personnel," *Business Marketing*, Vol. 71, No. 8 (August 1986), 84; and "Telephone Closes Are Up," *Personal Selling Power*, Vol. 14, No. 4 (May/June 1994), 20.

15. "Getting Past the Gatekeeper," *Selling Power* (July/August 2000), 56; Jan Gelman, "Gatekeeper," *Selling*, Vol. 2, No. 1 (July/August 1994), 54-56; and Nanci McCann, "Protocol," *Selling*, Vol. 1, No. 9 (May 1994), 79.

16. Michele Marchetti, "What a Sales Call Costs," *Sales & Marketing Management* (September 2000), 80-82.

17. Martin D. Shafiroff and Robert L. Shook, *Successful Telephone Selling in the '80s* (New York: Barnes & Noble Books, 1982), 9.

18. Adapted from George Walther's book, *Upside-Down Marketing.*

19. Wendy Weiss, "Top Ten Tips for Terminating Telephone Terror," *The American Salesman* (December 2000), 15-17.

20. June Johnson, "You Make a First Impression Only Once," *Selling Power* (June 2000), 42.

21. "Voice Concerns," *Personal Selling Power*, Vol. 13, No. 7 (October 1993), 44.

22. "Making a Telephone Investment," *Professional Selling*, Vol. 22, No. 5 (March 10, 1984), 1-2.

23. Jeffrey Jacobi, "Voice Power," Selling Power (October 2000), 66.

24. David Lill, "From phone to face-to-face," *Selling Power* (January/February 1998), 46-47.

25. Barry Z. Masser and William M. Leeds, *Power-Selling by Telephone* (West Nyack, NY: Parker Publishing Company, 1982), 56.

26. Shafiroff and Shook, *Successful Telephone Selling*, 36-37.

27. Paul O'Neil, "Selling Services: Using the Phone to Secure Face-to-face Appointments," *Salesdoctors Magazine* (October 25, 1999), 3; "Five Steps to Effective Telephone Sales," *Professional Selling*, Vol. 22, No. 13 (July 10, 1984), 2.

28. Information for this example came from an interview with Paula Wilson, District Manager in Nashville, TN, for TSI on June 15, 2000.

29. "Sixteen Ways to Improve Your Telemarketing Effort," *Personal Selling Power*, Vol. 12, No. 7 (October 1992), 42.

CHAPTER 9

1. Jenni Laidman, "Make it Count," *The Tennessean* (June 21, 2001), section D

of the Nashville newspaper, 1-2; George N. Kahn, "The Impression You Make," *Smooth Selling*, Vol. 62 (1967), 2.

2. Joan Leotta, "Dressed to Sell," *Selling Power* (October 2000), 89.

3. Anthony J. Alessandra and Phillip Wexler, *Nonmanipulative Selling* (Reston, VA: Reston Publishing, Inc., 1979), 87-93.

4. Joe Girard, *How to Sell Anything to Anybody* (New York: Warner Books, 1977), 143-144.

5. The exhibit was adapted from these sources:Elana Harris, "Dressing for Success, New Economy Style," *Sales & Marketing Management* (June 2000), 98; and Erika Rasmusson, "Corporate Casualties," *Sales & Marketing Management* (June 1997), 100-102.

6. Gerhard Gschwandtner, "Portrait of a World Class Sales Professional," *Personal Selling Power*, Vol. 12, No. 5 (July/August 1992), 60.

7. "Italian-Style Selling," *Sales & Marketing Management* (June 2001), 70.

8. Modified and adapted from the following sources: Melinda Ligos, "Does Image Matter," *Sales & Marketing Management* (March 2001), 53-56; Leo Green, "Ask an Expert: Five Do's and Don'ts for Dressing Down," *CA Magazine* (January/February 2001), 11; Geoffrey Brewer and Chad Kaydo, "Dressing for Success," *Sales & Marketing Management* (August 2000), 104.

9. Pat Shemek, "Super Duper Difference," *Selling Power* (July/August 2000), 56.

10. Melinda Ligos, "Does Image Matter?" *Sales & Marketing Management* (March 2001), 12.

11. Dorothea Johnson, director of The Protocol School of Washington, "Five Tips for International Handshaking," *Sales & Marketing Management* (July 1997), 90.

12. Henry Porter, "Opening for Every Occasion," *Sales Management*, Vol. 109, No. 9 (October 30,1972), 6-8.

13. "The Greeting," *American Salesman*, Vol. 27, No. 2 (February 1982), 20.

14. Karl Witsman, "No More What's His Name Again," *The American Salesman*, Vol. 32, No. 2 (February 1987), 25.

15. Adapted from "Here's an Easy Way to Remember Your Customers' Names," *Master Salesmanship* (Concordville, PA: Clement Communications, Inc., 1979) 3; and Nanci McCann, "When You Forget a Prospect's Name," *Selling* (March 1994), 101.

16. Adapted from Kevin Maney, "Take the Internet with you in a phone, watch or shoe," *USA TODAY* (March 18, 1998), 2B; George W. Colombo, "Need Info? Pick Up a Pen," *Selling* (May 1994), 24-26; Ginger Trumpio, "On-Line at

the Prudential," *Sales & Marketing Management* (June 1994), 42-44.

17. Phillip Proctor, "A Well–Bread Sale," *Selling Power* (September 2000), 20.

18. Paul P. Mok, "CST Influencing Model" from *CST: Communicating Styles Technology* (Dallas: T.A. Press, Inc., 1982), 13.

19. "Strange Tales of Sales," *Sales & Marketing Management*, Vol. 134, No. 8 (June 3,1985), 43.

CHAPTER 10

1. Bill Brooks, "What is the Difference Between What Customers Need and What They Really Want?" *The American Salesman* (January 2001), 3-5.

2. Ginger Trumfio, "Underlying Motivation," *Sales & Marketing Management* (June 1994), 71.

3. Erin Strout, "Throwing the Right Pitch," *Sales & Marketing Management* (April 2001), 63.

4. Art Sobczak, "Proposal Worthy," *Selling Power* (June 1997), 56; and Tim Connor, *The Soft Sell* (Crofton, MD: TR Training Associates Int'l., 1981), 64.

5. James Lorenzen, "Needs Analysis Replacing Product Presentation," *Marketing News*, Vol. 20, No. 9 (April 25, 1986), 180.

6. John O'Toole, "The Want Makes the Sale," *Selling* (June 1994), 43.

7. Camille P. Schuster and Jeffrey E. Davis, "Asking Questions: Some Characteristics of Successful Sales Encounters," *Journal of Personal Selling and Sales Management*, Vol. 6, No. 1 (May 1986), 17.

8. Wayne M. DeLozier, *The Marketing Communication Process* (New York: McGraw-Hill, 1976), 253.

9. Anthony Parinello, "Selling to VITO, the Very Important Top Officer" (Adams 1994), quoted in *Sales & Marketing Management* (August 1997), 108.

10. Ron Willingham, *The Best Seller* (Englewood Cliffs, NJ: Prentice-Hall, 1984), 37.

11. Anthony J. Alessandra and Phillip S. Wexler, *Non-Manipulative Selling* (Reston, VA.: Reston Publishing Co., 1979), adapted from 54-57.

12. Tim Connor, *The Soft Sell* (Crofton, MD: TR Training Associates Intl., 1981), 67.

13. Neil Rackham, *SPIN Selling* (New York: McGraw-Hill), 1988.

14. Ibid, 89.

15. Todd Youngblood, "Let Customers Sell Themselves," *Selling Power* (March 2001), 52.

16. William Kendy, "Probing For Real Customer Needs," *Selling Power* (January/February 2001), 26.

17. John M. Wilson, *Open the Mind, Close the Sale* (New York: McGraw-

Hill, 1953), 149.

18. Steve Atlas, "When and How to Use Your Favorite Close Effectively," *Selling Power* (September 2000), 48.

19. Doug Krumrei, "Poor Listeners — Disappointed Customers," *Bakery Production and Marketing* (March 15, 1998), 9; Max Messmer, "Improving Your Listening Skills," *Management Accounting* (March 1998), 14; and Marjorie Brody, "How To Listen To What's Really Being Said," *Personal Selling Power*, Vol. 14, No. 4 (May/June 1994), 65.

20. Murray Raphel, "Listening Correctly Can Increase Your Sales," *Direct Marketing*, Vol. 41, No. 11 (November 1982), 113.

21. Barry Elms, "Effective Listening is the Key to Identifying Buying Signals," *Selling Power* (March 2000), 40.

22. Rick Phillips, "Listen for More Sales," *Selling Power* (June 1996), 58-59; and Robert C. Immel, "Listen to What the Prospect is Telling You," *Sales & Marketing Executive Report IX*, Vol. 20 (October 1, 1986), 4-5.

23. George W. Colombo, "Need Info? Pick up a Pen," *Selling* (May 1994), 24-25.

24. Sarah Mahoney, "Hear Between the Lines," *Home Office Computing* (October 1997), 126-128; and Ken Thoreson, "Communicate to Sell," *Personal Selling Power*, Vol. 14, No. 1 (January/February 1993), 62.

CHAPTER 11

1. Bill Brooks, "What is the Difference Between What Customers Need and What They Really Want," *The American Salesman* (January 2001), 3-5.

2. This section culled from a book written by Dr. James Canton entitled, *Technofutures: How Leading Edge Technology Will Transform Business in the 21st Century* (Hay House, 1999).

3. "Presentations That Sell," *Sales & Marketing Management*. As adapted from Diane DiResta, *Knockout Presentations*, Chandler House Press, 1998.

4. William F. Kendy, "Presentations To Wow a Group," *Selling Power* (January/February 2001), 56.

5. Mack Hannan, "The Three C's of Selling: A Sure Cure for the Salesman's Curse," *Sales & Marketing Management*, Vol. 10, No. 7 (May 10, 1976), 93.

6. Ginger Trumfio, "Underlying Motivation," *Sales & Marketing Management* (June 1994), 71.

7. Robert F. Taylor, *Back to Basic Selling* (Englewood Cliffs, NJ: Prentice-Hall, 1985), 75.

8. Modified and adapted from: U.S. Census Bureau, Current Population Reports, 1993.

9. Gail S. Waisanen, "Cracking the Senior

Market," *Life Insurance Selling,* Vol. 69, No. 4 (April 1994), 173-190.

10. George N. Kahn, "You're on Stage," *Smooth Selling* (1975), 2.

11. Katherine Callan and Tom Stein, "Sales Arsenal," *Success* (May 1996), 24.

12. "Personal Touch Perks up Sales," In a special section entitled: Make Promotional Products Work For You, *Sales & Marketing Management* (October 1997), 7.

13. Staff of the National Sales Development Institute, *10 Steps to Greatness in Selling* (Waterford, CT: The National Sales Development Institute, 1980), 10-12.

14. Paul Piscitelli, "How to Wow an Audience," *Sales & Marketing Management* (June 1997), 63-69.

15. Adapted from Martha W. Holcombe and Judith K. Stein, "How to Deliver Dynamic Presentations: Use Visuals for Impact," *Business Marketing,* Vol. 71, No. 6 (June 1986), 163-164; and Richard Kern, "Making Visual Aids Work for You," *Sales & Marketing Management* (February 1989), 46-49.

16. Adapted from these articles: "Multi-Faceted Laser Disk Player," *Business Marketing* (June 1992), 36.; George W. Columbo, "Presenting: A New Tool," *Selling,* Vol. 1, No. 10 (June 1994), 29.

17. Heather Baldwin, "Let There Be Light," *Selling Power* (October 2000), 116.

18. Ibid, 118.

19. Karen Starr, "Plug and Play!" *Selling Power* (October 2000), 32-34.

20. Lisa Ferrari, "Sell Faster," *Selling Power* (January/February 2000), 96.

21. Erin Strout, "Throwing the Right Pitch," Sales & Marketing Management (April 2001), 62-63.

22. Bob Alexander, "How Laptops Put You in the Driver's Seat," *Personal Selling Power,* Vol. 10, No. 2 (March 1990), 53.

CHAPTER 12

1. For more detailed information on the art of Negotiation see these two articles: Gerhard Gschwandtner, "New York Negotiators," *Selling Power* (January/February 2000), 67-75; Ken Liebeskind, "You can be taught to negotiate," *Selling Power* (July/August 1997), 58.

2. Steve Atlas, "Demanding Customers," *Selling Power* (March 2001), 38.

3. James T. Healy, *Winning the High Tech Sales Game* (Reston, VA: Reston Publishing, 1985), 208.

4. Anthony Alessandra and Jim Cathcart, "Turn Objections into Sales," *Industrial Distribution,* Vol. 74, No. 1 (January

1985), 141.

5. Roger M. Pell, "The Road to Success is Paved with Objections," *Bank Marketing,* Vol. 22 (February 1990), 16.

6. Jack Kinder, Jr., Garry D. Kinder, and Roger Staubach, *Winning Strategies in Selling* (Englewood Cliffs, NJ: Prentice-Hall, 1981), 149.

7. Ron Willingham, *The Best Seller* (Englewood Cliffs, NJ: Prentice-Hall, 1984), 85.

8. Herman Harrow, "You Can Disagree without Being Disagreeable," *Sales & Marketing Management,* Vol. 123, No. 8 (December 10, 1979), 67.

9. Customer Objections: Do You Have the Answers?" *Professional Selling,* Vol. 22, No. 5 (March 10, 1984), 3.

10. "How do you address Objections? Here's a few ideas," *Life Association News* (November 1996), 16-18.

11. Myers Barnes, "Qualify Your Prospects To Avoid Stalls," *Selling Power* (March 2000), 33.

12. D. Forbes Ley, "The Stall—A Decision Not to Make a Decision," *The Selling Advantage* (May 14, 1991), 1-2.

13. Steve Atlas, "Listening for Hidden Objections," *Selling Power* (June 2000), 36.

14. R. G. McHugh, "Clearing Sales Hurdles: Here Are Key Questions," *Bank Marketing,* Vol. 18, No. 2 (February 1986), 10.

15. Graham Roberts-Phelps, "Objections Are Opportunities to Sell," *Personal Selling Power,* Vol. 12, No. 8 (November/December 1992), 34.

16. R.W. (Bill) Sharer, "When to Overcome Objections," *Industrial Distribution,* Vol. 73, No. 6 (March 1984), 34.

17. Dan Weadock, "Your Troops can Keep Control—and Close the Sale—by Anticipating Objections," *Sales & Marketing Management,* Vol. 124, No. 4 (March 17, 1980), 102-106.

18. Josh Gordon, *Tough Calls: Selling Strategies to Win Over Your Most Difficult Customers* (Amacom Publishing, 1997), 120.

19. Graham Roberts-Phelps, "Objections Are," 34.

20. Adapted and modified from *The Sales Question Book* published by *Personal Selling Power.* This was in the (November/December 1993) issue of the magazine on 43.

21. Frederic A. Russell, Frank H. Beach, and Richard H. Buskirk, *Selling: Principles and Practices* (New York: McGraw-Hill, 1982), 321; and Erika Rasmusson, "The Pitfalls of Price-Cutting," *Sales & Marketing Management* (May 1997), 17.

22. T. Scott Gross, "The Service Factor," *Selling Power* (October 2000), 45.

23. Rick Phillips, "Objection Prevention," *Selling Power* (July/ August 1997), 75.

24. Paul Goldner, "Overcoming Price Objection," *Agency Sales Magazine* (February 2000), 61.

25. John J. McCarthy, *Secrets of Super Selling* (New York: Boardroom Books, 1982), 324.

26. William F. Kendy, "Handling the Price Objection," *Selling Power* (September 2000), 41.

27. Rewritten from an article by Dr. David Lill, "Games negotiators play," Selling Power (September 1997), 90-91.

CHAPTER 13

1. "The Ingredients and Timing of the Perfect Close," *Sales Management,* Vol. 106, No. 12 (June 1971), 3.

2. Gerhard Gschwandtner, "On Closing the Sale," *Personal Selling Power,* Vol. 17, No. 5 (July/August 1987), 6.

3. Steve Atlas, "When and How to Use Your Favorite Close Effectively," *Selling Power* (September 2000), 48.

4. Paul H. Green, "Closing A Sale," (Web site – www.multiplex.com/Greensheet), July 9, 2001; and Gregg Berlie, "Anatomy of a Closing," *The American Salesman* (January 1986), 6.

5. Paul Frichtl, "Tactics for Tactics," *Industrial Distribution,* Vol. 75, No.7 (July 1986), 89.

6. Jeffrey Gitomer, "A funny thing happened to me on the way to closing a sale," (Web site – www.insiderbiz.com), July 15, 2001. Jeffrey Gitomer is author of *The Sales Bible* and *Customer Satisfaction is Worthless, Customer Loyalty is Priceless.*

7. "Sales Persistence: Pushing without Being Pushy," *Professional Selling,* Vol. 22, No. 6 (March 25, 1984), 2.

8. Tim Rudlaff, "The Power of Persistence," *Teamwork* (May 21, 1990), 1.

9. Graham Roberts-Phelps, "Make Persistence Pay," *Personal Selling Power,* Vol. 14, No. 4 (May/June 1994), 68.

10. Vincent Alonzo, "Addicted to Failure," *Sales & Marketing Management* (November 1997), 28.

11. William Kendy, "Handling Rejection," *Selling Power* (July/August 2000), 44; and Jack Falvey, "Adventures in No-Man's Land," *Selling* (April 1996), 83.

12. Adapted and modified from Pam Lontos, "Rejection Conditioning," *Selling Power* (June 1997), 78; and Tom Reilly, "Salespeople: Develop the Means to Handle Rejection," *Personal Selling Power,* Vol. 7, No. 5 (July/August 1987), 15.

13. Stephen Robinett, "The Final Step," *Success* (November 1986), 18.

14. Napolean Hill, "When Is the Psychological Moment to Close a Sale?," *Personal Selling Power,* Vol. 1, No. 3 (April 1991), 34. This article was orig-

inally written in the 1930's and reprinted in this issue.

15. Tom Reilly, "When You Ask for Commitment," *The Selling Advantage,* Vol. 4 (June 26, 1992), 1.

16. Cameron McPherson, "Remember: Ask for the Order," *Successful Closing Techniques* (Dartnell Corporation, 1986), 1.

17. Steve Atlas, "Listening For Buying Signals," *Selling Power* (March 2000), 38.

18. Adapted and modified from "Read the (closing) signs," *Selling Power* (September 1997), In the SELLING IDEAS section of the magazine, 108; and Adapted from William J. Tobin, "Watch for the Right Signal," *Telephony,* Vol. 197, No. 15 (October 8, 1979), 114-115.

19. William Kendy, "Body of Knowledge," *Selling Power* (March 2001), 68.

20. Jeanne Pritt, "Fifteen Secrets to Closing A Sale," *The Profit Zone Newsletter* (July 1998). From "The Profit Zone" – at www.profitzone.com

21. James J. Morrisey, "How to Use the Power of Silence," *Personal Selling Power,* Vol. 14, No. 55 (March 1994).

22. James O'Hara, "The Silent Barriers to Closing the Sale," *Selling* (May 1997), 9.

23. Andy Cohen, "Are Your Reps Afraid to Close?" *Sales & Marketing Management* (March 1996), 43.

CHAPTER 14

1. Kim Kinter, "No. 1 In Customer Satisfaction," *Selling* (April 1994), 98-100; and Daniel V. Byrne, "Delivering on a Guarantee: Perfect Service, No Exceptions," *Nation's Business* (August 1991), 6.

2. Ginger Trumfio, "Anything for a Client," *Sales & Marketing Management* (June 1994), 102; and Kate Bertrand, "In Service, Perception Counts," *Business Marketing* (April 1989), 44.

3. Paul R. Timm, *Customer Service: Career Success Through Customer Satisfaction* (New Jersey: Prentice-Hall, 1988), 45.

4. John Tschohl, "Exceptional Service—The Secret Weapon," *The Selling Advantage* (July 29, 1991), 2.

5. Steven Brown, "Service Recovery Through IT," *Marketing Management* (Fall 1997), 25-27; and Jan Carlzon, *Moments of Truth* (New York: Ballinger, 1987).

6. Jim Jewett, *Discovering Fast Track Success* (Columbus, OH: ESRL Press, 1988), 53.

7. Raymond Fisk, Stephen Grove, and Joby John, *Interactive Services Marketing* (New York: Houghton Mifflin Company, 2000), 181; Carl Sewell and Paul R. Brown, *Customers for Life* (New York

Pocket Books, 1990); Karl Albrecht and Ron Zemke, *Service America! Doing Business in the New Economy* (Homewood, IL: Richard D. Irwin, 1985), 6.

8. Kevin Freiberg and Jackie Freiberg, "Nuts! Southwest Airlines' Crazy Recipe for Business and Personal Success," 1996. *Adapted an insert in Selling Power* (September 1997), 103

9. Andy Cohen, "Changing Channels," *Sales & Marketing Management* (April 2001), 11.

10. "Get More From Current Customers," in the Selling Ideas section of *Selling Power* (October 2000), 62.

11. William Kendy, "How to Move the Customer to a Higher Purchasing Level," *Selling Power* (June 2000), 33-34.

12. Erika Rasmusson, "3M's Big Strategy For Big Accounts," *Sales & Marketing Management* (September 2000), 92-98.

13. Kathleen Cholewka, "CRM: Calling All Customers," *Sales & Marketing Management* (May 2001), 25-26.

14. Steve Atlas, "Focus on Solutions," *Selling Power* (March 2001), 40.

15. Dr. Ken Blanchard, "Get the Power," *Selling Power* (April 1998), 72; and "Promoting Your 'Service Differential,'" *Professional Selling,* Vol. 22, No.16 (August 15, 1984), 1.

16. Ray Dreyfack, "Good Complaints," in the Selling Ideas section of *Selling Power* (March 2000), 54.

17. Karl Albrecht and Ron Zemke, *Service America! Doing Business in the New Economy* (Homewood: Richard D. Irwin, 1985), 7-8.

18. Frederick H. Reichheld, "Learning from Customer Defections," *Harvard Business Review* (March/April 1996), 56-59; and Glenn DeSouza, "Designing a Customer Retention Plan," *The Journal of Business Strategy* (March/April 1992), 26.

19. Tricia Campbell, "Getting Personal With Customers," *Sales & Marketing Management* (January 1999), 68.

20. Geoffrey Brewer, "Winning Back Angry Customers," *Sales & Marketing Management* (October 1997), 131; and John R. Graham, "Why Customers Leave (and the reason they don't bother telling us why)," *The Selling Advantage* (June 12, 1992), Vol. 4, 2.

21. "Turn Conflict with a Customer Into a Selling Opportunity," *Personal Selling Power,* Vol. 12, No. 8 (September 1992), 73.

22. Dr. Ken Blanchard, "Mistake Proof," *Selling Power* (January/ February 1998), 42; and "Do You Deliver on Your Promises?," *Professional Selling,* Vol. 22, No. 10 (May 25, 1984), 4.

23. Anthony Urbaniak, "After the sale – what really happens to customer service," *The American Salesman* (February 2000), 14-17.

24. Steve Atlas, "Telephone Selling," in the Skills Workshop section of *Selling Power* (July/August 2000), 50.

25. Geoffrey Brewer, "How to Stay in Touch," *Sales & Marketing Management* (February 1998), 109.

26. Julie Puckett, "A Quick Thank-You," in the Reader To Reader Hot Tips section of *Selling Power* (September 2000), 60.

27. "Foxboro Trains Customers to Stay Loyal," *Sales & Marketing Management,* Vol. 133, No. 5 (October 8, 1984), 56-57.

CHAPTER 15

1. Ken Liebeskind, "Don't Squander Time," *Selling Power* (June 1997), 39.

2. Amy Feldman, "We'll Make You Scary," *Forbes* (February, 14, 1994), 96.

3. Joseph Block, "Just a Habit," *Personal Selling Power,* Vol. 14, No. 6 (September 1994), 90.

4. "Success is in her Makeup," *Selling Power* (November/December 1997), 96. A Tip from Mary Kay, Founder of Mary Kay Cosmetics.

5. L.B. Gschwandtner, "A Terrible Waste of Time," *Personal Selling Power* (July/August 1994), 52.

6. Loretta D. Foxman and Walter L. Polsky, "Five Steps to Get—and Stay—Organized," *Personnel Journal,* Vol. 63, No. 9 (August 1984), 18.

7. Thayer C. Taylor, "Giving Sales Leads a Leading Edge," *Sales and Marketing Management,* Vol. 127, No. 4 (September 14, 1981), 35.

8. Stuart Miller, "Beating the Clock – and Records," *Sales & Marketing Management* (February 1997), 21.

9. Carl Clayton, How to Manage Your Time and Territory for Better Sales Results," *Personal Selling Power,* Vol. 10, No. 2 (March 1990), 46.

10. Brian Jeffrey, "Make a List and Check It Twice," *Selling Power* (January/February 2000), 39; and Ed Brown, "Stephen Covey's New One-Day Seminar," *Fortune* (January 1999), 138.

11. "Goal Setting Basics," *Professional Selling, Bureau of Business Practice,* Vol. 127, No. 20 (October 25, 1989), 5.

12. Robert Tardiff, "Control Your Time," *Personal Selling Power* (May/June 1995), 72.

13. "Leader's Film Guide for Finding Time," prepared by Robin Schiff for CRM Productions, Inc., CRM McGraw-Hill Films, 13.

14. Foxman and Polsky, "Five Steps," 18.

15. William Kendy, "Eliminating Time Wasters," *Selling Power* (July/August 2000), 34.

16. Sarah Lorge, "Improving Time Management", *Sales & Marketing Man-*

agement (February 1998), 112.

17. Stephen Rush, "From Baseball to Business," *Nation's Business* (October 1996), 50.

18. Taken from an article by David Lill, "Time to Spare," *Selling Power,* (May 1997), 72-73.

19. R. A. Mackenzie, *The Time Trap* (New York: McGraw-Hill, 1975), 97.

20. Renee Zemanski, "Using your time on the road effectively," *Selling Power* (January/February 2000), 34.

21. Steve Atlas, "When the Customer Isn't Right," *Selling Power* (January/February 2001), 32.

22. For a more thorough discussion on "How to Run Your Territory Like a Business," See the booklet *Territory Management, Bureau of Business Practice, Inc.* (1989), 6-16.

23. Karen Starr, "Have PDA, Will Travel," *Selling Power* (March 2001), 28.

24. Melanie Berger, "Take a Right At the Light And..." *Sales & Marketing Management* (September 1997), 91-94.

25. Dan Gutman, "The Road More Traveled," *Success* (May 1996), 56.

26. Rich Bohn, "Territory Management Better Sales," *Sales & Field Force Automation* (April 1998), 76.

27. See these sources for more information on computer mapping systems: Niklas Von Daehne, "The Technology Edge," *Success* (May 1994), 53-54; Charles Lee Browne, "On the Road Again," *Personal Selling Power* (March 1994), 36; George W. Colombo, "Putting Sales on the Map," *Selling* (July/August 1994), 27-29; Thayer C. Taylor, "Mapping Out a Strategy," *Sales & Marketing Management* (February 1994), 51-52.

CHAPTER 16

1. Gerhard Gschwandtner, "World Class Sales," *Selling Power* (January/February 1998), 75.

2. Dr. Ken Blanchard, "Coaches, Facilitators and Cheerleaders," *Personal Selling Power,* Vol. 14, No. 1 (January/February 1994), 54-55.

3. Gilbert Churchill Jr. and Paul Peter, *Marketing*, 2nd ed. (New York: McGraw-Hill Irwin 1998), 515.

4. This section on Team Selling was modified from the following sources: Andy Ferguson, "Sales Departments Claim Marketers Could do Better," *Marketing Week* (September 11, 1997), 28-29; Mark McCormack," Doubles Anyone," *Sales & Marketing Management* (December 1993) 35-36; Tom Murray, "Team Selling: What's the Incentive?," *Sales & Marketing Management* (June 1991), 90; Jack Falvey, "Team Selling: What It Is and Isn't," *Sales & Marketing Management* (June 1990), 8-10; "Team Selling: A Team Approach to Increasing Sales," Small Business Report, April 1985), 23-25; and Calling in the Team," *Professional Selling*, (June 10, 1984), 1-3.

5. Malcolm Campbell, "How To Become a Top Performer," *Selling Power* (January/February 2000), 61.

6. Malcolm Fleschner, "Anatomy of a Sale," *Selling Power* (May 1998), 94-96.

7. Henry Canaday, "Flyaway Sales," *Selling Power* (October 2000), 110.

8. Erika Rasmusson, "Setting Your Sights on Videoconferencing," *Sales & Marketing Management* (September 1997), 106.

9. Mary boone, "The E-Vangelist: Face Time," *Sales & Marketing Management* (June 2001), 29.

10. Kathleen Cholewka, "Seven Signs You're Failing as a Manager and How to Avoid Them," *Sales & Marketing Management* (March 2001), 42.

11. Audrey Bottjen and Eduardo Canto, "Pep Talks That Inspire Reps," *Sales & Marketing Management* (June 2001), 66.

12. Melissa Campbell, "What Price Sales Force Satisfaction?," *Sales & Marketing Management* (July 1994), 37.

13. Julie Strugeon, "Wanted Successful Sales Manager," *Selling Power* (September 2000), 114.

14. Malcolm Fleschner, "Perfect Pitch," *Selling Power* (November/December 1997), 25.

15. Ray Mcdermott, "Targeting Top Customers," *Sales & Marketing Management* (February 1998), 114.

16. For a more detailed example and discussion of this useful approach, see Gilbert A. Churchill, Jr., Neil M. Ford, and Orville C. Walker, Jr., *Sales Force Management,* 4th ed. (Homewood, IL: Richard D. Irwin, Inc., 1993), 231-237.

17. Christen Heide, Dartnell's 29th "Survey of Sales Force Compensation, 1997-1998," reported in *Selling Power* (April 1998), 73.

18. Robert G. Head, "Select Salespeople Systematically," *Personal Selling Power,* Vol. 13, No. 4 (May/June 1993), 68-69; and Geoffrey Brewer, "Mind Reading: What Drives Top Salespeople to Greatness?," *Sales & Marketing Management* (May 1994), 86.

19. "Twenty-Sixth Survey of Sales Force Compensation," (Chicago, IL: 1990: The Dartnell Corporation). Reported in *Inc* magazine (August 1991), 82; and Dick Vink, "Can You Explain Your Comp Plan in 10 Minutes or Less?," *Sales & Marketing Management* (September 1992), 119; Jim M. Graber, Roger E. Breisch, and Walter E. Breisch, "Performance Appraisals and Deming: A Misunderstanding?," *Quality Progress* (June 1992), 59-62.

20. Henry Canaday, "What Are You Worth," *Selling Power* (January/February 2001), 83.

21. Patricia Zingheim, "Are your salespeople out of line?" *Selling Power* (July/August 2000), 81; Robert Head, "Restoring Balance to Sales compensation," *Sales & Marketing Management* (August 1992), 39-44; and James F. Carey, *The Complete Guide to Sales Force Compensation* (Business One Irwin, 1991).

22. Susan Greco, "The Customer Driven Bonus Plan," *Inc* magazine (September 1995), 89; Kerry Rottenberger and Richard Kern, "The Upside-Down Deming Principle," *Sales & Marketing Management* (June 1992), 39-44.

23. Todd Nelson, "Employee Compensation Likely to Change," *The Tennessean,* Section E (October 1, 1992), 4.

24. "Selling Without Commissions," *Sales & Marketing Management* (June 1994), 97.

25. Churchill, Ford, Walker, *Sales Force Management,* 486.

26. Edgar Speer, "The Role of Training at United States Steel," *Training and Development Journal,* Vol. 30, No. 6 (June 1976), 18-21.

27. Tricia Campbell, "Do Senior Reps Make Good Mentors?" *Sales & Marketing Management* (November 1997), 95.

28. Lawrence J. Tuttle, "A Training Revolution," *Personal Selling Power,* Vol. 14, No. 4 (May/June 1994), 32-33.

CREDITS

Written permission to reprint the following materials has been obtained from the appropriate rightsholders.

Sales & Marketing Management
Categories of Salespeople, Bill Communications, Inc.

Sales & Marketing Management
Ethics in Selling Honest (cartoon), Bill Communications, Inc.

Business Marketing
How to Reach Buyers in their Psychological Comfort Zones, Ingrasci, Hugh J.; Business Marketing, Crain Communications

Journal of Personal Selling & Sales Management
Rapport Building for Salespeople: A Neurolinguistic Approach, Nickels, William G, Robert F Everett and Robert Klein; Dr. Ron Michaels, Dept. of Marketing

Nancy cartoon, Scott, Jerry; United Feature Syndicate

Sales & Marketing Management
Dressed to Sell; Bill Communications, Inc.

How Important it is to Listen - pamphlet
cartoon, Unisys Corporation

Andy Capp cartoon, North America Syndicate

Cathy cartoon, Guisewite, Cathy; Universal Press

Adobe Image Library, *The Creative Professional's Catalog*, Volume 5/98. Adobe Systems Incorporated

Eyewire photography – I purchased over 300 pictures based on information gleaned from their Web site and received permission to use any one or all of them throughout the textbook. This was a tremendous source of images and pictures that are found on many pages of the book. The pictures that are used to begin Parts I to V in the book represent specific examples. Go to www.eyewire.com for specific catalogs of pictures that are available for purchase.

A special thanks and acknowledgement to Michael Reaggs, current Reprint Manager, and Lisa Abelson, former Reprint Manager, for *Sales & Marketing Management* magazine for giving me permission to modify and adapt exhibits, charts, articles and pictures from issues of the magazine. The pages listed here have items used from various issues of *Sales & Marketing Management* magazine: 6, 12, 19, 33, 36, 40, 53, 84, 135, 139, 146, 168, 170, 215, 216, 218, 229, 272, 275, 278, 343, 348, 376, 390, 401

INDEX